Philosophy Through Fiction and Film

Burton F. Porter

PEARSON

Prentice
Hall

UPPER SADDLE RIVER, NEW JERSEY 07458

Library of Congress Cataloging-in-Publication Data

Porter, Burton F.
    Philosophy through fiction and film / Burton F. Porter.— 1st ed.
        p. cm.
    ISBN 0-13-097506-0
    1. Literature and morals.   2. Motion pictures—Moral and ethical
aspects.   I. Title.
    PN49 .P675 2003
    809.93353—dc21

                                                2003004700

VP, Editorial Director: Charlyce Jones-Owen
Acquisition Editor: Ross Miller
Assistant Editor: Wendy Yurash
Editorial Assistant: Carla Worner
Senior Marketing Editor: Claire Bitting
Production Liaison: Fran Russello
Project Manager: Karen Berry/Pine Tree Composition, Inc.
Prepress and Manufacturing Buyer: Brian Mackey
Cover Designer: Bruce Kenselaar
Cover Photo: David James, Picture Desk, Inc./Kobal Collection
Marketing Manager: Claire Bitting
Marketing Assistant: Kimberly Daum

Credits and acknowledgments borrowed from other sources and reproduced,
with permission, in this textbook appear on pages 421–422.

Pearson Education LTD.
Pearson Education Singapore, Pte. Ltd
Pearson Education Canada, Ltd
Pearson Education–Japan
Pearson Education Australia PTY,
    Limited
Pearson Education North Asia Ltd.
Pearson Educación de Mexico, S.A.
    de C.V.
Pearson Education Malaysia, Pte. Ltd
Pearson Education, Upper Saddle
    River, New Jersey

10 9 8 7 6 5 4 3 2
ISBN: 0-13-097506-0

Contents

Preface

Philosophy Through Fiction and Film was written to introduce students to philosophy by means of literature and films as well as the systematic works of philosophers. The book therefore incorporates the perspectives of creative writers and film directors who express philosophic ideas. Through this multi-dimensional approach, the student is better able to understand philosophy, for the concepts are presented in a more immediate and lively way, one that shows various facets of ideas and appeals to different learning styles.

The works that are anthologized and summarized from philosophy, literature, and moving pictures are grouped under the major branches of philosophy, each in a separate chapter. Substantial introductions describe each of the branches and critically evaluate the basic concepts and theories within them. At the end of each chapter an extensive bibliography is provided for further exploration; this should be especially valuable for identifying films that contain philosophic themes.

The book therefore covers the major fields of philosophy including epistemology or theory of knowledge; metaphysics, the study of the nature of reality; ethics, the evaluation of our life purpose, conduct, and character; philosophy of religion, the critical analysis of religious belief; and political philosophy, theories of the ideal state. The introductions, as well as the headnotes preceding each selection, interpret the literature or film, explaining the rationale for grouping them under the various headings. In the case of film, synopses are provided that explain the philosophic points that they express. Study questions follow each selection to further point up the philosophic themes.

The principal of selection that was used is that of effectiveness in presenting fundamental philosophic ideas and high quality by world standards. As might be expected, employing this principle resulted in a diverse and multicultural group of selections from twelve countries including Russia, Japan, Canada, Nigeria, Ireland, Greece, Scotland, the United States, and so forth. Both men and women are represented, different races, and the ancient, Medieval, modern, and contemporary world. The bibliographies contain an even broader array of works from North America, South America, Europe, Africa, and Asia.

To view philosophy through literature can place the ideas within a human context. Philosophy and literature often have similar concerns, so the novel, play, or short story can offer a rich source for reflection, showing the basic issues of human life in a moving way. At the same time, all great literature is inherently philosophical, as George Santayana wrote, so the reading of literature can be illuminated by an awareness of its philosophic content.

In a similar way, films offer a unique and engaging introduction to philosophy. Movies are extremely prevalent in today's culture, resonating strongly with audiences, so their inclusion in summary form makes the philosophic ideas more current, personal, and accessible. Many students will be more familiar with the films than with either the literary or philosophic works, and the expositions will show the philosophic meaning of the movie.

Nevertheless, students who read the summary and excerpt from the screenplay should then view the film itself (or re-view it) whenever possible. For the impact of seeing the film far exceeds that of the synopsis or script, just as the musical score is meant to be performed and the written play takes on additional depth when staged in a theater. Classes can watch a film together in a viewing room in the library, or videotapes can be made available for viewing at home. This is especially valuable for long films and when class time is better used for explication and discussion. Additional viewing assignments could also be valuable in understanding philosophy through film. Students could watch 2 or 3 outside films during the term, drawn from the bibliography or current releases, and report on the philosophic ideas they contain. These could be individual or group projects, for presentation in class or in written form.

Philosophy Through Fiction and Film therefore offers an original approach to philosophy using literary and film narratives along with standard philosophic works. The fundamental fields of philosophy are covered but in a fresh way, using a wide range of sources and a variety of viewpoints. As Thomas Mann wrote, "All subject matter is boring unless ideas shine through it." The fiction and film enrich the philosophic dialogue, linking traditional philosophy to our contemporary experience, while the philosophic works ground the issues, showing their deeper significance. The result is that philosophy comes alive as something vivid and compelling.

Acknowledgment

I wish to thank the following individuals who reviewed the manuscript and offered numerous suggestions for its improvement: Scott D. Blackwell, Indiana University; Dan Flory, Montana State University; Richard Gilmore, Concordia College; Joseph H. Kupfer, Iowa State University; and Thomas E. Wartenberg, Mount Holyoke College. I also wish to acknowledge the fine work of the editors at Prentice Hall: Ross Miller, Acquisition Editor, who first believed in the concept and supported it with professional competence and personal concern, and Wendy Yurash, Assistant Editor, who guided the book to completion with a keen mind and a gentle hand.

Burton F. Porter
Amherst, Massachusetts

About the Author

Dr. Burton F. Porter is Professor of Philosophy at Western New England College in Massachusetts, having done his undergraduate work at the University of Maryland and his graduate work at St. Andrews University (Scotland) and Oxford University. He is the author of *The Voice of Reason* (2002), *The Good Life: Alternatives in Ethics, 3/e* (2000), *Philosophy: A Literary and Conceptual Approach, 3/e* (1998), *Religion and Reason* (1993), *Reasons for Living* (1988), *Personal Philosophy: Perspectives on Living* (1976), and *Deity and Morality* (1968).

The Aesthetic Experience of Film

In the following excerpt from Between the Frames: Thinking About Movies *we are not given a solemn and earnest discourse about film theory or aesthetics. The author, Heidi Dawidoff, does not analyze the art of cinema in terms of the lens, camera angle, cross-cutting, shot and frame, or the* mise-en-scene *of setting, lighting, costumes, and the movement of figures. Rather than being concerned with how the techniques produce their effects, or the way in which cinema compares to painting, theater, literature, or still photography, Dawidoff expresses her exuberant reaction to films, how they made her feel.*

In her personal account we recognize our own aesthetic response, and her reflections explain why we are affected so strongly and take away such vivid impressions and lessons. The illuminated images on the screen have the power to engage our emotions at an unconscious level, so that we are persuaded, thrilled, enlightened, shocked, gratified, pained or what have you by the visual show. Above all, it is the immediacy of films that enables us to feel we have undergone the experience ourselves and to keep them in our memories long after we emerge from the darkness into the light.

Between the Frames: Thinking About Movies

Heidi G. Dawidoff

Most children I grew up with followed the conventional cinematic course: they went weekly to the movies. In my rather strict and culturally lofty home, a trip to the movies resembled a carefully planned voyage:

undertaken only rarely; the stopping points chosen with marked decision. Other children went to local theaters on Saturday afternoons in
company with each other, ate popcorn during the show, and got to see
funny movies, silly movies, happy movies, energetic movies. I went
dressed up, accompanied by both parents, to early evening shows (evok-
ing in my parents' minds, perhaps, the annual gift to young Viennese
children of a night at the opera), and saw excellent movies, which were
invariably too adult for a little girl: *Wuthering Heights* one year; *The
Philadelphia Story* another; *The Green Years* yet another. Fed sparingly yet
well on such choice fare, I missed Hollywood's joyfully profuse productivity and the careless, roistering crowds of happy Americans who knew
how to relish mass entertainment with hearty appetites. Even so, I saw
what I was missing on the occasion of my first movie, *Wuthering Heights*,
when the *Movietone News*, featuring a smiling President Roosevelt swimming in the White House pool, was followed by the previews of *Meet Me
in St. Louis*. Three minutes of that movie revealed a way of life, a pace, an
attitude, a freedom of form, and a commitment to joy that the story of
gloom and thwarted passion, of course, could not. What was striking
about the experience, however, was precisely the contrast between the
aching drama of impossible love and the cheerful musical in which so
much was possible. It would probably have been the same if I had seen
Meet Me in St. Louis and had only glimpses of the darkly, broodingly romantic *Wuthering Heights*.

From his professorial height, my father determined the movies by
which I should be transported and, by extension, what I should remember and savor, for he screened everything I saw for suitability. The heavy
interim between movies bred in me a longing for them that he, in judi-
ciously concerning himself with the cultivation of my taste and judgment, may not have expected. Adolescence brought me some freedoms.
Trips to movies became jaunts, even weekly jaunts, with friends or by
myself, to first-run theaters, revival houses, Harvard's film societies—
any place where I could catch up. I saw *Johnny Belinda, Beat the Devil, A
Place in the Sun, Angels in the Outfield, Singin' in the Rain*, and finally, a
Bette Davis vehicle: *Of Human Bondage*; and again it was the rich sense of
movies' protean power brought out by the contrasts among such a sam-
pling that struck and delighted me.

Movies are made for entertainment, but so is all art. Part of the
entertainment is the transportation—what people, with reference to
movies, generally call escape—it makes possible. For a brief time, one is
taken beyond one's life. But the effect of the transportation lingers, and
that experience of remembering and savoring, once we've returned to
the business of our own lives, is also part of the entertainment. If art
failed to transport us, it wouldn't be art at all. Art is supposed to give us
life as we don't really live it; as we might live it; as we should like to live
it; as we never imagined we could live it; even sometimes as we daren't

or mustn't live it. That is the purpose of a movie's dissolve, which moves us silently and serenely from a completed scene to a new one, thus omitting the life between that we, in reality, hobble through minute by minute. That is the purpose of Busby Berkeley's dances—those unending metamorphoses formed by perfect patterns of beautiful girls, whose lovely figures and smiling faces outdo the kaleidoscopic fragments they imitate. That is the purpose of all the happy rescues, coincidences, endings; of all the ghouls, monsters, villains; of all the synchronization, stylization, composition. They water our imaginations, intensifying life's experience, spurring us to be less ordinary, not necessarily in what we do with life but certainly in how we think about it. For art is meant to give us ideas, to give us a heightened sense of possibility, to set us thinking.

Despite flaws in any or all of its component art forms—drama, acting, photography, music—the graceful union of these parts that comprises a whole movie pleased and prompted my young imagination in ways otherwise the prerogative of great art. Movies don't have to be, and mustn't try to be, great art in the usual sense of poised, still perfection captured by a great painting, for example, to achieve artistic grace and power. In fact, all too often, directors who have set out to create "an artistic masterpiece" along the lines of a great painting have succeeded only in foddering the art house crowd with fresh stupidities and boring the multitude with a massive piece of inert affectation weighed down by deathless (but nonetheless quite dead) symbols and poetic (but nonetheless quite prosaic) camera work. However beautiful particular shots may be, a movie requires cinematography; it won't do to give a slide show. A movie becomes art in its own way, a way that gains force and integrity by a lively amalgamation of several art forms, by its intrinsic promulgation of energy in motion. The movie, after all, sweeps us up in its moving pictures—those hours and hours of life imagined and arranged for us between countless frames whose organizing principle satisfies us while their borders remain as invisible as drawings beneath a painting or outlines behind a novel.

I make no secret of my preference for Hollywood movies of the '30s and '40s. Their wholehearted enthusiasm for and faith in a new art form prove ever irresistible to a person raised on New Deal optimism. In their profusion and variety, moreover, they deal with all of life's big subjects, sometimes tritely and formulaically, but, more often, imaginatively, honestly, and intelligently. They have something to say—the way any work of art has something to say about human life and the human spirit, something which transcends the particular occasion and becomes good for all time. It is life's big subjects—relationships between people being the biggest of all . . .

My early ventures in thinking about movies taught me that thinking has a great deal to do with keeping experiences alive long enough to understand them. Thinking may reveal sad truths or lead to dead ends, but its true function is to invigorate an idea, to enhance our attachment to a subject by confirming its importance in our minds. In this way, thinking gives life some shape and continuity, a narrative quality, as if our ideas, impelled by enthusiasm, were running through our minds like movies.

Introduction
The Basic Branches of Philosophy

The field of philosophy can be divided into several branches, although how these divisions should be made is a matter of some dispute. For the nature of philosophy is itself a philosophic issue, so different philosophers divide the field in different ways depending upon their philosophies.

One common classification, however, is to recognize five distinct branches: *epistemology*, the study of how to gain reliable knowledge; *metaphysics*, which is concerned with what is ultimately real; *ethics*, dealing with worthwhile actions and goals in living; *logic*, or systematic, rigorous reasoning; and *aesthetics*, the search for standards in judging art.

In addition, philosophers often include within the field the philosophic dimensions of other areas of knowledge. Thus we have the philosophy of politics, of science, of religion, of psychology, and so forth. (Sometimes aesthetics is categorized as the philosophy of art.) In each case, the philosopher is interested in exploring the presuppositions, methods, relations, implications, and basic nature of the academic area. What assumptions lie behind the theory of natural rights or a paternalistic theory of government? What evidence does the scientist use as opposed to the religious believer? What are the implications of regarding people as rational beings or as stimulus-response mechanisms?

In this introductory textbook, we will examine the basic branches of epistemology, metaphysics, and ethics. We will also study the philosophy of religion and political philosophy—two especially intriguing areas of philosophy.

I. Obtaining Reliable Knowledge: Epistemology

The main issue of epistemology is how to gain genuine knowledge. The epistemologist, as he or she is called, is not concerned with what we know but *how* we know, not what is real but the basis for asserting things are real. In what way does knowledge differ from personal belief, or understanding from mere matters of opinion? How can we differentiate between certainties, guesses, hypotheses, convictions, and self-evident truths?

We all maintain that certain things exist such as the mountain we see in the distance, the person we touch, the sunset or rainbow that we find beautiful, and so forth, but such claims are based on some means of knowing that we trust. When we question whether that means does disclose reality, then we are engaged in epistemological speculation.

The mountain appears small from a distance but huge if we have to climb it, and purple from far away but green with trees close up. Is the mountain small and purple or gigantic and green? We think we can touch other people, but from the standpoint of physics that never occurs. It is only that an electrical repulsion is set up between the atoms in our fingers and the atoms in the other person's body. We never touch the person at all. Furthermore, the sun does not actually set, rather we view the earth turning, and the colors we admire in the rainbow are only the refraction and reflection of the sun's rays in drops of rain. We will never find the pot of gold because, as we approach the end of the rainbow, the color is no longer visible. Has it faded to nothing or was it nothing to begin with?

Considerations of this kind make us wonder what we truly know, and in our most skeptical moments, we question whether we are equipped to grasp reality at all. The Chinese philosopher Lao-tze once

1

said, "The other night I dreamt I was a butterfly flitting from flower to flower. Now I do not know if I was a man dreaming I was a butterfly or whether I am now a butterfly dreaming I am a man."

In this chapter, we will address two epistemological questions: Can we distinguish between appearance and reality, and if so, what means of knowing should we consider the most trustworthy in understanding the world?

A. APPEARANCE AND REALITY: IS THE WORLD THE WAY IT SEEMS?

The preliminary problem of epistemology lies in separating the way things seem from what they are. How can we gain access to the real world rather than experience illusions of the senses and delusions of the mind? We know the magician is tricking us, but we would swear the woman was cut in half and that the rabbit came out of an empty hat. In the same way, we may be convinced that a table is solid and stationary whereas the physicist will tell us it consists mainly of space and of atoms in constant motion. A stick may look bent in water when in fact it is straight, and train tracks appear to come together in the distance even though parallel lines never meet. Sugar looks white to the naked eye, but under a microscope it appears black. In all objects, the greater the magnification, the greater the difference with ordinary perception, so we are never sure at what distance the actual object is perceived.

Similarly, the telescope enables astronomers to understand that the earth is rotating on its axis, orbiting the sun, wheeling through the cosmos as part of the Milky Way galaxy, and moving outwards in the continuing expansion of the universe, like dots on an inflating balloon. We are constantly moving in four directions at once while not being aware of any motion at all. To take another example from astronomy, because of the enormous distances between the stars and the earth, starlight can take years to reach us—even traveling at a speed of 186,281 miles per second. This means that we do not see the stars as they are but as they were. In fact, some of the stars we think we now see may have disappeared by the time we see them, so that we are looking at a ghostly image of the past.

At the individual level, we never know whether other people experience the same world that we do. We are not sure that another person sees the same hue of red in the flower, tastes the same delicious or awful flavor, or has identical emotions of love, depression, contentment, or sympathy. Can we ever share our feelings with others, or are we each trapped inside our skins, forever alone and confined to a private world? Perhaps the problem of communication stems from the fact that no two people experience the world the same way, so that when someone uses words such as beautiful, considerate, loyal, or democratic, he or she may mean very different things. Disputes over whether something is green or blue may only indicate that people learned to use the words differently.

Aside from such considerations (what is sometimes called the "egocentric predicament"), we have an additional problem in interpreting someone else's behavior. We may not know whether other people can be trusted, whether they are being sincere or manipulative, and whether they are enjoying our company or only pretending to for some devious purpose. A boy whose friend passes him by without saying hello may ask himself, "Did he deliberately ignore me or was he preoccupied with other things?" A girl in a romantic situation may wonder, "Why did he say that he loves me?"

Even greater problems occur when people believe in the fantastic, uncanny, or bizarre, claiming to have special knowledge that goes beyond ordinary comprehension. Then we have enormous problems in separating what seems so to that person from what is so. For example, suppose that someone maintains that déjà vu demonstrates we have all lived previous lives, that dreams are premonitions of disasters, maybe predestined disasters, or that the twenty-two tarot cards can be used for telling fortunes. Suppose people believe that there is a monster in Loch Ness, that ships disappear in the Bermuda Triangle, or Yetis (Abominable Snowmen) inhabit the Himalayas. How can such assertions be disproven? How can we separate superstition from religious beliefs that are also claimed to surpass all understanding?

To take Christianity, which is our dominant Western religion, we are asked to believe that Christ transformed water into wine, fed the multitude with a small amount of food, healed the sick and deformed, cast out demons, raised the dead, and was himself resurrected. What reasons can be offered to accept such miracles—reasons that differentiate them from absurd or even dangerous beliefs? Are these events to be taken literally or are they important just to show God at work in the world?

Fairly recently the members of a religious cult called Heaven's Gate committed mass suicide. They were convinced that creatures of superior intelligence were waiting for them in rocket ships in the tail of Hale-Bopp comet. Prior to that, members of a cult in Guyana drank Kool-Aid laced with poison on the orders of their leader, Jim Jones; nine hundred men, women, and children died. The epistemological question is how can we know when we are in receipt of divine revelation and when we are acting in a delusional or psychotic way?

In the first group of selections that follow, various figures discuss questions about appearance and reality, beginning with the theories of the ancient Greek philosopher Plato and continuing through the literary ideas of the German writer Rainer Maria Rilke, and the cinematic vision of the Japanese filmmaker Akira Kurosawa.

The Republic*
Plato

Plato (428–c. 347 B.C.) together with Aristotle (584–322 B.C.) stands as one of the most influential figures in Western philosophy. In addition to his contribution to epistemology, metaphysics, and ethics, Plato shaped both Christian and Jewish theology as well as medieval Islamic thought. A Neoplatonism flourished in the third century under Plotinus, and in the seventeenth century the Cambridge Platonists revived a number of Platonic concepts. According to the thinker Alfred North Whitehead, all subsequent philosophy has been merely "a series of footnotes to Plato."

Plato's writings were cast in dialogue form and consist of intellectual conversations on central philosophic topics. The early dialogues are probably genuine reports of the conversations of Socrates, Plato's teacher and the main figure, but the middle and later dialogues probably use Socrates as a vehicle for expressing Plato's own ideas. Paradoxically, although Plato produced some of the most artful writings in philosophy, he was suspicious of art as two steps removed from the world of Ideas, which is the fundamental reality.

Among the most celebrated of Plato's early dialogues are The Protagoras, *that claims virtue is knowledge and can be taught, and* The Euthyphro, *that separates ethics from religion. The significant dialogues of his middle period include* The Gorgias, *an analysis of ethical questions,* The Meno, *an examination of knowledge, and* The Apology, The Crito, *and* The Phaedo *that describe Socrates' defense in court, his refusal to escape from prison, and his death scene. In this period,* The Symposium, *concerning beauty and love, is Plato's most dramatically successful dialogue, and* The Republic *is his highest achievement, containing a discussion of justice in the individual and in the state. The late period includes* The Parmenides *and* The Sophist, *both of which deal with the theory of Ideas or Forms.*

In the excerpt from the famous philosophic dialogue, The Republic, *Plato presents an allegory of the human condition that is intended to show how the ordinary world we inhabit is largely one of illusion. At least it is less real than an eternal and perfect world that exists beyond our senses. To Plato, we are like prisoners in a cave who mistake the shadows for reality. The shadows represent the physical world of sense perception. To liberate ourselves from this world, we must realize there is light behind the shadows—light that represents Ideas which are the fundamental reality. Above*

---

*Translated by B. Jowett.

all, there is the sun at the pinnacle of light just as the Good stands as the foremost of the Ideas.

By the Ideas (or Forms or Universals), Plato means the general categories into which any group of objects can be placed. For example, apart from particular trees we know there is the idea of what a tree consists of. Through our senses we perceive oaks, elms, maples, pines, and so forth, but through our mind we understand that the idea of a tree is that of a woody, perennial plant with branches, leaves or needles, ordinarily growing to a considerable height. In the same way, we can see various horses from Clydesdales to Shetland ponies, and Appaloosas to Arabians, but rationally we can separate the idea of a horse as a large, four-legged, solid-hoofed, herbivorous mammal used for riding or pulling loads.

Therefore, behind every class of things is some idea that corresponds to it, and together they make up a world of Ideas. To Plato these ideas are more real than things, and just as the shadows should lead us to acknowledge the light, the objects in the world of sense should make us acknowledge the more fundamental ideas that lie behind them. More important than trees or horses, our physical experience should cause us to consider the ultimate ideas of truth, beauty, and justice, and what it is to be a human being.

Book VII

AND now, I said, let me show in a figure how far our nature is enlight- 514
ened or unenlightened:—Behold! human beings housed in an underground cave, which has a long entrance open towards the light and as
wide as the interior of the cave; here they have been from their childhood, and have their legs and necks chained, so that they cannot move b
and can only see before them, being prevented by the chains from turning round their heads. Above and behind them a fire is blazing at a distance, and between the fire and the prisoners there is a raised way; and
you will see, if you look, a low wall built along the way, like the screen
which marionette players have in front of them, over which they show
the puppets.

I see.

And do you see, I said, men passing along the wall carrying all sorts c
of vessels, and statues and figures of animals made of wood and stone 515
and various materials, which appear over the wall? While carrying
their burdens, some of them, as you would expect, are talking, others
silent.

You have shown me a strange image, and they are strange prisoners.

Like ourselves, I replied; for in the first place do you think they
have seen anything of themselves, and of one another, except the shadows which the fire throws on the opposite wall of the cave?

b   How could they do so, he asked, if throughout their lives they were never allowed to move their heads?

And of the objects which are being carried in like manner they would only see the shadows?

Yes, he said.

And if they were able to converse with one another, would they not suppose that the things they saw were the real things?[1]

Very true.

And suppose further that the prison had an echo which came from the other side, would they not be sure to fancy when one of the passers-by spoke that the voice which they heard came from the passing shadow?

No question, he replied.

c   To them, I said, the truth would be literally nothing but the shadows of the images.

That is certain.

And now look again, and see in what manner they would be released from their bonds, and cured of their error, whether the process would naturally be as follows. At first, when any of them is liberated and compelled suddenly to stand up and turn his neck round and walk and look towards the light, he will suffer sharp pains; the glare will distress him, and he will be unable to see the realities of which in his former state he had seen the shadows; and then conceive someone saying to him that

d what he saw before was an illusion, but that now, when he is approaching nearer to being and his eye is turned towards more real existence, he has a clearer vision,—what will be his reply? And you may further imagine that his instructor is pointing to the objects as they pass and requiring him to name them,—will he not be perplexed? Will he not fancy that the shadows which he formerly saw are truer than the objects which are now shown to him?

Far truer.

e   And if he is compelled to look straight at the light, will he not have a pain in his eyes which will make him turn away to take refuge in the objects of vision which he can see, and which he will conceive to be in reality clearer than the things which are now being shown to him?

True, he said.

And suppose once more, that he is reluctantly dragged up that steep and rugged ascent, and held fast until he is forced into the presence of the sun himself, is he not likely to be pained and irritated? When he

516 approaches the light his eyes will be dazzled, and he will not be able to see anything at all of what are now called realities.

Not all in a moment, he said.

---

[1][Text uncertain: perhaps 'that they would apply the name *real* to the things which they saw'.]

He will require to grow accustomed to the sight of the upper world. And first he will see the shadows best, next the reflections of men and other objects in the water, and then the objects themselves; and, when he turned to the heavenly bodies and the heaven itself, he would find it easier to gaze upon the light of the moon and the stars at night than to see b the sun or the light of the sun by day?

Certainly.

Last of all he will be able to see the sun, not turning aside to the illusory reflections of him in the water, but gazing directly at him in his own proper place, and contemplating him as he is.

Certainly.

He will then proceed to argue that this is he who gives the seasons and the years, and is the guardian of all that is in the visible world, and in a certain way the cause of all things which he and his fellows have been c accustomed to behold?

Clearly, he said, he would arrive at this conclusion after what he had seen.

And when he remembered his old habitation, and the wisdom of the cave and his fellow-prisoners, do you not suppose that he would felicitate himself on the change, and pity them?

Certainly, he would.

And if they were in the habit of conferring honours among themselves on those who were quickest to observe the passing shadows and to remark which of them went before and which followed after and which d were together, and who were best able from these observations to divine the future, do you think that he would be eager for such honours and glories, or envy those who attained honour and sovereignty among those men? Would he not say with Homer,

'Better to be a serf, labouring for a landless master',

and to endure anything, rather than think as they do and live after their manner?

Yes, he said, I think that he would consent to suffer anything rather e than live in this miserable manner.

Imagine once more, I said, such a one coming down suddenly out of the sunlight, and being replaced in his old seat; would he not be certain to have his eyes full of darkness?

To be sure, he said.

And if there were a contest, and he had to compete in measuring the shadows with the prisoners who had never moved out of the cave, while his sight was still weak, and before his eyes had become steady 517 (and the time which would be needed to acquire this new habit of sight might be very considerable), would he not make himself ridiculous? Men would say of him that he had returned from the place above with his eyes ruined; and that it was better not even to think of ascending; and if anyone tried to loose another and lead him up to the light, let them only catch the offender, and they would put him to death.

No question, he said.

This entire allegory, I said, you may now append, dear Glaucon, to b the previous argument; the prison-house is the world of sight, the light of the fire is the power of the sun, and you will not misapprehend me if you interpret the journey upwards to be the ascent of the soul into the intellectual world according to my surmise, which, at your desire, I have expressed—whether rightly or wrongly God knows. But, whether true or false, my opinion is that in the world of knowledge the Idea of good appears last of all, and is seen only with an effort; although, when seen, it is c inferred to be the universal author of all things beautiful and right, parent of light and of the lord of light in the visible world, and the immediate and supreme source of reason and truth in the intellectual; and that this is the power upon which he who would act rationally either in public or private life must have his eye fixed.

I agree, he said, as far as I am able to understand you.

Moreover, I said, you must agree once more, and not wonder that those who attain to this vision are unwilling to take any part in human affairs; for their souls are ever hastening into the upper world where they d desire to dwell; which desire of theirs is very natural, if our allegory may be trusted.

Yes, very natural.

And is there anything surprising in one who passes from divine contemplations to the evil state of man, appearing grotesque and ridiculous; if, while his eyes are blinking and before he has become accustomed to the surrounding darkness, he is compelled to fight in courts of law, or in other places, about the images or the shadows of images of justice, and e must strive against some rival about opinions of these things which are entertained by men who have never yet seen the true justice?

Anything but surprising, he replied.

518   Anyone who has common sense will remember that the bewilderments of the eyes are of two kinds and arise from two causes, either from coming out of the light or from going into the light, and, judging that the soul may be affected in the same way, will not give way to foolish laughter when he sees anyone whose vision is perplexed and weak; he will first ask whether that soul of man has come out of the brighter life and is unable to see because unaccustomed to the dark, or having turned from darkness to the day is dazzled by excess of light. And he b will count the one happy in his condition and state of being, and he will pity the other; or, if he have a mind to laugh at the soul which comes from below into the light, this laughter will not be quite so laughable as that which greets the soul which returns from above out of the light into the cave.

That, he said, is a very just distinction.

But then, if I am right, certain professors of education must be wrong when they say that they can put a knowledge into the soul which c was not there before, like sight into blind eyes.

They undoubtedly say this, he replied.

Whereas our argument shows that the power and capacity of learning exists in the soul already; and that just as if it were not possible to turn the eye from darkness to light without the whole body, so too the instrument of knowledge can only by the movement of the whole soul be turned from the world of becoming to that of being, and learn by degrees to endure the sight of being, and of the brightest and best of being, or in d other words, of the good.

Study Questions

1. In what way does the "Allegory of the Cave" illustrate Plato's epistemology?
2. When people are freed from the cave, what is it they understand?
3. Why would the liberated prisoners no longer want to participate in human affairs?
4. What does Plato mean when he says that "the power and capacity of learning exists in the soul already"?
5. To Plato, what is appearance and what is reality?

The Notebooks of Malte Laurids Brigge
Rainer Maria Rilke
(trans. by M. D. Herter Norton)

Rainer Maria Rilke (1875–1926) was an Austrian poet and prose writer who is best known for his poetic works The Duino Elegies *and* Sonnets to Orpheus *and two novels,* The Tale of Love and Death of Cornet Christopher Rilke *and* The Notebooks of Malte Laurids Brigge. *His ability to express abstract ideas in concrete images has influenced twentieth-century British and American poetry to a considerable extent.*

In The Notebooks of Malte Laurids Brigge, *Rilke refuses to identify the person with his body and appearance, distinguishing clothing, faces, and hands, in particular, as extraneous to self. Faces are masks, clothing is costume, and both are assumed by the individual in a continuous series of impersonations. They do not function as reflections of our nature, but are roles imposed upon us by society that we might be unable to stop playing when we try to be ourselves. Even hands are a part of the world, divorced from us to the point of having separate autonomy, and they bear a greater affinity to faces than to our volitional selves. To Rilke, the authentic self consists of internal forces, dynamic and spiritual, and* will *above all, which courses through men, nature, and objects.*

In his other writings, Rilke develops his concept of the primacy of inner forces. He describes cathedrals that have heaped themselves up until the molten rock crystalizes in the air while the surrounding houses are shocked into silence by the volcanic eruption. Trees surge toward the sky, the sap collecting and rising, the branches thrusting through the bark, the leaves unfolding and spreading. Single flowers stand up and shout "Red" in frightened voices, and houses grouped round a square pile on top of one another wanting to see everything. Rilke believes that it is the internal aspect of all things (human beings especially) which defines their nature, and that people must resist the self-alienation that comes from defining themselves by looking in a mirror. The "I" is known through "interior apprehension," which discloses indwelling spiritual centers as the essence of the individual.

Faces

Have I said it before? I am learning to see. Yes, I am beginning. It still goes badly. But I intend to make the most of my time.

To think, for instance, that I have never been aware before how many faces there are. There are quantities of human beings, but there are many more faces, for each person has several. There are people who wear the same face for years; naturally it wears out, it gets dirty, it splits at the folds, it stretches, like gloves one has worn on a journey. These are thrifty, simple people; they do not change their face, they never even have it cleaned. It is good enough, they say, and who can prove to them the contrary? The question of course arises, since they have several faces, what do they do with the others? They store them up. Their children will wear them. But sometimes, too, it happens that their dogs go out with them on. And why not? A face is a face.

Other people put their faces on, one after the other, with uncanny rapidity and wear them out. At first it seems to them they are provided for always; but they scarcely reach forty—and they have come to the last. This naturally has something tragic. They are not accustomed to taking care of faces, their last is worn through in a week, has holes, and in many places is thin as paper; and then little by little the under layer, the no-face, comes through, and they go about with that.

But the woman, the woman; she had completely collapsed into herself, forward into her hands. It was at the corner of rue Notre-Dame-des-Champs. I began to walk softly as soon as I saw her. When poor people are reflecting they should not be disturbed. Perhaps their idea will yet occur to them.

The street was too empty; its emptiness was bored; it caught my step from under my feet and clattered about with it hither and yon, as with a wooden clog. The woman startled and pulled away too quickly out of herself, too violently, so that her face remained in her two hands. I could see it lying in them, its hollow form. It cost me indescribable effort to stay with those hands and not to look at what had torn itself out of them. I shuddered to see a face from the inside, but still I was much more afraid of the naked flayed head without a face. . . .

Hands: A Childhood Experience

. . . I was drawing a knight, a solitary, easily recognizable knight, on a strikingly caparisoned horse. He became so gaily-colored that I had to change crayons frequently, but the red was most in demand, and for it I reached again and again. Now I needed it once more, when it rolled (I can see it yet) right across the lighted sheet to the edge of the table and, before I could stop it, fell past me and disappeared. I needed it really urgently, and it was very annoying to clamber down after it. Awkward as I was, I had to make all sorts of preparations to get down; my legs seemed to me far too long, I could not pull them out from under me; the too-prolonged kneeling posture had numbed my limbs; I could not tell what belonged to me, and what to the chair. At last I did arrive down there, somewhat bewildered, and found myself on a fur rug that stretched from under the table as far as the wall. But here a fresh difficulty arose. My eyes, accustomed to the brightness above and all inspired with the colors on the white paper, were unable to distinguish anything at all beneath the table, where the blackness seemed to me so dense that I was afraid I should knock against it. I therefore relied on my sense of touch, and kneeling, supported on my left hand, I combed around with my other hand in the cool, long-haired rug, which felt quite friendly; only that no pencil was to be found. I imagined I must be losing a lot of time, and was about to call to Mademoiselle and ask her to hold the lamp for me, when I noticed that to my involuntarily strained eyes the darkness was gradually growing more penetrable. I could already distinguish the wall at the back, which ended in a light-colored molding; I oriented myself with regard to the legs of the table; above all I recognized my own outspread hand moving down there all alone, a little like an aquatic animal, examining the ground. I watched it, as I remember still, almost with curiosity; it seemed as if it knew things I had never taught it, groping down there so independently, with movements I had never noticed in it before. I followed it up as it pressed forward, I was interested in it, ready for all sorts of things. But how should I have been prepared to see suddenly come to meet it out of the wall another hand, a larger, extraordinarily thin hand, such as I had never seen before. It came groping in similar fashion from the other side, and the two outspread hands moved blindly toward one another. My curiosity was not yet used up but suddenly it came to an end, and there was only terror. I felt that one of the hands belonged to me, and that it was committing itself to something irreparable. With all the authority I had over it, I checked it and drew it back flat and slowly, without taking my eyes off the other, which went on groping. I realized that it would not leave off; I cannot tell how I got up again. I sat deep in the armchair, my teeth chattered, and I had so little blood in my face that it seemed to me there could be no more blue in my eyes. . . .

Costumes: A Child's Game of Impersonation

It was then that I first learned to know the influence that can emanate directly from a particular costume itself. Hardly had I donned one of these suits, when I had to admit that it got me in its power; that it prescribed my movements, my facial expression, yes, even my ideas. My hand, over which the lace cuff fell and fell again, was anything but my usual hand; it moved like a person acting; I might even say that it was watching itself, exaggerated though that sounds. These disguises never, indeed, went so far as to make me feel a stranger to myself; on the contrary, the more varied my transformations, the more convinced did I become of myself. I grew bolder and bolder; I flung myself higher and higher; for my dexterity in recapture was beyond all doubt. I did not notice the temptation in this rapidly growing security. To my undoing, the last closet, which I had heretofore thought I could not open, yielded one day, to surrender to me, not specific costumes, but all kinds of random paraphernalia for mas- querades, the fantastic peradventures of which drove the blood to my cheeks. It is impossible to recount all I found there. In addition to a baútta that I remember, there were dominos in various colors, there were women's dresses that tinkled brightly with the coins with which they were sewn; there were pierrot-costumes that looked silly to me, and braided Turkish trousers, all folds, and Persian fezzes from which little camphor sacks slipped out, and coronets with stupid, expressionless stones. All these I rather despised; they were of such a shabby unreality and hung there so peeled-off and miserable and collapsed so will-lessly when one dragged them out into the light. But what transported me into a sort of intoxication were the capacious mantles, the wraps, the shawls, the veils, all those yielding, wide, unused fabrics, that were so soft and caressing, or so slithery that one could scarcely take hold of them, or so light that they flew by one like a wind, or simply heavy with all their own weight. In them I first discerned really free and infinitely mobile possibilities: being a slave-girl about to be sold, or being Jeanne d'Arc or an old king or a wizard; all this lay to hand, especially as there were also masks, large, threatening or astonished faces with real beards and full or high-drawn eyebrows. I had never seen masks before, but I understood at once what masks ought to be. I had to laugh when it occurred to me that we had a dog who looked as if he wore one. I recalled his affection- ate eyes, that always seemed to be looking as from behind into his hirsute visage. I was still laughing as I dressed up, and in the process I com- pletely forgot what I had intended to represent. No matter; it was novel and exciting not to decide till afterward before the mirror. The face I fas- tened on had a singularly hollow smell; it lay tight over my own face, but I was able to see through it comfortably, and not till the mask sat firm did I select all sorts of materials, which I wound about my head like a turban, in such a way that the edge of the mask, which reached downward into an immense yellow cloak, was almost entirely hidden also on top and at the sides. At length, when I could do no more, I considered myself suffi- ciently disguised. I seized in addition a large staff, which I made walk along beside me at arm's length, and in this fashion, not without diffi- culty, but, as it seemed to me, full of dignity, I trailed into the guest-room toward the mirror.

It was really grandiose, beyond all expectation. And the mirror gave it back instantly, it was too convincing. It would not have been at all nec- essary to move much; this apparition was perfect, even though it did nothing. But I wanted to discover what I actually was, so I turned a little and finally raised both arms: large, almost conjuring gestures were, I saw immediately, the only fitting ones. But just at this solemn moment I heard quite near me, muffled by my disguise, a very complicated noise; much frightened, I lost sight of the presence in the mirror and was badly upset to perceive that I had overturned a small round table with heaven knows what, probably very fragile objects. I bent down as well as I could and found my worst fears confirmed: it looked as though everything were in pieces. The two useless green-violet porcelain parrots were of course shattered, each in a different malign fashion. A box, from which rolled bonbons that looked like insects in silken cocoons, had cast its cover far away; only half of it was to be seen, and the other had totally disappeared. But most annoying of all was a scent-bottle that had been shivered into a thousand tiny fragments, from which the remainder of some sort of old essence had spurted that now formed a spot of very repulsive profile on the clear parquet. I wiped it up quickly with something or other that was hanging down about me, but it only became blacker and more unpleasant. I was indeed desperate. I picked myself up and tried to find something with which to repair the damage. But nothing was to be found. Besides I was so hampered in my vision and in every movement, that wrath rose in me against my absurd situation, which I no longer understood. I pulled at all my garments, but they clung only the tighter. The cords of the mantle strangled me, and the stuff on my head pressed as though more and more were being added to it. Furthermore the atmosphere had become dim and as though misty with the oldish fume of the spilled liquid.

Hot and angry, I rushed to the mirror and with difficulty watched through the mask the working of my hands. But for this the mirror had just been waiting. Its moment of retaliation had come. While I strove in boundlessly increasing anguish to squeeze somehow out of my disguise, it forced me, by what means I do not know, to lift my eyes and imposed on me an image, no, a reality, a strange, unbelievable and monstrous reality, with which, against my will, I became permeated: for now the mirror was the stronger, and I was the mirror. I stared at this great, terrifying unknown before me, and it seemed to me appalling to be alone with him. But at the very moment I thought this, the worst befell: I lost all sense, I simply ceased to exist. For one second I had an indescribable, painful and futile longing for myself, then there was only he: there was nothing but he.

I ran away, but now it was he that ran. He knocked against everything, he did not know the house, he had no idea where to go; he managed to get down a stairway, and in his course stumbled over someone who shouted in struggling free. A door opened, several persons came out: Oh, oh, what a relief it was to know them! There were Sieversen, the good Sieversen, and the housemaid and the butler: now for a decision. But they did not spring forward to the rescue; their cruelty knew no bounds. They stood there and laughed; my God, they could stand there and laugh. I wept, but the mask did not let the tears escape; they ran down inside over my cheeks and dried at once and ran again and dried. And at last I knelt before them, as no human being ever knelt; I knelt, and lifted up my hands, and implored them: "Take me out, if you still can, and keep me," but they did not hear; I had no longer any voice.

Study Questions

1. To Rilke, what is the relation between the face and the individual?
2. Do you think your hands are extraneous to yourself, express yourself, or are part of yourself?
3. Does Rilke consider clothing as costume for the roles we play or as a means of self-expression?
4. When you look in the mirror, do you see yourself as you really are or only your appearance? What is Rilke's view?
5. Do you think of your body as something real or a form you inhabit? How would you justify your position?

Rashomon

Director: Akira Kurosawa

Translator: Donald Richie

Screenplay: Akira Kurosawa and Shinobu Hashimoto

The basic cast of characters:

Tajomaru, the bandit
The Woman
The Samurai, her husband
The Woodcutter
The Priest
The Commoner

Akira Kurosawa (1910–1998) was a Japanese filmmaker who has directed over twenty-five films since 1942. They include High and Low, Red Beard, Dodes'ka-den, Ikiru, Yojimbo, *and* Rhapsody in August. *He has adapted several Shakespeare plays to film including* King Lear *as* Ran, *and* Macbeth *as* Throne of Blood, *and his* Seven Samurai *was remade by Hollywood as* The Magnificent Seven *just as his* The Hidden Fortress *was the basis for* Star Wars. *Kurosawa's film* Dersu Uzala *earned him an Academy Award as the best foreign language film, and* Kagemusha *won the Grand Prize at the Cannes film festival.*

Rashomon, here discussed and excerpted, was his first international success, garnering the Golden Lion in the Venice Film Festival and an Oscar for the Best Foreign Film in 1951. It usually appears on lists of the ten greatest films of all time.

Synopsis

Akira Kurosawa's films can be characterized as visually beautiful and dramatically strong, preoccupied with separating the true from the false in cinematic form. In *Rashomon*, Kurosawa investigates the question of appearance and reality, specifically the accuracy of memory and the interpretation of events. He offers several accounts of the same crime viewed from different perspectives, but rather than searching for the solution to the crime Kurosawa seeks insight into the elusive nature of truth itself.

The film is based on two short stories by Ryunosuke Akutagawa, "In the Grove" and "Roshomon," and was later remade by Hollywood as "Outrage" (starring Paul Newman as the bandit, from Mexico). As well as directing the film, Kurosawa was the principal author of the film script, and he employed the remarkable camera work of Kazuo Miya-gawa. The scenario, the editing, the music (by Fumio Hayakawa), the cast, the atmospheric effects, the camera angles, and cinematic techniques were all innovative for their time and are equally compelling today.

It is interesting to note that Kurosawa and his cast endured enor-mous hardships in the production. Most of the film was shot in a forest that was so full of leeches that the crew had to coat themselves with salt every day as protection. Black ink had to be added to the artificial rain to make it visible against the gray sky, and trees had to be chopped down to allow sufficient light for the cameras, When the film was first shown in Japan in the 1950s, people stood in lines a mile long in the pouring rain to buy a ticket.

The "Rashomon" from which the film takes its name was the largest gate in the capital city of Kyoto. First constructed in 789, it measured 106 feet wide, 26 feet deep, and its stone wall rose to a height of 75 feet. With the decline of Kyoto, the gate fell into disrepair, and by the twelfth century it had collapsed in many places, becoming a notorious hiding place for thieves.

The film moves back and forth between the Rashomon, where a group of people have taken shelter from the rain in the shadow of the gate, and the narrative they tell. To pass the time until the storm passes, a woodcutter and a priest relate the story of a rape and murder to a com-moner. Each of the characters involved in the events tells his or her ver-sion of the tale, with the scenes magically enacted before the viewer.

Apparently, while traveling in a forest, a samurai and his wife are waylaid by a notorious bandit named Tajomaru (Toshiro Mifune), who kills the husband (Masayuki Mori) and violates the wife (Machoko Kyo). This appears to be what occurred; however, discrepancies occur in the ac-counts given by the participants, so we are unsure which is correct. The rape and death are seen from four points of view, each of which seems convincing. The truth therefore appears relative, subjective, and partial, depending upon the narrator's perspective and needs.

According to the bandit's version, as told in a prison courtyard to a judge, he tied up the merchant, raped the wife, and later killed the hus-band in a fair duel. He swears this story is accurate: "No, I'm telling the truth," he declares. "I know you're going to cut off my head sooner or later—I'm not hiding anything. It was me, Tajomaru, who killed that man. Yes, I did it."

He adds enigmatically, "It was a hot afternoon, about three days ago, that I first saw them. And then all of a sudden there was this cool breeze. If it hadn't been for that breeze, maybe I wouldn't have killed them." This weak excuse makes the murder more a matter of chance than a premeditated act.

The scene begins with Tajomaru sleeping at the base of a huge tree, and the samurai coming down a hill leading a horse on which a woman is riding. The bandit awakens and sees the couple, noting the way the woman gently swings with the movement of the horse and how her veil is blown aside by the wind.

The couple move past him, but as Tajomaru tells the judge, "First I saw her, then she was gone—I thought I had seen an angel. And right then I decided I would take her, that I'd have her even if I had to kill the man . . . (he laughs,). But if I could do it without killing him then that would be all the better. So I decided not to kill him but to somehow get the woman alone."

A beautiful/horrible film sequence follows in which the Tajomaru tracks and chases the couple through the countryside. He then approaches them, circles the horse, and when he is challenged by the samurai pretends to offer him a sword. "Here, take it. Look at it," he says. "Near here I found this old tomb with lots of things like this in it . . . swords, daggers, mirrors . . . if you're interested I might sell some of them to you cheap."

The woman dismounts from the horse and settles herself on the grass near a brook while the samurai climbs the slope with Tajomaru to look at the cache of weapons. As soon as the samurai's back is turned, the bandit knocks him to the ground, overpowers the man, and ties him to a tree. He then rushes back to the woman, telling her that her husband has been bitten by a snake. As he describes it, "She became very pale and stared at me as though her eyes were frozen. She looked like a child when it turns suddenly serious. The sight of her made me jealous of that man, I started to hate him. I wanted to show her what he looked like, all tied up like that. I hadn't even thought of a thing like that before, but now I did."

The bandit pulls her up the hill after him, intent on displaying her husband's helplessness and humiliation. When the woman sees the situation she is transfixed at first but then charges the bandit with a dagger. Her thrust goes past him, and after she regains her balance she attacks him again, slashing wildly, even biting his forearm. Tajomaru is impressed by her desperation and finds her hysteria exciting.

After a short fight the woman collapses with exhaustion. Tajomaru pins her to the ground and begins to kiss her in front of the samurai, who bows his head. At first she struggles and claws at him, but gradually she closes her eyes and begins to caress him. The dagger drops from her hand and sticks point first in the ground.

"And so I had her—just as I had planned," the bandit tells the judge, "and without killing the husband. And that was how I did it. Besides, I hadn't intended to kill him."

But then, according to Tajomaru, the woman threw herself at his feet saying, "Wait. Stop. One of you must die. Either you or my husband . . . To be doubly disgraced, disgraced before two men, is more than I can bear." Consequently, the bandit frees the samurai, gives him back his sword, and the two men begin to duel. The battle goes on for some time, the men lunging in and out of the frame. Finally, the samurai stumbles, his sword becomes entangled in the undergrowth, and he is spitted on the bandit's sword.

Tajomaru explains, "I wanted to kill him honestly, since I had to kill him. And he fought really well. We crossed swords over twenty-three times. Think of that! No one had ever crossed over twenty with me. Then I killed him."

By Tajomaru's account he did intend to rape the woman, but he only killed the man because of the woman's sensibilities; she insisted that only one of them could live. In a sense, she was responsible for the death and he committed no crime. Furthermore, he gave the samurai a fair chance, and since he was the better swordsman he managed to win the fight; he implies that an even contest like that is hardly murder. Tajomaru therefore paints himself as an enthralling lover and a heroic fighter.

The wife, however, tells a different story, one that does involve her shame at being dishonored but not the possibility of remaining with the bandit. She recounts to the judge in the courtyard that after Tajomaru violated her before her husband's eyes, the bandit sneered and laughed then disappeared into the woods. She was left weeping on the ground, and after she had composed herself she threw her arms around her husband, sobbing on his chest.

However, he responded coldly and cynically. "Even now I remember his eyes," she says, "What I saw in them was not sorrow; not even anger. It was . . . a cold hatred of me." Frantically she implores him, "Don't look at me like that. Don't! Beat me, kill me if you must, but don't look at me like that. Please don't!" She retrieves the dagger from the ground, cuts his ropes, then extends the handle to him. "Then kill me if you will. Kill me with one stroke—quickly."

The husband remains implacable, and the woman faints after weaving in front of him with the dagger. "When I opened my eyes and looked around, I saw there, in my husband's chest, the dagger . . . I didn't know what to do. I ran through the forest—I must have, although I don't remember. Then I found myself standing by a pond . . . I threw myself into it. I tried to kill myself. But, I failed. (She sobs.) What should a poor helpless woman like me do?"

According to the wife, then, she killed her husband, although she does not remember doing so. Perhaps she could not bear his rejection of her for an act that was beyond her control. There is the suggestion that since she has no memory of the killing, maybe Tajomaru came back and stabbed him to death. All she knows is that when she regained consciousness the dagger was lodged in her husband's heart. The symbolism of his having pierced her heart, too, is unavoidable.

A third account is given by the dead husband through a medium (Fumiko Homma). With her long robes, flowing hair, and ethereal voice, the effect of her description is mesmerizing.

In this version, the bandit said to the woman that "after she had given herself, she would no longer be able to live with her husband—why didn't she go with him, the bandit, rather than remain behind to be unhappy with her husband? He said he had only attacked her because of his great love for her."

The samurai-medium goes on: "My wife looked at him, her face soft, her eyes veiled . . . Never, in all our life together, had I seen her more beautiful . . . And what did my beautiful wife reply to the bandit in front of her helpless husband? . . . 'Take me. Take me away with you.'"

"That is what she said," the samurai continues, "But that is not all she did, or else I would not now be in darkness. 'Kill him,' she said. 'As long as he is alive I cannot go with you. Kill him!'" In an anguished voice he adds, "I still hear those words. They are like a wind blowing me to the bottom of this dark pit. Has anyone ever uttered more pitiless words? Even the bandit was shocked to hear them."

Tajomaru does, in fact, feel disgust at her callousness, and he asks the husband, "What do you want me to do with this woman? Kill her? Spare her?" The samurai-medium remarks, "For these words, I almost forgave the bandit." Tajomaru throws the woman from him, who then disappears among the trees. Although the bandit chases her, she gets away, and when he returns he cuts the samurai's bonds.

The husband, in his grief, picks up the dagger from the ground and thrusts it into his own chest.

By this account the husband commited suicide, which can be a noble act in Japanese culture, and his death cannot be attributed to either Tajomaru or his wife. The bandit, in fact, is depicted as having some decency, and the woman is portrayed as unfaithful and self-serving.

Finally, a woodcutter reports that he witnessed the incident first-hand. He claims that while walking in a clearing he heard a woman crying, and when he investigated he saw a man tied up and the bandit crouching beside the woman. Tajomaru was saying "Until now, whenever I wanted to do anything bad, I always did it. It was for me and so it was good. But today is different. I've already taken you, but now I want you more and more—and I suffer. Go away with me. If you want, I'll marry you. Look. (He bows his head low.) I am Tajomaru, the famous bandit, known all over Miyako, and yet here I am, on my knees in front of you."

The woman only sobs harder. "Don't cry," Tajomaru tells her, "Answer. Tell me you'll be my wife . . . Tell me." The woman replies "But, how could I answer? How could I, a woman, answer a question like that?"

She yanks the dagger out of the ground, but instead of attacking the bandit she cuts her husband's bonds, then falls to the grass between the two men. Tajomaru prepares to fight, but the samurai says, "Stop! I refuse to risk my life for such a woman." He walks up to his wife contemptuously. "You shameless whore! Why don't you kill yourself?" Then turning to the bandit he declares, "If you want her I'll give her to you. I regret the loss of my horse much more than I will regret the loss of this woman."

The wife is visibly shaken, while the bandit looks at her with distaste as she wipes the perspiration from her face. She collapses in tears, but when Tajomaru says, "Women cannot help but cry . . . they are naturally weak," she lashes back. "It's not me, not me—it's you who are weak." To the samurai she says disparagingly, "If you are my husband then why don't you kill this man? Then you can tell me to kill myself. That is what a real man would do. But you aren't a real man. That is why I was crying. I'm tired, tired of this farce." She then crosses to the bandit, taunting him in turn. "I thought that Tajomaru might find some way out. I thought that if he would only save me I would do anything for him. But he's not a man, either. He's just like my husband! . . . A woman can be won only by strength—by the strength of the swords you are wearing."

Stung by her words the two men draw their weapons. They seem reluctant to fight, but their manliness and pride demand it. A furious and sustained battle then ensues at the end of which the samurai's sword becomes lodged in a stump. The bandit traps him as he tries to crawl into a thicket, and hurls his sword into the samurai's chest. Throughout the fight the men gasp for breath, and their terror, sweat, and exhaustion are almost palpable.

As Kurosawa writes in the screenplay, afterwards, "Tajomaru and the woman . . . stare at the body. Tajomaru, an idiotic expression on his face, rises and takes her hands, but she pulls them away and begins to back off frantically, ending near the tree stump where her husband's sword is still lodged. She utters little inarticulate cries. Tajomaru has followed stupidly, and now, half crazed, he pulls the dead man's sword free and swings it mightily at her as she flees."

On this reading, the bandit killed the husband at the wife's urging. She is the principal offender because she provoked the fight even though she did not strike the deathblow. At times she seems appalled at instigating the violence, but she is also seen "laughing and pointing gleefully." The men by comparison do not want to attack each other, although they are easily manipulated into doing so.

One major difference between the accounts of the bandit and the woodcutter is that, in the first, Tajomaru is heroic, skilled, and resourceful, whereas the second shows him lurching about in fear and desperation. Here as in earlier sequences, Mifune's performance as the bandit has been acclaimed by critics. He becomes almost the quintessence of evil, menacing, unpredictable, coarse, and vicious.

Toward the end we see the woodcutter, the priest, and the commoner sitting at the Rashomon gate as the rain subsides, trying to make sense of the four accounts. In effect, all three parties have claimed to be the killer, and the woodcutter's interpretation shows Tajomaru as responsible but blames the woman as well.

After the woodcutter finishes his story the cynical commoner remarks, "And I suppose that is supposed to be true."

> WOODCUTTER: I don't tell lies.
> COMMONER: Well, so far as that goes, no one tells lies after he has said he's going to tell one.*
> PRIEST: But it's horrible. If men don't trust one another then the earth becomes a kind of hell.
> COMMONER: You are right. The world we live in is hell.
> PRIEST: No I trust men . . . I don't want to believe that this world is hell.
> COMMONER: Which one of these stories do you believe?
> WOODCUTTER: I don't understand any of them. They don't make any sense.

The commoner is given the last word on the subject: "Well, don't worry about it. It isn't as though men were reasonable."

Kurosawa has remarked, "The human heart is hollow and full of filth," implying that lying and deceit make it nearly impossible to know what actually occurred.

Perhaps to mitigate the bleakness of this conclusion, Kurosawa adds a somewhat artificial ending to the film. A baby is heard crying, and although the commoner ignores it, the priest and woodcutter respond to its helplessness. The woodcutter, in fact, agrees to raise the child, showing that people are not entirely wicked.

In presenting the various versions of the story Kurosawa seems to be asserting that the truth can never be known. There is no recording angel to transcribe events as they actually occurred, and people have different memories of what happened—recollections that are often inconsistent. People may believe what they say, but their honesty does not guarantee it is true.

All of the characters in the film offer accounts that are favorable to themselves, and their shame at their role in the tragedy also reflects well on them. Kurosawa wrote in his autobiography, "Human beings are unable to be honest about themselves. They cannot talk about themselves without embellishing." In *Rashomon* perhaps he is illustrating this idea, that in place of the truth we have only favorable remembrances that help us live with ourselves.

---

*When we lie, we claim to be telling the truth.

Since the audience is seeing the action as well as hearing the testimonials, Kurosawa is also saying that you cannot always believe what you see. The four accounts do not match, but neither do the visual representations, and we come to doubt our own perception of reality. We may need certainty in our lives, but all we have is the ephemeral moment, flashed before our eyes. In the end, the puzzle posed by the film leaves us unsettled and unresolved, with neither a literary nor a cinematic solution.

Between words and action, however, Kurosawa tends to trust action. He was always impressed by the honest emotions shown in silent films, where facial expression and gestures took the place of dialogue. In *Rashomon* so much of the plot is visual, perhaps because the eye discerns more than the ear.

One important philosophic point must be kept in mind: To claim that no one can know the truth is not the same as saying there is no truth to be known. For practical purposes it makes no difference, nevertheless the conceptual distinction is important. If truth exists then we do not create it, although, as Kurosawa implies, we may not be able to discover it. Thinking would not make it so, but perhaps we cannot think our way through to the reality.

Rashomon seems to assert the relativity of truth in the sense that we never know where it lies or who possesses it. What people take to be true is a reflection of who they are, varying according to their pride; the absolute truth may be unknowable.

Study Questions

1. Which of the accounts given by the participants in the rape and murder do you find most persuasive? Why?
2. If you were on a jury, which person would you convict?
3. What is Kurosawa's view of truth? How would you define truth?
4. Would you agree with Kurosawa's contention that people remember events in a way flattering to themselves?
5. Do you think we know anything for certain? How certain are you of that?

B. Modes of Knowing: Perceiving, Reasoning, Intuiting

Not only is the epistemologist concerned with issues of appearance and reality but with finding the most trustworthy means of knowing.

1. Empiricism To most people, the evidence of the senses is most trustworthy, and to rely on sense perception as the foundation of knowledge is called empiricism. To take in the world people use their eyes and ears primarily, but they also use their sense of smell, taste, and touch. We say "seeing is believing," and we mean to include all of our senses as means of gaining understanding of the world. If someone asks, "How do you know there was an avalanche?" it is enough to say, "Because I saw it and heard it"; if someone asks, "What makes you say dinner is ready?" they will be satisfied if you answer, "Because I smelled the aroma, then tasted some of the food cooking in the kitchen." According to the conventional rules, a statement is proven if we can cite some sense experience as evidence for it.

Science, of course, depends upon the empirical method as the foundation of its claims. Through observation and experimentation, the physical and natural sciences reach results that we accept today as true. Science, in fact, is not so much a particular subject matter as a method for obtaining reliable knowledge. Both astronomy and astrology take the stars as their subject matter, but only one is a science; the same is true of chemistry and alchemy. Even though they all deal with the physical properties of matter, astronomy and chemistry use careful observation and precise measurement. They formulate hypotheses to account for known phenomena, then test these hypotheses to see whether the predicted results actually occur. In short, scientific method differentiates science from other things, and that method uses sense perception as its foundation.

However, as we have seen above, our senses can deceive us. The reality revealed by the telescope and the microscope is very different from that disclosed by our ordinary sense perception; we never see the stars any more than the molecules underlying matter. The table is not stationary and solid, the sun neither rises nor sets, and parallel train tracks never meet, although all these things appear true to our senses. Since mistakes of this kind are extremely common, perhaps our sense perception is not reliable after all.

Furthermore, empiricism may be too narrow in scope to capture every dimension of reality. People who make statements about historical or mathematical truths, or judgments about ethics or aesthetics, do not claim to *see* that their ideas are right. In the same way, religious people who claim that God exists, or who believe in angels, prayer, miracles, or an afterlife, do not cite the evidence of their senses as proof. Faith is thought to transcend our ordinary understanding.

2. Rationalism   Because the senses are fallible and limited, some philosophers have relied on other ways of establishing reality. Most notably, they have adopted a rationalistic theory of epistemology, which maintains that the rational mind should be trusted to provide sound knowledge.

The historian and mathematician mentioned above both use a rational means of knowing. The historian tries to amass information about a period, person, or event, and to draw conclusions based upon that material. He or she will reason out the best interpretation of the evidence, building a coherent picture of history. For example, to claim that Napoleon was proclaimed emperor of France in 1804 is consistent with the reforms instituted at that time and attributed to him. French law was standardized under the Napoleonic code; schools were centralized; the court system simplified; and the principle established of freedom of religion. The mathematician, too, will construct a rational system of thought. All of this is consistent with the claim about Napoleon. To take another example, if a number multiplied by 5 equals 60, then the equation would be $x \times 5 = 60, 5x = 60$, and x is 12. This simple algebraic problem is solved by pure reasoning, without reference to any evidence of the senses. The historian was not present in the nineteenth century, and algebraic notations are abstractions that no mathematician has ever seen.

However, an internally consistent system may not correspond to any reality. The historical facts and conclusion may all hang together, but perhaps things did not happen that way. The mathematical system, while making logical sense, may not diagram reality at all; it could be a castle in the air. Jorge Luis Borges, the Argentinian writer, is brilliant at constructing plausible but fictitious accounts of history, and we know that in mystery stories, where the evidence clearly points to someone as the guilty party, he or she often turns out to be innocent after all. Bertrand Russell, the British philosopher, has written, "If you follow empiricism you will be partly right, but if you are a rationalist you can be entirely wrong."*

3. Intuitionism   Because of the difficulties in empiricism and rationalism, some philosophers prefer an intuitional approach whereby we rely on some immediate apprehension or sudden awareness of the truth. Rather than using our senses or reason, we trust an inner sense, akin to an instinct, that something is so. Our emotions become paramount, our feelings not our perception, our heart rather than our head.

The intuition referred to is not the trite "women's intuition" of popular magazines but a type of revelation that carries with it a deep certainty. We simply know that something is true, and no one can persuade us through any arguments that we are mistaken.

---

*For an attempt at a reconciliation of the empiricist-rationalist controversy, see the writings of Immanuel Kant.

When we make claims of a moral, aesthetic, or religious kind, they are usually based on intuition. If we state that preserving life is morally better than taking life, or that roses or moonlight on the water is beautiful, we seem to know this immediately and unquestioningly. The judgment that Hitler was a bad leader or Picasso was a good painter is not based on the senses. Our senses may tell us what each did (if we have direct evidence), but to evaluate their actions requires a mental judgment. We do not *see* that the Holocaust is one of the most terrible acts of the twentieth century, but we judge it as such; we only see fragmented figures in Picasso's *Guernica,* but we judge it intuitively to be a great painting.

Religious people base their faith on similar feelings, although revelation is often cited as the specific source of understanding. They need to differentiate their beliefs from superstition (as discussed earlier), but their reasons for believing have nothing to do with sense perception or rational proof. In fact, believers do not base their faith on reason or anything seen, heard, touched, smelled, or tasted, but rather on some spiritual experience that lies beyond ordinary knowledge. Faith is thought to speak directly to our heart and soul. The theologian Blaise Pascal expressed this when he wrote, "The heart has its reasons that reason does not know" (*Le coeur a ses raisons que la raison ne connais point*).

However, intuition, too, has its weaknesses, which stem mainly from its private nature. That is, when someone uses intuition to back up a claim, he or she will not allow contrary evidence to count against it. The intuition is "self-authenticating," and the fact that it runs counter to experience or is irrational makes no difference. Usually no harm is done when a person claims to know intuitively that life should be preserved, but suppose someone intuits that life should be taken. The Inquisition, the Crusades, the witch trials, the burning of heretics, pogroms, and so forth were carried out by people who believed they were following God's will. The Muslim fanatics who flew airliners into the World Trade Center and the Pentagon were sincerely convinced it was a holy act. If empirical and rational factors are disqualified, there is no protection against such horrors.

Intuitive claims, then, are unverifiable by anything outside the person. Furthermore, they vary enormously between individuals, and the same person will maintain different things at different times based on new intuitions. Something that fickle and subjective is unreliable as a foundation for knowledge. We must be able to distinguish "God spoke to me in a dream" from "I dreamt that God spoke to me," or false beliefs and even atrocities could result.

Discovering the best way of knowing is therefore a difficult task. The problem is compounded by the fact that we must assume a way of knowing in choosing a way of knowing. That is, in deciding whether empiricism, rationalism, or intuitionism is most reliable, we must first have some epistemological foundation for our choice. This begs the question at issue; that is, we are assuming the point we are trying to prove. What basis for knowledge can we use, then, in determining the best basis for knowledge?

In the second group of selections that follow, we have examples of the empirical, rational, and intuitive means of knowing. The eighteenth-century British philosopher David Hume presents a strong empiricist position while the seventeenth-century French philosopher Rene Descartes endorses a rationalist approach. The German writer Hermann Hesse and the Italian filmmaker Federico Fellini then illustrate an intuitive mode of understanding.

An Enquiry Concerning Human Understanding

David Hume

David Hume (1711–1776) was a Scottish philosopher and historian who is best known for his book Enquiry Concerning Human Understanding. *The* Enquiry *is actually a condensation of his first and more important work* A Treatise of Human Nature, *but because of its difficult style it was not well received. Hume also wrote* Essays Moral and Political, Political Discourses, *and a three-volume* History of England, *the last a classic in its time.*

Hume lived in England and France, maintained a friendship for a time with Jean Jacques Rousseau, and held various public positions in Great Britain. Although he wanted to obtain a university post, his appointment was blocked because of his skeptical ideas. He rejected traditional religious beliefs, denied the notion of causation, and even questioned the customary concept of the self. To Hume, the self has no spiritual substance as its core but is "nothing but a bundle or collection of different perceptions." Despite his skepticism, Hume was an unusually generous and gracious man whom the Scots referred to as St. David.

In the Enquiry *excerpted here, Hume argues that all genuine thoughts originate from sense perception. Even thoughts of bizarre creatures only combine elements that have been experienced by the senses, and if one of our senses is defective then we cannot form any idea dependent on it: "A blind man can form no notion of colours; a deaf man of sounds." This means that an idea is meaningless if there is no sense experience corresponding to it.*

Hume then divides all thoughts into two types: relations of ideas and matters of fact. The first only shows the formal connection between ideas as in "three times five is equal to half of thirty." Subsequent philosophers referred to these as analytic propositions, which included sentences such as "Circles are round," "Bachelors are unmarried males," and "Murals are on walls." Such sentences only express the implications of words or concepts, and although they are certain they are also rather trivial.

Matters of fact are more interesting statements because they make some claim about the external world rather than referring to themselves. "The sun will rise," "Swans are white," and "People inhabit all regions of the earth," are examples of this type of statement. Not all matter-of-fact statements are true; for example, black swans are found in Australia, but to verify the truth of such statements we cite some cause for the belief. We claim someone is in the country because we received a letter from him, and we can say that someone must have been on an island because we find a watch there.

From these commonsense beginnings, Hume then reaches some surprising conclusions. He maintains that cause and effect, which is the basis for matter-of-fact statements, is merely a psychological association between two events not a necessary connection. That is, there is no hidden force in one event that compels another event to happen. The pin does not make the balloon pop; the lighted match does not ignite the paper; the hammer does not drive the nail into the wood; pulling the trigger does not force the gun to fire. Rather, our experience teaches us that two events have always occurred in succession, so we come to expect the second when we see the first. This is what we mean by causation, the association of two events established through "custom or habit." We must not assume that some mysterious, hidden power exists in one event that forces a subsequent one to occur.

Hume arrives at this conclusion because he is a consistent empiricist. He only accepts the evidence of the senses, and since we never perceive a cause we cannot assume that any such thing exists. All that we perceive are events following each other in time; we do not see that the first event made the second happen.

Section 2

Of the Origin of Ideas

EVERY one will readily allow, that there is a considerable difference between the perceptions of the mind, when a man feels the pain of excessive heat, or the pleasure of moderate warmth, and when he afterwards recalls to his memory this sensation, or anticipates it by his imagination. These faculties may mimic or copy the perceptions of the senses; but they never can entirely reach the force and vivacity of the original sentiment. The utmost we say of them, even when they operate with greatest vigour, is, that they represent their object in so lively a manner, that we could *almost* say we feel or see it: But, except the mind be disordered by disease or madness, they never can arrive at such a pitch of vivacity, as to render these perceptions altogether undistinguishable. All the colours of poetry, however splendid, can never paint natural objects in such a manner as to make the description be taken for a real landscape. The most lively thought is still inferior to the dullest sensation.

We may observe a like distinction to run through all the other perceptions of the mind. A man, in a fit of anger, is actuated in a very different manner from one who only thinks of that emotion. If you tell me, that any person is in love, I easily understand your meaning, and form a just conception of his situation; but never can mistake that conception for the real disorders and agitations of the passion. When we reflect on our past sentiments and affections, our thought is a faithful mirror, and copies its objects truly; but the colours which it employs are faint and dull, in comparison of those in which our original perceptions were clothed. It requires no nice discernment or metaphysical head to mark the distinction between them.

Here therefore we may divide all the perceptions of the mind into two classes or species, which are distinguished by their different degrees of force and vivacity. The less forcible and lively are commonly denominated THOUGHTS or IDEAS. The other species want a name in our language, and in most others; I suppose, because it was not requisite for any, but philosophical purposes, to rank them under a general term or appellation. Let us, therefore, use a little freedom, and call them IMPRESSIONS; employing that word in a sense somewhat different from the usual. By the term *impression,* then, I mean all our more lively perceptions, when we hear, or see, or feel, or love, or hate, or desire, or will. And impressions are distinguished from ideas, which are the less lively perceptions, of which we are conscious, when we reflect on any of those sensations or movements above-mentioned.

Nothing, at first view, may seem more unbounded than the thought of man, which not only escapes all human power and authority, but is not even restrained within the limits of nature and reality. To form monsters, and join incongruous shapes and appearances, costs the imagination no more trouble than to conceive the most natural and familiar objects. And while the body is confined to one planet, along which it creeps with pain and difficulty; the thought can in an instant transport us into the most distant regions of the universe; or even beyond the universe, into the unbounded chaos, where nature is supposed to lie in total confusion. What never was seen, or heard of, may yet be conceived; nor is any thing beyond the power of thought, except what implies an absolute contradiction.

But though our thought seems to possess this unbounded liberty, we shall find, upon a nearer examination, that it is really confined within very narrow limits, and that all this creative power of the mind amounts to no more than the faculty of compounding, transposing, augmenting, or diminishing the materials afforded us by the senses and experience. When we think of a golden mountain, we only join two consistent ideas, *gold,* and *mountain,* with which we were formerly acquainted. A virtuous horse we can conceive; because, from our own feeling, we can conceive virtue; and this we may unite to the figure and shape of a horse, which is an animal familiar to us. In short, all the materials of thinking are derived either from our outward or inward sentiment: The mixture and composition of these belongs alone to the mind and will. Or, to express myself in philosophical language, all our ideas or more feeble perceptions are copies of our impressions or more lively ones.

To prove this, the two following arguments will, I hope, be sufficient. *First,* When we analyze our thoughts or ideas, however compounded or sublime, we always find, that they resolve themselves into
such simple ideas as were copied from a precedent feeling or sentiment.
Even those ideas, which, at first view, seem the most wide of this origin,
are found, upon a nearer scrutiny, to be derived from it. The idea of
God, as meaning *an infinitely intelligent, wise, and good Being,* arises
from reflecting on the operations of our own mind, and augmenting,
without limit, those qualities of goodness and wisdom. We may prosecute this enquiry to what length we please; where we shall always find,
that every idea which we examine is copied from a similar impression.
Those who would assert, that this position is not universally true nor
without exception, have only one, and that an easy method of refuting it;
by producing that idea, which, in their opinion, is not derived from this
source. It will then be incumbent on us, if we would maintain our doctrine, to produce the impression or lively perception, which corresponds
to it.

Secondly, If it happen, from a defect of the organ, that a man is not
susceptible of any species of sensation, we always find, that he is as little
susceptible of the correspondent ideas. A blind man can form no notion
of colours; a deaf man of sounds. Restore either of them that sense, in
which he is deficient; by opening this new inlet for his sensations, you
also open an inlet for the ideas; and he finds no difficulty in conceiving
these objects. The case is the same, if the object, proper for exciting any
sensation, has never been applied to the organ. A LAPLANDER or NEGROE
has no notion of the relish of wine. And though there are few or no instances of a like deficiency in the mind, where a person has never felt or
is wholly incapable of a sentiment or passion, that belongs to his species;
yet we find the same observation to take place in a less degree. A man of
mild manners can form no idea of inveterate revenge or cruelty; nor can a
selfish heart easily conceive the heights of friendship and generosity. It is
readily allowed, that other beings may possess many senses, of which we
can have no conception; because the ideas of them have never been introduced to us, in the only manner, by which an idea can have access to the
mind, to wit, by the actual feeling and sensation.

There is, however, one contradictory phænomenon, which may
prove, that it is not absolutely impossible for ideas to arise, independent
of their correspondent impressions. I believe it will readily be allowed,
that the several distinct ideas of colour, which enter by the eye, or those
of sound, which are conveyed by the ear, are really different from each
other; though, at the same time, resembling. Now if this be true of different colours, it must be no less so of the different shades of the same
colour; and each shade produces a distinct idea, independent of the rest.
For if this should be denied, it is possible, by the continual gradation of
shades, to run a colour insensibly into what is most remote from it; and if

you will not allow any of the means to be different, you cannot, without absurdity, deny the extremes to be the same. Suppose, therefore, a person to have enjoyed his sight for thirty years, and to have become perfectly acquainted with colours of all kinds, except one particular shade of blue, for instance, which it never has been his fortune to meet with. Let all the different shades of that colour, except that single one, be placed before him, descending gradually from the deepest to the lightest; it is plain, that he will perceive a blank, where that shade is wanting, and will be sensible, that there is a greater distance in that place between the contiguous colours than in any other. Now I ask, whether it be possible for him, from his own imagination, to supply this deficiency, and raise up to himself the idea of that particular shade, though it had never been conveyed to him by his senses? I believe there are few but will be of opinion that he can: And this may serve as a proof, that the simple ideas are not always, in every instance, derived from the correspondent impressions; though this instance is so singular, that it is scarcely worth our observing, and does not merit, that for it alone we should alter our general maxim.

Here, therefore, is a proposition, which not only seems, in itself, simple and intelligible; but, if a proper use were made of it, might render every dispute equally intelligible, and banish all that jargon, which has so long taken possession of metaphysical reasonings, and drawn disgrace upon them. All ideas, especially abstract ones, are naturally faint and obscure: The mind has but a slender hold of them: They are apt to be confounded with other resembling ideas; and when we have often employed any term, though without a distinct meaning, we are apt to imagine it has a determinate idea, annexed to it. On the contrary, all impressions, that is, all sensations, either outward or inward, are strong and vivid: The limits between them are more exactly determined: Nor is it easy to fall into any error or mistake with regard to them. When we entertain, therefore, any suspicion, that a philosophical term is employed without any meaning or idea (as is but too frequent), we need but enquire, *from what impression is that supposed idea derived?* And if it be impossible to assign any, this will serve to confirm our suspicion. By bringing ideas into so clear a light, we may reasonably hope to remove all dispute, which may arise, concerning their nature and reality.[1] . . .

---

[1]It is probable, that no more was meant by those, who denied innate ideas, than that all ideas were copies of our impressions; though it must be confessed, that the terms, which they employed, were not chosen with such caution, nor so exactly defined, as to prevent all mistakes about their doctrine. For what is meant by *innate?* If innate be equivalent to natural, then all the perceptions and ideas of the mind must be allowed to be innate or natural, in whatever sense we take the latter word, whether in opposition to what is uncommon, artificial, or miraculous. If by *innate* be meant, *cotemporary to our birth,* the dispute seems to be frivolous; nor is it worth while to enquire at what time thinking begins, whether before, at, or after our birth. Again, the word *idea,* seems to be commonly taken in a very loose sense, by LOCKE and others; as standing for any of our perceptions, our sensations and passions, as

Section 4

Sceptical Doubts concerning the Operations
of the Understanding

Part 1

ALL the objects of human reason or enquiry may naturally be divided into two kinds, to wit, *Relations of Ideas* and *Matters of Fact*. Of the first kind are the sciences of Geometry, Algebra, and Arithmetic; and in short, every affirmation, which is either intuitively or demonstratively certain. *That the square of the hypothenuse is equal to the square of the two sides*, is a proposition, which expresses a relation between these figures. *That three times five is equal to the half of thirty*, expresses a relation between these numbers. Propositions of this kind are discoverable by the mere operation of thought, without dependence on what is any where existent in the universe. Though there never were a circle or triangle in nature, the truths, demonstrated by EUCLID, would for ever retain their certainty and evidence.

Matters of fact, which are the second objects of human reason, are not ascertained in the same manner; nor is our evidence of their truth, however great, of a like nature with the foregoing. The contrary of every matter of fact is still possible; because it can never imply a contradiction, and is conceived by the mind with the same facility and distinctness, as if ever so conformable to reality. *That the sun will not rise to-morrow* is no less intelligible a proposition, and implies no more contradiction, than the affirmation, *that it will rise*. We should in vain, therefore, attempt to demonstrate its falsehood. Were it demonstratively false, it would imply a contradiction, and could never be distinctly conceived by the mind.

It may, therefore, be a subject worthy of curiosity, to enquire what is the nature of that evidence, which assures us of any real existence and matter of fact, beyond the present testimony of our senses, or the records of our memory. This part of philosophy, it is observable, has been little cultivated, either by the ancients or moderns; and therefore our doubts and errors, in the prosecution of so important an enquiry, may be the more excusable; while we march through such difficult paths, without

---

well as thoughts. Now in this sense, I should desire to know, what can be meant by asserting, that self-love, or resentment of injuries, or the passion between the sexes is not innate?

But admitting these terms, *impressions* and *ideas*, in the sense above explained, and understanding by *innate*, what is original or copied from no precedent perception, then may we assert, that all our impressions are innate, and our ideas not innate.

To be ingenuous, I must own it to be my opinion, that LOCKE was betrayed into this question by the schoolmen, who, making use of undefined terms, draw out their disputes to a tedious length, without ever touching the point in question. A like ambiguity and circumlocution seem to run through that philosopher's reasonings on this as well as most other subjects.

any guide or direction. They may even prove useful, by exciting curiosity, and destroying that implicit faith and security, which is the bane of all reasoning and free enquiry. The discovery of defects in the common philosophy, if any such there be, will not, I presume, be a discouragement, but rather an incitement, as is usual, to attempt something more full and satisfactory, than has yet been proposed to the public.

All reasonings concerning matter of fact seem to be founded on the relation of *Cause* and *Effect*. By means of that relation alone we can go beyond the evidence of our memory and senses. If you were to ask a man, why he believes any matter of fact, which is absent; for instance, that his friend is in the country, or in FRANCE; he would give you a reason; and this reason would be some other fact; as a letter received from him, or the knowledge of his former resolutions and promises. A man, finding a watch or any other machine in a desert island, would conclude, that there had once been men in that island. All our reasonings concerning fact are of the same nature. And here it is constantly supposed, that there is a connexion between the present fact and that which is inferred from it. Were there nothing to bind them together, the inference would be entirely precarious. The hearing of an articulate voice and rational discourse in the dark assures us of the presence of some person: Why? Because these are the effects of the human make and fabric, and closely connected with it. If we anatomize all the other reasonings of this nature, we shall find, that they are founded on the relation of cause and effect, and that this relation is either near or remote, direct or collateral. Heat and light are collateral effects of fire, and the one effect may justly be inferred from the other.

If we would satisfy ourselves, therefore, concerning the nature of that evidence, which assures us of matters of fact, we must enquire how we arrive at the knowledge of cause and effect.

I shall venture to affirm, as a general proposition, which admits of no exception, that the knowledge of this relation is not, in any instance, attained by reasonings *a priori;* but arises entirely from experience, when we find, that any particular objects are constantly conjoined with each other. Let an object be presented to a man of ever so strong natural reason and abilities; if that object be entirely new to him, he will not be able, by the most accurate examination of its sensible qualities, to discover any of its causes or effects. ADAM, though his rational faculties be supposed, at the very first, entirely perfect, could not have inferred from the fluidity and transparency of water, that it would suffocate him, or from the light and warmth of fire, that it would consume him. No object ever discovers, by the qualities which appear to the senses, either the causes, which produced it, or the effects, which will arise from it; nor can our reason, unassisted by experience, ever draw any inference concerning real existence and matter of fact. . . .

Suppose a person, though endowed with the strongest faculties of reason and reflection, to be brought on a sudden into this world; he would, indeed, immediately observe a continual succession of objects, and one event following another; but he would not be able to discover any thing farther. He would not, at first, by any reasoning, be able to reach the idea of cause and effect; since the particular powers, by which all natural operations are performed, never appear to the senses; nor is it reasonable to conclude, merely because one event, in one instance, precedes another, that therefore the one is the cause, the other the effect. Their conjunction may be arbitrary and casual. There may be no reason to infer the existence of one from the appearance of the other. And in a word, such a person, without more experience, could never employ his conjecture or reasoning concerning any matter of fact, or be assured of any thing beyond what was immediately present to his memory and senses.

Suppose again, that he has acquired more experience, and has lived so long in the world as to have observed similar objects or events to be constantly conjoined together; what is the consequence of this experience? He immediately infers the existence of one object from the appearance of the other. Yet he has not, by all his experience, acquired any idea or knowledge of the secret power, by which the one object produces the other; nor is it, by any process of reasoning, he is engaged to draw this inference. But still he finds himself determined to draw it: And though he should be convinced, that his understanding has no part in the operation, he would nevertheless continue in the same course of thinking. There is some other principle, which determines him to form such a conclusion.

This principle is CUSTOM or HABIT. For wherever the repetition of any particular act or operation produces a propensity to renew the same act or operation, without being impelled by any reasoning or process of the understanding; we always say, that this propensity is the effect of *Custom.* By employing that word, we pretend not to have given the ultimate reason of such a propensity. We only point out a principle of human nature, which is universally acknowledged, and which is well known by its effects. Perhaps, we can push our enquiries no farther, or pretend to give the cause of this cause; but must rest contented with it as the ultimate principle, which we can assign, of all our conclusions from experience. It is sufficient satisfaction, that we can go so far; without repining at the narrowness of our faculties, because they will carry us no farther. And it is certain we here advance a very intelligible proposition at least, if not a true one, when we assert, that, after the constant conjunction of two objects, heat and flame, for instance, weight and solidity, we are determined by custom alone to expect the one from the appearance of the other. This hypothesis seems even the only one, which explains the difficulty, why we draw, from a thousand instances, an inference, which we are not able to draw from one instance, that is, in no respect, different from them. Reason is incapable of any such variation. The conclusions, which it draws from considering one circle, are the same which it would form upon surveying all the circles in the universe. But no man, having seen only one body move after being impelled by another, could infer, that every other body will move after a like impulse. All inferences from experience, therefore, are effects of custom, not of reasoning. . . .

Study Questions

1. On what grounds does Hume claim that all knowledge is derived from sense perception? Why would you agree or disagree?
2. Provide an original example of a statement that shows a "Relation of Ideas" and one that is a "Matter of Fact."
3. Explain Hume's theory of causation. Could you refute his contention with an example of some cause and effect that you have seen?
4. Do you think there are other valid ways of knowing besides empiricism? What would they be?
5. How would you argue against the skeptic who claims we can never gain reliable knowledge?

Meditations on First Philosophy
René Descartes

René Descartes (1596–1650) was a French philosopher often considered as the father of modern thought as opposed to medieval thinking. His philosophic works include Discourse on Method, Principles of Philosophy, *and* Meditations on First Philosophy, *included in part below. He also made important contributions to the fields of science, physiology, optics, and mathematics, especially analytic geometry and theory of equations.*

In Descartes' philosophizing, he adopts a rigorous methodology based on reason. Specifically, he tried to apply the methods of science to philosophy, and he trusted the rational understanding that each person is capable of exercising. He once wrote: "In our search for the direct road to truth, we should busy ourselves with no object about which we cannot attain a certitude equal to that of the demonstrations of arithmetic or geometry."

Medieval dogmas are based on authority, which is questionable, and the senses are fallible, therefore Descartes relies only on the mind. He wants knowledge that cannot be doubted, and reason alone can yield certainty. He even questions the most obvious sense data, for example, his awareness of sitting in his chair in front of a fire in a robe with a paper in his hands. Although the sensations seem self-evident, dreams can have a similar vividness, and a God or devil could conjure up illusions that would be indistinguishable from reality. Whether the deception is for benevolent or malevolent reasons, he cannot trust his senses to provide "clear and distinct" ideas about the world.

In his method of "systematic doubt," Descartes is even led to question his own existence, but here he draws the line. If he thinks, then he must exist. Even if he is doubting or being deceived, he must exist to doubt or be deceived. Therefore this rational proposition is necessarily true: "Cogito ergo sum"; I think, therefore I am.

The "I" in this proposition does not refer to the body, which is known by (fallible) sense perception but to the thinking mind. Descartes therefore asks "But what then am I?" and he answers "A thing which thinks . . . which doubts, understands, [conceives], affirms, denies, wills, refuses, which also imagines and feels." Reason leads us to this indubitable conclusion.

To Descartes, all things are known by the mind not by the senses, and to prove this he uses a comparison with wax. Although a piece of wax can change in its smell, color, shape, size, temperature, and sound (when struck), we still recognize it to be same piece of wax. Since the sense qualities can be different, we do not know it is the same wax by using our senses; we can only know it through our rational mind.

Descartes, incidentally, never explained the relation between mind and body in a satisfactory way but divided the two in a doctrine known as "Cartesian dualism." Ever since Descartes presented his theory, philosophers have been trying to show how two such radically different entities can interact to form a complete self.

Meditation I.

Of the things which may be brought within the sphere of the doubtful.

It is now some years since I detected how many were the false beliefs that I had from my earliest youth admitted as true, and how doubtful was everything I had since constructed on this basis; and from that time I was convinced that I must once for all seriously undertake to rid myself of all the opinions which I had formerly accepted, and commence to build anew from the foundation, if I wanted to establish any firm and permanent structure in the sciences. But as this enterprise appeared to be a very great one, I waited until I had attained an age so mature that I could not hope that at any later date I should be better fitted to execute my design. This reason caused me to delay so long that I should feel that I was doing wrong were I to occupy in deliberation the time that yet remains to me for action. To-day, then, since very opportunely for the plan I have in view I have delivered my mind from every care [and am happily agitated by no passions] and since I have procured for myself an assured leisure in a peaceable retirement, I shall at last seriously and freely address myself to the general upheaval of all my former opinions.

Now for this object it is not necessary that I should show that all of these are false—I shall perhaps never arrive at this end. But inasmuch as reason already persuades me that I ought no less carefully to withhold my assent from matters which are not entirely certain and indubitable than from those which appear to me manifestly to be false, if I am able to find in each one some reason to doubt, this will suffice to justify my rejecting the whole. And for that end it will not be requisite that I should examine each in particular, which would be an endless undertaking; for owing to the fact that the destruction of the foundations of necessity brings with it the downfall of the rest of the edifice, I shall only in the first place attack those principles upon which all my former opinions rested.

All that up to the present time I have accepted as most true and certain I have learned either from the senses or through the senses; but it is sometimes proved to me that these senses are deceptive, and it is wiser not to trust entirely to any thing by which we have once been deceived.

But it may be that although the senses sometimes deceive us concerning things which are hardly perceptible, or very far away, there are yet many others to be met with as to which we cannot reasonably have any doubt, although we recognise them by their means. For example, there is the fact that I am here, seated by the fire, attired in a dressing gown, having this paper in my hands and other similar matters. And how could I deny that these hands and this body are mine, were it not perhaps that I compare myself to certain persons, devoid of sense, whose cerebella are so troubled and clouded by the violent vapours of black bile, that they constantly assure us that they think they are kings when they are really quite poor, or that they are clothed in purple when they are really without covering, or who imagine that they have an earthenware head or are nothing but pumpkins or are made of glass. But they are mad, and I should not be any the less insane were I to follow examples so extravagant.

At the same time I must remember that I am a man, and that consequently I am in the habit of sleeping, and in my dreams representing to myself the same things or sometimes even less probable things, than do those who are insane in their waking moments. How often has it happened to me that in the night I dreamt that I found myself in this particular place, that I was dressed and seated near the fire, whilst in reality I was lying undressed in bed! At this moment it does indeed seem to me that it is with eyes awake that I am looking at this paper; that this head which I move is not asleep, that it is deliberately and of set purpose that I extend my hand and perceive it; what happens in sleep does not appear so clear nor so distinct as does all this. But in thinking over this I remind myself that on many occasions I have in sleep been deceived by similar illusions, and in dwelling carefully on this reflection I see so manifestly that there are no certain indications by which we may clearly distinguish wakefulness from sleep that I am lost in astonishment. And my astonishment is such that it is almost capable of persuading me that I now dream.

Now let us assume that we are asleep and that all these particulars, e.g. that we open our eyes, shake our head, extend our hands, and so on, are but false delusions; and let us reflect that possibly neither our hands nor our whole body are such as they appear to us to be. At the same time we must at least confess that the things which are represented to us in sleep are like painted representations which can only have been formed as the counterparts of something real and true, and that in this way those general things at least, i.e. eyes, a head, hands, and a whole body, are not imaginary things, but things really existent. For, as a matter of fact, painters, even when they study with the greatest skill to represent sirens and satyrs by forms the most strange and extraordinary, cannot give them natures which are entirely new, but merely make a certain medley of the members of different animals; or if their imagination is extravagant enough to invent something so novel that nothing similar has ever before been seen, and that then their work represents a thing purely fictitious and absolutely false, it is certain all the same that the colours of which this is composed are necessarily real. And for the same reason, although these general things, to wit, [a body], eyes, a head, hands, and such like, may be imaginary, we are bound at the same time to confess that there are at least some other objects yet more simple and more universal, which are real and true; and of these just in the same way as with certain real colours, all these images of things which dwell in our thoughts, whether true and real or false and fantastic, are formed.

To such a class of things pertains corporeal nature in general, and its extension, the figure of extended things, their quantity or magnitude and number, as also the place in which they are, the time which measures their duration, and so on.

That is possibly why our reasoning is not unjust when we conclude from this that Physics, Astronomy, Medicine and all other sciences which have as their end the consideration of composite things, are very dubious and uncertain; but that Arithmetic, Geometry and other sciences of that kind which only treat of things that are very simple and very general, without taking great trouble to ascertain whether they are actually existent or not, contain some measure of certainty and an element of the indubitable. For whether I am awake or asleep, two and three together always form five, and the square can never have more than four sides, and it does not seem possible that truths so clear and apparent can be suspected of any falsity [or uncertainty].

Nevertheless I have long had fixed in my mind the belief that an all-powerful God existed by whom I have been created such as I am. But how do I know that He has not brought it to pass that there is no earth, no heaven, no extended body, no magnitude, no place, and that nevertheless [I possess the perceptions of all these things and that] they seem to me to exist just exactly as I now see them? And, besides, as I sometimes imagine that others deceive themselves in the things which they think they know best, how do I know that I am not deceived every time that I add two and three, or count the sides of a square, or judge of things yet simpler, if anything simpler can be imagined? But possibly God has not desired that I should be thus deceived, for He is said to be supremely good. If, however, it is contrary to His goodness to have made me such that I constantly deceive myself, it would also appear to be contrary to His goodness to permit me to be sometimes deceived, and nevertheless I cannot doubt that He does permit this.

There may indeed be those who would prefer to deny the existence of a God so powerful, rather than believe that all other things are uncertain. But let us not oppose them for the present, and grant that all that is here said of a God is a fable; nevertheless in whatever way they suppose that I have arrived at the state of being that I have reached—whether they attribute it to fate or to accident, or make out that it is by a continual succession of antecedents, or by some other method—since to err and deceive oneself is a defect, it is clear that the greater will be the probability of my being so imperfect as to deceive myself ever, as is the Author to whom they assign my origin the less powerful. To these reasons I have certainly nothing to reply, but at the end I feel constrained to confess that there is nothing in all that I formerly believed to be true, of which I cannot in some measure doubt, and that not merely through want of thought or through levity, but for reasons which are very powerful and maturely considered; so that henceforth I ought not the less carefully to refrain from giving credence to these opinions than to that which is manifestly false, if I desire to arrive at any certainty [in the sciences].

But it is not sufficient to have made these remarks, we must also be careful to keep them in mind. For these ancient and commonly held opinions still revert frequently to my mind, long and familiar custom having given them the right to occupy my mind against my inclination and rendered them almost masters of my belief; nor will I ever lose the habit of deferring to them or of placing my confidence in them, so long as I consider them as they really are, i.e. opinions in some measure doubtful, as I have just shown, and at the same time highly probable, so that there is much more reason to believe in than to deny them. That is why I consider that I shall not be acting amiss, if, taking of set purpose a contrary belief, I allow myself to be deceived, and for a certain time pretend that all these opinions are entirely false and imaginary, until at last, having thus balanced by former prejudices with my latter [so that they cannot divert my opinions more to one side than to the other], my judgment will no longer be dominated by bad usage or turned away from the right knowledge of the truth. For I am assured that there can be neither peril nor error in this course, and that I cannot at present yield too much to distrust, since I am not considering the question of action, but only of knowledge.

I shall then suppose, not that God who is supremely good and the fountain of truth, but some evil genius not less powerful than deceitful, has employed whole energies in deceiving me; I shall consider that the heavens, the earth, colours, figures, sound, and all other external things are nought but the illusions and dreams of which this genius has availed himself in order to lay traps for my credulity; I shall consider myself as having no hands, no eyes, no flesh, no blood, nor any senses, yet falsely believing myself to possess all these things; I shall remain obstinately attached to this idea, and if by this means it is not in my power to arrive at the knowledge of any truth, I may at least do what is in my power [i.e. suspend my judgment], and with firm purpose avoid giving credence to any false thing, or being imposed upon by this arch deceiver, however powerful and deceptive he may be. But this task is a laborious one, and insensibly a certain lassitude leads me into the course of my ordinary life. And just as a captive who in sleep enjoys an imaginary liberty, when he begins to suspect that his liberty is but a dream, fears to awaken, and conspires with these agreeable illusions that the deception may be pro-longed, so insensibly of my own accord I fall back into my former opinions, and I dread awakening from this slumber, lest the laborious wakefulness which would follow the tranquillity of this repose should have to be spent not in daylight, but in the excessive darkness of the diffi-culties which have just been discussed.

Meditation II.

Of the Nature of the Human Mind; and that it is more easily known than the Body.

The Meditation of yesterday filled my mind with so many doubts that it is no longer in my power to forget them. And yet I do not see in what manner I can resolve them; and, just as if I had all of a sudden fallen into very deep water, I am so disconcerted that I can neither make certain of setting my feet on the bottom, nor can I swim and so support myself on the surface. I shall nevertheless make an effort and follow anew the same path as that on which I yesterday entered, i.e. I shall proceed by setting aside all that in which the least doubt could be supposed to exist, just as if I had discovered that it was absolutely false; and I shall ever follow in this road until I have met with something which is certain, or at least, if I can do nothing else, until I have learned for certain that there is nothing in the world that is certain. Archimedes, in order that he might draw the terrestrial globe out of its place, and transport it elsewhere, demanded only that one point should be fixed and immovable; in the same way I shall have the right to conceive high hopes if I am happy enough to dis-cover one thing only which is certain and indubitable.

I suppose, then, that all the things that I see are false; I persuade myself that nothing has ever existed of all that my fallacious memory represents to me. I consider that I possess no senses; I imagine that body, figure, extension, movement and place are but the fictions of my mind. What, then, can be esteemed as true? Perhaps nothing at all, unless that there is nothing in the world that is certain.

But how can I know there is not something different from those things that I have just considered, of which one cannot have the slightest doubt? Is there not some God, or some other being by whatever name we call it, who puts these reflections into my mind? That is not necessary, for is it not possible that I am capable of producing them myself? I myself, am I not at least something? But I have already denied that I had senses and body. Yet I hesitate, for what follows from that? Am I so dependent on body and senses that I cannot exist without these? But I was per-suaded that there was nothing in all the world, that there was no heaven, no earth, that there were no minds, nor any bodies: was I not then like-wise persuaded that I did not exist? Not at all; of a surety I myself did exist since I persuaded myself of something [or merely because I thought of something]. But there is some deceiver or other, very powerful and very cunning, who ever employs his ingenuity in deceiving me. Then without doubt I exist also if he deceives me, and let him deceive me as much as he will, he can never cause me to be nothing so long as I think that I am something. So that after having reflected well and carefully examined all things, we must come to the definite conclusion that this proposition: I am, I exist, is necessarily true each time that I pronounce it, or that I mentally conceive it.

But I do not yet know clearly enough what I am, I who am certain that I am; and hence I must be careful to see that I do not imprudently take some other object in place of myself, and thus that I do not go astray in respect of this knowledge that I hold to be the most certain and most evident of all I have formerly learned. That is why I shall now consider anew what I believed myself to be before I embarked upon these last reflections; and of my former opinions I shall withdraw all that might even in a small degree be invalidated by the reasons which I have just brought forward, in order that there may be nothing at all left beyond what is absolutely certain and indubitable.

What then did I formerly believe myself to be? Undoubtedly I believed myself to be a man. But what is a man? Shall I say a reasonable animal? Certainly not; for then I should have to inquire what an animal is, and what is reasonable; and thus from a single question I should insensibly fall into an infinitude of others more difficult; and I should not wish to waste the little time and leisure remaining to me in trying to unravel subtleties like these. But I shall rather stop here to consider the thoughts which of themselves spring up in my mind, and which were not inspired by anything beyond my own nature alone when I applied myself to the consideration of my being. In the first place, then, I considered myself as having a face, hands, arms, and all that system of members composed of bones and flesh as seen in a corpse which I designated by the name of body. In addition to this I considered that I was nourished, that I walked, that I felt, and that I thought, and I referred all these actions to the soul; but I did not stop to consider what the soul was, or if I did stop, I imagined that it was something extremely rare and subtle like a wind, a flame, or an ether, which was spread throughout my grosser parts. As to body I had no manner of doubt about its nature, but thought I had a very clear knowledge of it; and if I had desired to explain it according to the notions that I had then formed of it, I should have described it thus: By the body I understand all that which can be defined by a certain figure: something which can be confined in a certain place, and which can fill a given space in such a way that every other body will be excluded from it; which can be perceived either by touch, or by sight, or by hearing, or by taste, or by smell: which can be moved in many ways not, in truth, by itself, but by something which is foreign to it, by which it is touched [and from which it receives impressions]: for to have the power of self-movement, as also of feeling or of thinking, I did not consider to appertain to the nature of body: on the contrary, I was rather astonished to find that faculties similar to them existed in some bodies.

But what am I, now that I suppose that there is a certain genius which is extremely powerful, and, if I may say so, malicious, who employs all his powers in deceiving me? Can I affirm that I possess the least of all those things which I have just said pertain to the nature of the body? I pause to consider, I revolve all these things in my mind, and I find none of which I can say that it pertains to me. It would be tedious to stop to enumerate them. Let us pass to the attributes of soul and see if there is any one which is in me? What of nutrition or walking [the first mentioned]? But if it is so that I have no body it is also true that I can neither walk nor take nourishment. Another attribute is sensation. But one cannot feel without body, and besides I have thought I perceived many things during sleep that I recognised in my waking moments as not having been experienced at all. What of thinking? I find here that thought is an attribute that belongs to me; it alone cannot be separated from me. I am, I exist, that is certain. But how often? Just when I think; for it might possibly be the case if I ceased entirely to think, that I should likewise cease altogether to exist. I do not now admit anything which is not necessarily true: to speak accurately I am not more than a thing which thinks, that is to say a mind or a soul, or an understanding, or a reason, which are terms whose significance was formerly unknown to me. I am, however, a real thing and really exist; but what thing? I have answered: a thing which thinks.

And what more? I shall exercise my imagination [in order to see if I am not something more]. I am not a collection of members which we call the human body: I am not a subtle air distributed through these members, I am not a wind, a fire, a vapour, a breath, nor anything at all which I can imagine or conceive; because I have assumed that all these were nothing. Without changing that supposition I find that I only leave myself certain of the fact that I am somewhat. But perhaps it is true that these same things which I supposed were non-existent because they are unknown to me, are really not different from the self which I know. I am not sure about this, I shall not dispute about it now; I can only give judgment on things that are known to me. I know that I exist, and I inquire what I am, I whom I know to exist. But it is very certain that the knowledge of my existence taken in its precise significance does not depend on things whose existence is not yet known to me; consequently it does not depend on those which I can feign in imagination. And indeed the very term *feign* in imagination proves to me my error, for I really do this if I imagine myself a something, since to imagine is nothing else than to contemplate the figure or image of a corporeal thing. But I already know for certain that I am, and that it may be that all these images, and, speaking generally, all things that relate to the nature of body are nothing but dreams [and chimeras]. For this reason I see clearly that I have as little reason to say, 'I shall stimulate my imagination in order to know more distinctly what I am,' than if I were to say, 'I am now awake, and I perceive somewhat that is real and true: but because I do not yet perceive it distinctly enough, I shall go to sleep of express purpose, so that my dreams may represent the perception with greatest truth and evidence.' And, thus, I know for certain that nothing of all that I can understand by means of my imagination belongs to this knowledge which I have of myself, and that it is necessary to recall the mind from this mode of thought with the utmost diligence in order that it may be able to know its own nature with perfect distinctness.

But what then am I? A thing which thinks. What is a thing which thinks? It is a thing which doubts, understands, [conceives], affirms, denies, wills, refuses, which also imagines and feels.

Certainly it is no small matter if all these things pertain to my nature. But why should they not so pertain? Am I not that being who now doubts nearly everything, who nevertheless understands certain things, who affirms that one only is true, who denies all the others, who desires to know more, is averse from being deceived, who imagines many things, sometimes indeed despite his will, and who perceives many likewise, as by the intervention of the bodily organs? Is there nothing in all this which is as true as it is certain that I exist, even though I should always sleep and though he who has given me being employed all his ingenuity in deceiving me? Is there likewise any one of these attributes which can be distinguished from my thought, or which might be said to be separated from myself? For it is so evident of itself that it is I who doubts, who understands, and who desires, that there is no reason here to add anything to explain it. And I have certainly the power of imagining likewise; for although it may happen (as I formerly supposed) that none of the things which I imagine are true, nevertheless this power of imagining does not cease to be really in use, and it forms part of my thought. Finally, I am the same who feels, that is to say, who perceives certain things, as by the organs of sense, since in truth I see light, I hear noise, I feel heat. But it will be said that these phenomena are false and that I am dreaming. Let it be so; still it is at least quite certain that it seems to me that I see light, that I hear noise and that I feel heat. That cannot be false; properly speaking it is what is in me called feeling; and used in this precise sense that is no other thing than thinking.

From this time I begin to know what I am with a little more clearness and distinction than before; but nevertheless it still seems to me, and I cannot prevent myself from thinking, that corporeal things, whose images are framed by thought, which are tested by the senses, are much more distinctly known than that obscure part of me which does not come under the imagination. Although really it is very strange to say that I know and understand more distinctly these things whose existence seems to me dubious, which are unknown to me, and which do not belong to me, than others of the truth of which I am convinced, which are known to me and which pertain to my real nature, in a word, than myself. But I see clearly how the case stands: my mind loves to wander, and cannot yet suffer itself to be retained within the just limits of truth. Very good, let us once more give it the freest rein, so that, when afterwards we seize the proper occasion for pulling up, it may the more easily be regulated and controlled.

Let us begin by considering the commonest matters, those which we believe to be the most distinctly comprehended, to wit, the bodies which we touch and see; not indeed bodies in general, for these general ideas are usually a little more confused, but let us consider one body in particular. Let us take, for example, this piece of wax: it has been taken quite freshly from the hive, and it has not yet lost the sweetness of the honey which it contains; it still retains somewhat of the odour of the flowers from which it has been culled; its colour, its figure, its size are apparent; it is hard, cold, easily handled, and if you strike it with the finger, it will emit a sound. Finally all the things which are requisite to cause us distinctly to recognise a body, are met with in it. But notice that while I speak and approach the fire what remained of the taste is exhaled, the smell evaporates, the colour alters, the figure is destroyed, the size increases, it becomes liquid, it heats, scarcely can one handle it, and when one strikes it, no sound is emitted. Does the same wax remain after this change? We must confess that it remains; none would judge otherwise. What then did I know so distinctly in this piece of wax? It could certainly be nothing of all that the senses brought to my notice, since all these things which fall under taste, smell, sight, touch, and hearing, are found to be changed, and yet the same wax remains.

Perhaps it was what I now think, viz. that this wax was not that sweetness of honey, nor that agreeable scent of flowers, nor that particular whiteness, not that figure, nor that sound, but simply a body which a little while before appeared to me as perceptible under these forms, and which is now perceptible under others. But what, precisely, is it that I imagine when I form such conceptions? Let us attentively consider this, and, abstracting from all that does not belong to the wax, let us see what remains. Certainly nothing remains excepting a certain extended thing which is flexible and movable. But what is the meaning of flexible and movable? Is it not that I imagine that this piece of wax being round is capable of becoming square and of passing from a square to a triangular figure? No, certainly it is not that, since I imagine it admits of an infinitude of similar changes, and I nevertheless do not know how to compass the infinitude by my imagination, and consequently this conception which I have of the wax is not brought about by the faculty of imagination. What now is this extension? Is it not also unknown? For it becomes greater when the wax is melted, greater when it is boiled, and greater still when the heat increases; and I should not conceive [clearly] according to truth what wax is, if I did not think that even this piece that we are considering is capable of receiving more variations in extension than I have ever imagined. We must then grant that I could not even understand through the imagination what this piece of wax is, and that it is my mind alone which perceives it. I say this piece of wax in particular, for as to wax in general it is yet clearer. But what is this piece of wax which cannot be understood excepting by the [understanding or] mind? It is certainly the same that I see, touch, imagine, and finally it is the same which I have always believed it to be from the beginning. But what must particularly be observed is that its perception is neither an act of vision, nor of touch, nor of imagination, and has never been such although it may have appeared formerly to be so, but only an intuition of the mind, which may be imperfect and confused as it was formerly, or clear and distinct as it is at present, according as my attention is more or less directed to the elements which are found in it, and of which it is composed.

Yet in the meantime I am greatly astonished when I consider [the great feebleness of mind] and its proneness to fall [insensibly] into error; for although without giving expression to my thoughts I consider all this in my own mind, words often impede me and I am almost deceived by the terms of ordinary language. For we say that we see the same wax, if it is present, and not that we simply judge that it is the same from its having the same colour and figure. From this I should conclude that I knew the wax by means of vision and not simply by the intuition of the mind; unless by chance I remember that, when looking from a window and saying I see men who pass in the street, I really do not see them, but infer that what I see is men, just as I say that I see wax. And yet what do I see from the window but hats and coats which may cover automatic machines? Yet I judge these to be men. And similarly solely by the faculty of judgment which rests in my mind, I comprehend that which I believed I saw with my eyes.

A man who makes it his aim to raise his knowledge above the common should be ashamed to derive the occasion for doubting from the forms of speech invented by the vulgar; I prefer to pass on and consider whether I had a more evident and perfect conception of what the wax was when I first perceived it, and when I believed I knew it by means of the external senses or at least by the common sense as it is called, that is to say by the imaginative faculty, or whether my present conception is clearer now that I have most carefully examined what it is, and in what way it can be known. It would certainly be absurd to doubt as to this. For what was there in this first perception which was distinct? What was there which might not as well have been perceived by any of the animals? But when I distinguish the wax from its external forms, and when, just as if I had taken from it its vestments, I consider it quite naked, it is certain that although some error may still be found in my judgment, I can nevertheless not perceive it thus without a human mind.

But finally what shall I say of this mind, that is, of myself, for up to this point I do not admit in myself anything but mind? What then, I who seem to perceive this piece of wax so distinctly, do I not know myself, not only with much more truth and certainty, but also with much more distinctness and clearness? For if I judge that the wax is or exists from the fact that I see it, it certainly follows much more clearly that I am or that I exist myself from the fact that I see it. For it may be that what I see is not really wax, it may also be that I do not possess eyes with which to see anything; but it cannot be that when I see, or (for I no longer take account of the distinction) when I think I see, that I myself who think am nought. So if I judge that the wax exists from the fact that I touch it, the same thing will follow, to wit, that I am; and if I judge that my imagination, or some other cause, whatever it is, persuades me that the wax exists, I shall still conclude the same. And what I have here remarked of wax may be applied to all other things which are external to me [and which are met with outside of me]. And further, if the [notion or] perception of wax has seemed to me clearer and more distinct, not only after the sight or the touch, but also after many other causes have rendered it quite manifest to me, with how much more [evidence] and distinctness must it be said that I now know myself, since all the reasons which contribute to the knowledge of wax, or any other body whatever, are yet better proofs of the nature of my mind! And there are so many other things in the mind itself which may contribute to the elucidation of its nature, that those which depend on body such as these just mentioned, hardly merit being taken into account.

But finally here I am, having insensibly reverted to the point I desired, for, since it is now manifest to me that even bodies are not properly speaking known by the senses or by the faculty of imagination, but by the understanding only, and since they are not known from the fact that they are seen or touched, but only because they are understood, I see clearly that there is nothing which is easier for me to know than my mind. But because it is difficult to rid oneself so promptly of an opinion to which one was accustomed for so long, it will be well that I should halt a little at this point, so that by the length of my meditation I may more deeply imprint on my memory this new knowledge.

Study Questions

1. In Descartes' method of systematic doubt, why does he question the existence of objects of perception?
2. Why does Descartes believe we can confuse dreams with waking life?

3. If we assume God exists, wouldn't he guarantee the authenticity of our sense experience?
4. Explain what is meant by the Cartesian statement: "I think, therefore I am."
5. For Descartes, what does the example of wax illustrate?

Siddhartha

Hermann Hesse
(trans. by Hilda Rosner)

Hermann Hesse (1877–1962) was a German poet and novelist who is best known for Steppenwolf *and* Siddhartha. *Several of his other novels also attained considerable popular success, including* Magister Ludi (The Glass-Bead Game), Narcissus and Goldmund, *and* Demian. *In all of Hesse's works he is persistently concerned not with social issues but with problems of how the individual in his striving can build a harmonious personality and an adequate relationship to the world.*

In his novel Siddhartha, *excerpted below, Hesse presents an interpretation of the world view of Indian religion, and he does so in a serene and musical style suggestive of the eternal flow of life itself. Siddhartha advances in his spiritual development from the stage of self-denial in which home, family, and caste are ascetically abandoned, to the life of sensual love, wealth, and power, to the simple existence of a ferryman absorbing the lessons of eternality taught by the river itself. In this last stage of final enlightenment, Siddhartha reaches an awareness of the interconnectedness of all things, their simultaneity and oneness, and through the medium of mystical experience is able to impart his vision to others.*

Siddhartha's vision is essentially that of Indian scripture which comprehends the universe as an immense, all-encompassing, unified whole, with the individual soul (Atman) actually one with the Absolute or world spirit (Brahman). Any separation then, between self and world, subject and object is artificial; there is only the All. This is the essential view of Guatama, the Buddha, founder of Buddhism, whose given name was Siddhartha.

In the following passage, Siddhartha (as an old man), tells his boyhood friend, Govinda, of the truth he has found.

Govinda once spent a rest period with some other monks in the pleasure grove which Kamala, the courtesan, had once presented to the followers of Gotama. He heard talk of an old ferryman who lived by the river, a day's journey away, and whom many considered to be a sage. When Govinda moved on, he chose the path to the ferry, eager to see this ferryman, for although he had lived his life according to the rule and was also regarded with respect by the younger monks for his age and modesty, there was still restlessness in his heart and his seeking was unsatisfied.

He arrived at the river and asked the old man to take him across. When they climbed out of the boat on the other side, he said to the old man: "You show much kindness to the monks and pilgrims; you have taken many of us across. Are you not also a seeker of the right path?"

There was a smile in Siddhartha's old eyes as he said: "Do you call yourself a seeker, O venerable one, you who are already advanced in years and wear the role of Gotama's monks?"

"I am indeed old," said Govinda, "but I have never ceased seeking. I will never cease seeking. That seems to be my destiny. It seems to me that you also have sought. Will you talk to me a little about it, my friend?"

Siddhartha said: "What could I say to you that would be of value, except that perhaps you seek too much, that as a result of your seeking you cannot find."

"How is that?" asked Govinda.

"When someone is seeking," said Siddhartha, "it happens quite easily that he only sees the thing that he is seeking; that he is unable to find anything, unable to absorb anything, because he is only thinking of the thing he is seeking, because he has a goal, because he is obsessed with his goal. Seeking means: to have a goal; but finding means: to be free, to be receptive, to have no goal. You, O worthy one, are perhaps indeed a seeker, for in striving towards your goal, you do not see many things that are under your nose."

"I do not yet quite understand," said Govinda. "How do you mean?"

Siddhartha said: "Once, O worthy one, many years ago, you came to this river and found a man sleeping there. You sat beside him to guard him while he slept, but you did not recognize the sleeping man, Govinda."

Astonished and like one bewitched the monk gazed at the ferryman.

"Are you Siddhartha?" he asked in a timid voice. "I did not recognize you this time, too. I am very pleased to see you again, Siddhartha, very pleased. You have changed very much, my friend. And have you become a ferryman now?"

Siddhartha laughed warmly. "Yes, I have become a ferryman. Many people have to change a great deal and wear all sorts of clothes. I am one of those, my friend. You are very welcome, Govinda, and I invite you to stay the night in my hut."

Govinda stayed the night in the hut and slept in the bed that had once been Vasudeva's. He asked the friend of his youth many questions and Siddhartha had a great deal to tell him about his life.

When it was time for Govinda to depart the following morning, he said with some hesitation: "Before I go on my way, Siddhartha, I should like to ask you one more question. Have you a doctrine, belief or knowledge which you uphold, which helps you to live and do right?"

Siddhartha said: "You know, my friend, that even as a young man, when we lived with the ascetics in the forest, I came to distrust doctrines and teachers and to turn my back on them. I am still of the same turn of mind, although I have, since that time, had many teachers. A beautiful courtesan was my teacher for a long time, and a rich merchant and a dice player. On one occasion, one of the Buddha's wandering monks was my teacher. He halted in his pilgrimage to sit beside me when I fell asleep in the forest. I also learned something from him and I am grateful to him, very grateful. But most of all, I have learned from this river and from my predecessor, Vasudeva. He was a simple man; he was not a thinker, but he realized the essential as well as Gotama. He was a holy man, a saint."

Govinda said: "It seems to me, Siddhartha, that you still like to jest a little. I believe you and know that you have not followed any teacher, but have you not yourself, if not a doctrine, certain thoughts? Have you not discovered certain knowledge yourself that has helped you to live? It would give me great pleasure if you would tell me something about this."

Siddhartha said: "Yes, I have had thoughts and knowledge here and there. Sometimes, for an hour or for a day, I have become aware of knowledge, just as one feels life in one's heart. I have had many thoughts, but it would be difficult for me to tell you about them. But this is one thought that has impressed me, Govinda. Wisdom is not communicable. The wisdom which a wise man tries to communicate always sounds foolish."

"Are you jesting?" asked Govinda.

"No, I am telling you what I have discovered. Knowledge can be communicated, but not wisdom. One can find it, live it, be fortified by it, do wonders through it, but one cannot communicate and teach it. I suspected this when I was still a youth and it was this that drove me away from teachers. There is one thought I have had, Govinda, which you will again think is a jest or folly: that is, in every truth the opposite is equally true. For example, a truth can only be expressed and enveloped in words if it is one-sided. Everything that is thought and expressed in words is one-sided, only half the truth; it all lacks totality, completeness, unity. When the Illustrious Buddha taught about the world, he had to divide it into Sansara and Nirvana, into illusion and truth, into suffering and salvation. One cannot do otherwise, there is no other method for those who teach. But the world itself, being in and around us, is never one-sided. Never is a man or a deed wholly Sansara or wholly Nirvana; never is a man wholly a saint or a sinner. This only seems so because we suffer the illusion that time is something real. Time is not real, Govinda. I have realized this repeatedly. And if time is not real, then the dividing line that seems to lie between this world and eternity, between suffering and bliss, between good and evil, is also an illusion."

"How is that?" asked Govinda, puzzled.

"Listen, my friend! I am a sinner and you are a sinner, but someday the sinner will be Brahma again, will someday attain Nirvana, will someday become a Buddha. Now this 'someday' is illusion; it is only a comparison. The sinner is not on the way to a Buddha-like state; he is not evolving, although our thinking cannot conceive things otherwise. No, the potential Buddha already exists in the sinner; his future is already there. The potential hidden Buddha must be recognized in him, in you, in everybody. The world, Govinda, is not imperfect or slowly evolving along a long path to perfection. No, it is perfect at every moment; every sin already carries grace within it, all small children are potential old men, all sucklings have death within them, all dying people—eternal life. It is not possible for one person to see how far another is on the way; the Buddha exists in the robber and dice player; the robber exists in the Brahmin. During deep meditation it is possible to dispel time, to see simultaneously all the past, present and future, and then everything is good, everything is perfect, everything is Brahman. Therefore, it seems to me that everything that exists is good—death as well as life, sin as well as holiness, wisdom as well as folly. Everything is necessary, everything needs only my agreement, my assent, my loving understanding; then all is well with me and nothing can harm me. I learned through my body and soul that it was necessary for me to sin, that I needed lust, that I had to strive for property and experience nausea and the depths of despair in order to learn not to resist them, in order to learn to love the world, and no longer compare it with some kind of desired imaginary world, some imaginary vision of perfection, but to leave it as it is, to love it and be glad to belong to it. These, Govinda, are some of the thoughts that are in my mind."

Siddhartha bent down, lifted a stone from the ground and held it in his hand.

"This," he said, handling it, "is a stone, and within a certain length of time it will perhaps be soil and from the soil it will become plant, animal or man. Previously I should have said: This stone is just a stone; it has no value, it belongs to the world of Maya, but perhaps because within the cycle of change it can also become man and spirit, it is also of importance. That is what I should have thought. But now I think: This stone is stone; it is also animal, God and Buddha. I do not respect and love it because it was one thing and will become something else, but because it has already long been everything and always is everything. I love it just because it is a stone, because today and now it appears to me a stone. I see value and meaning in each one of its fine markings and cavities, in the yellow, in the grey, in the hardness and the sound of it when I knock it, in the dryness or dampness of its surface. There are stones that feel like oil or soap, that look like leaves or sand, and each one is different and worships Om in its own way; each one is Brahman. At the same time it is very much stone, oily or soapy, and that is just what pleases me and seems wonderful and worthy of worship. But I will say no more about it. Words do not express thoughts very well. They always become a little different immediately they are expressed, a little distorted, a little foolish. And yet it also pleases me and seems right that what is of value and wisdom to one man seems nonsense to another."

Govinda had listened in silence.

"Why did you tell me about the stone?" he asked hesitatingly after a pause.

"I did so unintentionally. But perhaps it illustrates that I just love the stone and the river and all these things that we see and from which we can learn. I can love a stone, Govinda, and a tree or a piece of bark. These are things and one can love things. But one cannot love words. Therefore teachings are of no use to me; they have no hardness, no softness, no colors, no corners, no smell, no taste—they have nothing but words. Perhaps that is what prevents you from finding peace, perhaps there are too many words, for even salvation and virtue. Sansara and Nirvana are only words, Govinda. Nirvana is not a thing; there is only the word Nirvana."

Govinda said: "Nirvana is not only a word, my friend; it is a thought."

Siddhartha continued: "It may be a thought, but I must confess, my friend, that I do not differentiate very much between thoughts and words. Quite frankly, I do not attach great importance to thoughts either. I attach more importance to things. For example, there was a man at this ferry who was my predecessor and teacher. He was a holy man who for many years believed only in the river and nothing else. He noticed that the river's voice spoke to him. He learned from it; it educated and taught him. The river seemed like a god to him and for many years he did not know that every wind, every cloud, every bird, every beetle is equally divine and knows and can teach just as well as the esteemed river. But when this holy man went off into the woods, he knew everything; he knew more than you and I, without teachers, without books, just because he believed in the river."

Govinda said: "But what you call thing, is it something real, something intrinsic? Is it not only the illusion of Maya, only image and appearance? Your stone, your tree, are they real?"

"This also does not trouble me much," said Siddhartha. "If they are illusion, then I also am illusion, and so they are always of the same nature as myself. It is that which makes them so lovable and venerable. That is why I can love them. And here is a doctrine at which you will laugh. It seems to me, Govinda, that love is the most important thing in the world. It may be important to great thinkers to examine the world, to explain and despise it. But I think it is only important to love the world, not to despise it, not for us to hate each other, but to be able to regard the world and ourselves and all beings with love, admiration and respect."

"I understand that," said Govinda, "but that is just what the Illustrious One called illusion. He preached benevolence, forbearance, sympathy, patience—but not love. He forbade us to bind ourselves to earthly love."

"I know that," said Siddhartha smiling radiantly, "I know that, Govinda, and here we find ourselves within the maze of meanings, within the conflict of words, for I will not deny that my words about love are in apparent contradiction to the teachings of Gotama. That is just why I distrust words so much, for I know that this contradiction is an illusion. I know that I am at one with Gotama. How, indeed, could he not know love, he who has recognized all humanity's vanity and transitoriness, yet loves humanity so much that he has devoted a long life solely to help and teach people? Also with this great teacher, the thing to me is of greater importance than the words; his deeds and life are more important to me than his talk, the gesture of his hand is more important to me than his opinions. Not in speech or thought do I regard him as a great man, but in his deeds and life."

The two old men were silent for a long time. Then as Govinda was preparing to go, he said: "I thank you, Siddhartha, for telling me something of your thoughts. Some of them are strange thoughts. I cannot grasp them all immediately. However, I thank you, and I wish you many peaceful days."

Inwardly, however, he thought: Siddhartha is a strange man and he expresses strange thoughts. His ideas seem crazy. How different do the Illustrious One's doctrines sound! They are clear, straightforward, comprehensible; they contain nothing strange, wild or laughable. But Siddhartha's hands and feet, his eyes, his brow, his breathing, his smile, his greeting, his gait affect me differently from his thoughts. Never, since the time our Illustrious Gotama passed into Nirvana, have I ever met a man with the exception of Siddhartha about whom I felt: This is a holy man! His ideas may be strange, his words may sound foolish, but his glance and his hand, his skin and his hair, all radiate a purity, peace, serenity, gentleness and saintliness which I have never seen in any man since the recent death of our illustrious teacher.

While Govinda was thinking these thoughts and there was conflict in his heart, he again bowed to Siddhartha, full of affection towards him. He bowed low before the quietly seated man.

"Siddhartha," he said, "we are now old men. We may never see each other again in this life. I can see, my dear friend, that you have found peace. I realize that I have not found it. Tell me one more word, my esteemed friend, tell me something that I can conceive, something I can understand! Give me something to help me on my way, Siddhartha. My path is often hard and dark."

Siddhartha was silent and looked at him with his calm, peaceful smile. Govinda looked steadily in his face, with anxiety, with longing. Suffering, continual seeking and continual failure were written in his look.

Siddhartha saw it and smiled.

"Bend near to me!" he whispered in Govinda's ear. "Come, still nearer, quite close! Kiss me on the forehead, Govinda."

Although surprised, Govinda was compelled by a great love and presentiment to obey him; he leaned close to him and touched his forehead with his lips. As he did this, something wonderful happened to him. While he was still dwelling on Siddhartha's strange words, while he strove in vain to dispel the conception of time, to imagine Nirvana and Sansara as one, while even a certain contempt for his friend's words conflicted with a tremendous love and esteem for him, this happened to him.

He no longer saw the face of his friend Siddhartha. Instead he saw other faces, many faces, a long series, a continuous stream of faces—hundreds, thousands, which all came and disappeared and yet all seemed to be there at the same time, which all continually changed and renewed themselves and which were yet all Siddhartha. He saw the face of a fish, of a carp, with tremendous painfully opened mouth, a dying fish with dimmed eyes. He saw the face of a newly born child, red and full of wrinkles, ready to cry. He saw the face of a murderer, saw him plunge a knife into the body of a man; at the same moment he saw this criminal kneeling down, bound, and his head cut off by an executioner. He saw the naked bodies of men and women in the postures and transports of passionate love. He saw corpses stretched out, still, cold, empty. He saw the heads of animals, boars, crocodiles, elephants, oxen, birds. He saw Krishna and Agni. He saw all these forms and faces in a thousand relationships to each other, all helping each other, loving, hating and destroying each other and become newly born. Each one was mortal, a passionate, painful example of all that is transitory. Yet none of them died, they only changed, were always reborn, continually had a new face: only time stood between one face and another. And all these forms and faces rested, flowed, reproduced, swam past and merged into each other, and over them all there was continually something thin, unreal and yet existing, stretched across like thin glass or ice, like a transparent skin, shell, form or mask of water—and this mask was Siddhartha's smiling face which Govinda touched with his lips at that moment. And Govinda saw that this mask-like smile, this smile of unity over the flowing forms, this smile of simultaneousness over the thousands of births and deaths—this smile of Siddhartha—was exactly the same as the calm, delicate, impenetrable, perhaps gracious, perhaps mocking, wise, thousand-fold smile of Gotama, the Buddha, as he had perceived it with awe a hundred times. It was in such a manner, Govinda knew, that the Perfect One smiled.

No longer knowing whether time existed, whether this display had lasted a second or a hundred years, whether there was a Siddhartha, or a Gotama, a Self and others, wounded deeply by a divine arrow which gave him pleasure, deeply enchanted and exalted, Govinda stood yet a while bending over Siddhartha's peaceful face which he had just kissed, which had just been the stage of all present and future forms. His countenance was unchanged after the mirror of the thousand-fold forms had disappeared from the surface. He smiled peacefully and gently, perhaps very graciously, perhaps very mockingly, exactly as the Illustrious One had smiled.

Govinda bowed low. Uncontrollable tears trickled down his old face. He was overwhelmed by a feeling of great love, of the most humble veneration. He bowed low, right down to the ground, in front of the man sitting there motionless, whose smile reminded him of everything that he had ever loved in his life, of everything that had ever been of value and holy in his life.

Study Questions

1. Explain the significance of Siddhartha's statement to Govinda that "as a result of your seeking you cannot find."
2. What does Siddhartha mean when he states that words can only express truths that are one-sided, whereas the world itself carries everything within it.
3. Why does Siddhartha regard the river, clouds, birds, and beetles as divine?
4. What happens when Govinda kisses Siddhartha on the forehead?
5. Do you agree that objects are not separate from each other, and that you and other people are one? Why?

Juliet of the Spirits

Director: Federico Fellini

Screenplay: Federico Fellini, Tullio Pinelli, and Brunello Rondi

The Italian film director Federico Fellini (1920–1993) first achieved inter-national acclaim for Il Vitelloni, *then won four academy awards for best foreign films; these include* 8^1/$_2$, Amarcord, Nights of Cabinia, *and* La Strada. *Numbered among his celebrated later works are* La Dolce Vita, Satyricon, *and* Juliet of the Spirits.

Fellini was first drawn to depictions of marginal people—drifters, prostitutes, and circus performers, especially in Il Vitelloni, *but later his narratives and images reflected his own life in surrealistic episodes. Some of his work displays sensuous, macabre, and phantasmagoric elements which Fellini uses to find imaginative understanding. Through his vital imagery Fellini is trying to penetrate to some truth for himself and the audience.*

In all his films, Fellini projects onto the screen events in his past, es-pecially those that haunt him as symbols; these are also strongly Jungian symbols. In Juliet of the Spirits *it is not an accident that his wife of twenty years, Giuletta Masina, plays Juliet. He also starred his wife in his early and celebrated films* La Strada *and* Nights of Cabiria, *but never in roles so close to their real relationship. Juliet's husband Giorgio, of course, is a surrogate for Fellini, but in caricature form—a self-parody of the charming philanderer with a bizarre group of followers.*

The fantasies in Fellini's films are usually those of the lead male, but in Juliet of the Spirits *the eroticism is reversed and becomes the heroine's adventures. Fellini intended the part as a gift to his wife, although all of his films are ultimately autobiographical. Luckily for the movie-going public, he has transmuted his history into art.*

When Juliet of the Spirits *was initially released it was given a Best Foreign Film award by the New York Film Critics and the National Board of Review. Considered a classic, it was recently restored in rich color by an Italian communications and broadcasting company.*

Synopsis

In his film *Juliet of the Spirits,* Fellini portrays a woman who turns away from conventional means of knowing in favor of the insights provided by feeling. An upper-class, middle-aged Italian wife named Juliet (Giulietta Masina) is shattered to learn that her husband Giorgio (Mario Pisu) has been unfaithful. At the same time, she fears the loneliness that would follow if he left her. To escape the painful reality of her situation, she takes refuge in a world of fantasies and dreams.

To some extent the images are projections of her own fears and wishes—desires that are felt so strongly they seem to come from outside herself. But she also moves in a somnambulistic way through actual experiences.

The dividing line between imagination and reality is never clearly drawn, and some of the scenes may be depictions of a psychic break-down, but Fellini orchestrates the plot so that Juliet's own emotional life is enhanced and celebrated. She learns to trust her feelings and through them to reach intuitive knowledge and some measure of peace.

From the start, Juliet seems unusually responsive to the spirit world, and we first see her participating in a séance conducted by her friend Valentina. Giorgio is seated in an armchair transcribing the messages, while three others, Alba, Raniero, and Chierichetta, are gathered round the table, their thumbs and little fingers intertwined to form a chain. The medium Valentina puts out the cat ("They attract restless spirits."), passes a stick of incense around their heads three times, and then inserts it into a chrysanthemum. The table trembles, tilts, and begins to tap on the carpet: The ghosts have arrived.

Juliet opens her eyes wide, incredulous, like someone who has had too much good luck. She looks at the others questioningly. Valentina mumbles, her forehead in a frown:

VALENTINA: It's a new spirit. I can tell from the way it moves the table. It's never manifested itself like this.

Juliet leans toward her and humbly, anxiously, like someone confessing a deep desire, says:

JULIET: Ask it something.

There is a silent pause.

VALENTINA: Can you tell us your name, spirit? (*The table beats out "I." Valentina successively calls out the letters, which Giorgio, in the armchair, writes down.*) I . . . R . . . I . . . S.
JULIET: Iris. What a beautiful name!
TABLE: I am beautiful.
VALENTINA: Have you a message for us, Iris?
TABLE: Love for all.
ALBA: Love for all? How lovely!
VALENTINA: Thank you, Iris. You're very sweet. Yours is a delightful message. Dear, would you like—

She stops herself because the table starts shaking violently. Juliet is very tense.

JULIET: What is it?

VALENTINA (*disconcerted*): I don't know. (*The table again shakes violently.*) Maybe it's an interference. Is that still you, Iris?

The table beats out a decisive "No."

CHIERICHETTA: It said no. Who can it be? . . .
VALENTINA: Can you tell us your name?

The table taps its message like a precise telegram. Quickly raising her head, Juliet is the first to interpret the message. With a holy attitude, she spells out:

JULIET: O . . . L . . . A . . . F.
CHIERICHETTA (*fascinated, approving*): It's Olaf, yes. . . .
ALBA: Have you a message for each one of us?
VALENTINA: Can you tell us something sweet, which might help us live, help us understand the meaning of our lives?
TABLE: Yes. . . .

Then suddenly the table taps out the name of Juliet. Alba, very excited, calls out:

ALBA: Juliet, a message for you.

Juliet turns pale.

TABLE: What are you up to? What's come into your head? Just what do you think you are? You're nothing; you don't count at all. You're of no importance to anyone . . . to anyone.

Juliet, now deathly pale, tries to say something. Doing her best to get up, she suddenly collapses, senseless.

ALBA: Juliet!
VALENTINA: Darling, darling. What are you doing? Stop. Don't break the chain.

Very excited, they all surround her, hold her up, call to her. With an almost sadistic compassion, Chierichetta exclaims:

CHIERICHETTA: She's going to die right here!
ALBA: A little water? . . .
GIORGIO: No, no. Wait. All right. It's over. All right. Juliet? Up, up.

Juliet opens her eyes with difficulty. She looks around as they call to her, smile at her, make her smell vinegar and gulp down a little water. She slowly recovers consciousness.

She looks at the faces of those around her, in an effort to recognize them. Finally, as if overcome by a sudden terror, her eyes search for her husband. She sees him and stares at him desperately. Suddenly she throws her arms around his neck, pulling him tightly toward her, with a muffled sob.

The judgment passed on Juliet by OLAF is obviously a reflection of her poor self-image, something she carries inside her rather than deriving it from the experience. When she clings to her husband in desperation it is probably out of insecurity, as well as fear at hearing the spirit's voice; she cannot imagine him staying with someone as inconsequential as herself.

Aside from séances (with echoes from *La Dolce Vita*), Juliet has a rich imaginative life of her own. She dreams wonderful/terrible images and is enthralled by the colorful scenes around her. Following the séance, when she is at the beach at Fregene with the local doctor, Don Raffaele, she refers to her inner-life as a girl.

> Sometimes, when I was a child, all I had to do was close my eyes and I saw—
> DON RAFFAELE: I see when I open my eyes, dear signora.
> JULIET: No, I mean . . . I used to see . . . people I didn't know . . . places. Now, instead . . .

Juliet closes her eyes as if to illustrate what she means and immediately feels a tremor. For a brief moment she has seen a flash of beautiful womanly faces.

Iris, perhaps?

Juliet opens her eyes again; she is upset and remains lost in emptiness while the doctor continues to speak.

> DON RAFFAELE: Such things are often digestive phenomena, dear signora. Digestion . . . the solar plexus slightly disturbed. Toxins, entering in a circle, reach the cerebral nervous centers. The hypophysis, in turn . . . a congestion forms.

Juliet's recounting of her visions and Don Raffaele's dismissal of them is interrupted by an image that seems magical. A helicopter flies over the umbrellas and lands on the beach nearby.

> From the cabin of the helicopter there emerges a beautiful half-dressed woman—Susy—who turns to wave goodbye to the pilot as the helicopter takes off.
> Susy keeps waving toward the sky; then, slowly, sure of herself, paying no attention to her surroundings, she crosses the beach and goes into the pine forest.
> Her passage has left breathless not only Juliet and her friends, but also the two or three young men scattered along the beach. It had been like an apparition of a superb feminine divinity.
> DON RAFFAELE (*recovering*): This, yes. This is an apparition I believe in.
> HIS WIFE (*chewing*): Last year I gave her massages. She has skin like silk. It disgusted me. (*She pauses, then speaks with hostility.*) She's the mistress of an industrialist. A man with white hair.

Later that same day, when the doctor and his wife have left and the beach is deserted, Juliet receives visions, and once again the realm of dreams, hallucinations, and actuality are indistinguishable.

Juliet closes her eyes and, from the deserted sea, right in front of her, there emerges from a large bubble of gray water, a large raft of wood and iron, loaded with ferocious and savage men. They carry weapons, barbaric armor, and daggers; they wear caps similar to the Fascist fezzes, with skull and crossbones, and bear strange flags covered with monsters and dragons. Their faces are those of Mongols, with drooping mustaches and rough-shaven beards. Juliet quickly opens her eyes, looking at the sea. The raft is there, in front of her; it is slowly approaching the shore. On its side, in large letters, is written OLAF.

Beyond the first raft, others are seen, these too loaded with mysterious warriors and with savage, shaggy horses.

Juliet tries to get up, terrified, with an instinctive desire to flee. She is at first unable to get to her feet and for a few moments crawls forward. Then she begins to run, stumbling as she does. Panting, frightened, she turns around. The rafts are still there, and now some of the warriors, naked, are on the beach, pulling the rafts to shore with huge ropes.

Juliet starts to run again, arriving almost at the dunes. Short of breath, she stops again, looking over her shoulder.

But now the rafts are gone, taking with them the savage warriors and horses, leaving behind no trace. The sea stretches out, calm and luminous, disappearing from sight.

In her relationship with her mother, Juliet is shown as deferential and subordinate, habitually criticized for her clothes and drab appearance. Massina plays Juliet as a rather mousy, insecure, dowdy, and dutiful housewife, immensely likable with her bright eyes, slight smile, and trim haircut, but sadly ordinary. Her mother (Caterina Boratto), on the other hand, is a beautiful and sophisticated woman who spends her time at the hairdresser and at glamorous gatherings. She seems to regard Juliet as a disappointment compared to her elegant daughter Adele, and always addresses her in a condescending way. The following scene is typical of the family dynamic:

A car has stopped in the little road near her. From it come two children, who greet her happily. They are her niece and nephew, children of her sister Adele, who is behind the wheel of the car. Next to Adele is Juliet's mother, an imposing woman, authoritative and cool, with a still-young face crowned by rich gray and blue hair. She is very elegant, as is Adele, who is beautiful, maternal, self-assured.

CHILDREN: Aunty. Hello, Aunty.

Juliet kisses them and goes to the car.

JULIET: Mamma, hello. Hello, Adele.

MOTHER: Where've you been? Whenever I come to see you, you're out. It's as if you did it on purpose. (*As Juliet leans over to kiss her, she pulls away.*) No, you're all wet.

JULIET: I was just going home. Let's go. Do you want some coffee?

MOTHER: It's too late now. (*She turns to Adele, speaking in a tone that implies the confidence of one friend speaking to another of things that concern only the two of them.*) What time do we have to be at Luciana's?

ADELE: At four. And first we have to stop off so that I can have my corset fitted.

MOTHER: Didn't Giorgio tell you? I called him myself.

ADELE: Where is your husband?

JULIET: In his office, working.

ADELE (*ironic, somewhat hostile*): He works so much! It's impossible to see him ever. Never a Sunday, never a vacation. Get in, children.

JULIET: What do you mean? In a month—he said he'll take a real rest. Maybe we'll take a cruise. To Spain or to Greece. We haven't decided yet, but I've got all the information. (*Her tone has suddenly become uncertain as she realizes that her mother is staring at her.*) What's wrong? Have I said something?

MOTHER: No, nothing. I was just looking. Don't you ever put cream on? You really don't take care of yourself. Give my best to Giorgio. So long. Call me tomorrow.

The car leaves.

One evening Juliet's worst nightmare is realized when she discovers that her husband has a mistress. He utters the name "Gabriella" in his sleep, and Juliet catches him speaking in an intimate tone to someone on the telephone; when he is challenged, Giorgio makes a lame excuse. The fact that he hardly tries to be convincing is itself a sign of contempt and indifference.

Distraught and fearful, Juliet begins to immerse herself in a world of the bizarre and fantastic. She has conversations with fey and exotic individuals, attends erotic parties given by her salacious, amoral neighbor Susy (Sandra Milo), and has an audience with Bhisma, an androgynous mystic.

Bhisma is the latest craze among the wealthy who are looking for the outlandish and thrilling. This man/woman is regarded as a seer in touch with the supernatural and dispensing inspired wisdom. Bhisma gives lectures on wise living dressed in exotic clothes and speaking in a thin, eerie voice, neither male nor female. On some occasions he/she also meets privately with people to help them with their personal problems, and in the following scene Valentina implores Bhisma to speak to Juliet.

BHISMA'S ROOM. INTERIOR. NIGHT.

VALENTINA: Maestro, my friend really wanted to talk to you. You can really help her. (*She encourages Juliet.*) Tell him, tell him. Do you want us to leave you alone with him? Speak to him, darling.

Bhisma stops staring at Juliet and goes to sit in an armchair. In the meantime, the assistant goes back and forth from the bathroom, after having taken the cup from Bhisma. Juliet, making a great effort, says in a low voice:

JULIET: No, nothing . . . There was something . . . something that . . . (*She is silent a moment; then, getting back her courage, she almost whispers.*) Since last night it has seemed to me that I have nothing. I'm afraid I lack everything. I'm afraid my husband has another woman.

Bhisma, calm, continues to smile. The assistant pours a liquid on her hands and begins to massage his head. But now Bhisma is staring intently at Juliet.

BHISMA: Anxiety . . . yes . . . but you must enter into another dimension. Another dimension. All things are only in three; in the fourth they rejoice. (*A moment of silence, then he begins again, strangely calm.*) It's the fourth dimension. The *Lapis Philosophorum.* "Make of a man and a woman a circle. And from this extract a square, and from the square a triangle."

He closes his eyes as if from the massage and remains silent. Alba, still excited, takes his hand and examines it.

ALBA: May I, Maestro? I would so like to . . . I draw. I am a painter. I would like to make a sketch of you. Even of your hand alone. I can come tomorrow.

Bhisma doesn't answer; he puts his head back and closes his eyes completely. There is a long silence, and the three women look at each other not knowing what to do. They watch the assistant, who is indicating to them that they should leave.

But suddenly Bhisma begins to act very oddly. Slow and increasingly effeminate movements from the arms and shoulders, accompanied by a stretching of—and a change in—the features of his face. An indefinable mask, almost too feminine, comes over his face. The assistant signals to the women not to move. Obviously the trance has begun. With a slow, soothing voice, the assistant asks:

ASSISTANT: Who are you, spirit?

BHISMA (*speaking in a strange voice, both sweet and sensual*): Iris.

Juliet starts; it is as if she perceived an extremely disturbing feminine presence around the shoulders of Bhisma. There is beauty and a sensuality of form and position. In the same voice, Bhisma begins again:

BHISMA-IRIS: Why don't you learn to please your husband, Juliet?

Juliet looks around. Upset, she answers in a hoarse voice, almost aggressively:

JULIET: I please my husband very much.

Bhisma breaks into laughter.

BHISMA-IRIS: I was born this way . . . a woman of love. Don't you find me beautiful? Speak freely.
JULIET (*after some hesitation, as if in a dream*): Yes. Very beautiful.
BHISMA-IRIS: Frankly, I too think I am beautiful. Yes, very beautiful. Have you seen my hair? I don't comb it; I caress it. I very much like to caress myself. I have such beautiful, fresh skin. When I'm in a bad mood, I go to the mirror and look at my back. I immediately become happy then. Have you bought stockings, Juliet?
JULIET: What stockings?
BHISMA-IRIS: Black net ones. All women want to be treated like fairies—and they don't know their job.
JULIET (*disturbed, aggressive*): Is love a job?
BHISMA-IRIS: I didn't say "job." I said "art." The art of loving. I had breasts when I was nine.
JULIET: No, I heard you very well. You said "job." A whore, then. Fine.

Once more a fresh and shameless laugh from the lips of Bhisma.

BHISMA-IRIS: Why don't you make yourself as beautiful as I am?

Bhisma's voice now fades out in a confused gurgle; the features of his face change again and another mask takes over, another voice comes from his lips. A masculine voice, persuasive and seductive, with a peculiar Spanish accent.

BHISMA: No one knows you, Juliet. No one sees you. Men no longer recognize real women. You are a real woman.
ASSISTANT: Who are you, spirit? Will you tell us your name?
BHISMA: I see all of you. Your breasts are beautiful, your hair is beautiful. Why are you afraid? You have extraordinary powers because your feminine sensuality is so refined. You are beautiful, Juliet. You are a real woman.
ASSISTANT: But who are you, who are you?

But Bhisma is coming to. He gurgles and stretches; his features return to normal.

The most seductive force in Juliet's life is her neighbor Susy, the woman who emerged from the helicopter on the beach, and Fellini treats their scenes as the most erotic and pungent in the film. The freedom Susy displays, the atmosphere of uninhibited sensuality, is almost irresistible to Juliet at this traumatic point in her life. She is strongly tempted to abandon her former, cautious nature and become more sexually adventurous under Susy's instruction.

Everything about Susy is lush and voluptuous. When she shows Juliet through the rooms of her villa they seem designed for love, and later, in the woods, she points out a tree house for rendezvous with men, complete with an elevator on a pulley; as Juliet watches, a man ascends to the nest. At a phantasmagoric party, Juliet is introduced to an unimagined world of sensual pleasure and self-indulgence, and she is encouraged to give herself to a beautiful boy reclining on silk cushions.

Juliet first contrives to meet Susy by returning her cat to the villa, and from the moment she enters the villa she feels the pull of the erotic.

THE GARDEN OF SUSY'S VILLA. EXTERIOR. DAYTIME.

The gate is half shut and—cat in arms—Juliet pushes it delicately and enters the rich garden. In the middle of the garden a shining, blue-tiled swimming pool surrounded by elegant outdoor furniture. With the cat held lovingly in her arms, Juliet timidly crosses the garden.

Scattered everywhere are the remains of a party. Abandoned party souvenirs, streamers, empty bottles. Everything very obvious, as if put there just to strike Juliet's imagination. A sense of total disorder under the covered terrace: many cushions still bearing the imprints of bodies, dirty dishes, records.

JULIET: May I—?

No one answers. Juliet enters the vast living room, a room full of all kinds of furniture, many sofas, curtains—disorder. Here the feeling of a party the night before is even stronger. A voice stops Juliet; it is Susy on the telephone. Though she would like to turn back, she is attracted by the voice and wants to listen. She stands, confused, in the veil of a curtain, which flutters around her face. She seems nailed there; she must listen.

Slowly, Susy's voice becomes clearer. A warm, sensual voice, interrupted by throaty laughter. A northern accent; from Ferrara.

SUSY (*on the telephone*): No, no, no. I just got up; how do you think I am? You can imagine. . . . This spring. . . . What? Let me think a moment. The smell. Yes, your skin smells a little of tobacco and of salt water, the sea. I realized that, yes. (*She laughs.*) It was obvious—couldn't you tell from the way I laughed? (*She sighs.*) You're impossible. Today? Maybe late in the afternoon. . . . I'm letting myself go. . . . Yes, you're a rat. . . . No, no complications for me. . . . Everything, everything, but no complications. It must be simple, because it is simple. Like the first time. Yes? Yes? Yes! Go back to the shower; you'll catch cold. (*A long silence. Susy, with a smile on her lips, looks around lasciviously and sees Juliet. But, as if she hadn't seen her, she continues to smile into space.*) Yes. . . . Yes. . . . Yes. (*Susy's voice is increasingly excited. Softly, she says a final "yes."*) Hold on one minute. (*She puts the mouthpiece of the phone on the sofa where she had been stretched out and gets up, smiling at Juliet.*) Oh, how sweet; you brought Rubirosa back. (*The cat jumps out of Juliet's arms and goes to Susy, who picks it up, kisses and pets it.*) My Rubirosa. Enormous Ruby, here, here, to your sweet mistress who wants to have all of you. Oh, come on, my thief, my troublemaker.

The cat miaows with pleasure. Without realizing it, Susy uses with him the same words she uses in her intimate moments with men; but she does it gracefully, in a low voice. Under a transparent robe, Susy is naked; her hair is uncombed—but the presence of Juliet doesn't embarrass her at all.

JULIET: He came into my garden. I thought I should bring him back. You know, they steal them.
SUSY (*detached, cutting it short*): Thank you. Isn't it true, Ruby, that we thank the lady? Imagine, they might steal you! Thank you, signora. Signora—
JULIET: My name is Juliet.
SUSY: I'm Susy. You like my Rubirosa. You know, he has a lot of names. Cloud, Pappone, Apollo—and, finally, Lover. Yes! Oh . . . (*She picks up the phone again.*) Are you still there? A woman who lives near here brought Rubirosa back. . . . Beautiful? Of course. (*She laughs.*) All my friends are beautiful. . . . Oh, that I don't know. (*Quietly*) Maybe. . . . Goodbye, goodbye. . . . Yes, yes, yes, yes. (*She hangs up the phone. Juliet is pleased. She feels that by her mere presence in this home she is living through an extraordinary adventure, a little like a prostitute. Susy continues to talk.*) Oh, how wonderful. Signora Juliet has come to bring the big, beautiful cat home. Do you want anything, signora? An apéritif?
JULIET (*hesitating, won over, finally accepting*): I don't know. No. Yes.

Susy gets up, now playing the role of the perfect, distinguished hostess—with complete ease.

SUSY: Yes? Good. So do I. What would you like? I find there is nothing better than a bottle of champagne. (*She takes a bottle of champagne from the bar refrigerator and expertly prepares to open it.*)

Do you like it? Yes? Do you know how to open it without letting all the foam out? Look. Like this. (*She opens the smoking bottle perfectly.*) You see? Done. (*She fills two glasses, gives one to Juliet.*) Chin-chin.
JULIET: Chin-chin.

Susy drinks with facetious greed.

SUSY: Good . . . Do you like the service? (*She points to the two glasses.*) It's a special crystal. I never serve champagne in goblets. It's boorish. Some more?
JULIET: No, thank you. It's delicious.

Noticing that Juliet is looking around her, Susy says:

SUSY: If you want to see the house, come along. Come on. (*Preceding Juliet, Susy takes a bunch of gladioli from a vase, smells them a moment; then, noticing that they are not really fresh, she holds her nose.*) Brrr, how awful! They smell of death.

Susy throws the flowers into a basket and leads Juliet down a hallway.

On the walls are little paintings in doubtful taste. Little sketches, they represent—as in a profane, blasphemous *"Via Crucis"*—the successive seasons of the love life of a woman. They are little scenes, episodes, colored anecdotes of incredible erotic ardor. Stopping in front of them, nose in the air, a bit shocked but clearly interested, Juliet examines them carefully.

Impatient, from the end of the hallway, Susy calls out, lightly tapping her foot on the floor.

SUSY: They're a gift from my fiancé. Filthy. But, the men . . . (*She stops in front of a door and opens it. In the room, stretched out on a bed, is a dark girl.*) Marisa, how are you? You want to eat in bed? (*The girl doesn't answer, nor does she turn around, Susy puts the cat on her bed and kisses her.*) I'm leaving you, Rubirosa. (*She closes the door and returns to the hallway.*) You know, that girl wanted to kill herself. I saved her by a miracle. I telephoned and telephoned and there was no answer. We had to break down her door. I can't tell you how awful it was. Now I keep her here. Gianni—you'll meet him—makes a big play for her, which keeps her distracted.
JULIET: Like Laura—a friend of mine from school. She was only seventeen. They made it look like an accident. She drowned for love. Oh, look, from here you can see my house.

Juliet, from the balcony, looks at the modest little house lost in the trees. It looks almost ridiculous to her. She smiles, pensive.

SUSY: You two make me feel so tender, when I see you. You're married, aren't you?
JULIET (*almost surprised*): Yes.

> SUSY: I envy those who can do it; it must be beautiful—only one man. But how can it be done?
> JULIET: It must also be beautiful to be free.

Susy opens a door onto a huge bedroom. A very low, wide bed, covered with delicate silk, contrasts with a thick dark-blue carpet. Susy falls gracefully on the bed and gestures Juliet to do the same. Reserved, rigid, dignified, Juliet sits on the edge of the bed, looking at the carpet—and at a pair of thick, furry men's slippers, which still seem warm from the feet of a man.

Susy's voice, over Juliet's shoulders, says quietly and cordially:

> SUSY: Try to lie down.

Susy's affectionate and light hand urges Juliet down to the bed. Supine, Juliet looks up. A kind of silk curtain covers the ceiling above the bed. Susy pulls a cord, opening the curtain, and reveals, above, an enormous mirror, which reflects Juliet's face and body. With a repressed exclamation of shock, Juliet half rises, as if her own image had hit her. She looks, fascinated, into the mirror.

> JULIET: Did you—find this here?
> SUSY'S VOICE: Oh, no, I had it built in. Isn't it amusing? Sometimes I get the impression that there are four of us. Now who knows what you think of me? But, you know, men like to enjoy themselves.

Susy's voice suddenly fades away. Juliet turns to look for her; she is gone. Her robe has been thrown on the bed. Only now does Juliet notice a large round hole in the floor, right next to the bed. From a distance there comes the muffled voice of Susy, together with a peculiar sound of rinsing.

> SUSY'S VOICE: Juliet! Signora!

Juliet looks into the hole and sees, at the bottom of a long slide, the bluish movement of the waters of a pool. Susy, half naked, is swimming; she appears and disappears as in the glass of a telescope. Her happy voice rises from the water.

> SUSY: Get undressed, and you come in too. The water is warm. Just so that right after making love with my fiancé we can come down here just as we are. It's beautiful. We take a bath—and then we can start again. Come on, Juliet. Dive in.

Fellini is here at his surrealist best in his sumptuous sets and costumes and brilliant imagery. The carnival music by Nina Rota, and the "waltzing camera" add to the whirling, opulent atmosphere. Critics have analyzed Fellini's symbolism as Freudian or Jungian, but whatever the psychological sources the viewer feels awash with vivid images that resonate emotionally. This was Fellini's first color film, and he uses strongly contrasting shades of primary colors to paint his scenes. In fact, "Feliniesque" has become a name for this combination of fantastical imagery and riotous color.

Religion is juxtaposed against Susy's sensuality, perhaps as another lure and trap. Specifically, Juliet recalls an incident from her childhood when her grandfather (Lou Gilbert) rescued her from a passion play. She was cast as a Christian martyr, tied to a grate and consumed by (paper) fire; she later ascends to heaven in a stage contraption. Her free-thinking grandfather stops the play and unties her, protesting against the primitive ecstasy of the pageant. He takes her in his arms, calling her "my little beefsteak," and carries her away to safety.

Perhaps this scene represents for Juliet a time when she felt small, passive, and deserving of abuse. She needs to separate herself from any such memories (or realities) that diminish her as a person.

Her hallucinations still crowd in on her though, and just as she saw the raft with savage men on the beach, she sees "bearded, invading warriors" throughout her house. They first appear on the veranda, then crowd into the bathroom, pantry, and dining room in overwhelming numbers. Juliet makes her way through the throng of bodies and armor, trying to escape into the pine forest.

GARDEN AND PINES EXTERIOR. TWILIGHT.

Juliet, having climbed over and pushed aside the massive, heavy bodies, emerges, out of breath, in the garden. But a forest of multicolored flags seems to surround it from every side. Troops of barbarians on horseback are lined up all around, leaving no avenue of escape. The horses neigh and paw the ground. Threatening shouts come from all over.

Juliet feels lost. But suddenly something makes her look up: A wavering, multicolored light falls from above, right over her head.

It is a large balloon that is descending into the garden, a balloon with many large flags and festoons of lanterns of many colors.

In the vessel someone is signaling to Juliet—two people, a man and a woman, are leaning over the basket and waving. The man is Juliet's grandfather; the woman is beautiful and shapely in a chanteuse's dress—it is his famous adventure, the ballerina of the singing café.

Juliet lets out a desperate call, full of unexpected hope.

JULIET: Grandfather!

The grandfather continues to wave his arms, while the balloon continues its descent toward the garden. When it is but a few feet away, the grandfather throws a rope ladder overboard and signals Juliet to hurry.

GRANDFATHER: Come on. Quickly!

Juliet runs breathlessly toward the balloon, grabs the rope ladder and climbs it.

Standing in the balloon, clinging tightly to the edge of the basket, Juliet rises above the world of anxieties, chatting happily with the ballerina and eating chocolates from a heart-shaped box. She is "filled with a sense of liberation, of well-being." Juliet and the ballerina sing and skip together, and although the balloon enters a cloud "the happy, impetuous song goes on." When Juliet asks her grandfather whether they are ever going back to earth he says, "Relax. Of course, we're going back whenever you like. I've always returned. One always does return home, but the world is large—full of things to see and do."

Juliet cannot remain in the fantasy world, but it refreshes her spirit and enables her to soar in her own way. She can then return to her circumstances in life with a wider and more tranquil perspective. She has rejected spiritism, promiscuity, and religion as being oppressive and foreign to her nature, and seems to have found harmony in her life through acceptance of herself. She is no longer bedeviled by visions, perhaps because she no longer needs them, and we later see her laughing and looking at her face in the mirror as if seeing it for the first time.

Although Juliet's descent into fantasy has been frightening, it has been liberating as well. As the psychotherapist R. D. Laing has said, breakdown can be breakthrough. Juliet's peaceful existence has been destroyed, but she is freer than ever before. It is as though she gave herself permission to go a little mad and to indulge in fantastic delusions. It protected her psyche against her husband's infidelity and was a means of becoming more whole.

The sun enters from the open window. Everything is calm; outside, the usual sounds of a radio, a hen, a car.

These are the usual, comforting noises. There are no signs of the nocturnal siege.

Juliet takes the newspaper and puts it on the bed, without even looking at the front-page headlines.

She goes to the dining room. Everything is in order, except for the dining room table, which still has the remains of the supper—bottles and dirty dishes, a crude reminder of what has happened. A slight grimace, a small shrug of the shoulder and she goes out into the garden.

Here too all is in order, with no trace of the siege.

The sun shining on the grass. An air of peace. The cats, as usual, sunning themselves.

The maid appears on the doorstep.

FORTUNATA: The coffee is ready. What should I make for lunch today?
JULIET: (*without turning around*): I don't know—whatever you like.
FORTUNATA: Will your husband be home for lunch?
JULIET: No, I don't think so. Nor this evening.

Juliet goes to the swing, gently swinging, her feet not leaving the ground.

She continues to swing this way, absorbed.

She looks through the pines at the luminous horizon of the sea, colored in reds and golds, acquiring a magic beat, but supremely normal, everyday.

A sail, in the midst of the horizon, comes gently into the path of the sun. The sun is rising, reddening, the sail now lighted by a marvelously warm reflection, but marvelously "natural."

Juliet is quiet, almost serene, as she lightly swings. She looks around her at a world that more and more takes on—in ways so simple, so stable—both the real and the unreal pulse of everyday magic.

A flight of swallows passes high in the sky. Juliet raises her eyes and sees the swallows also slowly enter into the golden refraction of the sun's rays.

Juliet seems to be whispering something under her breath, but for the first time not in order to call or surprise anyone. She seems at peace with this pure world, filled with marvelous realities, which spring to life around her.

She hears a cry from above—it could be the sound of a group of birds, or the call of the swallows.

She raises her eyes, shields them from the powerful sun with the back of her hand. She tries to puzzle out the meaning of this faintly heard sound.

But she sees only the very blue sky—a blue as deep as a marine abyss—and the golden rays of the sun.

Juliet smiles, bends her head and continues to sway on the swing, in the rustling of a light wind. It is as if she no longer cares about the origins of the sounds, the images she has seen, whether they be part of a natural mystery or part of a supernatural secret. Everything in her is now anchored in peaceful harmony, beyond the mystifying ghosts that have until now besieged her; she is concerned with the daily miracle of simple reality.

Juliet smiles, liberated, at peace.

Study Questions

1. Would you ever trust your feelings more than reason and good sense, your heart over your head? How would you protect yourself from being mistaken?

2. If you were Juliet, how would you tell the difference between hallucinations, memories, fantasies, dreams, and reality? Could you separate "I dreamt of a spirit" from "A spirit visited me in a dream"?

3. How would you know when to trust the advice of an alleged seer such as Bhisma or messages received during a seance?

4. Would Juliet be happier if she were more like her neighbor Susy? Would religion be her salvation?

5. In what way does Juliet change from the beginning to the end of the film?

Bibliography of Philosophy, Literature, and Films

I. Obtaining Reliable Knowledge: Epistemology

Philosophy

Appearance and Reality	F. H. Bradley
Critique of Practical Reason	Immanuel Kant
Critique of Pure Reason	Immanuel Kant
Enquiry Concerning Human Understanding	David Hume
Essay Concerning Human Understanding	John Locke
Essays in Pragmatism	William James
Fact, Fiction, and Forecast	Nelson Goodman
Genealogy of Morals	Friedrich Nietzsche
A History of Philosophy	F. C. Copleston
Human Knowledge	Bertrand Russell
A Hundred Years of Philosophy	John Passmore
Meditations on First Philosophy	René Descartes
Mysticism	Evelyn Underhill
Parmenides, Republic, Sophist, Theaetetus	Plato
Philosophical Investigations	Ludwig Wittgenstein
Philosophical Method	R. G. Collingwood
Philosophical Papers	G. E. Moore
The Philosophy of Perception	G. J. Warnock
Sensations and Perceptions	D. W. Hamlyn
Some Main Problems of Philosophy	G. E. Moore
A Treatise Concerning the Principles of Human Knowledge	George Berkeley
A Treatise of Human Nature	David Hume
Word and Object	W. V. O. Quine

Literature

The Aleph and Other Stories	Jorge Luis Borges
The Balcony	Jean Genet
Brand	H. Ibsen
Candide	Voltaire
The Castle	Franz Kafka
City Life	Donald Barthelme
Confessions of a Mask	Yukio Mishima
Dr. Faustus	Thomas Mann
The Ebony Tower	John Fowles
Endgame	Samuel Beckett
Exit the King	Eugene Ionesco
Faust	Johann Wolfgang Goethe
Finnegan's Wake	James Joyce

Flow My Tears, The Policeman Said	Philip K. Dick
The Flowers of Evil	Charles Baudelaire
The Fox	D. H. Lawrence
The French Lieutenant's Woman	John Fowles
It Is So (If You Think So)	Luigi Pirandello
Labyrinths	Jorge Luis Borges
Nausea	Jean-Paul Sartre
One Hundred Years of Solitude	Gabriel Garcia Marquez
"The Real Thing"	Henry James
Remembrance of Things Past	Marcel Proust
Ulysses	James Joyce
V	Thomas Pynchon
Waiting for Godot	Samuel Beckett
Wide Sargasso Sea	Jean Rhys

Films

All About Eve	Joseph Mankiewicz
The Andalusian Dog (Un Chien Andalov)	Luis Bunuel
Beauty and the Beast	Jean Cocteau
Bladerunner	Ridley Scott
The Cabinet of Dr. Caligari	Robert Wiene
David and Lisa	Frank and Eleanor Perry
8 1/2	Federico Fellini
Les Enfant du Paradis	Marcel Carne
Juliet of the Spirits	Federico Fellini
Laura	Otto Preminger
North by Northwest	Alfred Hitchcock
Rashomon	Akira Kurosawa
Rear Window	Alfred Hitchcock
The Return of Martin Guerre	Daniel Vigne
The Third Man	Carol Reed
The Truman Show	Peter Weir
Twelve Angry Men	Sidney Lumet

II. Exploring the Nature of Reality: Metaphysics

As defined earlier, metaphysics tries to discover the fundamental nature of reality. Some philosophers regard it as a comprehensive study of what is fundamental to all existence, while others define it as the study of first principles or ultimate truths, or the effort to comprehend the universe, not simply piecemeal or by fragments, but somehow as a whole. In more contemporary terms, metaphysics gives us a new way of regarding the world, a shift of vision in our paradigm of reality. All of these academic definitions help, to some extent, in understanding the field, but metaphysics affects each of us on a more personal level.

In our more reflective moments, when we pause to consider our lives, we often experience a profound curiosity about the universe we inhabit. We wonder about the overall scheme of things and our part in it. Although it may make our head swim, we feel a need to understand the meaning of our individual lives and of human existence in general.

When we begin to think in a more deliberate way, we question whether we exist as an accident of physical forces or whether purpose governs the universe, directing us toward some end. This may lead us to wonder whether the world is basically empty and meaningless or whether a cosmic intelligence is at work, a benevolent God who created us for a reason. We also ask if the values we believe in have any objective foundation. Are right and wrong grounded in some genuine ethical truth, or do they merely reflect our times, our society, and our personal tastes? If life is meaningless in itself, perhaps we can invest it with meaning through our choices, and by our creative act bring purpose into being.

We also want to know whether space has a limit and, if so, what lies beyond it, and whether the universe had a beginning and what existed before it. If life on earth comes to an end, will that be with a bang or a whimper, in a fiery apocalypse when the sun explodes or through the gradual loss of available energy in accordance with the law of entropy? The concept of time can perplex us also, for the past resembles a dream, the future a fantasy, so we are left with the knife-edge instant of the present which seems impossible to hold; the minute we say now it is then. Can we locate our lives within the flux of time or do we watch the river of time flow by?

In addition, we are curious to know the basic substance of the universe, that is, whether it is spiritual or material, and to discover its inherent structure and the process by which it operates. We may regard the process as mechanical or organic, evolution or devolution, a cyclical, spiral, linear, or stepwise progression. Or we may come to believe in the expansion and contraction of the entire universe, a pulsing or breathing like some enormous organism.

Metaphysicians wonder about the nature of reality in the same way, but they try to be systematic and logical in approaching the problems. They also use evidence from the sciences as the basis for their speculations, exploring the meaning and implications of scientific discoveries in a rigorous way. Although each person who engages in metaphysical thinking must find his or her own answers, we can gain insights from outstanding minds that have contemplated these fundamental questions.

A. The Self: Questioning Its Identity and Freedom

One basic metaphysical question has to with our own selves. In a sense, nothing seems more obvious than our very self, but when we attempt to define its nature we tend to become confused. Part of the problem is that we ourselves are analyzing our selves, which is rather like trying to point a flashlight at its own beam of light. The principal problem, however, stems from the complex nature of the self which makes it difficult to characterize.

On the one hand, we think of the self as a physical entity that exists in the same tangible form as a horse or a tree, and whose existence is verified by sense perception. We recognize our own self and other selves as corporeal beings, acting in a concrete world of objects and events. In short, the self can be conceived of as physical; our bodies are something we are rather than something we have.

On the other hand, this definition of the self does not seem to capture its essence. It seems superficial and almost irrelevant to selfhood. We often feel that the self is more adequately described as that spiritual entity lying beneath our physical appearance; it is the nonbodily source of our actions. In this view, the essential self is known through introspection whereby we look inside ourselves and discover our spiritual center. The body serves as a shell or housing within which the self resides, issuing orders, receiving impressions, storing memories, reflecting and deliberating. In short, the self is here identified with our spirit or mind, and our bodies as something we have but not what we are.

However, this concept of self is difficult to defend in scientific terms. Furthermore, it resembles some extreme religious beliefs that also claim to be based on private knowledge. We cannot be sure, therefore, whether the self is a real psychic entity surpassing all scientific understanding, or whether such a belief is a delusion. Perhaps we just like to think of ourselves as spiritual entities rather than animals.

These alternatives, of identifying the self with the body or with the mind, are thus fraught with problems; nevertheless, they are natural and persistent ways of thinking. They are also two major theories in metaphysics as to the nature of self and, for these reasons, deserve further discussion.

The theory that the self is the same as the physical body falls within the theory of *materialism*; the view that the self is explicable in terms of the mind or spirit is called *idealism*.

Materialism rejects the notion of mind altogether and explains all activities in terms of mechanical, physical sequences. "Brain" is substituted for "mind" as the agency responsible for actions, and the self is treated as identical with the bodily organism, which includes the brain as well as the nerves, muscles, organs, skin, and so on. According to this theory, we are nothing but our anatomical parts and physiological processes.

Not only is a physical explanation thought to be sufficient to account for all activities of the self, but the concept of mind is vigorously challenged on the grounds that there can be no possible evidence of its existence. It is argued that mind, by its very nature, belongs to a permanently unknowable realm beyond the reach of empirical evidence. It cannot be seen, touched, heard, smelled, or tasted; in fact, no conceivable test could detect its presence within the body. For example, if a woman reaches for a fork, then a train of physiological events can be described in a cause-and-effect pattern: Her muscles contracted on certain nerve impulses that were triggered by neural events occurring in her brain. But no evidence can be offered to prove that a nonphysical entity called "mind" was responsible for the movement of her arm.

Sometimes the materialist charges that the existence of mind can only be asserted using an *argumentum ad ignorantiam*: We do not know what lies behind the physiological processes (assuming that something must), consequently we claim that mind is this agency. This is logically invalid, for a lack of knowledge cannot be taken as grounds for any conclusion; a theory is neither proven by not having been disproven nor disproven by not having been proven. If we do not know the cause of action, we cannot conclude that the cause must be the mind.

Perhaps we are being unduly influenced by the structure of the English language that requires a subject for sentences. We say "It is raining" or "It is five o'clock." The word "It" is a grammatical fiction, and maybe "I" functions the same way, making us think of ourselves as the spirit behind our actions.

On the basis of these points, the (reductive) materialist rejects the notion of mind and defines the self strictly in terms of its physical components; the "I" is entirely reduced to the physical body, without any spiritual or mental part.

Idealism, the opposite theory, maintains that the self is basically spiritual or psychical in nature; even our physical body is thought to be in some way mental. Rather than the mind being in the body, the body is contained in the mind.

Idealism rejects the materialistic view of self and regards it as having arisen from a prejudice for scientific explanations—a prejudice that is inconsistent with our experiences of remembering, desiring, deliberating, reflecting, and acting in accordance with conscious purpose. To reduce phenomena of this sort to physiological terms does violence to our deep feeling that something other than a physical process is occurring when, for example, we are experiencing happiness or love. The materialistic explanation also diminishes human beings by declaring that they cannot be anything other than that which is empirically verifiable, that is, known by sense experience. Such a reduction is not only repugnant but depends upon an unfounded criterion for genuine knowledge.

As an alternative theory, the idealist declares that the essential self consists of mind, soul, or spirit, and that the reality of any physical aspect of self can be doubted. Viewed from this context, a supposedly physical event such as drinking wine is only the sense of mellowness and well-being; a morning swim is the feeling of invigoration; and both experiences are increased by anticipation and recollection, which also belong to the mental realm.

According to the idealist, all "physical" occurrences ultimately come down to internal experiences and are nothing but these experiences. If our skin is cut or burned, for example, that injury is only a mental event of experiencing pain. There is no physical self that has been injured but only a mental self that is suffering; the *consciousness* of pain is what being injured means. The same is said to be true of any bodily event.

The idealist also argues that everyone recognizes himself or herself to be that spiritual being within the animal form rather than the form itself. We know this through firsthand knowledge that gives us immediate and direct assurance that our mind not our body constitutes the core of our self.

Some idealists go so far as to claim that, by analogy with the human self, the entire range of objects in the world—from animals to plants to rocks—might possess an internal spirit and some degree of awareness. For just as we know our own self to lie behind that which appears externally, other entities, too, could possess centers of consciousness within. In the case of flowers and trees, the level of awareness would be quite low; for fish and birds it would be somewhat higher, for chimpanzees and apes considerably higher. But a mode of consciousness might reside within every object in the universe, with the sum total of these spiritual centers constituting reality.

Whether or not we feel persuaded to adopt this position, it does seem plausible to trust our primary awareness that our minds exist. We may not be willing to accept the theory that mind is the only reality, or attribute consciousness to inanimate objects, but we do tend to believe that our minds, as well as our bodies, are real.

Once we assert the reality of mind and body, we are faced with the Cartesian problem of how interaction can occur between such radically different entities, but at least we are in harmony with our understanding that the self includes both. In idealism and materialism, a certain consistency is gained at the expense of common sense, when neither our mental part nor our physical part seems reducible to the other.

If the self does embrace both mind and body, then a further set of questions becomes relevant: to what extent are we physical beings and to what extent mental?* The self cannot be identified wholly with the body since we are more than the sum of our physical parts; nevertheless, the body seems to be a definite part of the self. And although the self is closely identified with the mind, it is not just mind but something more encompassing.†

What then are the boundaries of the self? How much or what part of our bodies would have to be lost before we felt a diminution of selfhood? If we have our hair cut or lose a tooth, do we leave part of ourself behind? When our bodies grow, decay, and otherwise change throughout our lives, are we ourselves expanding or deteriorating? How can the self reflect upon itself, be both subject and object; how can "I" contemplate "me"?

Related to these questions are others concerning the relation of the self to the nonself, especially the limits of the self in "space." What should be included as essential to the self and what should be excluded as extraneous to it? What lies outside the circle of the self as object and what resides within as subject?

---

*It is one thing, incidentally to distinguish between mind and body, and quite another to say that mind can exist after the body has decayed. Belief in the distinction between mind and body does not logically entail belief in disembodied existence; a separate argument is needed to prove the immortality of the spirit.

†(If self were only that series of mental phenomena making up mind then it would be impossible to account for the fact of self-awareness. To quote John Stuart Mill, we would have to "accept the paradox that something which *ex hypothesi* is but a series of feelings, can be aware of itself as a series"; or that "I feel" is the same as "I know that I feel." That is, consciousness cannot be the same as self-consciousness.)

The self has sometimes been said to include the people one loves, so that their successes are our successes, their pain our own. It might also include personal property, especially objects such as tools worn from a lifetime of use, one's land and home, special books or paintings, a musical instrument or favorite chair, or clothing that has conformed to the body from repeated wearing. As Henry David Thoreau writes in *Walden:*

> Kings and queens who wear a suit but once, though made by some tailor or dressmaker to their majesties, cannot know the comfort of wearing a suit that fits. They are no better than wooden horses to hang the clean clothes on. Every day our garments become more assimilated to ourselves, receiving the impress of the wearer's character, until we hesitate to lay them aside, . . . even as our bodies.

Or one can enlarge the self to embrace the whole of mankind within one's consciousness, as the English poet John Donne declares in his *Meditation XVII*:

> No man is an island, entire of itself; every man is a piece of the continent, a part of the main; if a clod be washed away by the sea, Europe is the less, as well as if a promontory were; as well as if a manor of the friends or of thine own; any man's death diminishes me, because I am involved in mankind; and therefore never send to know for whom the bell tolls; it tolls for thee.

The question is that of deciding the extent of the self: How wide or narrow can we interpret it to be? Perhaps we can accept the idea that an individual is the sum of all that he can call his.

Just as we may question the extent of the self in "space," we may also wonder about the persistence of the self through "time." Here we wish to determine what personal essence survives all the changes to ourselves that take place during our lifetime. Seemingly every facet of our being changes without any thread of continuity existing throughout. Our thoughts, attitudes, aspirations, and values change between childhood and old age. Our memories may grow dim; our disposition can vary from extreme compassion to bitter cynicism; our bodies undergo a virtual metamorphosis as every cell is replaced; and growth and degeneration occur continually between birth and death. What, then, remains constant? In temporal terms, the self is whatever entitles us to declare we are the same person throughout our lifetime, legitimately referred to by the same name. Our essential self is the constant element, that principle of personal unity underlying all change, but it is hard to determine what that golden thread might be.

As a final point, it should be mentioned that some philosophic systems of a mystical nature have denied the reality of the self altogether. Most notably, Indian philosophies will often make this claim, treating the self as an illusion (*maya*). It is argued that the enlightened person understands that there are no separate selves and no difference between people and the world. Reality is one, without inner and outer parts, and no distinction exists between our individual soul and the world soul. Indian philosophy further maintains that we can experience the unitary character of reality in privileged moments of heightened awareness. If our spirit is properly prepared, then the Oneness of the universe can be revealed to us in a transcendental experience. Here our sensations are melted and fused, our bones become liquefied, and we are absorbed into the cosmic All.

To conceive of the self in this way, as undifferentiated and consequently unreal, is extremely appealing when we long for escape from suffering. Nevertheless, we are aware of our selves with a vividness, immediacy, and power that seems to guarantee authenticity. To deny that we ourselves exist seems far-fetched. Western philosophers generally argue that if the "I" is not real, then everything is an illusion, for few things strike us as more certain. As we have seen, Descartes argues for the indubitability of the self.

If we are prepared to assert the self's reality, we then face the more puzzling issue of defining its nature. In the selections from the literary and philosophic works and the films that follow, various facets of selfhood are presented, as both a philosophic problem and a highly personal issue.

In the first set of selections in Part A, the philosopher Thomas Reid affirms the existence of the self, mainly using an argument from memory and continuity. The celebrated Canadian writer Margaret Atwood then explores the way gender defines the self, and the film director Stanley Kubrick raises questions as to the difference between people and machines.

Essays on the Intellectual Powers of Man
"Of the Nature and Origin of our Notion of Personal Identity"
Thomas Reid

Thomas Reid (1710–1796) was a Scottish philosopher and the founder of the common sense school of philosophy. He was appointed Professor at King's College at the University of Aberdeen, then taught at the University of Glasgow. His books include Inquiry into the Human Mind, Essays on the Active Powers of Man, *and* Essays on the Intellectual Powers of Man.

Reid endorsed what is sometimes called "naïve realism." Contrary to philosophers such as George Berkeley (discussed below), he maintained that the external world would exist even without being perceived, and contrary to David Hume (discussed previously), that causality is a correct judgment of the mind. Although a minor philosopher, he stands as a practical corrective to philosophic claims that violate our common sense view of the world.

In keeping with his down-to-earth philosophy, Reid maintained that the self is evident to every person who cares to reflect on it. In his Essays on the Intellectual Powers of Man *(here excerpted), he presents a metaphysical account of the nature of the self. Reid writes "My personal identity . . . implies the continued existence of that indivisible thing which I call* myself." *Although his thoughts, actions, and feelings change, "that self, or I, to which they belong, is permanent."*

Evidence for this continuous self can be found in such things as memory (although failing to remember something does not mean it did not occur). Reid also asserts that the self is not a changing succession of impressions and ideas because a mind must exist to have those impressions and ideas. There cannot be thoughts without a thinker, reason without a reasoner.

Of Identity in General

The conviction which every man has of his identity, as far back as his memory reaches, needs no aid of philosophy to strengthen it; and no philosophy can weaken it, without first producing some degree of insanity.

The philosopher, however, may very properly consider this conviction as a phenomenon of human nature worthy of his attention. If he can discover its cause, an addition is made to his stock of knowledge; if not, it must be held as a part of our original constitution, or an effect of that constitution produced in a manner unknown to us.

That we may form as distinct a notion as we are able of this phenomenon of the human mind, it is proper to consider what is meant by identity in general, what by our own personal identity, and how we are led into that invincible belief and conviction which every man has of his own personal identity, as far as his memory reaches.

Identity in general I take to be a relation between a thing which is known to exist at one time, and a thing which is known to have existed at another time. If you ask whether they are one and the same, or two different things, every man of common sense understands the meaning of your question perfectly. Whence we may infer with certainty, that every man of common sense has a clear and distinct notion of identity.

If you ask a definition of identity, I confess I can give none; it is too simple a notion to admit of logical definition: I can say it is a relation, but I cannot find words to express the specific difference between this and other relations, though I am in no danger of confounding it with any other. I can say that diversity is a contrary relation, and that similitude and dissimilitude are another couple of contrary relations, which every man easily distinguishes in his conception from identity and diversity.

I see evidently that identity supposes *an uninterrupted continuance of existence*. That which has ceased to exist cannot be the same with that which afterwards begins to exist; for this would be to suppose a being to exist after it ceased to exist, and to have had existence before it was produced, which are manifest contradictions. Continued uninterrupted existence is therefore necessarily implied in identity. Hence we may infer, that identity cannot, in its proper sense, be applied to our pains, our pleasures, our thoughts, or any operation of our minds. The pain felt this day is not the same individual pain which I felt yesterday, though they may be *similar* in kind and degree, and have the same cause. The same may be said of every feeling, and of every operation of mind. They are all successive in their nature, like time itself, no two moments of which can be the same moment. It is otherwise with the parts of absolute space. They always are, and were, and will be the same. So far, I think, we proceed upon clear ground in fixing the notion of identity in general.

Of Our Idea of Personal Identity

It is perhaps more difficult to ascertain with precision the meaning of *personality*: but it is not necessary in the present subject: it is sufficient for our purpose to observe, that all mankind place their personality in something that *cannot be divided, or consist of parts*. A part of a person is a manifest absurdity. When a man loses his estate, his health, his strength, he is still the same person, and has lost nothing of his personality. If he has a leg or an arm cut off, he is the same person he was before. The amputated member is no part of his person, otherwise it would have a right to a part of his estate, and be liable for a part of his engagements. It would be entitled to a share of his merit and demerit, which is manifestly absurd. A person is something indivisible, and is what Leibnitz calls a *monad*.

My personal identity, therefore, implies the continued existence of that indivisible thing which I call *myself*. Whatever this self may be, it is something which thinks, and deliberates, and resolves, and acts, and suffers. I am not thought, I am not action, I am not feeling; I am something that thinks, and acts, and suffers. My thoughts, and actions, and feelings, change every moment; they have no continued, but a successive, existence; but that *self*, or *I*, to which they belong, is permanent, and has the same relation to all the succeeding thoughts, actions, and feelings which I call mine.

Such are the notions that I have of my personal identity. But perhaps it may be said, this may all be fancy without reality. How do you know— what evidence have you—that there is such a permanent self which has a claim to all the thoughts, actions, and feelings which you call yours?

To this I answer, that the proper evidence I have of all this is *remembrance*. I remember that twenty years ago I conversed with such a person; I remember several things that passed in that conversation: my memory testifies, not only that this was done, but that it was done by me who now remembers it. If it was done by me, I must have existed at that time, and continued to exist from that time to the present: if the identical person whom I call myself had not a part in that conversation, my memory is fallacious; it gives a distinct and positive testimony of what is not true. Every man in his senses believes what he distinctly remembers, and everything he remembers convinces him that he existed at the time remembered.

Although memory gives the most irresistible evidence of my being the identical person that did such a thing, at such a time, I may have other good evidence of things which befell me, and which I do not remember: I know who bore me, and suckled me, but I do not remember these events.

It may here be observed (though the observation would have been unnecessary, if some great philosophers had not contradicted it), that it is not my remembering any action of mine that *makes* me to be the person who did it. This remembrance makes me to *know* assuredly that I did it; *but I might have done it, though I did not remember it*. That relation to me, which is expressed by saying that *I did it*, would be the same, though I had not the least remembrance of it. To say that my remembering that I did such a thing, or, as some choose to express it, my being conscious that I did it, makes me to have done it, appears to me as great an absurdity as it would be to say, that my belief that the world was created made it to be created.

When we pass judgment on the identity of other persons than ourselves, we proceed upon other grounds, and determine from a variety of circumstances, which sometimes produce the firmest assurance, and sometimes leave room for doubt. The identity of persons has often furnished matter of serious litigation before tribunals of justice. But no man of a sound mind ever doubted of his own identity, as far as he distinctly remembered.

The identity of a person is a perfect identity: wherever it is real, it admits of no degrees; and it is impossible that a person should be in part the same, and in part different; because a person is a *monad*, and is not divisible into parts. The evidence of identity in other persons than ourselves does indeed admit of all degrees, from what we account certainty, to the least degree of probability. But still it is true, that the same person is perfectly the same, and cannot be so in part or in some degree only.

For this cause, I have first considered personal identity, as that which is perfect in its kind, and the natural measure of that which is imperfect.

We probably at first derive our notion of identity from that natural conviction which every man has from the dawn of reason of *his own* identity and continued existence. The operations of our minds, are all successive, and have no continued existence. But the thinking being has a continued existence, and we have an invincible belief, that it remains the same when all its thoughts and operations change.

Our judgments of the identity of objects of sense seem to be formed much upon the same grounds as our judgments of the identity of *other persons* than ourselves. Wherever we observe great *similarity*, we are apt to presume identity, if no reason appears to the contrary. Two objects ever so like, when they are perceived at the same time, cannot be the same; but if they are presented to our senses at different times, we are apt to think them the same, merely from their similarity.

Whether this be a natural prejudice, or from whatever cause it proceeds, it certainly appears in children from infancy; and when we grow up, it is confirmed in most instances by experience: for we rarely find two individuals of the same species that are not distinguishable by obvious differences. A man challenges a thief whom he finds in possession of his horse or his watch, only on similarity. When the watchmaker swears that he sold this watch to such a person, his testimony is grounded on similarity. The testimony of witnesses to the identity of a person is commonly grounded on no other evidence.

Thus it appears, that the evidence we have of our own identity, as far back as we remember, is totally of a different kind from the evidence we have of the identity of other persons, or of objects of sense. The first is grounded on *memory*, and gives undoubted certainty. The last is grounded on *similarity*, and on other circumstances, which in many cases are not so decisive as to leave no room for doubt. It may likewise be observed, that the identity of *objects of sense* is never perfect. All bodies, as they consist of innumerable parts that may be disjoined from them by a great variety of causes, are subject to continual changes of their own substance, increasing, diminishing, changing insensibly. When such alterations are gradual, because language could not afford a different name for every different state of such a changeable being, it retains the same name, and is considered as the same thing. Thus we say of an old regiment, that it did such a thing a century ago, though there now is not a man alive who then belonged to it. We say a tree is the same in the seed-bed and in the forest. A ship of war, which has successively changed her anchors, her tackle, her sails, her masts, her planks, and her timbers, while she keeps the same name, is the same.

The identity, therefore, which we ascribe to bodies, whether natural or artificial, is not perfect identity; it is rather something which, for the convenience of speech, we call identity. It admits of a great change of the subject, providing the change be *gradual*; sometimes, even of a total change. And the changes which in common language are made consistent with identity differ from those that are thought to destroy it, not in *kind*, but in *number* and *degree*. It has no fixed nature when applied to bodies; and questions about the identity of a body are very often questions about words. But identity, when applied to persons, has no ambiguity, and admits not of degrees, or of and less. It is the foundation of all rights and obligations, and of all accountableness; and the notion of it is fixed and precise.

Thought Requires a Thinker

The thoughts of which I am conscious are the thoughts of a being which I call MYSELF, my MIND, my PERSON.

The thoughts and feelings of which we are conscious are continually changing, and the thought of this moment is not the thought of the last; but something which I call *myself* remains under this change of thought. This self has the same relation to all the successive thoughts I am conscious of; they are all *my* thoughts; and every thought which is not my thought must be the thought of some other person.

If any man asks a proof of this, I confess I can give none; there is an evidence in the proposition itself which I am unable to resist. Shall I think, that thought can stand by itself without a thinking being? or that ideas can feel pleasure or pain? My nature dictates to me that it is impossible. And that nature has dictated the same to all men appears from the structure of all languages: for in all languages men have expressed thinking, reasoning, willing, loving, hating, by *personal* verbs, which from their nature require a person who thinks, reasons, wills, loves, or hates. From which it appears, that men have been taught by nature to believe that thought requires a thinker, reason a reasoner, and love a lover.

Here we must leave Mr. Hume, who conceives it to be a vulgar error, that, besides the thoughts we are conscious of, there is a mind which is the subject of those thoughts. If the mind be anything else than impressions and ideas, it must be a word without a meaning. The mind, therefore, according to this philosopher, is a word which signifies a bundle of perceptions; or, when he defines it more accurately, "it is that succession of related ideas and impressions, of which we have an intimate memory and consciousness."

I am, therefore, that succession of related ideas and impressions of which I have the intimate memory and consciousness. But who is the *I* that has this memory and consciousness of a succession of ideas and impressions? Why, it is nothing but that succession itself. Hence I learn, that this succession of ideas and impressions intimately remembers, and is conscious of itself. I would wish to be further instructed, whether the impressions remember and are conscious of the ideas, or the ideas remember and are conscious of the impressions, or if both remember and are conscious of both? and whether the ideas remember those that come after them, as well as those that were before them? These are questions naturally arising from this system, that have not yet been explained.

This, however, is clear, that this succession of ideas and impressions not only remembers and is conscious, but that it judges, reasons, affirms, denies; nay, that it eats and drinks, and is sometimes merry and sometimes sad. If these things can be ascribed to a succession of ideas and impressions, in a consistency with common sense, I should be very glad to know what is nonsense.

Study Questions

1. Explain Reid's conception of the identity of the self.
2. Why does identity require "an uninterrupted continuance of existence"?
3. Why does Reid believe we must be more than our impressions and ideas?
4. Does your personal identity consist of your characteristics or that being which has characteristics?
5. If you love people presumably it is for such qualities as their attractiveness, their abilities, and their personality. Could you still love them if, in old age, they became unattractive, lost their skills, and their personality changed?

The Edible Woman
Margaret Atwood

Margaret Atwood (1939–) is a renowned Canadian novelist, poet, and short story writer whose works have received considerable critical acclaim as well as a wide popular audience. In her early books of poetry, such as Double Persephone *and* The Circle Game, *she describes relationships as both a trap and a shelter, nature as both menacing and liberating, and explores dualities such as self and others, subject and object, male and female. In her novels* The Handmaid's Tale, Bodily Harm, Life Before Man, *and* The Edible Woman *(here anthologized), she sounds the strong feminist themes of a modern woman who finds herself isolated, exploited, adrift, and suffering.*

*   The Edible Woman* describes the rebellion of Marian McAlpin *against her forthcoming marriage which threatens to be too conventional and confining. She ultimately rejects the image of herself as a commodity or comestible, something to absorb and assimilate like food (cupcake, sugar, honey, sweetie pie, in short, edible).*

"THERE'S jelly, salmon, peanut butter and honey, and egg salad," Mrs. Grot said, shoving the platter almost under Marian's nose—not because she was being rude but because Marian was sitting on the chesterfield and Mrs. Grot was standing up, and the assemblage of vertebrae, inflexible corsetry, and desk-oriented musculature that provided Mrs. Grot with her vertical structure would not allow her to bend very far over.

Marian drew herself back into the soft chintz cushions. "Jelly, thanks," she said, taking one.

It was the office Christmas party, which was being held in the ladies' lunchroom where they could be, as Mrs. Gundridge had put it, "more comfy." So far their comfiness, all-permeating as it was in these close quarters, had been tempered by a certain amount of suppressed resentment. Christmas fell on a Wednesday this year, which meant that they all had to come back to work on Friday, missing by a single day the chance of a gloriously long weekend. It was the knowledge of this fact however that had, Marian was sure, put the twinkle in Mrs. Grot's spectacles and even infused her with gaiety enough to sustain this unprecedentedly-social sandwich-passing. It's because she wants to take a good close look at our sufferings, Marian thought, watching the rigid figure as it progressed around the room.

The office party seemed to consist largely of the consumption of food and the discussion of ailments and bargains. The food had all been brought by the ladies themselves: each of them had agreed to provide a certain item. Even Marian had been pressured into promising some chocolate brownies, which she had actually bought at a bakery and switched to a different bag. She had not felt much like cooking lately. The food was heaped on the table that stood at one end of the lunchroom— much more food than they needed really, salads and sandwiches and fancy breads and desserts and cookies and cakes. But since everyone had brought something, everyone had to eat at least some of everything, or else the contributor would feel slighted. From time to time one or another of the ladies would shriek, "Oh, Dorothy, I just *have* to try some of your Orange-Pineapple Delight!" or "Lena, your Luscious Fruit Sponge looks just scrummy!" and heave to her feet and trundle to the table to re-fill her paper plate.

Marian gathered that it had not always been like this. For some of the older girls, there was a memory, fast fading to legend, of a time when the office party had been a company-wide event; that was when the company had been much smaller. In those far-off days, Mrs. Bogue said mistily, the men from upstairs had come down, and they even had drinks. But the office had expanded, finally things reached a stage at which nobody knew everybody any longer, and the parties started to get out of hand. Small ink-stained girls from Mimeo were pursued by wandering executives, there were untimely revelations of smouldering lusts and concealed resentments, and elderly ladies had a papercupful too much and hysterics. Now, in the interests of allover office morale, each department had its own office party; and Mrs. Gundridge had volunteered earlier that afternoon that it was a lot comfier this way anyhow, just all us girls here together, a comment which had produced glutinous murmurs of assent.

Marian was sitting wedged between two of the office virgins; the third was perched on the arm of the chesterfield. In situations like this, the three of them huddled together for self-protection: they had no children whose cutenesses could be compared, no homes whose furnishings were of much importance, and no husbands, details of whose eccentricities and nasty habits could be exchanged. Their concerns were other, though Emmy occasionally contributed an anecdote about one of her illnesses to the general conversation. Marian was aware that her own status among them was doubtful—they knew that she was on the fringe of matrimony and therefore regarded her as no longer genuinely single, no longer able to empathize with their problems—but in spite of their slight coolness towards her she still preferred being with them to joining any of the other groups. There was little movement in the room. Apart from the platter-passers, most of the ladies remained seated, in various clusters and semi-circles, re-clumping themselves every now and then by an exchange of chairs. Mrs. Bogue alone circulated, bestowing a sociable smile here, a mark of attention or a cookie there. It was her duty.

She was working at it the more assiduously because of the cata-
clysm that had taken place earlier in the day. The giant citywide instant
tomato juice taste-test, in the offing since October but constantly delayed
for further refinements, had been due to go out that morning. A record
number of interviewers, almost the whole available crew, were to have
descended on the unwary front porches of the housewives with card-
board trays on strings around their necks, like cigarette girls (privately, to
Lucy, Marian had suggested bleaching them all and dressing them up in
feathers and net stockings), carrying small paper cups of real canned
tomato juice and small paper cups of Instant tomato juice powder and
small pitchers of water. The housewife was to take a sip of the real juice,
watch the interviewer mix the Instant right before her astounded eyes,
and then try the result, impressed, possibly, by its quickness and ease:
"One Stir and you're Sure!" said the tentative advertisement sketches. If
they'd done it in October it might have worked.

Unfortunately the snow that had been withholding itself during five
uniformly overclouded grey days had chosen that morning at ten o'clock
to begin to fall, not in soft drifting flakes or even intermittent flurries, but
in a regular driving blizzard. Mrs. Bogue had tried to get the higher-ups
to postpone the test, but in vain. "We're working with humans, not with
machines," she had said on the phone, her voice loud enough so that they
could hear it through the closed door of her cubicle. "It's utterly impossible out there!" But there was a deadline to be met. The thing had already
been postponed for so long that it could be kept back no longer, and furthermore a delay of one day at this point would mean an actual delay of
three because of the major inconvenience of Christmas. So Mrs. Bogue's
flock had been driven, bleating faintly, out into the storm.

For the rest of the morning the office had resembled the base of a
mercy-mission in a disaster-area. Phone-calls flooded in from the hapless
interviewers. Their cars, anti-freeze and snow-tireless, balked and stalled,
stranded themselves in blowing drifts, and slammed their doors on
hands and their trunk-lids on heads. The paper cups were far too light to
withstand the force of the gale, and whirled away over the lanes and
hedges, emptying their blood-red contents on the snow, on the interviewers, and, if the interviewers had actually made it as far as a front door, on
the housewife herself. One interviewer had her whole tray ripped from
her neck and lifted into the air like a kite; another had tried to shelter hers
inside her coat, only to have it tipped and spewn against her body by the
wind. From eleven o'clock on, the interviewers themselves had come
straggling in, wild-haired and smeared with red, to resign or explain or
have their faith in themselves as scientific and efficient measures of public opinion restored, depending on temperament; and Mrs. Bogue had
had to cope in addition with the howls of rage from the broadloomed
Olympics above who refused to recognize the existence of any storm not
of their own making. The traces of the fray were still evident on her face

as she moved among the eating women. When she was pretending to be flustered and upset, she was really serene; but now, attempting serenity, she reminded Marian of a club-lady in a flowered hat making a gracious speech of thanks, who has just felt a small many-legged creature scamper up her leg.

Marian gave up half-listening to several conversations at once and let the sound of voices filling the room wash across her ears in a blur of meaningless syllables. She finished her jelly sandwich and went for a piece of cake. The loaded table made her feel gluttonous: all that abundance, all those meringues and icings and glazes, those coagulations of fats and sweets, that proliferation of rich glossy food. When she returned with a piece of spongecake Lucy, who had been talking with Emmy, had turned and was now talking with Millie, so that after she had taken her place again Marian found herself in the middle of their conversation.

"Well naturally they just didn't know what to do about it," Lucy was saying. "You just don't ask someone would they please take a bath. I mean it's not very polite."

"And London's so dirty too," Millie said sympathetically. "You see the men in the evenings, the collars of their white shirts are black, just black. It's all the soot."

"Yes well, and this went on and it got worse and worse, it was getting so bad they were ashamed to even ask their friends in. . . ."

"Who's this?" Marian asked.

"Oh this *girl* who was living with some friends of mine in England and she just stopped *washing*. Nothing else was wrong with her, she just didn't wash, even her *hair* even, or change her clothes or anything, for the longest time, and they didn't want to say anything because she seemed perfectly *normal* in every other way, but obviously underneath it she must have been really *sick*."

Emmy's narrow peaked face swung round at the word, "sick," and the story was repeated to her.

"So what happened, then?" Millie asked, licking chocolate icing from her fingers.

"Well," said Lucy, nibbling daintily at a morsel of shortcake, "it got pretty horrible. I mean, she was wearing the same *clothes*, you can imagine. And I guess it must have been three or four months."

There was a murmur of "Oh no's," and she said, "Well, at least two. And they were just about to ask her for god's sake either take a bath or move out. I mean, wouldn't you? But one day she came home and just took off those clothes and burnt them, and had a bath and everything, and she's been perfectly normal ever since. Just like that."

"Well that *is* queer!" Emmy said in a disappointed voice. She had been expecting a severe illness, or perhaps even an operation.

"Of course they're all a lot dirtier Over There, you know," Millie said in a woman-of-the-world tone.

"But *she* was from Over Here!" Lucy exclaimed. "I mean she'd been brought up the right way, she was from a good family and all; it wasn't as if they didn't have a *bath*room, *they* were always perfectly clean!"

"Maybe it was one of those things we sort of all go through," said Millie philosophically. "Maybe she was just immature, and being away from home like that and all. . . ."

"I think she was *sick*," Lucy said. She was picking the raisins out of a piece of Christmas-cake, preparatory to eating it.

Marian's mind grasped at the word "immature," turning it over like a curious pebble found on a beach. It suggested an unripe ear of corn, and other things of a vegetable or fruitlike nature. You were green and then you ripened: became mature. Dresses for the mature figure. In other words, fat.

She looked around the room at all the women there, at the mouths opening and shutting, to talk or to eat. Here, sitting like any other group of women at an afternoon feast, they no longer had the varnish of official-dom that separated them, during regular office hours, from the vast anonymous ocean of housewives whose minds they were employed to explore. They could have been wearing housecoats and curlers. As it was, they all wore dresses for the mature figure. They were ripe, some rapidly becoming overripe, some already beginning to shrivel; she thought of them as attached by stems at the tops of their heads to an invisible vine, hanging there in various stages of growth and decay . . . in that case, thin elegant Lucy, sitting beside her, was merely at an earlier stage, a spring-time green bump or nodule forming beneath the careful golden calyx of her hair. . . .

She examined the women's bodies with interest, critically, as though she had never seen them before. And in a way she hadn't, they had just been there like everything else, desks, telephones, chairs, in the space of the office: objects viewed as outline and surface only. But now she could see the roll of fat pushed up across Mrs. Gundridge's back by the top of her corset, the ham-like bulge of thigh, the creases round the neck, the large porous cheeks; the blotch of varicose veins glimpsed at the back of one plump crossed leg, the way her jowls jellied when she chewed, her sweater a woolly teacosy over those rounded shoulders; and the others too, similar in structure but with varying proportions and tex-tures of bumpy permanents and dune-like contours of breast and waist and hip; their fluidity sustained somewhere within by bones, without by a carapace of clothing and makeup. What peculiar creatures they were; and the continual flux between the outside and the inside, taking things in, giving them out, chewing, words, potato-chips, burps, grease, hair, ba-bies, milk, excrement, cookies, vomit, coffee, tomato-juice, blood, tea, sweat, liquor, tears, and garbage. . . .

For an instant she felt them, their identities, almost their substance, pass over her head like a wave. At some time she would be—or no, already she was like that too; she was one of them, her body the same, identical, merged with that other flesh that choked the air in the flowered room with its sweet organic scent; she felt suffocated by this thick sargasso-sea of femininity. She drew a deep breath, clenching her body and her mind back into her self like some tactile sea-creature withdrawing its tentacles: she wanted something solid, clear: a man; she wanted Peter in the room so that she could put her hand out and hold on to him to keep from being sucked down. Lucy had a gold bangle on one arm. Marian focussed her eyes on it, concentrating on it as though she was drawing its hard gold circle around herself, a fixed barrier between herself and that liquid amorphous other.

She became aware of a silence in the room. The henyard gabble had ceased. She lifted her head: Mrs. Bogue was standing at the end of the room near the table, holding up her hand.

"Now that we're all gathered together here in this unofficial way," she said, smiling benignly, "I'd like to take this opportunity to make a very pleasant announcement. I've learned recently through the grapevine that one of our girls will soon be getting married. I'm sure we'll all wish Marian McAlpin the very best in her new life."

There were preliminary squeals and chirps and burbles of excitement; then the whole mass rose up and descended upon her, deluging her with moist congratulations and chocolate-crumbed inquiries and little powdery initiatory kisses. . . .

In the supermarket she went methodically up and down the aisles, relentlessly out-manoeuvring the muskrat-furred ladies, edging the Saturday children to the curb, picking the things off the shelves. Her image was taking shape. Eggs, Flour, Lemons for the flavour. Sugar, icing-sugar, vanilla, salt, food-colouring. She wanted everything new, she didn't want to use anything that was already in the house. Chocolate—no, cocoa, that would be better. A glass tube full of round silver decorations. Three nesting plastic bowls, teaspoons, aluminum cake-decorator and a cake tin. Lucky, she thought, they sell almost everything in supermarkets these days. She started back towards the apartment, carrying her paper bag.

Sponge or angel-food? she wondered. She decided on sponge. It was more fitting.

She turned on the oven. That was one part of the kitchen that had not been over-run by the creeping skin-disease-covering of dirt, mostly because they hadn't been using it much recently. She tied on an apron and rinsed the new bowls and the other new utensils under the tap, but did not disturb any of the dirty dishes. Later for them. Right now she didn't have time. She dried the things and began to crack and separate the eggs, hardly thinking, concentrating all her attention on the movements of her hands, and then when she was beating and sifting and folding, on the relative times and the textures. Spongecake needed a light hand. She poured the batter into the tin and drew a fork sideways through it to break the large air-bubbles. As she slid the tin into the oven she almost hummed with pleasure. It was a long time since she had made a cake.

While the cake was in the oven baking she re-washed the bowls and mixed the icing. An ordinary butter icing, that would be the best. Then she divided the icing into three parts in the three bowls. The largest portion she left white, the next one she tinted a bright pink, almost red, with the red food-colouring she had bought, and the last one she made dark brown by stirring cocoa into it.

What am I going to put her on? she thought when she had finished. I'll have to wash a dish. She unearthed a long platter from the very bottom of the stack of plates in the sink and scoured it thoroughly under the tap. It took quite a lot of detergent to get the scum off.

She tested the cake; it was done. She took it out of the oven and turned it upside-down to cool.

She was glad Ainsley wasn't home: she didn't want any interference with what she was going to do. In fact it didn't look as though Ainsley had been home at all. There was no sign of her green dress. In her room a suitcase was lying open on the bed where she must have left it the night before. Some of the surface flotsam was eddying into it, as though drawn by a vortex. Marian wondered in passing how Ainsley was ever going to cram the random contents of the room into anything as limited and rectilinear as a set of suitcases.

While the cake was cooling she went into the bedroom and tidied her hair, pulling it back and pinning it to get rid of the remains of the hairdresser's convolutions. She felt lightheaded, almost dizzy: it must be the lack of sleep and the lack of food. She grinned into the mirror, showing her teeth.

The cake wasn't cooling quickly enough. She refused to put it into the refrigerator though. It would pick up the smells. She took it out of the tin and set it on the clean platter, opened the kitchen window, and stuck it out on the snowy sill. She knew what happened to cakes that were iced warm—everything melted.

She wondered what time it was. Her watch was still on the top of the dresser where she had left it the day before but it had run down. She didn't want to turn on Ainsley's transistor, that would be too distracting. She was getting jittery already. There used to be a number you could phone . . . but anyway she would have to hurry.

She took the cake off the sill, felt it to see if it was cool enough, and put it on the kitchen table. Then she began to operate. With the two forks she pulled it in half through the middle. One half she placed flat side down on the platter. She scooped out part of it and made a head with the section she had taken out. Then she nipped in a waist at the sides. The other half she pulled into strips for the arms and legs. The spongy cake was pliable, easy to mould. She stuck all the separate members together with white icing, and used the rest of the icing to cover the shape she had constructed. It was bumpy in places and had too many crumbs in the skin, but it would do. She reinforced the feet and ankles with tooth-picks.

Now she had a blank white body. It looked slightly obscene, lying there soft and sugary and featureless on the platter. She set about clothing it, filling the cake-decorator with bright pink icing. First she gave it a bikini, but that was too sparse. She filled in the midriff. Now it had an ordinary bathing-suit, but that still wasn't exactly what she wanted. She kept extending, adding to top and bottom, until she had a dress of sorts. In a burst of exuberance she added a row of ruffles around the neckline, and more ruffles at the hem of the dress. She made a smiling lush-lipped pink mouth and pink shoes to match. Finally she put five pink fingernails on each of the amorphous hands.

The cake looked peculiar with only a mouth and no hair or eyes. She rinsed out the cake-decorator and filled it with chocolate icing. She drew a nose, and two large eyes, to which she appended many eyelashes and two eyebrows, one above each eye. For emphasis she made a line demarcating one leg from the other, and similar lines to separate the arms from the body. The hair took longer. It involved masses of intricate baroque scrolls and swirls, piled high on the head and spilling down over the shoulders.

The eyes were still blank. She decided on green—the only other possibilities were red and yellow, since they were the only other colors she had—and with a toothpick applied two irises of green food-colouring.

Now there were only the globular silver decorations to add. One went in each eye, for a pupil. With the others she made a floral design on the pink dress, and stuck a few in the hair. Now the woman looked like an elegant antique china figurine. For an instant she wished she had bought some birthday candles; but where could they be put? There was really no room for them. The image was complete.

Her creation gazed up at her, its face doll-like and vacant except for the small silver glitter of intelligence in each green eye. While making it she had been almost gleeful, but now, contemplating it, she was pensive. All that work had gone into the lady and now what would happen to her?

"You look delicious," she told her. "Very appetizing. And that's what will happen to you; that's what you get for being food." At the thought of food her stomach contracted. She felt a certain pity for her creature but she was powerless now to do anything about it. Her fate had been decided. Already Peter's footsteps were coming up the stairs.

Marian had a swift vision of her own monumental silliness, of how infantile and undignified she would seem in the eyes of any rational observer. What kind of game did she think she was playing? But that wasn't the point, she told herself nervously, pushing back a strand of hair. Though if Peter found her silly she would believe it, she would accept his version of herself, he would laugh and they would sit down and have a quiet cup of tea.

She smiled gravely at Peter as he came up out of the stairwell. The expression on his face, a scowl combined with a jutting chin, meant he was still angry. He was wearing a costume suitable for being angry in: the suit stern, tailored, remote, but the tie a paisley with touches of sullen maroon.

"Now what's all this . . ." he began.

"Peter, why don't you go into the living-room and sit down? I have a surprise for you. Then we can have a talk if you like." She smiled at him again.

He was puzzled, and forgot to sustain his frown; he must have been expecting an awkward apology. But he did as she suggested. She remained in the doorway for a moment, looking almost tenderly at the back of his head resting against the chesterfield. Now that she had seen him again, the actual Peter, solid as ever, the fears of the evening before had dwindled to foolish hysteria and the flight to Duncan had become a stupidity, an evasion; she could hardly remember what he looked like. Peter was not the enemy after all, he was just a normal human being like most other people. She wanted to touch his neck, tell him that he shouldn't get upset, that everything was going to be all right. It was Duncan that was the mutation.

But there was something about his shoulders. He must have been sitting with his arms folded. The face on the other side of that head could have belonged to anyone. And they all wore clothes of real cloth and had real bodies: those in the newspapers, those still unknown, waiting for their chance to aim from the upstairs window; you passed them on the streets every day. It was easy to see him as normal and safe in the afternoon, but that didn't alter things. The price of this version of reality was testing the other one.

She went into the kitchen and returned, bearing the platter in front of her, carefully and with reverence, as though she was carrying something sacred in a procession, an icon or the crown on a cushion in a play. She knelt, setting the platter on the coffee-table in front of Peter.

"You've been trying to destroy me, haven't you," she said. "You've been trying to assimilate me. But I've made you a substitute, something you'll like much better. This is what you really wanted all along, isn't it? I'll get you a fork," she added somewhat prosaically.

Peter stared from the cake to her face and back again. She wasn't smiling.

His eyes widened in alarm. Apparently he didn't find her silly.

When he had gone—and he went quite rapidly, they didn't have much of a conversation after all, he seemed embarrassed and eager to leave and even refused a cup of tea—she stood looking down at the figure. So Peter hadn't devoured it after all. As a symbol it had definitely failed. It looked up at her with its silvery eyes, enigmatic, mocking, succulent.

Suddenly she was hungry. Extremely hungry. The cake after all was only a cake. She picked up the platter, carried it to the kitchen table and located a fork. "I'll start with the feet," she decided.

She considered the first mouthful. It seemed odd but most pleasant to be actually tasting and chewing and swallowing again. Not bad, she thought critically; needs a touch more lemon though.

Already the part of her not occupied with eating was having a wave of nostalgia for Peter, as though for a style that had gone out of fashion and was beginning to turn up on the sad Salvation Army clothes racks. She could see him in her mind, posed jauntily in the foreground of an elegant salon with chandeliers and draperies, impeccably dressed, a glass of scotch in one hand; his foot was on the head of a stuffed lion and he had an eyepatch over one eye. Beneath one arm was strapped a revolver. Around the margin was an edging of gold scrollwork and slightly above Peter's left ear was a thumbtack. She licked her fork meditatively. He would definitely succeed.

She was halfway up the legs when she heard footsteps, two sets of them, coming up the stairs. Then Ainsley appeared in the kitchen doorway with Fischer Smythe's furry head behind her. She still had on her bluegreen dress, much the worse for wear. So was she: her face was haggard and in only the past twenty-four hours her belly seemed to have grown noticeably rounder.

"Hi," said Marian, waving her fork at them. She speared a chunk of pink thigh and carried it to her mouth.

Fischer had leaned against the wall and closed his eyes as soon as he reached the top of the stairs, but Ainsley focussed on her. "Marian, what have you got there?" She walked over to see. "It's a woman—a woman made of cake!" She gave Marian a strange look.

Marian chewed and swallowed. "Have some," she said, "it's really good. I made it this afternoon."

Ainsley's mouth opened and closed, fishlike, as though she was trying to gulp down the full implication of what she saw. "Marian!" she exclaimed at last, with horror. "You're rejecting your femininity!"

Marian stopped chewing and stared at Ainsley, who was regarding her through the hair that festooned itself over her eyes with wounded concern, almost with sternness. How did she manage it, that stricken attitude, that high seriousness? She was almost as morally earnest as the lady down below.

Marian looked back at her platter. The woman lay there, still smiling glassily, her legs gone. "Nonsense," she said. "It's only a cake." She plunged her fork into the carcass, neatly severing the body from the head.

Study Questions

1. Do you believe Margaret Atwood is right in thinking that men regard women as equivalent to food?
2. The office party consists mainly of eating, and many of the women are fat. What meaning do you ascribe to this?
3. Why did Marian bake a cake for Peter that is in the shape of a woman?
4. What is the relationship between Marian and Ainsley?
5. To what extent do you think people's identities are determined by their gender? You can forget whether people you've met wore glasses, or had brown or blonde hair. Can you forget whether they were male or female?

2001, A Space Odyssey

Director: Stanley Kubrick

Screenwriters: Stanley Kubrick and Arthur C. Clarke

Stanley Kubrick (1928–1999) was a celebrated film director with a number of artistic and box office successes to his credit. His first major film, Paths of Glory, *received the Grand Prix de la Critique in Belgium, and it was followed by* Spartacus, *a star-studded epic that grossed twelve million dollars. Kubrick then directed a series of celebrated motion pictures, many adapted from books, including* Lolita *(from the Vladimir Nabakov novel),* A Clockwork Orange *(from the Anthony Burgess novel), and* The Shining *(from the Stephen King novel). Kubrick also wrote, produced, and directed* Dr. Strangelove, Barry Lyndon, *and* Full Metal Jacket.

Kubrick's 2001, A Space Odyssey *is often regarded as the best science fiction film ever made. He does not show laser attacks by alien empires, dog fights between spaceships traveling at the speed of light, or exploding meteors or civilizations. His sci-fi world is unlike* Star Wars, Battlehip Gallactica, *or* Red Planet, *or* Blade Runner, Robotech, *or* Tron. *Kubrick presents a more poetic and reflective film of space, with attention to pacing, music, and images, one that is understated but lasts in our visual memory.*

Synopsis

As a philosophic film, *2001, A Space Odyssey* prompts us to reflect on human evolution and destiny, our intrinsic nature and our place within the cosmos. Human beings seem an amalgam of angels, beasts, and machines, both body and spirit, just as the universe appears to be composed of the material and nonmaterial. We pride ourselves on being the rational animals, dominating the planet through our brain, but if computers surpass us in intelligence then we have lost our uniqueness and superiority. We often value logic over feeling and don't want to behave like animals, but that puts us closer to mechanical computers. When these machines outperform us in computation, memory, and data organization as well as overall speed of "thinking," we are left wondering about our distinctness.

In 1997 the reigning World Chess Champion, Gary Kasparov, played a chess match against IBM's supercomputer, Deep Blue. He lost the match, and since chess is considered the paradigm of human reasoning, this event was thought to demonstrate the emerging superiority of machine intelligence. We had already witnessed mechanical devices that surpassed their bodily counterparts: pumps that were better than the heart, cameras that captured images better than the eye, electric wires that functioned better than nerves, and so forth. Now the human brain was threatened by artificial intelligence (AI).

Throughout the 1980s and the 1990s enormous advances were made in computers and their offshoots of robots, cyborgs, and androids. In addition to business applications, computers are now employed to forecast the weather, clean up toxic waste, design cars and buildings, model financial data, develop drug therapies, make medical diagnoses, facilitate communications, and perform multiple other functions. The computer program Eliza functions as a psychotherapist, and some computers can run programs for the computers on which they are running. NASA has ongoing projects in pattern recognition, automated scheduling and planning, imaging and mapping, the identification, mining and classification of knowledge, resource management systems, and human/machine interface. In 1969, a year after the release of *2001*, our technology was sophisticated enough for Apollo 11 to land men on the moon.

These scientific achievements raise questions about the identity of human beings. Are we simply machines, clever enough to invent machines brighter than ourselves, or spiritual beings created in the image of God? Are we input/output mechanisms programmed by heredity and environment, or souls with a divine spark on the verge of transcending the limitations of matter?

We even wonder whether we can draw a line between computers and humans since some are able to pass an intelligence test as designed by Alan Turing. According to the "Turing test," suppose you had two keyboards in front of you, one connected to a computer, the other leading to a person. When you type a question, each responds with an answer on your screen. If you cannot tell which is the person and which the machine, then you must consider the computer to be intelligent.

2001, A Space Odyssey reflects on such questions and can be considered a meditation on the nature of humankind. The Odyssey of the title is an internal journey as well as an external one, traveling outward to the stars but also exploring our interior nature and evolving state.

The two-hour and twenty-minute film is highly imagistic with only forty minutes of dialogue, and it proceeds at a leisurely pace that requires patience and encourages contemplation. The atmosphere is cold, detached, and impersonal, with the vastness of space producing a tranquil and majestic effect that is also slightly menacing. The space ship and the astronauts inside float weightless in a slow-motion ballet. Strauss's lush music (and the score by Alex North) suggests the beauty and mystery of space, especially the "Blue Danube" waltz as the shuttle docks, and

"Thus Spake Zarathustra," which is the central theme.* The first five opening notes are heroic, signifying the emergence of man to a higher level of being.

The film is divided into four parts, "Dawn of Man," "The Lunar Journey," "Jupiter Mission," and "Jupiter and Beyond the Infinite." After the camera pans from the pitted surface of the moon and shows the sun, earth, and moon in alignment, the "Dawn of Man" begins with shots of Australopithecines foraging for edible grasses in an arid landscape. A leopard attacks one of the ape-men, and after a fade out, we see a clan establish its dominance over a watering hole under the leadership of Moonwatcher (Daniel Richter). The scenes are probably intended to show the precarious and violent character of prehistoric life.

In the morning light we see a polished, black, erect, rectangular slab that has mysteriously appeared in the clan's den, emitting a strange humming sound. When curiosity overcomes his fear, Moonwatcher reaches out to the alien object, followed by all the clan members, and their lives seem transformed by touching the monolith. Later, when Moonwatcher is searching for food, he picks up a large bone from an antelope's skeleton and, in an ecstatic moment of discovery, begins to wield it like a club. He smashes the rest of the skeleton, then uses the weapon for hunting and defense, and the music builds along with his newfound intelligence and power. As the fragments of bone scatter in all directions and the club is thrown triumphantly into the air, the image dissolves into a spaceship floating through space four million years later.

According to some anthropologists, human life began with the ability to use tools (homo faber), made possible by our cerebral cortex and opposable thumb and forefinger, so the line between wielding a bone and building a spacecraft is continuous. The evolution of civilization is compressed in time and shown in microcosm; in both cases inhospitable environments are controlled through technology.

However, the role of the monolithic slab in the film is more puzzling. No explanation is provided in the dialogue, which does not start until nearly thirty minutes into the film, but commentators have given two principal interpretations.

One of the screenwriters, Arthur Clarke, treats the monolith as a highly advanced machine sent to earth by aliens to assist in our evolution. If it isn't a sign from an advanced civilization, the object could symbolize knowledge and technology, showing early man that his world is not just given but can be made. The other interpretation is a religious one;

---

*Some interpreters see an implied reference to the book of the same name by the German philosopher Friedrich Nietzsche, and to the religion of Zoroastrianism that claims the prophet Zoroaster will come again after nine thousand years of history.

the monolith could be a mirror reflecting the face of God. We advance from animal to human state once we come in contact with the divine, as in the painting by Michelangelo where God brings Adam to life by touching his finger. This would be in keeping with the theological ideas of Teilhard de Chardin who saw in science, technology, and evolution a positive direction leading to final holiness.

In "The Lunar Journey," we are projected into a space shuttle bound for the moon by way of a staging area, the wheel-shaped revolving Space Station 5, then into the lunar lander for the trip to the Clavius base. The camera focuses on a Dr. Heywood R. Floyd (William Sylvester) within the spacecrafts and space station, and in meetings with scientists on the moon, and we are treated to both familiar and exotic images. A flight attendant must wear suction shoes in the weightless atmosphere, and she turns upside-down while delivering trays of food, but then the shuttle and spacecraft are Pan American, we see advertisements for Hilton and Howard Johnson in a hallway, and Floyd speaks to his daughter at home on a Bell video phone while the earth drifts majestically by the window. An announcement is made with an unfamiliar content but a familiar ring:

> Despite an excellent and continually improving safety record there are certain risks inherent in space travel and an extremely high cost of payload. Because of this it is necessary for the Space Carrier to advise you that it cannot be responsible for the return of your body to Earth should you become deceased on the Moon or en route to the moon. However, it wishes to advise you that insurance covering this contingency is available in the Main Lounge. Thank you.

The purpose of Dr. Floyd's visit to the moon is to investigate a strange monolith under the lunar surface that has been transmitting radio signals. When he encounters the object, buried four million years ago, he reaches out to touch it as Moonwatcher did, and as the earth, sun, and moon are in conjunction it emits a piercing sound. The monolith looks the same as the one that prehistoric men discovered on earth, but the signal is beamed at the planet Jupiter (the Roman Zeus).

The third and longest section of the film, "Jupiter Mission," takes place on the spaceship "Discovery" as it travels to this distant planet. As in many journeys, a physical quest becomes a spiritual one. David Bowman (Keir Dullea) and Frank Poole (Gary Lockwood) are the chief astronauts on board with three scientists cryogenically suspended in transparent cylinders. A supercomputer HAL-9000, which stands for Heuristic Algorithmic Computer, constitutes the brain of the ship, and as critics have pointed out, HAL is one letter up from IBM.

Of the three, HAL is the most interesting character. His interactive eye suggests an all-seeing Cyclops, and his voice (Douglas Rain) is soft, mellifluous, and restrained—more expressive than Dave or Frank who speak in a lifeless monotone. He (not it) displays emotion and has a complex, conflicted character that becomes sympathetic in the tragic ending; he "really likes people." On board the ship he handles routine tasks such as navigation and systems maintenance, and he plays chess with the men, programmed to lose 50 percent of the time to make the game interesting. However, at some point during the space journey he malfunctions, and the most dramatic sequence in the film consists of the struggle between HAL and Dave for control of the spacecraft, a conflict played out against the nothingness of outer-space.

As explained by Mission Control, HAL became deranged because of a built-in inconsistency. Although he was generally programmed to be truthful, he was also instructed to lie to the astronauts about the purpose of the mission. The astronauts believed they were carrying out a mission that was part of the general space program when, in fact, they were sent to investigate the meaning of the monolith's signal from the moon. For reasons of national security, the truth was kept from them.

In an earlier version of the screenplay, Bowman and Poole grow suspicious at one point, and question HAL:

> POOLE: . . . I heard there's something about the mission we weren't told.
> BOWMAN: That's very unlikely . . . Of course, it would be very easy for us to find out now.
> POOLE: How?
> BOWMAN: Just ask HAL. It's conceivable they might keep something from us, but they'd never keep anything from HAL.
> POOLE: That's true.
> BOWMAN: Well . . . it's silly, but . . . if you want to, why don't you?

Poole walks to the HAL 9000 computer.

> POOLE: HAL . . . Dave and I believe that there's something about the mission that we weren't told. Something that the rest of the crew know and that you know. We'd like to know whether this is true.
> HAL: I'm sorry, Frank, but I don't think I can answer that question without knowing everything that all of you know.
> BOWMAN: He's got a point . . .
> POOLE: Right. HAL, tell me whether the following statements are true or false.
> HAL: I will if I can, Frank.
> POOLE: Our Mission Profile calls for Discovery going to Saturn. True or false?
> HAL: True.
> POOLE: Our transit time is 257 days. Is that true?

> HAL: That's true.
> POOLE: At the end of a hundred days of exploration, we will all go into hibernation. Is that true?
> HAL: That's true.
> POOLE: Approximately five years after we go into hibernation, the recovery vehicle will make rendezvous with us and bring us back. Is this true?
> HAL: That's true.
> POOLE: There is no other purpose for this mission than to carry out a continuation of the space program and to further our general knowledge of the planets. Is that true?
> HAL: That's true.
> POOLE: Thank you very much, HAL.
> HAL: I hope I've been able to be of some help.

Both men look at each other rather sheepishly.

In reaction to the double bind, which causes paranoia, and because he thinks the mission is threatened, HAL begins killing the astronauts. "This mission is too important for me to allow you to jeopardize it," he states to Dave. He lures Frank Poole out of the spaceship on the pretext that the "AO-unit" in the guidance system needs to be replaced; we then see Frank tumbling and receding into space. HAL also kills the crew asleep in the "Hibernaculum," and almost kills David Bowman by opening some pod bay doors and generating an explosion.

At this point, Dave realizes that HAL is wholly untrustworthy, and in the most dramatic moment in the film (which also contains gallows humor and a certain pathos) he proceeds to disconnect him. Here HAL's emotions are closest to that of humans.

> Bowman has worked his way to the solid logic program storage area, and he begins turning HAL off by inserting a tool into the electronic mechanism.
>
> HAL: Just what do you think you are doing, Dave? Dave, I really think I'm entitled to an answer to that question.
>
> Bowman does not answer.
>
> HAL: I know everything hasn't been quite right with me, but I can assure you now, very confidently, that it's going to be all right again. I feel much better now, I really do.
>
> Bowman does not answer.
>
> HAL: Look Dave, I can see you're really upset about this. I honestly think you ought to sit down calmly, take a stress pill, and think things over.

HAL: I know I've made some really poor decisions recently but I can give you my complete assurance that my work will be back to normal. I've still got the greatest enthusiasm and confidence in the mission, and I want to help you.

Bowman works swiftly.

HAL: Dave, stop. Stop, will you? Stop, Dave. Will you stop, Dave? Stop, Dave.

Bowman ignores him.

HAL: I'm afraid. I'm afraid, Dave.

Bowman does not answer.

HAL: Dave, my mind is going. I can feel it. My mind is going. There is no question about it. I can feel it. I can feel it.
HAL: I'm afraid.

Bowman keeps turning the tool.

HAL: Good afternoon, gentlemen. I am HAL 9000 computer. I became operational at the HAL plant in Urbana, Illinois, on the 12th of January, 1992. My first instructor was Mr. Langley. He taught me to sing a song. If you'd like to hear it, I can sing it for you.
BOWMAN: Yes, I'd like to hear it HAL. Sing it for me.
HAL: Daisy, Daisy, give me your answer do. I'm half crazy all for the love of you . . .

Computer continues to sing the song, becoming more and more childish and making mistakes and going off-key. It finally stops completely.

In a philosophic sense, we wonder whether HAL could be considered a person. He certainly has many of the qualities of a human being and may be entitled to human rights. He can think logically and rapidly, remember vast amounts of information, learn from experience, express his personality, communicate with others, and act in self-defense. He is capable of spying and deceiving, and he is willing to kill to accomplish his purpose. Furthermore, he possesses not just consciousness but self-consciousness, and he feels strong emotions, including fear when he is being shut down.

HAL's persona raises very basic issues as to the theoretical difference between human beings and machines. The question is not whether people now do things that computers do not, but what can people do that computers will never be able to do? What human states are they incapable of having by their very nature?

Computers may be creative but could they be inspired? They can be programmed to laugh, but will they ever find things funny? They can reproduce themselves (computers that beget computers that beget computers), but could they feel passion or love in the act of procreation? If a computer is programmed to be deceitful, could it feel ashamed of itself and tell the truth despite the programming (conditioning)? Computers can receive data and store it in memory, but is that the same as understanding or wisdom? They can differentiate between colors, but could they be enthralled by the beauty of a sunset? They can diagnose a disease, but could they experience pain and suffering, or grief at a personal loss? They can fail in a task, but could they feel badly about themselves and wonder if they've made a mess of their lives? Computers can scan a document, duplicate it, and place it on a disk or hard drive, but could they ever understand what it means? They can describe God and religion, but could they appreciate the human need for worship and immortality? Is it theoretically impossible for computers to have dignity, loyalty, insight, hope, or awareness, or a sense of despair, fairness, remorse, pleasure, or compassion? Is it a matter of developing more sophisticated systems, or are some human states unique to people and inaccessible to machines?

When Dave is disconnecting him, HAL pleads for his life saying, "I'm scared, Dave," but those feelings may lie outside the capacity of any computer. It might only happen in the movies.

After HAL's demise, Dave Bowman then takes over manual control of the spacecraft, and the final segment of the film, "Jupiter and Beyond the Infinite," projects us into a mystical and surrealistic realm. The "Discovery" encounters another monolith, this one larger and floating through space, and when Bowman enters it in a pod we see him suddenly transported beyond the physical universe in a kaleidoscope display of psychedelic lights and startling colors. Following a fantastic journey through inner- or outer-space, we see him alone in a Louis XVI–style bedroom suite, eating his meals, napping, becoming feeble and bedridden, and when he becomes a very old man, turning into a fetal infant. The fetus is then transformed into a star-child, floating in a time warp between the earth and the moon.

The ending is intentionally obscure and cryptic, leaving viewers without a clear resolution. Is Kubrick asserting a cyclical theory of reincarnation, that in the ending is the beginning? Is he saying that ultimate reality lies beyond our comprehension? Is he showing the relation between human beings and higher forms of life? Is the film's message that, instead of seeking masculine control through tools like Hal, we must become as little children in order to be authentically human? Maybe the film is recounting the classic war between man and machine, with the human being emerging triumphant. (HAL says, "I can't do that Dave," which signals his revolt.) If Kubrick is anti-technology, showing that machines can kill, it would be paradoxical to create a high-tech film to make the argument, and if he is anti-religion the film should not offer something of a religious experience as its culmination.

Perhaps the most persuasive interpretation centers round evolution, which is the film's guiding theme. Maybe we are shown the future development of humans from physical beings to pure forms of energy as we rely increasingly on our minds. At each stage of history, people learn to think instead of reacting to their physical needs, and human consciousness keeps making giant leaps forward. Kubrick has, in fact, referred to human progress from "biological species, which are fragile shells for the mind at best, into immortal machine entities," of being transformed from "the chrysalis of matter into beings of pure energy and spirit."

In the final analysis, the conclusion is inconclusive. Kubrick intended the ending to be enigmatic because as he stated, "*2001* attempts to communicate more to the subconscious and to the feelings than it does to the intellect . . . I tried to create a visual experience, one that bypasses verbalized pigeonholing and directly penetrates the subconscious with an emotional and philosophic content."

The film, therefore, was meant to generate reflection about the nature of human life and its place in the universe, and to do so through a fable rendered in sensory images. As Kubrick stated in an interview,

> I think that if *2001* succeeds at all, it is in reaching a wide spectrum of people who would not often give a thought to man's destiny, his role in the cosmos and his relationship to higher forms of life. But even in the case of someone who is highly intelligent, certain ideas found in *2001* would, if presented as abstractions, fall rather lifelessly and be automatically assigned to pat intellectual categories; experienced in a moving visual and emotional context, however, they can resonate within the deepest fibers of one's being.

Study Questions

1. What is the relationship between Dave Bowman and HAL? Do you think people can feel affection or even love for a machine?
2. What interpretation would you offer of the monolith? Defend your answer.
3. How would you differentiate between human beings and computers? Bear in mind that human beings can be regarded as input/output mechanisms, with the body as hardware and psychological conditioning as our programming.
4. Which of the various explanations of the film's ending do you find most convincing? Why?
5. In the light of the considerations raised in *2001* how do you see the essence of your identity as a human being? What is it without which you would no longer be human?

B. THE UNIVERSE: WHAT IS ULTIMATELY REAL?

The pre-Socratic Greek philosopher Thales in the sixth century B.C. was the first man known to history to speculate about the basic "stuff" of the universe. In an imaginative leap of understanding, Thales reasoned that despite the apparent diversity of things around us there might well be a single substance common to all matter. Thales identified water as the essential substance underlying everything, and he used numerous ingenious arguments to prove his case,* but his particular choice of water and his "proofs" are philosophically and scientifically irrelevant. What matters is that Thales tried to reduce the multiplicity of objects to a unity, the seeming heterogeneity to a homogeneity, which means that he saw beyond appearances and accounted for why things exist as they do.

After Thales had broken the ground, a contemporary named Anaximander posited the Boundless or Indefinite as the primary source of matter, that "out of which all things arise and to which all return," but which does not itself possess determinate characteristics. And after Anaximander, Pythagoras declared numbers as basic, not just because everything could be expressed numerically but because numbers were thought to be fundamental entities with magnitude. Following these philosophers were some fifth-century pre-Socratics who were impressed with the idea of constancy and change—Heraclitus, for whom *logos* (that is, process or measure) characterized everything, and Parmenides, who asserted that change is an illusion. For Parmenides and his follower Zeno, the universe is motionless, a fixed and frozen block. Finally, Anaxagoras and Democritus spoke of particles that come into collision, mix, and combine to produce the physical world; Democritus, amazingly enough, offered an early theory of atomic interaction.

All of these metaphysical theories are little more than historical curiosities today, but they led to the more profound theories of the celebrated Greek philosophers Plato and Aristotle, and to the theories of modern philosophers, such as Bertrand Russell and Alfred North Whitehead. All subsequent philosophers addressed themselves to similar problems, using these early speculations as stepping stones. And when we ourselves begin asking metaphysical questions, we encounter the same problems. We, too, ask about the reality underlying appearances, the basis of things, and what remains constant throughout the flux of life. In short, metaphysical

---

*Thales argued that water transformed itself into air and earth through evaporation and into fire during lightning storms. Water underlies the earth as can be seen in wells and earthquakes, the latter caused by storms at sea. Furthermore, water is essential to all life and actually creates life as can be seen by the organisms left wriggling in half-dried mud pools. With regard to the last, Thales is not far wrong, for life began as specks of protoplasmic jelly in the scum of tides.

questions are the most perennial of all, for they are rooted in the human condition, and no thinking person can avoid reflecting on them.

As metaphysics has developed, certain theories have crystallized as dominant and persuasive. They are theories concerning the nature of the universe, but as might be expected, they also correspond to theories of the self. According to the *materialist* or *naturalist* theory the universe can be understood in wholly natural terms without any recourse to supernatural explanation. Human beings are a part of the natural order, and even though they have evolved to a position of supremacy among other animals, they are not unique creations outside of nature.

In contrast to the materialist, the *idealist* or *spiritualist* believes that soul or spirit constitutes the ultimate reality. Matter is thought to be dependent on some spiritual force for its existence, including a holy, omniscient, almighty, eternal God.*

We will see examples of these and other conceptions of reality in the readings, but let us explore here one pressing problem in metaphysics, namely whether people are free or compelled in their actions. More precisely, metaphysicians wonder whether human beings possess free will or whether they are determined in their choices. Are people able to decide between alternative courses of action as we usually assume?

The *determinist* takes the absolute position that all actions, including those people think they deliberately choose, are the inevitable result of prior factors. In a sense, all choices have already been made and a free decision is an illusion. The factors that are operative may be internal or external, but they completely govern human actions in accordance with physical laws. Once these laws are fully known, all behavior will be predictable. It is only because of incomplete knowledge that we cannot predict conduct with complete accuracy at present.

The *libertarian* admits that people often do behave in predictable ways and that statistical probabilities are possible, but claims people are not forced to act as they do; they are always free to behave differently. In brief, the libertarian maintains that the causes of human choice lie with the human being, or differently put, that reasons for decisions cannot be reduced to causes.

Thus the lines are drawn, and various arguments are used by the two sides to support their positions.

The determinist, first of all, admits that decisions are usually thought to be free, but claims that this is a false assumption caused by pride and ignorance. Once we scientifically analyze the full range of factors behind our choices, then we realize that we are determined

---

*Spiritualism and *idealism* are sometimes treated as synonymous, but spiritualism has a definite religious character whereas idealism regards all of existence as ideas or mind.

throughout. Freedom is seen as a delusion to feed our ego, a popular misconception that must give way before scientific truth.

Among the causal factors cited by the determinist is our genetic inheritance, including our body type, nervous system, skeletal structure, brain capacity, glandular secretions, and so forth. Each of these biological factors affects the way we live. Our body type, for example, whether round, large boned and muscular, or tall and thin, determines whether we choose sedentary or energetic activities, and the predisposition of our brain, for example, whether analytic or imaginative, determines the type of occupation we follow. In addition to genetic factors, the determinist also points to geographic and climatic conditions that exert an influence on our behavior. People who live in mountainous regions tend to be hardier and more independent than those who live on the plains, and more energetic people come from cold climates rather than areas of hot, humid weather.

Even more important than these factors, the determinist claims, are the effects of a person's social environment. For, each society determines the character of its members by the customs and mores that it holds, its religious and philosophical ideas, and the social, economic, and political structures that it embodies. As a consequence, the Eskimos differ from the French, and the Africans from the Chinese, irrespective of physical characteristics, climate, or geography. If people are raised in the American Midwest, they are likely to be religious, conservative, and patriotic; the reverse would be true on the East coast. Other factors that are said to determine people's personality and decisions are their family upbringing, formal and informal education, and the unique experiences they have undergone in their lives.

The list could be extended, but the determinist maintains that once all of these factors are taken into account, the causes of a person's actions are revealed; we can then see why a person had to act as he or she did. What's more, the better we know someone the more confident we become that the person will behave in certain consistent ways. Social interaction is predicated upon these expectations, and when someone surprises us, we conclude that we did not know the person as well as we thought. Knowing someone, then, means being able to predict what the person will do. That is, we know the determining factors and the conduct that will follow because of them.

Determinists further argue that science is founded upon the assumption of an orderly universe, shot throughout with causal laws. Surely human actions lie within this natural scheme and cannot be exempted as having special status. Behaviorist psychology in particular, by its use of the stimulus-response model, assumes that conduct has causal determinants. This model has been employed with considerable success in describing and predicting behavior. As a result of research, the behaviorist claims that alleged choices are actually responses to given stimuli;

when other stimuli are present, different choices are made. The conclusion must be that causal conditions lie behind human actions; that all
events occur according to deterministic laws.

The libertarian responds to the determinist's indictment by first arguing that factors of biology, climate, geography, and so forth, will only
control the individual until they are brought to the level of consciousness.
At that point, they become influences not determinants. Once individuals
are aware of the forces operating upon them they are free to respond positively or negatively to their influence. That is, individuals are always
free to choose once they are conscious of the factors that affect them.

Furthermore, knowing people and having confidence in them does
not mean knowing what they are forced to do, but knowing the choices
they consistently make. We depend upon people in the sense that we
know what they usually do, not what they must do. Freedom of the will,
then, is perfectly consistent with the ability to predict someone's behavior. To say that people are free does not mean that they behave unpre-
dictably, but only that their choices, while falling into a pattern, are
decided by themselves.

With regard to universal causation, the libertarian maintains that
perhaps man is a unique being, capable of reflection and conscious deliberation prior to action. Even within the causal framework, belief in free
will can be maintained, for we might be the cause of our own actions.
Various forces may play upon us, but we make the final decision. In other
words, a person's free choice is the ultimate causal factor.

Libertarians also take the offensive and level some criticisms
against the determinist theory. They charge, for example, that determinism renders moral and legal obligations meaningless by assuming that
individuals are not responsible for their actions. For, if all behavior is determined, and events could not have been otherwise, then no one is accountable for what happens; people can neither be praised not blamed.
As Immanuel Kant, the eighteenth-century German philosopher taught
us, "ought implies can." In order to recommend that an action *ought* to be
performed, we must assume that the person *can* do what is asked. If an
individual has no choice but is compelled by forces beyond his or her
control, then all moral judgments become futile. No legal responsibility
can be assigned, and courts and prisons should close. The criminal becomes a victim not a free agent, and he or she cannot be held responsible
for any crimes. The libertarian is arguing that since these consequences of
determinism are unacceptable, the theory cannot be valid.

Finally, determinists are charged with self-contradiction for they
claim that all decisions are caused by factors beyond the individual's control, yet by arguing for this position, they assume people are free to accept or reject the theory. In other words, if people can judge the truth of
determinism, then they cannot be regarded as determined, and the more
the determinist tries to convince people to accept the theory, the more

apparent it becomes that the theory cannot be true. Determinists give the game away by presenting a case for determinism, for they acknowledge that people are free to change their minds.

These are some of the principal arguments used on both sides. Yet, the libertarian does not necessarily have the last word. With regard to legal punishment, for example, the determinist sometimes claims that criminals can still be imprisoned even if they are not thought to be responsible for their crimes. Prison can simply function to condition the criminal against performing future crimes and, at the same time, to deter potential criminals in the society. In a determinist system, we cannot blame people for what they have done, but we can administer punishment as reinforcement, that is, to keep them from doing it again. We do not slap their wrist but take their pulse and prisons become hospitals.

Determinists also defend themselves against the charge of self-contradiction. They claim that if libertarians change their mind in response to determinist arguments it will be because they could not do otherwise; the arguments forced them to agree. The entire process, therefore, is further proof of determinism, for the strongest factors always win.

The libertarian has counter-arguments to these points, but we must leave the matter here.*

Metaphysics, then, tries to penetrate the core of reality with questions about human free will, the nature of the self, and general issues of the structure, process, and substance of the universe.

The second set of selections that follow present various views of the nature of reality, some of which have implications for the free will/determinism controversy. The British philosopher George Berkeley, who is classified as a subjective idealist, claims that spirit constitutes the essential reality, and he offers ingenious arguments in support of his theory. The writer Stephen Crane then shows us an opposite view—that the natural world of physical forces and accident make up the real world, and it contains no mercy or purpose. Finally, the filmmakers Larry and Andy Wachowski present a virtual world generated by computers, causing us to questions whether our ordinary conception of reality is sound.

---

*To explore the matter further, the distinction between hard and soft determinism should be examined.

Three Dialogues Between Hylas and Philonous

George Berkeley

George Berkeley (1685–1753) was an Irish philosopher and clergyman who was Fellow of Trinity College, Dublin, and also served as Bishop of Cloyne. His first philosophic work, The Principles of Human Knowledge, *was not well received but his subsequent work,* Three Dialogues Between Hylas and Philonous, *was more successful in convincing people of his theory.*

Berkeley (pronounced Barkley) is generally regarded as the founder of idealism—the theory that takes mind, soul, or spirit as the ultimate reality. Epistemologically, he is often grouped with David Hume and John Locke as one of the British empiricists, since he maintained that all knowledge is derived from sense perception.

In the excerpt that follows, Berkeley explains his theory that no material world exists; our knowledge of the external world wholly depends on the perceptions of the mind or "myself." To say that something exists only means that we have seen, heard, felt, touched, or tasted it, and we cannot claim anything exists that has not been sensed. Esse est percipi, *Berkeley writes: "To be is to be perceived."*

One objection that was raised to Berkeley's theory is that things seem to have a material existence apart from a perceiver. If we leave a room where a fire is burning and return some time later, the logs seem to have been consumed in our absence. Furthermore, different people perceive the same object, so reality cannot be a function of individual perception. Berkeley argues, however, that although objects cannot exist unperceived, the ultimate perceiver is God who regards everything in the world continuously.

This, in fact, becomes a proof for the existence of God for Berkeley. That is, the only way to account for the constancy of the world is to postulate a God who perceives everything at every moment.

The First Dialogue

HYL. You were represented in last night's conversation as one who maintained the most extravagant opinion that ever entered into the mind of man, to wit, that there is no such thing as *material substance* in the world.

PHIL. That there is no such thing as what philosophers call "material substance," I am seriously persuaded; but if I were made to see anything absurd or skeptical in this, I should then have **the** same reason to renounce this that I imagine I have now to reject the contrary opinion.

HYL. What! can anything be more fantastical, more repugnant to common sense or a more manifest piece of skepticism than to believe there is no such thing as matter?

PHIL. Softly, good Hylas. What if it should prove that you, who hold there is, are, by virtue of that opinion, a greater skeptic and maintain more paradoxes and repugnancies to common sense than I who believe no such thing?

HYL. You may as soon persuade me the part is greater than the whole, as that, in order to avoid absurdity and skepticism, I should ever be obliged to give up my opinion in this point.

PHIL. Well, then, are you content to admit that opinion for true which, upon examination, shall appear most agreeable to common sense and remote from skepticism?

HYL. With all my heart. Since you are for raising disputes about the plainest things in nature, I am content for once to hear what you have to say.

PHIL. Pray, Hylas, what do you mean by a "skeptic"? . . .

HYL. I mean what all men mean, one that doubts of everything . . . but I should have added: or who denies the reality and truth of things.

PHIL. What things? Do you mean the principles and theorems of sciences? But these you know are universal intellectual notions, and consequently independent of matter; the denial therefore of this does not imply the denying them.

HYL. I grant it. But are there no other things? What think you of distrusting the senses, of denying the real existence of sensible things, or pretending to know nothing of them. Is not this sufficient to denominate a man a skeptic?

PHIL. Shall we therefore examine which of us it is that denies the reality of sensible things or professes the greatest ignorance of them, since, if I take you rightly, he is to be esteemed the greatest skeptic?

HYL. That is what I desire.

PHIL. This point then is agreed between us—that sensible things are those only which are immediately perceived by sense. You will further inform me whether we immediately perceive by sight anything besides light and colors and figures; or by hearing, anything but sounds; by the palate, anything besides tastes; by the smell, besides odors; or by the touch, more than tangible qualities.

HYL. We do not.

PHIL. It seems, therefore, that if you take away all sensible qualities, there remains nothing sensible?

HYL. I grant it.

PHIL. Sensible things therefore are nothing else but so many sensible qualities or combinations of sensible qualities?

HYL. Nothing else.

PHIL. Heat is then a sensible thing?

HYL. Certainly.

PHIL. Does the reality of sensible things consist in being perceived, or is it something distinct from their being perceived, and that bears no relation to the mind?

HYL. To exist is one thing, and to be perceived is another.

PHIL. I speak with regard to sensible things only; and of these I ask, whether by their real existence you mean a subsistence exterior to the mind and distinct from their being perceived?

HYL. I mean a real absolute being, distinct from and without any relation to their being perceived.

PHIL. Heat therefore, if it be allowed a real being, must exist without the mind?

HYL. It must

PHIL. Tell me, Hylas, is this real existence equally compatible to all degrees of heat, which we perceive, or is there any reason why we should attribute it to some and deny it to others? And if there be, pray let me know that reason.

HYL. Whatever degree of heat we perceive by sense, we may be sure the same exists in the object that occasions it.

PHIL. What! the greatest as well as the least?

HYL. I tell you, the reason is plainly the same in respect of both: they are both perceived by sense; nay, the greater degree of heat is more sensibly perceived; and consequently, if there is any difference, we are more certain of its real existence than we can be of the reality of a lesser degree.

PHIL. But is not the most vehement and intense degree of heat a very great pain?

HYL. No one can deny it.

PHIL. And is any unperceiving thing capable of pain or pleasure?

HYL. No, certainly.

PHIL. Is your material substance a senseless being or a being endowed with sense and perception?

HYL. It is senseless, without doubt.

PHIL. It cannot, therefore, be the subject of pain?

HYL. By no means.

PHIL. Nor, consequently, of the greatest heat perceived by sense, since you acknowledge this to be no small pain?

HYL. I grant it.

PHIL. What shall we say then of your external object: is it a material substance, or no?

HYL. It is a material substance with the sensible qualities inhering in it.

PHIL. How then can a great heat exist in it, since you own it cannot in a material substance? I desire you would clear this point.

HYL. Hold, Philonous, I fear I was out in yielding intense heat to be a pain. It should seem rather that pain is something distinct from heat, and the consequence or effect of it.

PHIL. Upon putting your hand near the fire, do you perceive one simple uniform sensation or two distinct sensations?

HYL. But one simple sensation.

PHIL. Is not the heat immediately perceived?

HYL. It is.

PHIL. And the pain?

HYL. True.

PHIL. Seeing therefore they are both immediately perceived at the same time, and the fire affects you only with one simple or un-compounded idea, it follows that this same simple idea is both the intense heat immediately perceived and the pain; and, consequently, that the intense heat immediately perceived is nothing distinct from a particular sort of pain.

HYL. It seems so.

PHIL. Again, try in your thoughts, Hylas, if you can conceive a vehement sensation to be without pain or pleasure.

HYL. I cannot.

PHIL. Or can you frame to yourself an idea of sensible pain or pleasure, in general, abstracted from every particular idea of heat, cold, tastes, smells, etc.?

HYL. I do not find that I can.

PHIL. Does it not therefore follow that sensible pain is nothing distinct from those sensations or ideas—in an intense degree?

HYL. It is undeniable; and, to speak the truth, I begin to suspect a very great heat cannot exist but in a mind perceiving it. . . .

PHIL. Suppose now one of your hands hot, and the other cold, and that they are both at once put into the same vessel of water, in an intermediate state, will not the water seem cold to one hand, and warm to the other?

HYL. It will.

PHIL. Ought we not therefore, by your principles, to conclude it is really both cold and warm at the same time, that is, according to your own concession, to believe an absurdity?

HYL. I confess it seems so.

PHIL. Consequently, the principles themselves are false, since you have granted that no true principle leads to an absurdity.

HYL. But, after all, can anything be more absurd than to say, "there is no heat in the fire"?

PHIL. To make the point still clearer; tell me whether, in two cases exactly alike, we ought not to make the same judgment?

HYL. We ought.

PHIL. When a pin pricks your finger, does it not rend and divide the fibers of your flesh?

HYL. It does.

PHIL. And when a coal burns your finger, does it any more?

HYL. It does not.

PHIL. Since, therefore, you neither judge the sensation itself occasioned by the pin, nor anything like it to be in the pin, you should not, conformably to what you have now granted, judge the sensation occasioned by the fire, or anything like it, to be in the fire.

HYL. Well, since it must be so, I am content to yield this point and acknowledge that heat and cold are only sensations existing in our minds. But there still remain qualities enough to secure the reality of external things.

PHIL. But what will you say, Hylas, if it shall appear that the case is the same with regard to all other sensible qualities, and that they can no more be supposed to exist without the mind than heat and cold?

HYL. Then, indeed, you will have done something to the purpose; but that is what I despair of seeing proved.

PHIL. Let us examine them in order. What think you of tastes—do they exist without the mind, or no?

HYL. Can any man in his senses doubt whether sugar is sweet, or wormwood bitter?

PHIL. Inform me, Hylas. Is a sweet taste a particular kind of pleasure or pleasant sensation, or is it not?

HYL. It is.

PHIL. And is not bitterness some kind of uneasiness or pain?

HYL. I grant it.

PHIL. If, therefore, sugar and wormwood are unthinking corporeal substances existing without the mind, how can sweetness and bitterness, that is, pleasure and pain, agree to them? . . .

May we not therefore conclude of smells, as of the other forementioned qualities, that they cannot exist in any but a perceiving substance or mind?

HYL. I think so.

PHIL. Then as to sounds, what must we think of them, are they accidents really inherent in external bodies or not?

HYL. That they inhere not in the sonorous bodies is plain from hence; because a bell struck in the exhausted receiver of an air pump [i.e., a vacuum] sends forth no sound. The air, therefore, must be thought the subject of sound.

PHIL. What reason is there for that, Hylas?

HYL. Because, when any motion is raised in the air, we perceive a sound greater or lesser, in proportion to the air's motion; but without some motion in the air we never hear any sound at all.

PHIL. And granting that we never hear a sound but when some motion is produced in the air, yet I do not see how you can infer from thence that the sound itself is in the air.

HYL. It is this very motion in the external air that produces in the mind the sensation of sound. For, striking on the drum of the ear, it causes a vibration which by the auditory nerves being communicated to the brain, the soul is thereupon affected with the sensation called "sound."

PHIL. What! is sound then a sensation?

HYL. I tell you, as perceived by us it is a particular sensation in the mind.

PHIL. And can any sensation exist without the mind?

HYL. No, certainly.

PHIL. How then can sound, being a sensation, exist in the air if by the "air" you mean a senseless substance existing without the mind? . . .

HYL. To deal ingenuously, I do not like it. And, after the concessions already made, I had as well grant that sounds, too, have no real being without the mind.

PHIL. And I hope you will make no difficulty to acknowledge the same of colors.

HYL. Pardon me; the case of colors is very different. Can anything be plainer than that we see them on the objects?

PHIL. The objects you speak of are, I suppose, corporeal substances existing without the mind?

HYL. They are.

PHIL. And have true and real colors inhering in them?

HYL. Each visible object has that color which we see in it.

PHIL. How! is there anything visible but what we perceive by sight?

HYL. There is not. . . .

PHIL. What! are then the beautiful red and purple we see on yonder clouds really in them? Or do you imagine they have in themselves any other form than that of a dark mist or vapor?

HYL. I must own, Philonous, those colors are not really in the clouds as they seem to be at this distance. They are only apparent colors.

PHIL. "Apparent" call you them? How shall we distinguish these apparent colors from real?

HYL. Very easily. Those are to be thought apparent which, appearing only at a distance, vanish upon a nearer approach.

PHIL. And those, I suppose, are to be thought real which are discovered by the most near and exact survey.

HYL. Right.

PHIL. Is the nearest and exactest survey made by the help of a microscope or by the naked eye?

HYL. By a microscope, doubtless.

PHIL. But a microscope often discovers colors in an object different from those perceived by the unassisted sight. And, in case we had microscopes magnifying to any assigned degree, it is certain that no object whatsoever, viewed through them, would appear in the same color which it exhibits to the naked eye.

HYL. I confess there is something in what you say.

PHIL. Besides, it is not only possible but manifest that there actually are animals whose eyes are by nature framed to perceive those things which by reason of their minuteness escape our sight. What think you of those inconceivably small animals perceived by glasses? Must we suppose they are all stark blind? Or, in case they see, can it be imagined their sight has not the same use in preserving their bodies from injuries which appears in that of all other animals? And if it has, is it not evident they must see particles less than their own bodies, which will present them with a far different view in each object from that which strikes our senses? Even our own eyes do not always represent objects to us after the same manner. In the jaundice everyone knows that all things seem yellow. Is it not therefore highly probable those animals in whose eyes we discern a very different texture from that of ours, and whose bodies abound with different humors, do not see the same colors in every object that we do? From all which should it not seem to follow that all colors are equally apparent, and that none of those which we perceive are really inherent in any outward object?

HYL. It should.

PHIL. The point will be past all doubt if you consider that, in case colors were real properties or affections inherent in external bodies, they could admit of no alteration without some change wrought in the very bodies themselves; but is it not evident from what has been said that, upon the use of microscopes, upon a change happening in the humors of the eye, or a variation of distance, without any manner of real alteration in the thing itself, the colors of any object are either changed or totally disappear? Nay, all other circumstances remaining the same, change but the situation of some objects and they shall present different colors to the eye. The same thing happens upon viewing an object in various degrees of light. And what is more known than that the same bodies appear differently colored by candlelight from what they do in the open day? Add to these the experiment of a prism which, separating the heterogeneous rays of light, alters the color of any object and will cause the whitest to appear of a deep blue or red to the naked eye. And now tell me whether you are still of opinion that every body has its true real color inhering in it; and if you think it has, I would fain know further from you what certain distance and position of the object, what peculiar texture and formation of the eye, what degree or kind of light is necessary for ascertaining that true color and distinguishing it from apparent ones. . . .

HYL. I frankly own, Philonous, that it is in vain to stand out any longer. Colors, sounds, tastes, in a word, all those termed "secondary qualities," have certainly no existence without the mind. But by this acknowledgment I must not be supposed to derogate anything from the reality of matter or external objects; seeing it is no more than several philosophers maintain, who nevertheless are the farthest imaginable from denying matter. For the clearer understanding of this you must know sensible qualities are by philosophers divided into *primary* and *secondary.* The former are extension, figure, solidity, gravity, motion, and rest. And these they hold exist really in bodies. The latter are those above enumerated, or, briefly, all sensible qualities besides the primary, which they assert are only so many sensations or ideas existing nowhere but in the mind. But all this, I doubt not, you are already apprised of. For my part I have been a long time sensible there was such an opinion current among philosophers, but was never thoroughly convinced of its truth till now.

PHIL. You are still then of opinion that *extension* and *figure* are inherent in external unthinking substances?

HYL. I am.

PHIL. But what if the same arguments which are brought against secondary qualities will hold good against these also?

HYL. Why then I shall be obliged to think they too exist only in the mind. . . .

PHIL. Is it not the very same reasoning to conclude there is no extension or figure in an object because to one eye it shall seem little, smooth, and round, when at the same time it appears to the other great, uneven, and angular?

HYL. The very same. But does this latter fact ever happen?

PHIL. You may at any time make the experiment by looking with one eye bare, and with the other through a microscope.

HYL. I know not how to maintain it, and yet I am loath to give up *extension;* I see so many odd consequences following upon such a concession. . . .

PHIL. Then as for *solidity*; either you do not mean any sensible quality by that word, and so it is beside our inquiry; or if you do, it must be either hardness or resistance. But both the one and the other are plainly relative to our senses: it being evident that what seems hard to one animal may appear soft to another who has greater force and firmness of limbs. Nor is it less plain that the resistance I feel is not in the body.

Study Questions

1. Why is Berkeley classified as a subjective idealist?
2. Why does Berkeley say that we cannot claim objects exist unless they are perceived?
3. If you put a red sweater away and close the drawer, how do you know it is still red? What would Berkeley say?
4. How would you decide the well known philosophic question: If a tree falls in the forest and there's no one there to hear it, is there any noise?
5. Do you think the ultimate reality consists of ideas or material objects? Why?

The Open Boat
Stephen Crane

Stephen Crane (1871–1900) was an American journalist, novelist, and short story writer who, together with Frank Norris, Jack London, and Theodore Dreiser originated the movement of literary naturalism in this country. Although Crane is best known for his Civil War novel The Red Badge of Courage, *and received critical acclaim for his realistic novel* Maggie: A Girl of the Streets, *his major achievements are in the genre of the short story. His Western tales such as "The Blue Hotel," "One Dash-Horses," and "The Bride Comes to Yellow Sky," are celebrated for the tragic atmosphere they create and for their rich symbolism. Crane's war stories surpass* The Red Badge of Courage, *especially "Death and the Child," "The Price of the Harness," "The Upturned Face," and "An Episode of War."*

"The Open Boat" that appears below presents Crane's naturalistic or materialistic view of reality. It sounds many of his literary themes including isolation, endurance, companionship, courage, chance, and death. In philosophic terms, the story shows the insignificance of man and the indifference of nature to his fate. The people in the boat do not deserve their suffering, and there is no reason why they should live or die. Everything happens by accident, not according to the will of a benevolent God. Crane pictures life as a series of absurdities, devoid of meaning or justice; to withstand its terrors we must band together in decency and comradeship. As Crane once wrote, there is only "this terrible and inscrutable wrath of nature."

As an interesting side note, the story is based on Crane's own experience when he was shipwrecked on his way to Cuba. He survived the ordeal but died a few years later of tuberculosis; he was twenty-eight.

I

None of them knew the color of the sky. Their eyes glanced level, and were fastened upon the waves that swept toward them. These waves were of the hue of slate, save for the tops, which were of foaming white, and all of the men knew the colors of the sea. The horizon narrowed and widened, and dipped and rose, and at all times its edge was jagged with waves that seemed thrust up in points like rocks.

Many a man ought to have a bathtub larger than the boat which here rode upon the sea. These waves were most wrongfully and barbarously abrupt and tall, and each froth-top was a problem in small-boat navigation.

The cook squatted in the bottom, and looked with both eyes at the six inches of gunwale which separated him from the ocean. His sleeves were rolled over his fat forearms, and the two flaps of his unbuttoned vest dangled as he bent to bail out the boat. Often he said, "Gawd! that was a narrow clip." As he remarked it he invariably gazed eastward over the broken sea.

The oiler, steering with one of the two oars in the boat, sometimes raised himself suddenly to keep clear of water that swirled in over the stern. It was a thin little oar, and it seemed often ready to snap.

The correspondent, pulling at the other oar, watched the waves and wondered why he was there.

The injured captain, lying in the bow, was at this time buried in that profound dejection and indifference which comes, temporarily at least, to even the bravest and most enduring when, willy-nilly, the firm fails, the army loses, the ship goes down. The mind of the master of a vessel is rooted deep in the timbers of her, though he command for a day or a decade; and this captain had on him the stern impression of a scene in the grays of dawn of seven turned faces, and later a stump of a topmast with a white ball on it, that slashed to and fro at the waves, went low and lower, and down. Thereafter there was something strange in his voice. Although steady, it was deep with mourning, and of a quality beyond oration or tears.

"Keep 'er a little more south, Billie," said he.

"A little more south, sir," said the oiler in the stern.

A seat in this boat was not unlike a seat upon a bucking broncho, and by the same token a broncho is not much smaller. The craft pranced and reared and plunged like an animal. As each wave came, and she rose for it, she seemed like a horse making at a fence outrageously high. The manner of her scramble over these walls of water is a mystic thing, and, moreover, at the top of them were ordinarily these problems in white water, the foam racing down from the summit of each wave requiring a new leap, and a leap from the air. Then, after scornfully bumping a crest, she would slide and race and splash down a long incline, and arrive bobbing and nodding in front of the next menace.

A singular disadvantage of the sea lies in the fact that after successfully surmounting one wave you discover that there is another behind it just as important and just as nervously anxious to do something effective in the way of swamping boats. In a ten-foot dinghy one can get an idea of the resources of the sea in the line of waves that is not probable to the average experience, which is never at sea in a dinghy. As each salty wall of water approached, it shut all else from the view of the men in the boat, and it was not difficult to imagine that this particular wave was the final outburst of the ocean, the last effort of the grim water. There was a terrible grace in the move of the waves, and they came in silence, save for the snarling of the crests.

In the wan light the faces of the men must have been gray. Their eyes must have glinted in strange ways as they gazed steadily astern. Viewed from a balcony, the whole thing would doubtless have been weirdly picturesque. But the men in the boat had no time to see it, and if they had had leisure, there were other things to occupy their minds. The sun swung steadily up the sky, and they knew it was broad day because the color of the sea changed from slate to emerald-green streaked with amber lights, and the foam was like tumbling snow. The process of the breaking day was unknown to them. They were aware only of this effect upon the color of the waves that rolled toward them.

In disjointed sentences the cook and the correspondent argued as to the difference between a life-saving station and a house of refuge. The cook had said: "There's a house of refuge just north of the Mosquito Inlet Light, and as soon as they see us they'll come off in their boat and pick us up."

"As soon as who see us?" said the correspondent.

"The crew," said the cook.

"Houses of refuge don't have crews," said the correspondent. "As I understand them, they are only places where clothes and grub are stored for the benefit of shipwrecked people. They don't carry crews."

"Oh, yes, they do," said the cook.

"No, they don't," said the correspondent.

"Well, we're not there yet, anyhow," said the oiler, in the stern.

"Well," said the cook, "perhaps it's not a house of refuge that I'm thinking of as being near Mosquito Inlet Light; perhaps it's a lifesaving station."

"We're not there yet," said the oiler in the stern.

II

As the boat bounced from the top of each wave the wind tore through the hair of the hatless men, and as the craft plopped her stern down again the spray slashed past them. The crest of each of these waves was a hill, from the top of which the men surveyed for a moment a broad tumultuous expanse, shining and wind-riven. It was probably splendid, it was probably glorious, this play of the free sea, wild with lights of emerald and white and amber.

"Bully good thing it's an on shore wind," said the cook. "If not, where would we be? Wouldn't have a show."

"That's right," said the correspondent.

The busy oiler nodded his assent.

Then the captain, in the bow, chuckled in a way that expressed humor, contempt, tragedy, all in one. "Do you think we've got much of a show now, boys?" said he.

Whereupon the three were silent, save for a trifle of hemming and hawing. To express any particular optimism at this time they felt to be childish and stupid, but they all doubtless possessed this sense of the situation in their minds. A young man thinks doggedly at such times. On the other hand, the ethics of their condition was decidedly against any open suggestion of hopelessness. So they were silent.

"Oh, well," said the captain, soothing his children, "we'll get ashore all right."

But there was that in his tone which made them think; so the oiler quoth, "Yes! if this wind holds."

The cook was bailing. "Yes! if we don't catch hell in the surf."

Canton-flannel gulls flew near and far. Sometimes they sat down on the sea, near patches of brown seaweed that rolled over the waves with a movement like carpets on a line in a gale. The birds sat comfortably in groups, and they were envied by some in the dinghy, for the wrath of the sea was no more to them than it was to a covey of prairie chickens a thousand miles inland. Often they came very close and stared at the men with black bead-like eyes. At these times they were uncanny and sinister in their unblinking scrutiny, and the men hooted angrily at them, telling them to be gone. One came, and evidently decided to alight on the top of the captain's head. The bird flew parallel to the boat and did not circle, but made short sidelong jumps in the air in chicken fashion. His black eyes were wistfully fixed upon the captain's head. "Ugly brute," said the oiler to the bird. "You look as if you were made with a jackknife." The cook and the correspondent swore darkly at the creature. The captain naturally wished to knock it away with the end of the heavy painter, but he did not dare do it, because anything resembling an emphatic gesture would have capsized this freighted boat; and so, with his open hand, the captain gently and carefully waved the gull away. After it had been discouraged from the pursuit the captain breathed easier on account of his hair, and others breathed easier because the bird struck their minds at this time as being somehow gruesome and ominous.

In the meantime the oiler and the correspondent rowed. And also they rowed. They sat together in the same seat, and each rowed an oar. Then the oiler took both oars; then the correspondent took both oars; then the oiler; then the correspondent. They rowed and they rowed. The very ticklish part of the business was when the time came for the reclining one in the stern to take his turn at the oars. By the very last star of truth, it is easier to steal eggs from under a hen than it was to change seats in the dinghy. First the man in the stern slid his hand along the thwart and moved with care, as if he were of Sèvres. Then the man in the rowingseat slid his hand along the other thwart. It was all done with the most extraordinary care. As the two sidled past each other, the whole party kept watchful eyes on the coming wave, and the captain cried: "Look out, now! Steady, there!"

The brown mats of seaweed that appeared from time to time were like islands, bits of earth. They were traveling, apparently, neither one way nor the other. They were, to all intents, stationary. They informed the men in the boat that it was making progress slowly toward the land.

The captain, rearing cautiously in the bow after the dinghy soared on a great swell, said that he had seen the lighthouse at Mosquito Inlet. Presently the cook remarked that he had seen it. The correspondent was at the oars then, and for some reason he too wished to look at the lighthouse; but his back was toward the far shore, and the waves were important, and for some time he could not seize an opportunity to turn his head. But at last there came a wave more gentle than the others, and when at the crest of it he swiftly scoured the western horizon.

"See it?" said the captain.

"No," said the correspondent, slowly; "I didn't see anything."

"Look again," said the captain. He pointed. "It's exactly in that direction."

At the top of another wave the correspondent did as he was bid, and this time his eyes chanced on a small, still thing on the edge of the swaying horizon. It was precisely like the point of a pin. It took an anxious eye to find a lighthouse so tiny.

"Think we'll make it, Captain?"

"If this wind holds and the boat don't swamp, we can't do much else," said the captain.

The little boat, lifted by each towering sea and splashed viciously by the crests, made progress that in the absence of seaweed was not apparent to those in her. She seemed just a wee thing wallowing, miraculously top up, at the mercy of five oceans. Occasionally a great spread of water, like white flames, swarmed into her.

"Bail her, cook," said the captain, serenely.

"All right, Captain," said the cheerful cook.

III

It would be difficult to describe the subtle brotherhood of men that was here established on the seas. No one said that it was so. No one mentioned it. But it dwelt in the boat, and each man felt it warm him. They were a captain, an oiler, a cook, and a correspondent, and they were friends—friends in a more curiously ironbound degree than may be common. The hurt captain, lying against the water jar in the bow, spoke always in a low voice and calmly; but he could never command a more ready and swiftly obedient crew than the motley three of the dinghy. It was more than a mere recognition of what was best for the common safety. There was surely in it a quality that was personal and heartfelt. And after this devotion to the commander of the boat, there was this comradeship, that the correspondent, for instance, who had been taught to be cynical of men, knew even at the time was the best experience of his life. But no one said that it was so. No one mentioned it.

"I wish we had a sail," remarked the captain. "We might try my overcoat on the end of an oar, and give you two boys a chance to rest." So the cook and the correspondent held the mast and spread wide the overcoat; the oiler steered; and the little boat made good way with her new rig. Sometimes the oiler had to scull sharply to keep a sea from breaking into the boat, but otherwise sailing was a success.

Meanwhile the lighthouse had been growing slowly larger. It had now almost assumed color, and appeared like a little gray shadow on the sky. The man at the oars could not be prevented from turning his head rather often to try for a glimpse of this little gray shadow.

At last, from the top of each wave, the men in the tossing boat could see land. Even as the lighthouse was an upright shadow on the sky, this land seemed but a long black shadow on the sea. It certainly was thinner than paper. "We must be about opposite New Smyrna," said the cook, who had coasted this shore often in schooners. "Captain, by the way, I believe they abandoned that lifesaving station there about a year ago."

"Did they?" said the captain.

The wind slowly died away. The cook and the correspondent were not now obliged to slave in order to hold high the oar. But the waves continued their old impetuous swooping at the dinghy, and the little craft, no longer under way, struggled woundily over them. The oiler or the correspondent took the oars again.

Shipwrecks are *apropos* of nothing. If men could only train for them and have them occur when the men had reached pink condition, there would be less drowning at sea. Of the four in the dinghy none had slept any time worth mentioning for two days and two nights previous to embarking in the dinghy, and in the excitement of clambering about the deck of a foundering ship they had also forgotten to eat heartily.

For these reasons, and for others, neither the oiler nor the correspondent was fond of rowing at this time. The correspondent wondered ingenuously how in the name of all that was sane could there be people who thought it amusing to row a boat. It was not an amusement; it was a diabolical punishment, and even a genius of mental aberrations could never conclude that it was anything but a horror to the muscles and a crime against the back. He mentioned to the boat in general how the amusement of rowing struck him, and the weary-faced oiler smiled in full sympathy. Previously to the foundering, by the way, the oiler had worked a double watch in the engine room of the ship.

"Take her easy now, boys," said the captain. "Don't spend yourselves. If we have to run a surf you'll need all your strength, because we'll sure have to swim for it. Take your time."

Slowly the land arose from the sea. From a black line it became a line of black and a line of white—trees and sand. Finally the captain said that he could make out a house on the shore. "That's the house of refuge, sure," said the cook. "They'll see us before long, and come out after us."

The distant lighthouse reared high. "The keeper ought to be able to make us out now, if he's looking through a glass," said the captain. "He'll notify the lifesaving people."

"None of those other boats could have got ashore to give word of this wreck," said the oiler, in a low voice, "else the lifeboat would be out hunting us."

Slowly and beautifully the land loomed out of the sea. The wind came again. It had veered from the northeast to the southeast. Finally a new sound struck the ears of the men in the boat. It was the low thunder of the surf on the shore. "We'll never be able to make the lighthouse now," said the captain. "Swing her head a little more north, Billie."

"A little more north, sir," said the oiler.

Whereupon the little boat turned her nose once more down the wind, and all but the oarsman watched the shore grow. Under the influence of this expansion doubt and direful apprehension were leaving the minds of the men. The management of the boat was still most absorbing, but it could not prevent a quiet cheerfulness. In an hour, perhaps, they would be ashore.

Their backbones had become thoroughly used to balancing in the boat, and they now rode this wild colt of a dinghy like circus men. The correspondent thought that he had been drenched to the skin, but happening to feel in the top pocket of his coat, he found therein eight cigars. Four of them were soaked with seawater; four were perfectly scatheless. After a search, somebody produced three dry matches; and thereupon the four waifs rode impudently in their little boat and, with an assurance of an impending rescue shining in their eyes, puffed at the big cigars, and judged well and ill of all men. Everybody took a drink of water.

IV

"Cook," remarked the captain, "there don't seem to be any signs of life about your house of refuge."

"No," replied the cook. "Funny they don't see us!"

A broad stretch of lowly coast lay before the eyes of the men. It was of low dunes topped with dark vegetation. The roar of the surf was plain, and sometimes they could see the white lip of a wave as it spun up the beach. A tiny house was blocked out black upon the sky. Southward, the slim lighthouse lifted its little gray length.

Tide, wind, and waves were swinging the dinghy northward. "Funny they don't see us," said the men.

The surf's roar was here dulled, but its tone was nevertheless thunderous and mighty. As the boat swam over the great rollers the men sat listening to this roar. "We'll swamp sure," said everybody.

It is fair to say here that there was not a lifesaving station within twenty miles in either direction; but the men did not know this fact, and in consequence they made dark and opprobrious remarks concerning the eyesight of the nation's lifesavers. Four scowling men sat in the dinghy and surpassed records in the invention of epithets.

"Funny they don't see us."

The light-heartedness of a former time had completely faded. To their sharpened minds it was easy to conjure pictures of all kinds of incompetency and blindness and, indeed, cowardice. There was the shore of the populous land, and it was bitter and bitter to them that from it came no sign.

"Well," said the captain, ultimately, "I suppose we'll have to make a try for ourselves. If we stay out here too long, we'll none of us have strength left to swim after the boat swamps."

And so the oiler, who was at the oars, turned the boat straight for the shore. There was a sudden tightening of muscles. There was some thinking.

"If we don't all get ashore," said the captain—"if we don't all get ashore, I suppose you fellows know where to send news of my finish?"

They then briefly exchanged some addresses and admonitions. As for the reflections of the men, there was a great deal of rage in them. Perchance they might be formulated thus: "If I am going to be drowned—if I am going to be drowned—if I am going to be drowned, why, in the name of the seven mad gods who rule the sea, was I allowed to come thus far and contemplate sand and trees? Was I brought here merely to have my nose dragged away as I was about to nibble the sacred cheese of life? It is preposterous. If this old ninny-woman, Fate, cannot do better than this, she should be deprived of the management of men's fortunes. She is an old hen who knows not her intention. If she has decided to drown me, why did she not do it in the beginning and save me all this trouble? The whole affair is absurd. . . . But no; she cannot mean to drown me. She dare not drown me. She cannot drown me. Not after all this work." Afterward the man might have had an impulse to shake his fist at the clouds. "Just you drown me, now, and then hear what I call you!"

The billows that came at this time were more formidable. They seemed always just about to break and roll over the little boat in a turmoil of foam. There was a preparatory and long growl in the speech of them. No mind unused to the sea would have concluded that the dinghy could ascend these sheer heights in time. The shore was still afar. The oiler was a wily surfman. "Boys," he said swiftly, "she won't live three minutes more, and we're too far out to swim. Shall I take her to sea again, Captain?"

"Yes; go ahead!" said the captain.

This oiler, by a series of quick miracles and fast and steady oarsmanship, turned the boat in the middle of the surf and took her safely to sea again.

There was a considerable silence as the boat bumped over the furrowed sea to deeper water. Then somebody in gloom spoke: "Well, anyhow, they must have seen us from the shore by now."

The gulls went in slanting flight up the wind toward the gray, desolate east. A squall, marked by dingy clouds and clouds brick-red, like smoke from a burning building, appeared from the southeast.

"What do you think of those lifesaving people? Ain't they peaches?"

"Funny they haven't seen us."

"Maybe they think we're out here for sport! Maybe they think we're fishin'. Maybe they think we're damned fools."

It was a long afternoon. A changed tide tried to force them southward, but wind and wave said northward. Far ahead, where coastline, sea, and sky formed their mighty angle, there were little dots which seemed to indicate a city on the shore.

"St. Augustine?"

The captain shook his head. "Too near Mosquito Inlet."

And the oiler rowed, and then the correspondent rowed; then the oiler rowed. It was a weary business. The human back can become the seat of more aches and pains than are registered in books for the composite anatomy of a regiment. It is a limited area, but it can become the theater of innumerable muscular conflicts, tangles, wrenches, knots, and other comforts.

"Did you ever like to row, Billie?" asked the correspondent.

"No," said the oiler; "hang it!"

When one exchanged the rowing-seat for a place in the bottom of the boat, he suffered a bodily depression that caused him to be careless of everything save an obligation to wiggle one finger. There was cold seawater swashing to and fro in the boat, and he lay in it. His head, pillowed on a thwart, was within an inch of the swirl of a wavecrest, and sometimes a particularly obstreperous sea came inboard and drenched him once more. But these matters did not annoy him. It is almost certain that if the boat had capsized he would have tumbled comfortably out upon the ocean as if he felt sure that it was a great soft mattress.

"Look! There's a man on the shore!"

"Where?"

"There! See 'im? See 'im?"

"Yes, sure! He's walking along."

"Now he's stopped. Look! He's facing us!"

"He's waving at us!"

"So he is! By thunder!"

"Ah, now we're all right! Now we're all right! There'll be a boat out here for us in half an hour."

"He's going on. He's running. He's going up to that house there."

The remote beach seemed lower than the sea, and it required a searching glance to discern the little black figure. The captain saw a floating stick, and they rowed to it. A bath towel was by some weird chance in the boat, and, tying this on the stick, the captain waved it. The oarsman did not dare turn his head, so he was obliged to ask questions.

"What's he doing now?"

"He's standing still again. He's looking, I think. . . . There he goes again—toward the house. . . . Now he's stopped again."

"Is he waving at us?"

"No, not now; he was, though."

"Look! There comes another man!"

"He's running."

"Look! at him go, would you!"

"Why, he's on a bicycle. Now he's met the other man. They're both waving at us. Look!"

"There comes something up the beach."

"What the devil is that thing?"

"Why, it looks like a boat."

"Why, certainly, it's a boat."

"No; it's on wheels."

"Yes, so it is. Well, that must be the lifeboat. They drag them along shore on a wagon."

"That's the lifeboat, sure."

"No, by God, it's—it's an omnibus."

"I tell you it's a lifeboat."

"It is not! It's an omnibus. I can see it plain. See? One of these big hotel omnibuses."

"By thunder, you're right. It's an omnibus, sure as fate. What do you suppose they are doing with an omnibus? Maybe they are going around collecting the life-crew, hey?"

"That's it, likely. Look! There's a fellow waving a little black flag. He's standing on the steps of the omnibus. There come those other two fellows. Now they're all talking together. Look at the fellow with the flag. Maybe he ain't waving it!"

"That ain't a flag, is it? That's his coat. Why, certainly, that's his coat."

"So it is; it's his coat. He's taken it off and is waving it around his head. But would you look at him swing it!"

"Oh, say, there isn't any lifesaving station there. That's just a winter-resort hotel omnibus that has brought over some of the boarders to see us drown."

"What's that idiot with the coat mean? What's he signaling, anyhow?"

"It looks as if he were trying to tell us to go north. There must be a lifesaving station up there."

"No; he thinks we're fishing. Just giving us a merry hand. See? Ah, there, Willie!"

"Well, I wish I could make something out of those signals. What do you suppose he means?"

"He don't mean anything; he's just playing."

"Well, if he'd just signal us to try the surf again, or to go to sea and wait, or go north, or go south, or go to hell, there would be some reason in it. But look at him! He just stands there and keeps his coat revolving like a wheel. The ass!"

"There come more people."

"Now there's quite a mob. Look! Isn't that a boat?"

"Where? Oh, I see where you mean. No, that's no boat."

"That fellow is still waving his coat."

"He must think we like to see him do that. Why don't he quit it? It don't mean anything."

"I don't know. I think he is trying to make us go north. It must be that there's a lifesaving station there somewhere."

"Say, he ain't tired yet. Look at 'im wave!"

"Wonder how long he can keep that up. He's been revolving his coat ever since he caught sight of us. He's an idiot. Why aren't they getting men to bring a boat out? A fishing boat—one of those big yawls—could come out here all right. Why don't he do something?"

"Oh, it's all right now."

"They'll have a boat out here for us in less than no time, now that they've seen us."

A faint yellow tone came into the sky over the low land. The shadows on the sea slowly deepened. The wind bore coldness with it, and the men began to shiver.

"Holy smoke!" said one, allowing his voice to express his impious mood, "if we keep on monkeying out here! If we've got to flounder out here all night!"

"Oh, we'll never have to stay here all night! Don't you worry. They've seen us now, and it won't be long before they'll come chasing out after us."

The shore grew dusky. The man waving a coat blended gradually into this gloom, and it swallowed in the same manner the omnibus and the group of people. The spray, when it dashed uproariously over the side, made the voyagers shrink and swear like men who were being branded.

"I'd like to catch the chump who waved the coat. I feel like socking him one, just for luck."

"Why? What did he do?"

"Oh, nothing, but then he seemed so damned cheerful."

In the meantime the oiler rowed, and then the correspondent rowed, and then the oiler rowed. Gray-faced and bowed forward, they mechanically, turn by turn, plied the leaden oars. The form of the lighthouse had vanished from the southern horizon, but finally a pale star appeared, just lifting from the sea. The streaked saffron in the west passed before the all-merging darkness, and the sea to the east was black. The land had vanished, and was expressed only by the low and drear thunder of the surf.

"If I am going to be drowned—if I am going to be drowned—if I am going to be drowned, why, in the name of the seven mad gods who rule the sea, was I allowed to come thus far and contemplate sand and trees? Was I brought here merely to have my nose dragged away as I was about to nibble the sacred cheese of life?"

The patient captain, drooped over the water jar, was sometimes obliged to speak to the oarsman.

"Keep her head up! Keep her head up!"

"Keep her head up, sir." The voices were weary and low.

This was surely a quiet evening. All save the oarsman lay heavily and listlessly in the boat's bottom. As for him, his eyes were just capable of noting the tall black waves that swept forward in a most sinister silence, save for an occasional subdued growl of a crest.

The cook's head was on a thwart, and he looked without interest at the water under his nose. He was deep in other scenes. Finally he spoke. "Billie," he murmured, dreamfully, "what kind of pie do you like best?"

V

"Pie!" said the oiler and the correspondent, agitatedly. "Don't talk about those things, blast you!"

"Well," said the cook, "I was just thinking about ham sandwiches, and—"

A night on the sea in an open boat is a long night. As darkness settled finally, the shine of the light, lifting from the sea in the south, changed to full gold. On the northern horizon a new light appeared, a small bluish gleam on the edge of the waters. These two lights were the furniture of the world. Otherwise there was nothing but waves.

Two men huddled in the stern, and distances were so magnificent in the dinghy that the rower was enabled to keep his feet partly warm by thrusting them under his companions. Their legs indeed extended far under the rowing-seat until they touched the feet of the captain forward. Sometimes, despite the efforts of the tired oarsman, a wave came piling into the boat, an icy wave of the night, and the chilling water soaked them anew. They would twist their bodies for a moment and groan, and sleep the dead sleep once more, while the water in the boat gurgled about them as the craft rocked.

The plan of the oiler and the correspondent was for one to row until he lost the ability, and then arouse the other from his sea-water couch in the bottom of the boat.

The oiler plied the oars until his head drooped forward and the overpowering sleep blinded him; and he rowed yet afterward. Then he touched a man in the bottom of the boat, and called his name. "Will you spell me for a little while?" he said meekly.

"Sure, Billie," said the correspondent, awaking and dragging himself to a sitting position. They exchanged places carefully, and the oiler, cuddling down in the seawater at the cook's side, seemed to go to sleep instantly.

The particular violence of the sea had ceased. The waves came without snarling. The obligation of the man at the oars was to keep the boat headed so that the tilt of the rollers would not capsize her, and to preserve her from filling when the crests rushed past. The black waves were silent and hard to be seen in the darkness. Often one was almost upon the boat before the oarsman was aware.

In a low voice the correspondent addressed the captain. He was not sure that the captain was awake, although this iron man seemed to be always awake. "Captain, shall I keep her making for that light north, sir?"

The same steady voice answered him. "Yes. Keep it about two points off the port bow."

The cook had tied a lifebelt around himself in order to get even the warmth which this clumsy cork contrivance could donate, and he seemed almost stove-like when a rower, whose teeth invariably chattered wildly as soon as he ceased his labor, dropped down to sleep.

The correspondent, as he rowed, looked down at the two men sleeping underfoot. The cook's arm was around the oiler's shoulders, and, with their fragmentary clothing and haggard faces, they were the babes of the sea—a grotesque rendering of the old babes in the wood.

Later he must have grown stupid at his work, for suddenly there was a growling of water, and a crest came with a roar and a swash into the boat, and it was a wonder that it did not set the cook afloat in his lifebelt. The cook continued to sleep, but the oiler sat up, blinking his eyes and shaking with the new cold.

"Oh, I'm awful sorry, Billie," said the correspondent, contritely.

"That's all right, old boy," said the oiler, and lay down again and was asleep.

Presently it seemed that even the captain dozed, and the correspondent thought that he was the one man afloat on all the oceans. The wind had a voice as it came over the waves, and it was sadder than the end.

There was a long, loud swishing astern of the boat, and a gleaming trail of phosphorescence, like blue flame, was furrowed on the black waters. It might have been made by a monstrous knife.

Then there came a stillness, while the correspondent breathed with open mouth and looked at the sea.

Suddenly there was another swish and another long flash of bluish light, and this time it was alongside the boat, and might almost have been reached with an oar. The correspondent saw an enormous fin speed like a shadow through the water, hurling the crystalline spray and leaving the long glowing trail.

The correspondent looked over his shoulder at the captain. His face was hidden, and he seemed to be asleep. He looked at the babes of the sea. They certainly were asleep. So, being bereft of sympathy, he leaned a little way to one side and swore softly into the sea.

But the thing did not then leave the vicinity of the boat. Ahead or astern, on one side or the other, at intervals long or short, fled the long sparkling streak, and there was to be heard the *whirroo* of the dark fin. The speed and power of the thing was greatly to be admired. It cut the water like a gigantic and keen projectile.

The presence of this biding thing did not affect the man with the same horror that it would if he had been a picnicker. He simply looked at the sea dully and swore in an undertone.

Nevertheless, it is true that he did not wish to be alone with the thing. He wished one of his companions to awake by chance and keep him company with it. But the captain hung motionless over the water jar, and the oiler and the cook in the bottom of the boat were plunged in slumber.

VI

"If I am going to be drowned—if I am going to be drowned—if I am going to be drowned, why, in the name of the seven mad gods who rule the sea, was I allowed to come thus far and contemplate sand and trees?"

During this dismal night, it may be remarked that a man would conclude that it was really the intention of the seven mad gods to drown him, despite the abominable injustice of it. For it was certainly an abominable injustice to drown a man who had worked so hard, so hard. The man felt it would be a crime most unnatural. Other people had drowned at sea since galleys swarmed with painted sails, but still—

When it occurs to a man that nature does not regard him as important, and that she feels she would not maim the universe by disposing of him, he at first wishes to throw bricks at the temple, and he hates deeply the fact that there are no bricks and no temples. Any visible expression of nature would surely be pelleted with his jeers.

Then, if there be no tangible thing to hoot, he feels, perhaps, the desire to confront a personification and indulge in pleas, bowed to one knee, and with hands supplicant, saying, "Yes, but I love myself."

A high cold star on a winter's night is the word he feels that she says to him. Thereafter he knows the pathos of his situation.

The men in the dinghy had not discussed these matters, but each had, no doubt, reflected upon them in silence and according to his mind. There was seldom any expression upon their faces save the general one of complete weariness. Speech was devoted to the business of the boat.

To chime the notes of his emotion, a verse mysteriously entered the correspondent's head. He had even forgotten that he had forgotten this verse, but it suddenly was in his mind.

> A soldier of the Legion lay dying in Algiers;
> There was lack of woman's nursing, there was dearth of woman's tears;
> But a comrade stood beside him, and he took that comrade's hand,
> And he said, "I never more shall see my own, my native land."

In his childhood the correspondent had been made acquainted with the fact that a soldier of the Legion lay dying in Algiers, but he had never regarded the fact as important. Myriads of his schoolfellows had informed him of the soldier's plight, but the dinning had naturally ended by making him perfectly indifferent. He had never considered it his affair that a soldier of the Legion lay dying in Algiers, nor had it appeared to him as a matter for sorrow. It was less to him than the breaking of a pencil's point.

Now, however, it quaintly came to him as a human, living thing. It was no longer merely a picture of a few throes in the breast of a poet, meanwhile drinking tea and warming his feet at the grate; it was an actuality—stern, mournful, and fine.

The correspondent plainly saw the soldier. He lay on the sand with his feet out straight and still. While his pale left hand was upon his chest in an attempt to thwart the going of his life, the blood came between his fingers. In the far Algerian distance, a city of low square forms was set against a sky that was faint with the last sunset hues. The correspondent, plying the oars and dreaming of the slow and slower movements of the lips of the soldier, was moved by a profound and perfectly impersonal comprehension. He was sorry for the soldier of the Legion who lay dying in Algiers.

The thing which had followed the boat and waited had evidently grown bored at the delay. There was no longer to be heard the slash of the cutwater, and there was no longer the flame of the long trail. The light in the north still glimmered, but it was apparently no nearer to the boat. Sometimes the boom of the surf rang in the correspondent's ears, and he turned the craft seaward then and rowed harder. Southward, some one had evidently built a watch fire on the beach. It was too low and too far to be seen, but it made a shimmering, roseate reflection upon the bluff in back of it, and this could be discerned from the boat. The wind came stronger, and sometimes a wave suddenly raged out like a mountain cat, and there was to be seen the sheen and sparkle of a broken crest.

The captain, in the bow, moved on his water jar and sat erect. "Pretty long night," he observed to the correspondent. He looked at the shore. "Those lifesaving people take their time."

"Did you see that shark playing around?"

"Yes, I saw him. He was a big fellow, all right."

"Wish I had known you were awake."

Later the correspondent spoke into the bottom of the boat. "Billie!" There was a slow and gradual disentanglement. "Billie, will you spell me?"

"Sure," said the oiler.

As soon as the correspondent touched the cold, comfortable sea-water in the bottom of the boat and had huddled close to the cook's lifebelt he was deep in sleep, despite the fact that his teeth played all the popular airs. This sleep was so good to him that it was but a moment before he heard a voice call his name in a tone that demonstrated the last stages of exhaustion. "Will you spell me?"

"Sure, Billie."

The light in the north had mysteriously vanished, but the correspondent took his course from the wide-awake captain.

Later in the night they took the boat farther out to sea, and the captain directed the cook to take one oar at the stern and keep the boat facing the seas. He was to call out if he should hear the thunder of the surf. This plan enabled the oiler and the correspondent to get respite together. "We'll give those boys a chance to get into shape again," said the captain. They curled down and, after a few preliminary chatterings and trembles, slept once more the dead sleep. Neither knew they had bequeathed to the cook the company of another shark, or perhaps the same shark.

As the boat caroused on the waves, spray occasionally bumped over the side and gave them a fresh soaking, but this had no power to break their repose. The ominous slash of the wind and the water affected them as it would have affected mummies.

"Boys," said the cook, with the notes of every reluctance in his voice, "she's drifted in pretty close. I guess one of you had better take her to sea again." The correspondent, aroused, heard the crash of the toppled crests.

As he was rowing, the captain gave him some whiskey-and-water, and this steadied the chills out of him. "If I ever get ashore and anybody shows me even a photograph of an oar—"

At last there was a short conversation.

"Billie! . . . Billie, will you spell me?"
"Sure," said the oiler.

VII

When the correspondent again opened his eyes, the sea and the sky were each of the gray hue of the dawning. Later, carmine and gold was painted upon the waters. The morning appeared finally, in its splendor, with a sky of pure blue, and the sunlight flamed on the tips of the waves.

On the distant dunes were set many little black cottages, and a tall white windmill reared above them. No man, nor dog, nor bicycle appeared on the beach. The cottages might have formed a deserted village.

The voyagers scanned the shore. A conference was held in the boat. "Well," said the captain, "if no help is coming, we might better try a run through the surf right away. If we stay out here much longer we will be too weak to do anything for ourselves at all." The others silently acquiesced in this reasoning. The boat was headed for the beach. The correspondent wondered if none ever ascended the tall wind-tower, and if then they never looked seaward. This tower was a giant, standing with its back to the plight of the ants. It represented in a degree, to the correspondent, the serenity of nature amid the struggles of the individual—nature in the wind, and nature in the vision of man. She did not seem cruel to him then, nor beneficent, nor treacherous, nor wise. But she was indifferent, flatly indifferent. It is, perhaps, plausible that a man in this situation, impressed with the unconcern of the universe, should see the innumerable flaws of his life, and have them taste wickedly in his mind, and wish for another chance. A distinction between right and wrong seems absurdly clear to him, then, in this new ignorance of the grave-edge, and he understands that if he were given another opportunity he would mend his conduct and his words, and be better and brighter during an introduction or at a tea.

"Now boys," said the captain, "she is going to swamp sure. All we can do is work her in as far as possible, and then when she swamps, pile out and scramble for the beach. Keep cool now, and don't jump until she swamps sure."

The oiler took the oars. Over his shoulders he scanned the surf. "Captain," he said, "I think I'd better bring her about and keep her head-on to the seas and back her in."

"All right Billie," said the captain. "Back her in." The oiler swung the boat then and, seated in the stern, the cook and the correspondent were obliged to look over their shoulders to contemplate the lonely and indifferent shore.

The monstrous inshore rollers heaved the boat high until the men were again enabled to see the white sheets of water scudding up the slanted beach. "We won't get in very close," said the captain. Each time a man could wrest his attention from the rollers, he turned his glance toward the shore, and in the expression of the eyes during the contemplation there was a singular quality. The correspondent, observing the others, knew that they were not afraid, but the full meaning of their glances was shrouded.

As for himself, he was too tired to grapple fundamentally with the fact. He tried to coerce his mind into thinking of it, but the mind was dominated at this time be the muscles, and the muscles said they did not care. It merely occurred to him that if he should drown it would be a shame.

There were no hurried words, no pallor, no plain agitation. The men simply looked at the shore. "Now, remember to get well clear of the boat when you jump," said the captain.

Seaward the crest of a roller suddenly fell with a thunderous crash, and the long white comber came roaring down upon the boat.

"Steady now," said the captain. The men were silent. They turned their eyes from the shore to the comber and waited. The boat slid up the incline, leaped at the furious top, bounced over it, and swung down the long back of the wave. Some water had been shipped, and the cook bailed it out.

But the next crest crashed also. The tumbling, boiling flood of white water caught the boat and whirled it almost perpendicular. Water swarmed in from all sides. The correspondent had his hands on the gunwale at this time, and when the water entered at that place he swiftly withdrew his fingers, as if he objected to wetting them.

The little boat, drunken with this weight of water, reeled and snuggled deeper into the sea.

"Bail her out, cook! Bail her out!" said the captain.

"All right, Captain," said the cook.

"Now, boys, the next one will do for us sure," said the oiler. "Mind to jump clear of the boat."

The third wave moved forward, huge, furious, implacable. It fairly swallowed the dinghy, and almost simultaneously the men tumbled into the sea. A piece of lifebelt had lain in the bottom of the boat, and as the correspondent went overboard he held this to his chest with his left hand.

The January water was icy, and he reflected immediately that it was colder than he had expected to find it off the coast of Florida. This appeared to his dazed mind as a fact important enough to be noted at the time. The coldness of the water was sad; it was tragic. This fact was somehow mixed and confused with his opinion of his own situation, so that it seemed almost a proper reason for tears. The water was cold.

When he came to the surface he was conscious of little but the noisy water. Afterward he saw his companions in the sea. The oiler was ahead in the race. He was swimming strongly and rapidly. Off to the correspondent's left, the cook's great white and corked back bulged out of the water; and in the rear the captain was hanging with his one good hand to the keel of the overturned dinghy.

There is a certain immovable quality to a shore, and the correspondent wondered at it amid the confusion of the sea.

It seemed also very attractive; but the correspondent knew that it was a long journey, and he paddled leisurely. The piece of life preserver lay under him, and sometimes he whirled down the incline of a wave as if he were on a hand-sled.

But finally he arrived at a place in the sea where travel was beset with difficulty. He did not pause swimming to inquire what manner of current had caught him, but there his progress ceased. The shore was set before him like a bit of scenery on a stage, and he looked at it and understood with his eyes each detail of it.

As the cook passed, much farther to the left, the captain was calling to him, "Turn over on your back, cook! Turn over on your back and use the oar."

"All right, sir." The cook turned on his back, and, paddling with an oar, went ahead as if he were a canoe.

Presently the boat also passed to the left of the correspondent, with the captain clinging with one hand to the keel. He would have appeared like a man raising himself to look over a board fence if it were not for the extraordinary gymnastics of the boat. The correspondent marveled that the captain could still hold to it.

They passed on nearer to shore—the oiler, the cook, the captain—and following them went the water jar, bouncing gally over the seas.

The correspondent remained in the grip of this strange new enemy—a current. The shore, with its white slope of sand and its green bluff topped with little silent cottages, was spread like a picture before him. It was very near to him then, but he was impressed as one who, in a gallery, looks at a scene from Brittany or Algiers.

He thought: "I am going to drown? Can it be possible? Can it be possible? Can it be possible?" Perhaps an individual must consider his own death to be the final phenomenon of nature.

But later a wave perhaps whirled him out of this small deadly current, for he found suddenly that he could again make progress toward the shore. Later still he was aware that the captain, clinging with one hand to the keel of the dinghy, had his face turned away from the shore and toward him, and was calling his name. "Come to the boat! Come to the boat!"

In his struggle to reach the captain and the boat, he reflected that when one gets properly wearied drowning must really be a comfortable arrangement—a cessation of hostilities accompanied by a large degree of relief; and he was glad of it, for the main thing in his mind for some moments had been horror of the temporary agony. He did not wish to be hurt.

Presently he saw a man running along the shore. He was undressing with most remarkable speed. Coat, trousers, shirt, everything flew magically off him.

"Come to the boat!" called the captain.

"All right, Captain." As the correspondent paddled, he saw the captain let himself down to bottom and leave the boat. Then the correspondent performed his one little marvel of the voyage. A large wave caught him and flung him with ease and supreme speed completely over the boat and far beyond it. It struck him even then as an event in gymnastics and a true miracle of the sea. An overturned boat in the surf is not a plaything to a swimming man.

The correspondent arrived in water that reached only to his waist, but his condition did not enable him to stand for more than a moment. Each wave knocked him into a heap, and the undertow pulled at him.

Then he saw the man who had been running and undressing, and undressing and running, come bounding into the water. He dragged ashore the cook, and then waded toward the captain; but the captain waved him away and sent him to the correspondent. He was naked— naked as a tree in winter; but a halo was about his head, and he shone like a saint. He gave a strong pull, and a long drag, and a bully heave at the correspondent's hand. The correspondent, schooled in the minor formulae, said, "Thanks, old man." But suddenly the man cried, "What's that?" He pointed a swift finger. The correspondent said, "Go."

In the shallows, face downward, lay the oiler. His forehead touched sand that was periodically, between each wave, clear of the sea.

The correspondent did not know all that transpired afterward. When he achieved safe ground he fell, striking the sand with each particular part of his body. It was as if he had dropped from a roof, but the thud was grateful to him.

It seems that instantly the beach was populated with men with blankets, clothes, and flasks, and women with coffeepots and all the remedies sacred to their minds. The welcome of the land to the men from the sea was warm and generous; but a still and dripping shape was carried slowly up the beach, and the land's welcome for it could only be the different and sinister hospitality of the grave.

When it came night, the white waves paced to and fro in the moonlight, and the wind brought the sound of the great sea's voice to the men on the shore, and they felt that they could then be interpreters.

Study Questions

1. What is the relationship and interaction of the men in the boat?

2. Is the sea regarded as benevolent, malevolent, or indifferent to the fate of the men?
3. When people on shore spot the dinghy, why don't they send help?
4. What is Crane's view of God as implied by the story?
5. Do you think this naturalistic account is an accurate depiction of reality?

The Matrix

Directors and Screenwriters: Larry and Andy Wachowski

The directors Larry and Andy Wachowski are comparative newcomers to film. They wrote Assassins *or* Day of Reckoning, *then directed* Bound. *However,* The Matrix *was their first major success as filmmakers, and the two current sequels also achieved recognition:* The Matrix Reloaded *and* Matrix 3.

In The Matrix, *a futuristic thriller, our notion of reality is challenged by a world of virtual reality that human beings accept as genuine. People have been deceived by a series of simulated figures and events generated by computer. Since film itself is an illusion (along with other arts and cyberspace experiences), the viewer can appreciate the subtle boundary between fantasy and reality. We take the events on the screen as actual, suspending our disbelief, and when the lights come on, the real world may be hard to accept.*

The story has been criticized as somewhat simplistic and derivative, trading on themes of human beings vs. robots, good vs. evil and, particularly, the salvation of man through Christ (Neo in the film). However, The Matrix *does present fascinating questions about the nature of reality and whether we are being deluded in our understanding of it. The film may be an uneasy amalgam of science fiction, mysticism, video games, comic books, and vague Zen notions, but it is held together by the suspense and philosophic questions. The Kung Fu action and the visual technology alone keep the film entertaining, and in the end the viewer is led to reflection of a metaphysical kind.*

Synopsis

The central premise of the sci-fi thriller *The Matrix* is that, in this post-apocalyptic world, the reality experienced by human beings exists only in their minds. All events and feelings are actually images hardwired into their brains. People live entirely in this dream-like, virtual state, while imagining they are living in the late-twentieth century. They go about their business in the usual way, oblivious to the fact that their brains have been hooked-up by computer to a simulated reality. They would find it absurd to think that they are floating in comas, suspended in incubators, and that all their experiences are a complex network of delusions. Nevertheless, that is their condition. The plot of *The Matrix* consists in exposing the deception, and in overthrowing the forces that have enslaved people through this mass hallucination.

The film trades on a philosophic problem called the *ego-centric predicament*, which was first identified and named by Ralph Barton Perry in *Present Philosophical Tendencies*. According to the ego-centric predicament, the mind is confined to the circle of its own ideas, so that it is difficult, and perhaps impossible, to know the external world. That is, we cannot get outside our own minds to know whether our ideas correspond to anything external. No standpoint exists from which we can view the external world and see whether the notions in our mind correspond to it. We are trapped within the boundaries of our being and cannot get outside ourselves to verify the reality of anyone or anything else. Given this condition, we could be skeptical about whether there exists an external world, independent of our own thoughts and images.

Perry describes it this way: "No one can report on the nature of things without being on hand himself. It follows that whatever thing he reports does as a matter of fact stand in relation to him, as an idea, object of knowledge or experience."

As we have seen, George Berkeley used this viewpoint to declare *"esse est percipi,"* to be is to be perceived. He claimed that reality is nothing other than our mental ideas, and that no material world exists. Berkeley's theory, however, has been extensively criticized by a number of philosophers. They have pointed out that although things must be mentally experienced in order to be known, that does not prove that reality is nothing but the ideas in our mind. Things can exist without our thinking about them; we simply would not know of their existence. In other words, all knowledge depends on our conscious ideas, but that does not prove the ideas themselves are the reality and that nothing else exists.

In *The Matrix* human beings do take their mental experience as reality, and the viewer along with the protagonist gradually learn that they are deceived. Not only does the real world lie outside their consciousness, but their consciousness is of a virtual reality and not a reflection of the actual world at all.

After a preliminary action sequence, the main plot of the film begins with shots of a computer programmer, Thomas Anderson (Keanu Reeves), working late at night in an apartment littered with technological equipment. Anderson works for a software development firm but, in addition, he commits computer crimes under the name "Neo," hiring himself out as a hacker. This night, as he half-dozes, a mysterious message appears on his screen, seemingly from the computer itself: "The Matrix has you," it states, and "Follow the white rabbit" (like Alice).

A client named Choi then appears with his girlfriend, and asks Neo to take on a job for him, which Neo agrees to do. In thanking him Choi says "Hallelujah! You are my savior, man! My own personal Jesus Christ." With equal significance Neo replies, "You ever have the feeling that you're not sure if you're awake or still dreaming?"

Choi invites Neo to a rave, which he first declines to do, then accepts when he sees a small white rabbit on the girl's jacket. At the party he meets Trinity (Carrie-Ann Moss), a sleekly attractive, mysterious woman dressed in black vinyl, who tells him he is being watched and in danger.

> TRINITY: Please. Just listen. I know why you're here, Neo . . . You're looking for him.

[Her body is against his; her lips very close to his ear.]

> TRINITY: I know because I came looking for the same thing, but when he found me he told me I wasn't really looking for him. I was looking for an answer.

[There is a hypnotic quality to her voice and Neo feels the words, like a drug, seeping into him.]

> TRINITY: It's the question that brought you here. You know the question just as I did. It is a hacker's question.
> NEO: What is the Matrix?
> TRINITY: When I asked him, he said that no one could ever be told the answer to that question. They have to see it to believe it.

[She leans close, her lips almost touching his ear.]

> TRINITY: The answer is out there, Neo, it's looking for you and it will find you, if you want it to.

The next day at work Neo receives a call from Morpheus, a mythical hacker he has longed to meet. Morpheus tells him, "They're coming for you," and as two agents and police come onto the floor, he gives Neo exact instructions on how to escape: into an empty cubicle, then through a window, onto a ledge, and down a scaffold. However, Neo balks at the leap to the scaffold and is captured by the police.

Agent Smith (Hugo Weaving), the chief villain of the film, subsequently interrogates Neo. After telling him that he knows about his criminal activities as a hacker, Smith offers to wipe the slate clean in return for Neo's cooperation in bringing a terrorist to justice. When Neo refuses, he inserts into his navel a fiberoptic wire tap in the form of an organic worm/insect.

Unsure afterwards whether or not it was a nightmare, Neo agrees to meet with Morpheus. "You're the One," Morpheus tells him. "You see, you may have spent the last few years looking for me, but I've spent most of my life looking for you." In the car that is sent for him, Trinity removes the electronic "bug" from his stomach with a cylindrical probe, and they continue on for the meeting with Morpheus in room 1313 of a decayed hotel.

Morpheus is dressed in a long black coat with his eyes invisible behind dark glasses, which is in keeping with the noir style of the film.

MORPHEUS: Let me tell you why you are here. You have come because you know something. What you know you can't explain
but you feel it. You've felt it your whole life, felt that something
is wrong with the world. You don't know what, but it's there . . .
Do you know what I'm talking about?
NEO: The Matrix?
MORPHEUS: Do you want to know what it is?

[Neo swallows hard and nods.]

MORPHEUS: The Matrix is everywhere, it's all around us, here
even in this room. You can see it out your window or on your
television. You can feel it when you go to work, or go to church
or pay your taxes. It is the world that has been pulled over your
eyes to blind you from the truth.
NEO: What truth?
MORPHEUS: That you are a slave, Neo. Like everyone else, you
were born into bondage, kept inside a prison that you cannot
smell, taste, or touch. A prison for your mind.

Morpheus then offers him a choice of two pills: the blue will take
him home; the red will lead him to the truth about the Matrix. Without
much hesitation, Neo swallows the red pill. Morpheus then asks "Have
you ever had a dream, Neo, that you were so sure was real?" . . . "What if
you were unable to wake from that dream, Neo? How would you know
the difference between the dream world and the real world?"

Subsequently Neo undergoes a traumatic and painful process to
free him from his illusions. A mirror envelops him in silvery strands,
melting like gel and spreading across his body. He then finds himself in
an oval capsule filled with red gelatin, a coaxial cable plugged into the
base of his skull. All around him are other people also in pods with the
same tubes feeding into a metal stem. A machine drops in front of him,
paralyzes his muscles, and disengages the main cable. Immediately he is
sucked into a black hole, drawn through sewer pipes and grease traps,
and finally pulled into the belly of a futuristic hovercraft.

Morpheus and Trinity are there together with a man named Dozer,
who is rebuilding Neo's atrophied muscles, and various members of the
crew—Mouse, Cypher, Apoc, Switch, Tank, and so forth. His eyes hurt
because, as Morpheus explains, he has never used them before, so he is
given dark glasses like the others.

Morpheus then reveals to Neo that the year is about 2197 not 1997.
Using the jack at the back of his neck, he hooks him into a computer program that shows the Chicago he is familiar with and the Chicago that has
come to be. He begins to explain that in the early twenty-first century
human beings invented machines that were incredibly smart, but their intelligence enabled them to revolt and take over the planet. In order to

supply their need for power they required an energy source besides the sun, so they began "farming" human beings. "The human body generates more bioelectricity than a 120-volt battery and over 25,000 B.T.U.'s of body heat," Morpheus explains. Consequently, it was a perfect source of power.

The machines therefore started using people as batteries, and to keep the human race ignorant of its condition and under control, the Matrix was created—a computer-generated, virtual world. Almost everyone, including Neo, had been living within the illusions created by the cyber intelligence, while Morpheus and a few others who had escaped, were free from the deception. They were battling to wrest control back from the machines.

When Neo refuses to believe that these are the real circumstances, Morpheus asks rhetorically, "What is real? How do you define real? If you're talking about your senses, what you feel, taste, smell, or see, then all you're talking about are electrical signals interpreted by your brain."

He also discloses that Neo has been born with special powers that would enable him to manipulate the Matrix and defeat the machines. An Oracle had prophesied that a man would return to free humankind, bring about enlightenment and man's salvation. The obvious reference is to Christ, and Neo is seen as the promised Messiah. Morpheus tells him "There is a greatness inside of you, Neo. A greatness that is going to lift you to unimaginable heights and that in time will change the world."

To prepare for his role mentally and physically, discs are loaded into Neo's supplemental drive, including savate, jujitsu, Ken Po, and kung fu. He spars with Morpheus using the martial arts programmed inside him, moving with incredible speed and strength, defying the law of gravity with his leaps and dodges. However, Neo fails in a crucial jump, and people wonder if he is the One; apparently, Morpheus had been mistaken before.

To make sure of his identity, Neo is taken to see the Oracle, someone with the eyes of a sphinx who is never wrong. "The Matrix cannot tell you who you are," Morpheus declares, "but an oracle can . . . She sees beyond the relativity of time. For her there is no past, present, or future. There is only what is." When Neo is skeptical, saying that he doesn't believe in this stuff, Morpheus replies, "Faith is beyond the reach of whys and why nots. These things are not a matter of cause and effect, Neo. I do not believe things with my mind. I believe them with my heart. In my gut." Religion is thus given precedence over science, feelings over the rationality that created the Matrix.

Contrary to expectations, the Oracle seems to deny that Neo is the One, although like most seers, soothsayers, and prophets her words are ambiguous. She does foretell that, Morpheus will attempt to give up his life so Neo can live; then Neo will have to decide which of the two will die.

Fast-paced action scenes follow as agents of the Matrix, who are machines in human form, swarm into the headquarters of the rebels. Several of the rebels are killed, and amidst blasts of gunfire Neo, Morpheus, Trinity, and Cypher try to escape through the crawlspace between the walls. Agent Smith momentarily catches Neo, but Morpheus explodes through the lath and plaster and grabs Smith by the throat. He tells Trinity to leave him behind and save Neo, so the two of them slide inside the wall to the basement where they escape through an opening to the sewers.

Meanwhile Morpheus is captured, and Agent Smith begins extracting information from him using a serum that attacks his neuro-systems. To avoid having their entire operation destroyed, Tank and Trinity reluctantly decide that Morpheus must be killed, which they can do remotely. However, Neo will not agree. He realizes that this is the moment the Oracle predicted, when either he or Morpheus would die, and he decides to risk his life in attempting a rescue. Trinity insists on going with him, so the two of them are propelled inside the Matrix.

More fast action follows as Neo and Trinity penetrate the government building where Morpheus is being held, killing a number of guards with their guns, fists, and explosives. They then steal a helicopter and attack the room where Morpheus is imprisoned. Neo manages to extract Morpheus by dangling from a rope, and they carry him to safety, landing on the roof of a skyscraper.

In the final scene that begins in a subway station, Neo and Agent Smith fight a furious battle, each twisting, bending, and ducking faster than the bullets coming at them. They land powerful blows, kick box and hurl each other into walls, exhibiting uncanny suppleness and speed. Although Smith is hit by an oncoming train, he metamorphoses into an identical agent, and begins to chase Neo through the city. Several agents join in the pursuit, appearing from the midst of crowds, from behind tent flaps, crates, fish counters. Neo ducks into buildings, sprints down corridors, through apartments, and scrambles up a fire escape as bullets whiz around him. But when he throws open the door to one room Agent Smith is waiting for him; he kills Neo with one shot.

One would think the rebel struggle would be over with the Matrix emerging victorious, but Neo miraculously comes back to life. He hears Trinity's voice saying,

> The Oracle, she told me that I'd fall in love and that man, the man I loved would be the One. You see? You can't be dead, Neo, you can't be because I love you. You hear me? I love you!

At this, Neo rises to his feet, and effortlessly overcomes Agent Smith, even making bullets stop in their tracks. The Matrix is thereby defeated, love overcoming hate, and as the camera rises above the city Neo ascends still faster, traveling upwards at an unearthly speed.

We can see in the film a strong religious allegory. The symbolism alone is hard to miss: Neo as a Christ figure, the Messiah come to save the world, Trinity, a demigoddess of the New Age variety, and Morpheus, the god of dreams in Ovid's *Metamorphosis*. Several interpreters have seen further Christian elements in the film, some of which have already been mentioned. For example, "Neo" has been taken as an anagram for eon and One; he is born into the world anew, like the virgin birth of Christ; Morpheus can be seen as John the Baptist who foretold Christ's coming; the hovercraft is called Nebuchadnezzar, and the core of the planet where human survivors live is "Zion," both of which are biblical references; Cypher is a Judas who gave up Morpheus to Agent Smith (a Roman centurion); at the end of the film, Neo rises into the sky just as Christ ascended to heaven; and Neo's death and resurrection are foretold just as Christ prophesied he would be killed and raised from the dead.

For our purposes, *The Matrix* offers a fascinating approach to the question of reality. It may be far-fetched to think that a master computer is feeding perceptions into our brain, so that we are experiencing a virtual world, but we do sometimes wonder whether reality exists only in our minds. We may not be computer viruses or batteries for computers, but in today's world perhaps we are increasingly being told what to think. It is more than paranoia to fear control by drugs, technology, advertising, and government bureaus, so we are sympathetic to the notion that our minds could be manipulated from outside.

Limited as we are to the private space inside our heads, we are never certain how much contact we have with anything objective, or whether the internal or the external is real. In the modern world of implants, virtual objects, cyberspace, holograms, robotics, bioengineering, and artificial intelligence, what we take to be true might just be illusions of the senses or delusions of the mind. In a sense, our mental life forms a world in itself, and even if it's phony that may be all we have. As Morpheus asks, if we were unable to awaken from a dream, how would we know the difference between the dream world and the real world?

The Matrix raises such questions within the context of an entertaining, high-tech drama. Using special effects such as computer animation, wire stunts, and impossible martial arts, the film create an exciting visual fantasy. It crosses the boundary between the cyberpunk and the reflective, ultimately offering us a metaphysical thriller.

Study Questions

1. Define the nature of the Matrix.
2. Do you think there is any way of telling the difference between virtual reality and actual life?

3. In what way is *The Matrix* a Christian parable?
4. Why do the agents fight so hard to perpetuate the false reality.
5. If you were Neo, would you take the red or blue pill? Would you rather know the harsh truth or believe the comforting delusion?

Bibliography of Philosophy, Literature, and Films

II. Exploring the Nature of Reality: Metaphysics

Philosophy

The Analysis of Mind	Bertrand Russell
Being and Nothingness	Jean-Paul Sartre
Body and Mind	Godfrey Vesey
The Bondage of the Will	Martin Luther
Cartesian Meditations	Edmund Husserl
The Concept of Mind	Gilbert Ryle
The Concept of a Person	A. J. Ayer
De Anima, Metaphysics	Aristotle
Determinism and Freedom	Sidney Hook
Essays on the Freedom of the Will	Arthur Schopehauer
Essays on the Intellectual Powers of Man	Thomas Reid
Freedom and Reason	R. M. Hare
Freedom of the Individual	Stuart Hampshire
Freedom of the Will	Jonathan Edwards
In Defense of Free Will	C. A. Campbell
Individuals	P. F. Strawson
Intention	G. E. M. Anscombe
Materialist Theory of Mind	D. M. A. Armstrong
The Mind and Its Place in Nature	C. D. Broad
The Mind-Brain Identity Theory	Clive V. Borst
Minds and Machines	Alan R. Anderson
The Nature of Woman	Mary Anne Warren
On Free Choice of the Will	St. Augustine
On Human Freedom	John Laird
Other Minds	John Wisdom
The Philosophy of Mind	Alan R. White
The Problems of Philosophy	Bertrand Russell
Problems of the Self	Bernard Williams
Reconstruction in Philosophy	John Dewey
The Self and Its Brain	Karl Popper
Person and Object	Roderick Chisholm
Time and Free Will	Henri Bergson
The Philosophy of Mind	Stuart Hampshire
The Problem of the Self	Henry Johnstone
The Revolt Against Dualism	Arthur Lovejoy
The Second Sex	Simone de Beauvoir

Literature

The Age of Reason, Nausea	Jean-Paul Sartre
Alcestis, Iphigenia, Medea	Euripides

A Man's a Man	Bertolt Brecht
Antigone	Sophocles
An American Tragedy	Theodore Dreiser
And Quiet Flows the Don	Mikhail Sholokhov
Buddenbrooks	Thomas Mann
Candide	Voltaire
The Castle, The Trial	Franz Kafka
Chance	Joseph Conrad
The Common Reader	Virginia Woolf
Death of a Salesman	Arthur Miller
Dice Thrown Never Will Annul Chance	Stephane Mallarme
Do With Me What You Will	Joyce Carol Oates
A Doll's House	Henrik Ibsen
The Double, Notes from Underground	Fedor Dostoevski
The Edible Woman	Margaret Atwood
The Egoist	George Meredith
Ficciones	Jorge Luis Borges
Free Fall	William Golding
Gravity's Rainbow	Thomas Pynchon
The Gulag Archipelago	Alexander Solzhenitsyn
Hamlet	William Shakespeare
Hedda Gabler	Henrik Ibsen
Henry VI	William Shakespeare
Invisible Cities	Italo Calvino
Jacob's Room	Virginia Wolf
Labyrinths	Jorge Luis Borges
Magic Mountain	Thomas Mann
The Magus	John Fowles
The Man Without Qualities	Robert Musil
One Hundred Years of Solitude	Gabriel Garcia Marquez
Othello	William Shakespeare
Phaedra	Jean Baptiste Racine
The Picture of Dorian Gray	Oscar Wilde
Pygmalion	George Bernard Shaw
Portrait of the Artist as a Young Man	James Joyce
Remembrance of Things Past	Marcel Proust
Richard III	William Shakespeare
The Secret Sharer	Joseph Conrad
Sapho	Alphonse Daudet
The Story of Gosta Berling	Selma Lagerlof
The Stranger	Albert Caus
The Time Machine	H. G. Wells
"A Very Old Man With Enormous Wings"	Gabriel Garcia Marquez

Walden Two	B. F. Skinner
Ward No. 6	Anton Chekhov
The Way of All Flesh	Samuel Butler
The Wild Duck	Henrik Ibsen

Films

Alien	Ridley Scott
Altered States	Ken Russell
The Andalusian Dog	Luis Bunuel
The Andromeda Strain	Robert Wise
Babbitt	Sinclair Lewis
The Ballad of Narayame	Shohei Imamura
Beauty and the Beast	Jean Cocteau
Billy Liar	John Schlesinger
Blade Runner	Ridley Scott
Brazil	Terry Gillian
Captains Courageous	Victor Fleming
Close Encounters of the Third Kind	Steven Spielberg
Coccoon	Ron Howard
The Crying Game	Neil Jordan
Dead Man Walking	Tim Robbins
East of Eden	Elia Kazan
The Four Hundred Blows	Francois Truffaut
Frankenstein	James Whale
Gattaca	Andrew Niccol
The Golden Age	Luis Bunuel
The Graduate	Mike Nichols
Groundhog Day	Harold Ramis
Hedwig and the Angry Inch	John Cameron Mitchell
The Hustler	Robert Rossen
Jurassic Park	Steven Spielberg
Lord of the Flies	Peter Brooks
Lost Horizon	Frank Capra
Love and Death	Woody Allen
A Man for All Seasons	Fred Zinneman
Memento	Christopher Nolan
Metropolis	Fritz Lang
Minority Report	Steven Spielberg
Nosferatu	F. W. Murneau
The Matrix	Wachowski Brothers
Orpheus	Jean Cocteau
The Passion of Ana	Ingmar Bergman
Pather Panchali	Satyajit Ray
Slaughterhouse Five	George Roy Hill

Star Trek	Robert Wise
Star Wars	George Lucas
2001, A Space Odyssey	Stanley Kubrick
The Unbearable Lightness of Being	Philip Kaufman
Woman in the Dunes	Hiroshi Teshigahara

III. Judging the Value of Conduct: Ethics

In addition to epistemology and metaphysics, the field of ethics is considered another major branch of philosophy. Ethics is concerned with both the right and the good, that is, the right way to behave and the good in life overall. The ethicist tries to answer questions such as how much should we sacrifice for someone else's welfare and how much can we take from life for ourselves? Should we always keep promises, tell the truth, and preserve life or would it be morally permissible under certain conditions, to break promises, deceive others, and to take life? Do we know what is right by that still small voice called conscience, by our personal experience, by reason, by the traditions in our society, or by authorities such as parents, teachers, or sacred books? Is an act wrong because it is illegal or illegal because it is wrong? Should we judge actions in terms of the intention of the agent, the intrinsic nature of the act, or the ultimate harm or benefit that results? What goals or ideals are worth pursuing as our purpose in living?

Although everyone must decide these questions for themselves, that does not mean one person's opinion is as good as another's. The person who is aware of the various options, thinks logically, and knows the kinds of considerations that apply in evaluating them, is in a much better position to reach a sound conclusion. An informed decision is far better than accepting the popular notions of our time or the opinions we assimilated as children. As Socrates said, "The unexamined life is not worth living." Once we have examined the various directions we can take, and understand what makes them right or wrong, good or bad, then we are truly in command of our life choices.

A. Relativism and Objectivism: Are There Universal Values?

One primary question in ethics is whether our values only reflect our culture or whether they have an objective basis. According to the *relativist* view, when we make a value judgment we are only stating the attitudes and prejudices of our society. To the *objectivist*, we may be identifying something genuinely right or wrong, good or bad. For example, when we blame someone for lying, the relativist sees this as an expression of our culture's disapproval; our particular society favors honesty and condemns dishonesty. The objectivist would argue that we are stating an objective truth: that lying, by its very nature, is wrong; society depends upon mutual trust.

Some relativists point out that our judgments are also a matter of personal taste as well as a reflection of societal norms. What is right to one person may be wrong to another; values are an individual matter. John may believe that sex is only permissible within marriage whereas Bill may think premarital sex is perfectly acceptable. Just as we have different tastes in food we have different sets of values, and no one can be judged wrong either for liking broccoli or for being sexually promiscuous. As the Romans said, *"de gustibus non est disputandum"*; about taste there can be no dispute.

All standards are relative to a particular person or society, and they have no general validity outside that context. Therefore, to deliberate about which values are really worthwhile is a pointless exercise. Everything is relative to the individual, the culture, the time, and the place.

Relativists often argue for their theory by citing the variety of value systems across the world, each different and each supported by people who believe themselves right. In some cultures, a man gains esteem by having several wives while in other cultures polygamy is considered immoral; in some societies, drugs are taken for pleasure and insight, while in others using drugs is a crime; in some places, a woman must cover her body completely in a burka with netting over her eyes, while in others, women can wear attractive clothes and bikinis on the beach. In the past, many cultures practiced slavery whereas today it is considered immoral, and war was thought heroic, but now we regard it as tragic. Old age used to be respected and even venerated, but currently youth is celebrated as the ideal, just as piety and wisdom were once highly valued, but now we prize wealth and status. Because of the multiplicity of cultural perspectives the relativist concludes that morality is a matter of history and geography.

At the extreme, the relativist theory maintains that values are a matter of opinion. Whatever a person thinks is right becomes right because the person thinks so. We tell one another, "It's all a matter of opinion, it's how you feel," or "What gives you the right to judge?" or "Who's to say?" The implication is that whatever people believe to be true is true for them, and no outside judgment can prove them wrong. As Shakespeare declares in *Hamlet*, "There is nothing either good or bad, but thinking makes it so."

The impulses behind relativism seem to be admirable. First, there is the desire for *tolerance* and open-mindedness toward other people's ideas—including those that are different from our own. In a democracy, everyone has a right to his or her opinion as well as a right to be heard, and we should not presume that our ideas are the only correct ones. Such an attitude smacks of arrogance and righteousness. Furthermore, we should be wary of people who are sure they are right because such certainty can result in inquisitions, witch burnings, crusades, pogroms, purges, ethnic cleansing, and so forth.

A second source of relativism lies in our wish to maximize our *freedom*. If there are correct moral principles then we are compelled to acknowledge them, whether we like it or not, whereas if right and wrong depend upon how we feel then we have a great deal of personal control. We are then free to choose our values, and all ethical decisions become a function of our preferences. We do not choose that which is valuable but whatever we choose becomes valuable because we've chosen it.

A third motive for accepting relativism is our *uncertainty* in today's world as to which values are worth accepting and defending. History has proven us wrong too often with regard to political doctrines, social theories, or religious beliefs, so we have lost confidence in the truth of our ideas. Furthermore, our awareness of diverse values in a multicultural world casts doubt on any one theory of what is right or good.

Our uncertainty is increased by the scientific approach to knowledge, which has nearly eclipsed every other way of knowing. As science operates, only empirical statements are capable of being verified, which implies that all value judgments are a matter of opinion. Added to this are specific scientific findings such as Einstein's theory of relativity, which takes space and time as relative phenomena. Although relativity theory only applies to physics, people have taken it as evidence for the relativity of ethical values as well.

It appears, then, that every value judgment we make should be tentative and qualified. The sense of being sure about what is right has now been lost, and we are acutely conscious that every moral statement we make is potentially false. Furthermore we want to give ourselves maximum freedom in deciding how to live, and, in addition, to be tolerant toward other people's choices. Therefore it seems correct to say that everything is relative.

Persuasive as the case for relativism might be, many philosophers accept the opposite position of objectivism. According to the objectivist theory, we can identify particular acts as right, others as wrong, and certain purposes in living as more desirable than others. Societies do not create values but can reach an understanding about them, and individuals do not invent values but discover them. When we make a moral judgment we are not revealing something about ourselves or our culture's attitudes but expressing insight into the moral nature of an act.

For example, the judgment that stealing is wrong tells us something about the inherent nature of stealing. To take someone else's property, especially something they have worked hard to acquire, is to cause them injury. Therefore it is wrong, not just for us but for anyone. Whether we are in Africa, Europe, or America, in the fourth, the sixteenth, or the twenty-first century, we should not take what does not belong to us.

The objectivist, therefore, believes that we as human beings should follow certain standards of behavior because they are right in themselves. We should not be self-righteous, of course, and assume we know what those standards are, but we can have confidence that such standards exist. That gives direction to our search, and through rational discussion we can hope to get closer to the truth of things.

The objectivist also rejects many of the specific arguments used by the relativist. For instance, the objectivist points out that although values differ between cultures that does not imply that all values are relative. The differences can be attributed to one society being more backward or enlightened than another, seeing values more dimly or clearly. To take an analogy from science, the fact that people thought the earth was flat at one time, and round at another, does not mean that each idea is right. Rather, people came to understand that although they believed the earth was flat, it really is round. In the same way, people have come to realize that women should be treated with absolute equality, that enslaving people is wrong in any society, and that we should respect minority rights. Prejudice and discrimination is not wrong in some cultures and right in others; it is wrong whenever and wherever it occurs.

In addition, the objectivist argues that the diversity of values between cultures may be more apparent than real. A wide area of moral agreement exists between cultures across the earth. For example, one society may condone a husband killing his wife's lover, another may condemn it, and this seems like a major difference. However, both societies will probably have laws prohibiting murder and a strong belief in the protection of human life. They will differ only in their definition of murder, that is, taking life unjustifiably. In the same way, one society may be hostile to strangers, another warm and welcoming, but both may believe in the value of hospitality. The difference is that one applies the rules of hospitality only to families within the society, the other extends them to outsiders as well.

Objectivists will sometimes cite the golden rule as a major example of a cross-cultural value. In Christianity we read, "Whatsoever ye would that men should do unto you, do ye even so to them"; in Judaism, "What is hateful to yourself, don't do to your fellow man"; in Buddhism, "Hurt not others with that which pains oneself"; and in Hinduism, "Do naught to others which if done to thee would cause pain." Confucianism tells us, "What you don't want done to yourself, don't do to others"; Zoroastrianism says, "Do not do unto others all that which is not well for oneself"; Sikhism declares, "Treat others as thou wouldst be treated thyself"; and even Plato advises himself, "May I do unto others as I would that they should do unto me." Perhaps all societies do have a substratum of shared values.

The objectivist also points out a variety of logical criticisms showing that relativism is self-contradictory. For one thing, the relativist claims that the statement, "Everything is relative" is really true, but if everything is relative then nothing is really true, including that statement. It may be true relative to one's culture or according to one's tastes, but to say it is objectively true contradicts the theory itself.

Plato identifies another type of contradiction in a dialogue called the *Theatetus*. Here Socrates says to Protagoras, "and the best of the joke is that he acknowledges the truth of their opinions who believe his own opinions to be false for he admits that the opinions of all men are true." In other words, if everyone is right, then the person who thinks you are wrong must be right.

Finally, there is the self-contradiction with regard to tolerance (which was mentioned as one of the supports for relativism). Relativists claim that their position has the virtue of fostering tolerance because no value is considered really worthwhile. However, by extolling tolerance, relativists are assuming it possesses value. The relativists thereby give the game away, for tolerance at least is considered objectively valuable.

The relativist/objectivist controversy is an ongoing one, and in the selections that follow the two positions are argued and exemplified. The philosopher Jean-Paul Sartre presents a relativist view as contained in his existential philosophy. Then a short story by Ursula K. Le Guin poses questions about the limits of relativism, and the director Elia Kazan presents a clash of cultural values. Both of the latter two imply that right and wrong are objective; we become aware of right and wrong in life situations.

The Humanism of Existentialism
Jean-Paul Sartre

Jean-Paul Sartre (1905–1980) was a French philosopher, novelist, and playwright who is generally considered the foremost figure in the twentieth-century movement of existentialism. In his writings, he stressed the existential tenet that for human beings "existence precedes essence," which means that first we exist then we develop our essential character. We do not come into being with any basic human nature, but become a particular kind of person during our lifetime.

Sartre developed and popularized the existential philosophy in a number of books, most notably his Being and Nothingness. *His other major works in philosophy and literature include* The Flies, No Exit, Nausea, The Age of Reason, Troubled Sleep, Saint Genet, *and* The Words. *He was awarded the Nobel Prize for Literature but refused it because he thought it might compromise his integrity as a writer.*

In the selection that follows, Sartre affirms the doctrine of ethical relativism, or more precisely subjectivism, by maintaining that, "Man is nothing else but what he makes of himself." We create our own values and purposes, and determine the kind of person we want to become. To Sartre, God does not exist to authenticate any conduct; neither are there any ethical principles inherent in the universe or a destiny we must fulfill. As human beings, we exist in total solitude without any objective principles to guide our behavior. However, whatever we choose to do we thereby make valuable, and we are responsible for the decisions we make. Life has no meaning in itself, but we can invest life with meaning through our free commitments.

What can be said from the very beginning is that by existentialism we mean a doctrine which makes human life possible and, in addition, declares that every truth and every action implies a human setting and a human subjectivity.

As is generally known, the basic charge against us is that we put the emphasis on the dark side of human life. Someone recently told me of a lady who, when she let slip a vulgar word in a moment of irritation, excused herself by saying, "I guess I'm becoming an existentialist." Consequently, existentialism is regarded as something ugly; that is why we are said to be naturalists; and if we are, it is rather surprising that in this day and age we cause so much more alarm and scandal than does naturalism, properly so called. The kind of person who can take in his stride such a novel as Zola's *The Earth* is disgusted as soon as he starts reading an existentialist novel; the kind of person who is resigned to the wisdom of the ages—which is pretty sad—finds us even sadder. Yet, what can be more disillusioning than saying "true charity begins at home" or "a scoundrel will always return evil for good"?

We know the commonplace remarks made when this subject comes up, remarks which always add up to the same thing: we shouldn't struggle against the powers-that-be; we shouldn't resist authority; we shouldn't try to rise above our station; any action which doesn't conform to authority is romantic; any effort not based on past experience is doomed to failure; experience shows that man's bent is always toward trouble, that there must be a strong hand to hold him in check, if not, there will be anarchy. There are still people who go on mumbling these melancholy old saws, the people who say, "It's only human!" whenever a more or less repugnant act is pointed out to them, the people who glut themselves on *chansons réalistes;* these are the people who accuse existentialism of being too gloomy, and to such an extent that I wonder whether they are complaining about it, not for its pessimism, but much rather its optimism. Can it be that what really scares them in the doctrine I shall try to present here is that it leaves to man a possibility of choice? To answer this question, we must re-examine it on a strictly philosophical plane. What is meant by the term *existentialism?*

Most people who use the word would be rather embarrassed if they had to explain it, since, now that the word is all the rage, even the work of a musician or painter is being called existentialist. A gossip columnist in *Clartés* signs himself *The Existentialist,* so that by this time the word has been so stretched and has taken on so broad a meaning, that it no longer means anything at all. It seems that for want of an advanced-guard doctrine analogous to surrealism, the kind of people who are eager for scandal and flurry turn to this philosophy which in other respects does not at all serve their purposes in this sphere.

Actually, it is the least scandalous, the most austere of doctrines. It is intended strictly for specialists and philosophers. Yet it can be defined easily. What complicates matters is that there are two kinds of existentialists; first, those who are Christian, among whom I would include Jaspers and Gabriel Marcel, both Catholic; and on the other hand the atheistic existentialists among whom I class Heidegger, and then the French existentialists and myself. What they have in common is that they think that existence precedes essence, or, if you prefer, that subjectivity must be the starting point.

Just what does that mean? Let us consider some object that is manufactured, for example, a book or a paper-cutter: here is an object which has been made by an artisan whose inspiration came from a concept. He referred to the concept of what a paper-cutter is and likewise to a known method of production, which is part of the concept, something which is, by and large, a routine. Thus, the paper-cutter is at once an object produced in a certain way and, on the other hand, one having a specific use; and one cannot postulate a man who produces a paper-cutter but does not know what it is used for. Therefore, let us say that, for the paper-cutter, essence—that is, the ensemble of both the production routines and the properties which enable it to be both produced and defined—precedes existence. Thus, the presence of the paper-cutter or book in front of me is determined. Therefore, we have here a technical view of the world whereby it can be said that production precedes existence.

When we conceive God as the Creator, He is generally thought of as a superior sort of artisan. Whatever doctrine we may be considering, whether one like that of Descartes or that of Leibniz, we always grant that will more or less follows understanding or, at the very least, accompanies it, and that when God creates He knows exactly what He is creating. Thus, the concept of man in the mind of God is comparable to the concept of a paper-cutter in the mind of the manufacturer, and, following certain techniques and a conception, God produces man, just as the artisan, following a definition and a technique, makes a paper-cutter. Thus, the individual man is the realization of a certain concept in the divine intelligence.

In the eighteenth century, the atheism of the *philosophers* discarded the idea of God, but not so much for the notion that essence precedes existence. To a certain extent, this idea is found everywhere; we find it in Diderot, in Voltaire, and even in Kant. Man has a human nature; this human nature, which is the concept of the human, is found in all men, which means that each man is a particular example of a universal concept, man. In Kant, the result of this universality is that the wild-man, the natural man, as well as the bourgeois, are circumscribed by the same definition and have the same basic qualities. Thus, here too the essence of man precedes the historical existence that we find in nature.

Atheistic existentialism, which I represent, is more coherent. It states that if God does not exist, there is at least one being in whom existence precedes essence, a being who exists before he can be defined by any concept, and that this being is man, or, as Heidegger says, human reality. What is meant here by saying that existence precedes essence? It means that, first of all, man exists, turns up, appears on the scene, and, only afterwards, defines himself. If man, as the existentialist conceives him, is indefinable, it is because at first he is nothing. Only afterward will he be something, and he himself will have made what he will be. Thus, there is no human nature, since there is no God to conceive it. Not only is man what he conceives himself to be, but he is also only what he wills himself to be after this thrust toward existence.

Man is nothing else but what he makes of himself. Such is the first principle of existentialism. It is also what is called subjectivity, the name we are labeled with when charges are brought against us. But what do we mean by this, if not that man has a greater dignity than a stone or table? For we mean that man first exists, that is, that man first of all is the being who hurls himself toward a future and who is conscious of imagining himself as being in the future. Man is at the start a plan which is aware of itself, rather than a patch of moss, a piece of garbage, or a cauliflower; nothing exists prior to this plan; there is nothing in heaven; man will be what he will have planned to be. Not what he will want to be. Because by the word "will" we generally mean a conscious decision, which is subsequent to what we have already made of ourselves. I may want to belong to a political party, write a book, get married; but all that is only a manifestation of an earlier, more spontaneous choice that is called "will." But if existence really does precede essence, man is responsible for what he is. Thus, existentialism's first move is to make every man aware of what he is and to make the full responsibility of his existence rest on him. And when we say that a man is responsible for himself, we do not only mean that he is responsible for his own individuality, but that he is responsible for all men.

The word subjectivism has two meanings, and our opponents play on the two. Subjectivism means, on the one hand, that an individual chooses and makes himself; and, on the other, that it is impossible for man to transcend human subjectivity. The second of these is the essential meaning of existentialism. When we say that man chooses his own self, we mean that every one of us does likewise; but we also mean by that that in making this choice he also chooses all men. In fact, in creating the man that we want to be, there is not a single one of our acts which does not at the same time create an image of man as we think he ought to be. To choose to be this or that is to affirm at the same time the value of what we choose, because we can never choose evil. We always choose the good, and nothing can be good for us without being good for all.

If, on the other hand, existence precedes essence, and if we grant that we exist and fashion our image at one and the same time, the image is valid for everybody and for our whole age. Thus, our responsibility is much greater than we might have supposed, because it involves all mankind. If I am a workingman and choose to join a Christian trade-union rather than be a communist, and if by being a member I want to show that the best thing for man is resignation, that the kingdom of man is not of this world, I am not only involving my own case—I want to be resigned for everyone. As a result, my action has involved all humanity. To take a more individual matter, if I want to marry, to have children; even if this marriage depends solely on my own circumstances or passion or wish, I am involving all humanity in monogamy and not merely myself. Therefore, I am responsible for myself and for everyone else. I am creating a certain image of man of my own choosing. In choosing myself, I choose man.

This helps us understand what the actual content is of such rather grandiloquent words as anguish, forlornness, despair. As you will see, it's all quite simple.

First, what is meant by anguish? The existentialists say at once that man is anguish. What that means is this: the man who involves himself and who realizes that he is not only the person he chooses to be, but also a lawmaker who is, at the same time, choosing all mankind as well as himself, cannot help escape the feeling of his total and deep responsibility. Of course, there are many people who are not anxious; but we claim that they are hiding their anxiety, that they are fleeing from it. Certainly, many people believe that when they do something, they themselves are the only ones involved, and when someone says to them, "What if everyone acted that way?" they shrug their shoulders and answer, "Everyone doesn't act that way." But really, one should always ask himself, "What would happen if everybody looked at things that way?" There is no escaping this disturbing thought except by a kind of double-dealing. A man who lies and makes excuses for himself by saying "Not everybody does that," is someone with an uneasy conscience, because the act of lying implies that a universal value is conferred upon the lie.

Anguish is evident even when it conceals itself. This is the anguish that Kierkegaard called the anguish of Abraham. You know the story: an angel has ordered Abraham to sacrifice his son; if it really were an angel who has come and said, "You are Abraham, you shall sacrifice your son," everything would be all right. But everyone might first wonder, "Is it really an angel, and am I really Abraham? What proof do I have?"

There was a madwoman who had hallucinations; someone used to speak to her on the telephone and give her orders. Her doctor asked her, "Who is it who talks to you?" She answered, "He says it's God." What proof did she really have that it was God? If an angel comes to me, what proof is there that it's an angel? And if I hear voices, what proof is there that they come from heaven and not from hell, or from the subconscious, or a pathological condition? What proves that they are addressed to me? What proof is there that I have been appointed to impose my choice and my conception of man on humanity? I'll never find any proof or sign to convince me of that. If a voice addresses me, it is always for me to decide that this is the angel's voice; if I consider that such an act is a good one, it is I who will choose to say that it is good rather than bad.

Now, I'm not being singled out as an Abraham, and yet at every moment I'm obliged to perform exemplary acts. For every man, everything happens as if all mankind had its eyes fixed on him and were guiding itself by what he does. And every man ought to say to himself, "Am I really the kind of man who has the right to act in such a way that humanity might guide itself by my actions?" And if he does not say that to himself, he is masking his anguish.

There is no question here of the kind of anguish which would lead to quietism, to inaction. It is a matter of a simple sort of anguish that anybody who has had responsibilities is familiar with. For example, when a military officer takes the responsibility for an attack and sends a certain number of men to death, he chooses to do so, and in the main he alone makes the choice. Doubtless, orders come from above, but they are too broad; he interprets them, and on this interpretation depend the lives of ten or fourteen or twenty men. In making a decision he cannot help having a certain anguish. All leaders know this anguish. That doesn't keep them from acting; on the contrary, it is the very condition of their action. For it implies that they envisage a number of possibilities, and when they choose one, they realize that it has value only because it is chosen. We shall see that this kind of anguish, which is the kind that existentialism describes, is explained, in addition, by a direct responsibility to the other men whom it involves. It is not a curtain separating us from action, but is part of action itself.

When we speak of forlornness, a term Heidegger was fond of, we mean only that God does not exist and that we have to face all the consequences of this. The existentialist is strongly opposed to a certain kind of secular ethics which would like to abolish God with the least possible expense. About 1880, some French teachers tried to set up a secular ethics which went something like this: God is a useless and costly hypothesis; we are discarding it; but, meanwhile, in order for there to be an ethics, a society, a civilization, it is essential that certain values be taken seriously and that they be considered as having an *a priori* existence. It must be obligatory, *a priori,* to be honest, not to lie, not to beat your wife, to have children, etc., etc. So we're going to try a little device which will make it possible to show that values exist all the same, inscribed in a heaven of ideas, though otherwise God does not exist. In other words—and this, I believe, is the tendency of everything called reformism in France—nothing will be changed if God does not exist. We shall find ourselves with the same norms of honesty, progress, and humanism, and we shall have made of God an outdated hypothesis which will peacefully die off by itself.

The existentialist, on the contrary, thinks it very distressing that God does not exist, because all possibility of finding values in a heaven of ideas disappears along with Him; there can no longer be an *a priori* Good, since there is no infinite and perfect consciousness to think it. Nowhere is it written that the Good exists, that we must be honest, that we must not lie; because the fact is we are on a plane where there are only men. Dostoievsky said, "If God didn't exist, everything would be possible." That is the very starting point of existentialism. Indeed, everything is permissible if God does not exist, and as a result man is forlorn, because neither within him nor without does he find anything to cling to. He can't start making excuses for himself.

If existence really does precede essence, there is no explaining things away by reference to a fixed and given human nature. In other words, there is no determinism, man is free, man is freedom. On the other hand, if God does not exist, we find no values or commands to turn to which legitimize our conduct. So, in the bright realm of values, we have no excuse behind us, nor justification before us. We are alone, with no excuses.

That is the idea I shall try to convey when I say that man is condemned to be free. Condemned, because he did not create himself, yet, in other respects is free; because, once thrown into the world, he is responsible for everything he does. The existentialist does not believe in the power of passion. He will never agree that a sweeping passion is a ravaging torrent which fatally leads a man to certain acts and is therefore an excuse. He thinks that man is responsible for his passion.

The existentialist does not think that man is going to help himself by finding in the world some omen by which to orient himself. Because he thinks that man will interpret the omen to suit himself. Therefore, he thinks that man, with no support and no aid, is condemned every moment to invent man. Ponge, in a very fine article, has said, "Man is the future of man." That's exactly it. But if it is taken to mean that this future is recorded in heaven, that God sees it, then it is false, because it would really no longer be a future. If it is taken to mean that, whatever a man may be, there is a future to be forged, a virgin future before him, then this remark is sound. But then we are forlorn.

To give you an example which will enable you to understand forlornness better, I shall cite the case of one of my students who came to see me under the following circumstances: his father was on bad terms with his mother, and, moreover, was inclined to be a collaborationist; his older brother had been killed in the German offensive of 1940, and the young man, with somewhat immature but generous feelings, wanted to avenge him. His mother lived alone with him, very much upset by the half-treason of her husband and the death of her older son; the boy was her only consolation.

The boy was faced with the choice of leaving for England and joining the Free French Forces—that is, leaving his mother behind—or remaining with his mother and helping her to carry on. He was fully aware that the woman lived only for him and that his going-off—and perhaps his death—would plunge her into despair. He was also aware that every act that he did for his mother's sake was a sure thing, in the sense that it was helping her to carry on, whereas every effort he made toward going off and fighting was an uncertain move which might run aground and prove completely useless; for example, on his way to England he might, while passing through Spain, be detained indefinitely in a Spanish camp; he might reach England or Algiers and be stuck in an office at a desk job. As a result, he was faced with two very different kinds of action: one, concrete, immediate, but concerning only one individual; the other concerned an incomparably vaster group, a national collectivity, but for that very reason was dubious, and might be interrupted en route. And, at the same time, he was wavering between two kinds of ethics. On the one hand, an ethics of sympathy, of personal devotion; on the other, a broader ethics, but one whose efficacy was more dubious. He had to choose between the two.

Who could help him choose? Christian doctrine? No. Christian doctrine says, "Be charitable, love your neighbor, take the more rugged path, etc., etc." But which is the more rugged path? Whom should he love as a brother? The fighting man or his mother? Which does the greater good, the vague act of fighting in a group, or the concrete one of helping a particular human being to go on living? Who can decide *a priori*? Nobody. No book of ethics can tell him. The Kantian ethics says, "Never treat any person as a means, but as an end." Very well, if I stay with mother, I'll treat her as an end and not as a means; but by virtue of this very fact, I'm running the risk of treating the people around me who are fighting, as means; and, conversely, if I go to join those who are fighting, I'll be treating them as an end, and, by doing that, I run the risk of treating my mother as a means.

If values are vague, and if they are always too broad for the concrete and specific case that we are considering, the only thing left for us is to trust our instincts. That's what this young man tried to do; and when I saw him, he said, "In the end, feeling is what counts. I ought to choose whichever pushes me in one direction. If I feel that I love my mother enough to sacrifice everything else for her—my desire for vengeance, for action, for adventure—then I'll stay with her. If, on the contrary, I feel that my love for my mother isn't enough, I'll leave."

But how is the value of a feeling determined? What gives his feeling for his mother value? Precisely the fact that he remained with her. I may say that I like so-and-so well enough to sacrifice a certain amount of money for him, but I may say so only if I've done it. I may say "I love my mother well enough to remain with her" if I have remained with her. The only way to determine the value of this affection is, precisely, to perform an act which confirms and defines it. But, since I require this affection to justify my act, I find myself caught in a vicious circle.

On the other hand, Gide has well said that a mock feeling and a true feeling are almost indistinguishable; to decide that I love my mother and will remain with her, or to remain with her by putting on an act, amount somewhat to the same thing. In other words, the feeling is formed by the acts one performs; so, I can not refer to it in order to act upon it. Which means that I can neither seek within myself the true condition which will impel me to act, nor apply to a system of ethics for concepts which will permit me to act. You will say, "At least, he did go to a teacher for advice." But if you seek advice from a priest, for example, you have chosen this priest; you already knew, more or less, just about what advice he was going to give you. In other words, choosing your adviser is involving yourself. The proof of this is that if you are a Christian, you will say, "Consult a priest." But some priests are collaborating, some are just marking time, some are resisting. Which to choose? If the young man chooses a priest who is resisting or collaborating, he has already decided on the kind of advice he's going to get. Therefore, in coming to see me he knew the answer I was going to give him, and I had only one answer to give: "You're free, choose, that is, invent." No general ethics can show you what is to be done; there are no omens in the world. The Catholics will reply, "But there are." Granted—but, in any case, I myself choose the meaning they have.

When I was a prisoner, I knew a rather remarkable young man who was a Jesuit. He had entered the Jesuit order in the following way: he had had a number of very bad breaks; in childhood, his father died, leaving him in poverty, and he was a scholarship student at a religious institution where he was constantly made to feel that he was being kept out of charity; then, he failed to get any of the honors and distinctions that children like; later on, at about eighteen, he bungled a love affair; finally, at twenty-two, he failed in military training, a childish enough matter, but it was the last straw.

This young fellow might well have felt that he had botched everything. It was a sign of something, but of what? He might have taken refuge in bitterness or despair. But he very wisely looked upon all this as a sign that he was not made for secular triumphs, and that only the triumphs of religion, holiness, and faith were open to him. He saw the hand of God in all this, and so he entered the order. Who can help seeing that he alone decided what the sign meant?

Some other interpretation might have been drawn from this series of setbacks; for example, that he might have done better to turn carpenter or revolutionist. Therefore, he is fully responsible for the interpretation. Forlornness implies that we ourselves choose our being. Forlornness and anguish go together.

As for despair, the term has a very simple meaning. It means that we shall confine ourselves to reckoning only with what depends upon our will, or on the ensemble of probabilities which make our action possible. When we want something, we always have to reckon with probabilities. I may be counting on the arrival of a friend. The friend is coming by rail or street-car; this supposes that the train will arrive on schedule, or that the street-car will not jump the track. I am left in the realm of possibility; but possibilities are to be reckoned with only to the point where my action comports with the ensemble of these possibilities, and no further. The moment the possibilities I am considering are not rigorously involved by my action, I ought to disengage myself from them, because no God, no scheme, can adapt the world and its possibilities to my will.

When Descartes said, "Conquer yourself rather than the world," he meant essentially the same thing.

The Marxists to whom I have spoken reply, "You can rely on the support of others in your action, which obviously has certain limits because you're not going to live forever. That means: rely on both what others are doing elsewhere to help you, in China, in Russia, and what they will do later on, after your death, to carry on the action and lead it to its fulfillment, which will be the revolution. You even *have* to rely upon that, otherwise you're immoral." I reply at once that I will always rely on fellow-fighters insofar as these comrades are involved with me in a common struggle, in the unity of a party or a group in which I can more or less make my weight felt; that is, one whose ranks I am in as a fighter and whose movements I am aware of at every moment. In such a situation, relying on the unity and will of the party is exactly like counting on the fact that the train will arrive on time or that the car won't jump the track. But, given that man is free and that there is no human nature for me to depend on, I can not count on men whom I do not know by relying on human goodness or man's concern for the good of society. I don't know what will become of the Russian revolution; I may make an example of it to the extent that at the present time it is apparent that the proletariat plays a part in Russia that it plays in no other nation. But I can't swear that this will inevitably lead to a triumph of the proletariat. I've got to limit myself to what I see.

Given that men are free and that tomorrow they will freely decide what man will be, I cannot be sure that, after my death, fellow-fighters will carry on my work to bring it to its maximum perfection. Tomorrow, after my death, some men may decide to set up Fascism, and the others may be cowardly and muddled enough to let them do it. Fascism will then be the human reality, so much the worse for us.

Actually, things will be as man will have decided they are to be. Does that mean that I should abandon myself to quietism? No. First, I should involve myself; then, act on the old saw, "Nothing ventured, nothing gained." Nor does it mean that I shouldn't belong to a party, but rather that I shall have no illusions and shall do what I can. For example, suppose I ask myself, "Will socialization, as such, ever come about?" I know nothing about it. All I know is that I'm going to do everything in my power to bring it about. Beyond that, I can't count on anything. Quietism is the attitude of people who say, "Let others do what I can't do." The doctrine I am presenting is the very opposite of quietism, since it declares, "There is no reality except in action." Moreover, it goes further, since it adds, "Man is nothing else than his plan; he exists only to the extent that he fulfills himself; he is therefore nothing else than the ensemble of his acts, nothing else than his life."

According to this, we can understand why our doctrine horrifies certain people. Because often the only way they can bear their wretchedness is to think, "Circumstances have been against me. What I've been and done doesn't show my true worth. To be sure, I've had no great love, no great friendship, but that's because I haven't met a man or woman who was worthy. The books I've written haven't been very good because I haven't had the proper leisure. I haven't had children to devote myself to because I didn't find a man with whom I could have spent my life. So there remains within me, unused and quite viable, a host of propensities, inclinations, possibilities, that one wouldn't guess from the mere series of things I've done."

Now, for the existentialist there is really no love other than one which manifests itself in a person's being in love. There is no genius other than one which is expressed in works of art; the genius of Proust is the sum of Proust's works; the genius of Racine is his series of tragedies. Outside of that, there is nothing. Why say that Racine could have written another tragedy, when he didn't write it? A man is involved in life, leaves his impress on it, and outside of that there is nothing. To be sure, this may seem a harsh thought to someone whose life hasn't been a success. But, on the other hand, it prompts people to understand that reality alone is what counts, that dreams, expectations, and hopes warrant no more than to define a man as a disappointed dream, as miscarried hopes, as vain expectations. In other words, to define him negatively and not positively. However, when we say, "You are nothing else than your life," that does not imply that the artist will be judged solely on the basis of his works of art; a thousand other things will contribute toward summing him up. What we mean is that a man is nothing else than a series of undertakings, that he is the sum, the organization, the ensemble of the relationships which make up these undertakings.

When all is said and done, what we are accused of, at bottom, is not our pessimism, but an optimistic toughness. If people throw up to us our works of fiction in which we write about people who are soft, weak, cowardly, and sometimes even downright bad, it's not because these people are soft, weak, cowardly, or bad; because if we were to say, as Zola did, that they are that way because of heredity, the workings of environment, society, because of biological or psychological determinism, people would be reassured. They would say, "Well, that's what we're like, no one can do anything about it." But when the existentialist writes about a coward, he says that this coward is responsible for his cowardice. He's not like that because he has a cowardly heart or lung or brain; he's not like that on account of his physiological make-up; but he's like that because he has made himself a coward by his acts. There's no such thing as a cowardly constitution; there are nervous constitutions; there is poor blood, as the common people say, or there are strong constitutions. But the man whose blood is poor is not a coward on that account, for what makes cowardice is the act of renouncing or yielding. A constitution is not an act; the coward is defined on the basis of the acts he performs.

People feel, in a vague sort of way, that this coward we're talking about is guilty of being a coward, and the thought frightens them. What people would like is that a coward or a hero be born that way.

One of the complaints most frequently made about *The Ways of Freedom** can be summed up as follows: "After all, these people are so spineless, how are you going to make heroes out of them?" This objection almost makes me laugh, for it assumes that people are born heroes. That's what people really want to think. If you're born cowardly, you may set your mind perfectly at rest; there's nothing you can do about it; you'll be cowardly all your life, whatever you may do. If you're born a hero, you may set your mind just as much at rest; you'll be a hero all your life; you'll drink like a hero and eat like a hero. What the existentialist says is that the coward makes himself cowardly, that the hero makes himself heroic. There's always a possibility for the coward not to be cowardly any more and for the hero to stop being heroic. What counts is total involvement; some one particular action or set of circumstances is not total involvement.

Thus, I think we have answered a number of the charges concerning existentialism. You see that it can not be taken for a philosophy of quietism, since it defines man in terms of action; nor for a pessimistic description of man—there is no doctrine more optimistic, since man's destiny is within himself; nor for an attempt to discourage man from acting, since it tells him that the only hope is in his acting and that action is the only thing that enables a man to live. Consequently, we are dealing here with an ethics of action and involvement.

Study Questions

1. In what way does Sartre present a subjectivist theory of ethics?
2. What is Sartre's view of the role of God in human affairs?
3. Define the meaning of "existence precedes essence."
4. What is the source of anguish and forlornness?
5. Explain Sartre's concept of human freedom.

Les Chemins de la Liberté, Sartre's trilogy of novels—TRANS.

The Ones Who Walk Away from Omelas
Ursula K. Le Guin

Ursula K. Le Guin (1929–) is usually classified as a science fiction writer although a more accurate label might be mythological fantasist. The Left Hand of Darkness *is arguably her finest book, exploring life in an androgynous world, and another critically acclaimed work,* The Dispossessed, *imagines a perfect anarchic society. Le Guin has written over seventeen novels, eleven children's books, more than one hundred short stories, two collections of essays, five works of poetry, and two volumes of translation and screenplays of her works.*

To Le Guin's credit she has won five Hugo awards, five Nebulas, the Kafka Award, and a Pushcart Prize, as well as the National Book Award for Children's Literature (for The Farthest Shore*). Among her best known works are* City of Illusions, The Beginning Place, The Lathe of Heaven, The Compass Rose, Unlocking the Air, *and* The Wind's Twelve Quarters *(in which the short story appears that is anthologized here).*

Le Guin is primarily a storyteller but one who tells her tales in a restrained, subtle, evocative way that induces thoughtfulness in the reader. Her stories do not end but resolve themselves in metaphor; her last lines in particular inspire reflection. For example, "But he had not brought anything. His hands were empty, as they had always been" (The Dispossessed*), and "Gravely she walked beside him up the white streets of Havnor, holding his hand like a child coming home" (* The Tombs of Atuan*).*

In "The Ones Who Walk Away from Omelas" Le Guin takes an idea first presented in the great Russian novel The Brothers Karamazov *by Fedor Dostoevsky and later developed by the American philosopher William James in "The Moral Philosopher and the Moral Life." As James expresses it, "If the hypothesis were offered us of a world in which . . . millions [are] kept permanently happy on the simple condition that a certain lost soul on the far-off edge of things should lead a life of lonely torment, . . . how hideous a thing would be its enjoyment when deliberately accepted as the fruit of such a bargain."*

Le Guin paints just such a picture in the literary work that follows, raising a host of ethical questions: Are we justified in denying the rights of one person to attain the well-being of the majority? Are there humane principles that cannot be violated regardless of the good that accrues to humankind? If most people approve of a practice, does that legitimize it as moral—even in a democracy? Does right consists of whatever a culture approves of, as the relativists claim, or are there objective standards against which a society's ethics can be measured? Such questions should be kept in mind in reading Le Guin's short story.

With a clamor of bells that set the swallows soaring, the Festival of Summer came to the city Omelas, bright-towered by the sea. The rigging of the boats in harbor sparkled with flags. In the streets between houses with red roofs and painted walls, between old moss-grown gardens and under avenues of trees, past great parks and public buildings, processions moved. Some were decorous: old people in long stiff robes of mauve and grey, grave master workmen, quiet, merry women carrying their babies and chatting as they walked. In other streets the music beat faster, a shimmering of gong and tambourine, and the people went dancing, the procession was a dance. Children dodged in and out, their high calls rising like the swallows' crossing flights over the music and the singing. All the processions wound towards the north side of the city, where on the great water-meadow called the Green Fields boys and girls, naked in the bright air, with mud-stained feet and ankles and long, lithe arms, exercised their restive horses before the race. The horses wore no gear at all but a halter without bit. Their manes were braided with streamers of silver, gold, and green. They flared their nostrils and pranced and boasted to one another; they were vastly excited, the horse being the only animal who has adopted our ceremonies as his own. Far off to the north and west the mountains stood up half encircling Omelas on her bay. The air of morning was so clear that the snow still crowning the Eighteen Peaks burned with white-gold fire across the miles of sunlit air, under the dark blue of the sky. There was just enough wind to make the banners that marked the racecourse snap and flutter now and then. In the silence of the broad green meadows one could hear the music winding through the city streets, farther and nearer and ever approaching, a cheerful faint sweetness of the air that from time to time trembled and gathered together and broke out into the great joyous clanging of the bells.

Joyous! How is one to tell about joy? How describe the citizens of Omelas?

They were not simple folk, you see, though they were happy. But we do not say the words of cheer much any more. All smiles have become archaic. Given a description such as this one tends to make certain assumptions. Given a description such as this one tends to look next for the King, mounted on a splendid stallion and surrounded by his noble knights, or perhaps in a golden litter borne by great-muscled slaves. But there was no king. They did not use swords, or keep slaves. They were not barbarians. I do not know the rules and laws of their society, but I suspect that they were singularly few. As they did without monarchy and slavery, so they also got on without the stock exchange, the advertisement, the secret police, and the bomb. Yet I repeat that these were not simple folk, not dulcet shepherds, noble savages, bland utopians. They were not less complex than us. The trouble is that we have a bad habit, encouraged by pedants and sophisticates, of considering happiness as something rather stupid. Only pain is intellectual, only evil interesting. This is the treason of the artist: a refusal to admit the banality of evil and the terrible boredom of pain. If you can't lick 'em, join 'em. If it hurts, repeat it. But to praise despair is to condemn delight, to embrace violence is to lose hold of everything else. We have almost lost hold; we can no longer describe a happy man, nor make any celebration of joy. How can I tell you about the people of Omelas? They were not naïve and happy children—though their children were, in fact, happy. They were mature, intelligent, passionate adults whose lives were not wretched. O miracle! but I wish I could describe it better. I wish I could convince you. Omelas sounds in my words like a city in a fairy tale, long ago and far away, once upon a time. Perhaps it would be best if you imagined it as your own fancy bids, assuming it will rise to the occasion, for certainly I cannot suit you all. For instance, how about technology? I think that there would be no cars or helicopters in and above the streets; this follows from the fact that the people of Omelas are happy people. Happiness is based on a just discrimination of what is necessary, what is neither necessary nor destructive, and what is destructive. In the middle category, however—that of the unnecessary but undestructive, that of comfort, luxury, exuberance, etc.—they could perfectly well have central heating, subway trains, washing machines, and all kinds of marvelous devices not yet invented here, floating light-sources, fuelless power, a cure for the common cold. Or they could have none of that: it doesn't matter. As you like it. I incline to think that people from towns up and down the coast have been coming in to Omelas during the last days before the Festival on very fast little trains and double-decked trams, and that the train station of Omelas is actually the handsomest building in town, though plainer than the magnificent Farmers' Market. But even granted trains, I fear that Omelas so far strikes some of you as goody-goody. Smiles, bells, parades, horses, bleh. If so, please add an orgy. If an orgy would help, don't hesitate. Let us not, however, have temples from which issue beautiful nude priests and priestesses already half in ecstasy and ready to copulate with any man or woman, lover or stranger, who desires union with the deep godhead of the blood, although that was my first idea. But really it would be better not to have any temples in Omelas—at least, not manned temples. Religion yes, clergy no. Surely the beautiful nudes can just wander about, offering themselves like divine soufflés to the hunger of the needy and the rapture of the flesh. Let them join the processions. Let tambourines be struck above the copulations, and the glory of desire be proclaimed upon the gongs, and (a not unimportant point) let the offspring of these delightful rituals be beloved and looked after by all. One thing I know there is none of in Omelas is guilt. But what else should there be? I thought at first there were no drugs, but that is puritanical. For those who like it, the faint insistent sweetness of *drooz* may perfume the ways of the city, *drooz* which first brings a great lightness and brilliance to the mind and limbs, and then after some hours a dreamy languor, and wonderful visions at last of the very arcana and inmost secrets of the Universe, as well as exciting the pleasure of sex beyond all belief; and it is not habit-forming. For more modest tastes I think there ought to be beer. What else, what else belongs in the joyous city? The sense of victory, surely, the celebration of courage. But as we did without clergy, let us do without soldiers. The joy built upon successful slaughter is not the right kind of joy; it will not do; it is fearful and it is trivial. A boundless and generous contentment, a magnanimous triumph felt not against some outer enemy but in communion with the finest and fairest in the souls of all men everywhere and the splendor of the world's summer: this is what swells the hearts of the people of Omelas, and the victory they celebrate is that of life. I really don't think many of them need to take *drooz*.

Most of the processions have reached the Green Fields by now. A marvelous smell of cooking goes forth from the red and blue tents of the provisioners. The faces of small children are amiably sticky; in the benign grey beard of a man a couple of crumbs of rich pastry are entangled. The youths and girls have mounted their horses and are beginning to group around the starting line of the course. An old woman, small, fat, and laughing, is passing out flowers from a basket, and tall young men wear her flowers in their shining hair. A child of nine or ten sits at the edge of the crowd, alone, playing on a wooden flute. People pause to listen, and they smile, but they do not speak to him, for he never ceases playing and never sees them, his dark eyes wholly rapt in the sweet, thin magic of the tune.

He finishes, and slowly lowers his hands holding the wooden flute.

As if that little private silence were the signal, all at once a trumpet sounds from the pavilion near the starting line: imperious, melancholy, piercing. The horses rear on their slender legs, and some of them neigh in answer. Sober-faced, the young riders stroke the horses' necks and soothe them, whispering, "Quiet, quiet, there my beauty, my hope. . . ." They begin to form in rank along the starting line. The crowds along the racecourse are like a field of grass and flowers in the wind. The Festival of Summer has begun.

Do you believe? Do you accept the festival, the city, the joy? No? Then let me describe one more thing.

In a basement under one of the beautiful public buildings of Omelas, or perhaps in the cellar of one of its spacious private homes, there is a room. It has one locked door, and no window. A little light seeps in dustily between cracks in the boards, secondhand from a cobwebbed window somewhere across the cellar. In one corner of the little room a couple of mops, with stiff, clotted, foul-smelling heads, stand near a rusty bucket. The floor is dirt, a little damp to the touch, as cellar dirt usually is. The room is about three paces long and two wide: a mere broom closet or disused tool room. In the room a child is sitting. It could be a boy or a girl. It looks about six, but actually is nearly ten. It is feeble-minded. Perhaps it was born defective, or perhaps it has become imbecile through fear, malnutrition, and neglect. It picks its nose and occasionally fumbles vaguely with its toes or genitals, as it sits hunched in the corner farthest from the bucket and the two mops. It is afraid of the mops. It finds them horrible. It shuts its eyes, but it knows the mops are still standing there; and the door is locked; and nobody will come. The door is always locked; and nobody ever comes, except that sometimes—the child has no understanding of time or interval—sometimes the door rattles terribly and opens, and a person, or several people, are there. One of them may come in and kick the child to make it stand up. The others never come close, but peer in at it with frightened, disgusted eyes. The food bowl and the water jug are hastily filled, the door is locked, the eyes disappear. The people at the door never say anything, but the child, who has not always lived in the tool room, and can remember sunlight and its mother's voice, sometimes speaks. "I will be good," it says. "Please let me out. I will be good!" They never answer. The child used to scream for help at night, and cry a good deal, but now it only makes a kind of whining, "eh-haa, eh-haa," and it speaks less and less often. It is so thin there are no calves to its legs; its belly protrudes; it lives on a half-bowl of corn meal and grease a day. It is naked. Its buttocks and thighs are a mass of festered sores, as it sits in its own excrement continually.

They all know it is there, all the people of Omelas. Some of them have come to see it, others are content merely to know it is there. They all know that it has to be there. Some of them understand why, and some do not, but they all understand that their happiness, the beauty of their city, the tenderness of their friendships, the health of their children, the wisdom of their scholars, the skill of their makers, even the abundance of their harvest and the kindly weathers of their skies, depend wholly on this child's abominable misery.

This is usually explained to children when they are between eight and twelve, whenever they seem capable of understanding; and most of those who come to see the child are young people, though often enough an adult comes, or comes back, to see the child. No matter how well the matter has been explained to them, these young spectators are always shocked and sickened at the sight. They feel disgust, which they had thought themselves superior to. They feel anger, outrage, impotence, despite all the explanations. They would like to do something for the child. But there is nothing they can do. If the child were brought up into the sunlight out of that vile place, if it were cleaned and fed and comforted, that would be a good thing, indeed; but if it were done, in that day and hour all the prosperity and beauty and delight of Omelas would wither and be destroyed. Those are the terms. To exchange all the goodness and grace of every life in Omelas for that single, small improvement: to throw away the happiness of thousands for the chance of the happiness of one: that would be to let guilt within the walls indeed.

The terms are strict and absolute; there may not even be a kind word spoken to the child.

Often the young people go home in tears, or in a tearless rage, when they have seen the child and faced this terrible paradox. They may brood over it for weeks or years. But as time goes on they begin to realize that even if the child could be released, it would not get much good of its freedom: a little vague pleasure of warmth and food, no doubt, but little more. It is too degraded and imbecile to know any real joy. It has been afraid too long ever to be free of fear. Its habits are too uncouth for it to respond to humane treatment. Indeed, after so long it would probably be wretched without walls about it to protect it, and darkness for its eyes, and its own excrement to sit in. Their tears at the bitter injustice dry when they begin to perceive the terrible justice of reality, and to accept it. Yet it is their tears and anger, the trying of their generosity and the acceptance of their helplessness, which are perhaps the true source of the splendor of their lives. Theirs is no vapid, irresponsible happiness. They know that they, like the child, are not free. They know compassion. It is the existence of the child, and their knowledge of its existence, that makes possible the nobility of their architecture, the poignancy of their music, the profundity of their science. It is because of the child that they are so gentle with children. They know that if the wretched one were not there snivelling in the dark, the other one, the flute-player, could make no joyful music as the young riders line up in their beauty for the race in the sunlight of the first morning of summer.

Now do you believe in them? Are they not more credible? But there is one more thing to tell, and this is quite incredible.

At times one of the adolescent girls or boys who go to see the child does not go home to weep or rage, does not, in fact, go home at all. Sometimes also a man or woman much older falls silent for a day or two, and then leaves home. These people go out into the street, and walk down the street alone. They keep walking, and walk straight out of the city of Omelas, through the beautiful gates. They keep walking across the farmlands of Omelas. Each one goes alone, youth or girl, man or woman. Night falls; the traveler must pass down village streets, between the houses with yellow-lit windows, and on out into the darkness of the fields. Each alone, they go west or north, towards the mountains. They go on. They leave Omelas, they walk ahead into the darkness, and they do not come back. The place they go towards is a place even less imaginable to most of us than the city of happiness. I cannot describe it at all. It is possible that it does not exist. But they seem to know where they are going, the ones who walk away from Omelas.

Study Questions

1. Is Le Guin expressing a relativist or objectivist view of ethics?
2. Why do some people leave Omelas?
3. Isn't it justified to allow a few to suffer if by doing so the society as a whole is better off?
4. Does it make a moral difference that the person locked in the cellar is a child?
5. Could an action be wrong even if the majority of people in a society agree to it?

On the Waterfront

Director: Elia Kazan

Screenplay: Budd Schulberg

Elia Kazan (1909–) is an American theater and film director as well as a novelist. He directed a number of stage plays including A Streetcar Named Desire, Death of a Salesman, *and* Cat on a Hot Tin Roof, *but he is best known as a director of films such as* A Tree Grows in Brooklyn, *and* East of Eden. *Kazan received Academy Awards as best director for* Gentleman's Agreement *and* On the Waterfront, *and he made successful motion pictures of several of his novels including* America, America *and* The Arrangement. *In his later years he wrote a series of novels,* The Assassins, The Understudy, *and* The Anatolian, *and he published an autobiography entitled* Elia Kazan, A Life.

On the Waterfront *usually makes the critics' list of "best films," and it has been placed on the National Film Registry of the Library of Congress. Among the numerous awards the film has received are the following:* 1954 Academy Awards: *Best Picture, Best Director (Elia Kazan), Best Actor (Marlon Brando), Best Supporting Actress (Eva Marie Saint), Best Art Direction/Set Decoration (B&W), Best Black and White Cinematography, Best Film Editing, Best Story and Screenplay;* 1954 Directors Guild of America Awards: *Best Director (Kazan);* 1955 Golden Globe Awards: *Best Actor—Drama (Marlon Brando), Best Director (Elia Kazan), Best Film—Drama;* 1954 National Board of Review Awards: *Ten Best Films of the Year;* 1954 New York Film Critics Awards: *Best Actor (Marlon Brando), Best Director (Elia Kazan), Best Film;* 1954 Academy Award Nominations: *Best Supporting Actor (Lee J. Cobb, Karl Malden, and Rod Steiger), Best Original Score.*

Synopsis

On the Waterfront explores the world of corrupt labor unions and racketeering bosses, the dockworkers they intimidate through violence, and those with the courage to break the code of silence and stand up to the mob. The intense and dynamic performances by the cast make the film extremely realistic, especially the role played by Marlon Brando using the techniques of method acting. The authenticity of the film is further enhanced by being filmed on the docks of New York City and Hoboken, New Jersey, in cargo holds of ships, the rooftops of tenements, gritty church basements, and working-class bars; actual longshoreman were used as extras. A black-and-white format was deliberately chosen to heighten the sense of the stark environment without comforting color or ambiguity.

The director, Elia Kazan, actually meant the film as self-vindication for his informing on communists before the House Un-American Activities Committee. At that time in 1954, members of the Communist Party and "fellow travelers" were being "purged" from Hollywood and blacklisted from working in films. Although Kazan himself was once sympathetic to communism, he came to regard the system as a threat to American life. He then felt obligated to give evidence against people in the movie industry who were card-carrying communists.

While Kazan regarded his testimony as patriotic, his left-wing friends branded it as traitorous and ostracized him for "ratting" on his friends. Subsequently, when his film won eight Oscars, he felt absolved of those charges, assuming that the awards meant acceptance of the film's premise: we have a moral responsibility to inform on evil organizations. In his 1988 autobiography he writes, "I was tasting vengeance that night and enjoying it. *On the Waterfront* is my own story; every day I worked on that film, I was telling the world where I stood."

Although Kazan may have been justifying himself and settling scores with his enemies, his film does not need any private symbolic significance; it has meaning in its own right. Perhaps the hero is a surrogate for Kazan, and the hoodlums stand for the communist mob that tried to silence him, but overtly the story is about corruption on the docks in the 1950s and about those who act on their conscience against racketeers and thugs. Budd Schulberg's screenplay is, in fact, based on a series of Pulitzer Prize–winning articles published in the *New York Sun* that exposed the union bosses and their connection to organized crime.

The story turns on the growing awareness of Terry Malloy (Marlon Brando), a washed-up boxer who works for the racketeers who control the docks. Specifically, Terry runs errands for the union boss whose name ironically is Johnny Friendly (Lee J. Cobb), and for a lieutenant and lawyer in the organization, Charley Malloy (Rod Steiger), who is Terry's brother.

Terry is part of a system of intimidation and oppression. The mob forces the longshoremen to borrow money at exorbitant rates of interest, extorts a daily payment qualifying them to work, and runs the "shape-up," the morning meetings where hiring bosses decide who will have a job that day. The "tabs" or medallions that entitle a man to work are distributed according to loyalty, not by seniority or performance, and this system of favoritism leaves them little incentive or self-respect. In more ruthless actions, the gangsters beat or kill anyone who threatens their operation, especially those who "squeal" to the authorities. In the end, Terry joins with the sister of a murder victim and an activist priest to destroy the system and restore decency to the working community.

The opening scene of the film shows Johnny Friendly walking up the gangplank from the union shack on the docks followed by a deferential Terry Malloy. A longshoreman named Joey Doyle is planning to testify to the crime commission, and Terry is told to lure him into a trap. Like a number of blue-collar workers at the time, Terry keeps pigeons on the roof, so he uses that as bait. "Joey, Joey Doyle...Hey, I got one of your birds. I recognize him by the band...He flew into my coop. You want him?"

When Joey goes up to claim his pigeon, he is met by two of Friendly's goons who throw him off the roof. The thugs make jokes about Joey's death saying, "I think somebody fell off the roof. He thought he was gonna sing for the Crime Commission. He won't." and "A canary. Maybe he could sing but he couldn't fly."

Terry meanwhile is shocked to witness the murder. "I thought they was gonna talk to him and get him to dummy up," he says, "I figured the worst they was gonna do was lean on him a little bit." The incident signals the start of Terry's moral reflections and a sea change in his attitudes.

The crowd that gathers around Joey's body is also stunned, particularly the major characters: the priest Father Barry (Karl Malden), the boy's sister Edie Doyle (Eva Marie Saint), and his father Pop Doyle (John Hamilton). Edie screams in grief and outrage, "I want to know who killed my brother," but the father is resigned to his death as a way of life on the docks. "Kept telling him. Don't say nothin'. Keep quiet. You'll live longer."

The longshoremen have adopted a relativistic ethic and feel they must conform to the ethos of the waterfront out of self-preservation, while Edie, Father Barry, and eventually Terry recognize more fundamental values that compel them to combat the violence and unfairness.

In a sleazy bar afterwards, Johnny Friendly tries to explain the situation to Terry, realizing he is shaken by the murder.

> You know, takin' over this local took a little doin'. There's some pretty rough fellas in the way. They gave me this (he displays an ugly scar on his neck) to remember them by . . . I got two thousand dues-payin' members in this local—that's $72,000 a year *legitimate* and when each one of 'em puts in a couple of bucks a day just to make sure they work steady—well you figure it out. And that's just for openers. We got the fattest piers in the fattest harbor in the world. Everything moves in and out—we take our cut...You don't suppose I can afford to be boxed out of a deal like this, do ya? A deal I sweated and bled for, on account of one lousy cheese-eater, that Doyle bum, who thinks he can go squealin' to the crime commission? Do ya? Well, DO YA?

"Uncle Johnny" then gives Terry a fifty-dollar bill and promises him a cushy job on the docks. "You check in and you goof off on the coffee bags. OK?" His brother, "Charley the Gent," reinforces the message. "Hey, you got a real friend here. Now don't forget it." Terry seems mollified, and the next day when he is approached by agents from the Waterfront Crime Commission he tells them, "I don't know nothin', I ain't seen nothin', I'm not sayin' nothin'."

Father Barry and Edie Doyle are present at the shape-up the following morning, because as the priest says, "I don't know how much I can do, but I'll never find out unless I come down here and take a good look for myself." Terry is attracted to Edie and awed by the fact that she attends college, while at the same time feeling guilty for his part in her brother's death. When Father Barry offers the basement of his church as a place where the longshoremen can discuss their grievances, Charley gives Terry the special assignment of taking the names of those who attend the meeting.

Although Terry expresses reservations about the job, saying he doesn't want to be a stool pigeon, Charley explains that this is different. "Let me tell you what stooling is. Stooling is when you rat on your friends, the guys you're with." Nevertheless, Terry remains unresolved, and the issue of when squealing is justified comes up repeatedly throughout the film. Should Joey Doyle have informed about the union racketeering, or is that something that should stay within the family? Should the dock workers have told the investigators about Doyle's murder or was it Doyle's own fault because "he couldn't learn to keep his mouth shut"? In response to Father Barry's plea for help, one longshoreman says, "Deaf and dumb. No matter how much we hate the torpedoes, we don't rat."

The code of silence dictates that one shouldn't be a canary, a squealer, a cheese-eater, or a stool pigeon but just "D and D." That principle of not telling your business to anyone "outside," operates even within companies, military, schools, the government, prisons, hospitals, police departments, and so forth, leaving many people conflicted. Obedience, privacy, and safety lie in one direction, conscience in another. If your cause is just, is it then right to inform? Does that override the virtue of loyalty?

Terry does not know if he should betray his friends, or even who his friends are, because his loyalties are divided, his values confused. After he attends the church meeting, which is disrupted by the mob's strong-arm men, Terry tells Friendly "It was a big nothin'. The priest did all the talking." Perhaps this signals a shift in his allegiances.

Edie Doyle and Father Barry are the instruments for Terry's redemption. Through them and the events that unfold, the film takes on a mythic quality while at the same time preserving its raw realism. Their conversations with Terry enable him to grasp the moral depth of the situation, so that he can say to his brother, "There's more to this than I thought, Charley."

At first Terry cannot fathom Edie's generous view of people, raised as he was in a Children's Home on an ethic of self-interest. When she asks him "Which side are you with?" he answers "Me? I'm with me, Terry." The difference in their perspectives is pointed up in several scenes, with Terry finding it increasingly difficult to defend his standpoint. For example, when Terry tells her about his brutal schooling, how the sisters "thought they were going to beat an education into me," she replies

> EDIE: Maybe they just didn't know how to handle you.
> TERRY: How would you have done it?
> EDIE: With a little more patience and kindness. That's what makes people mean and difficult. People don't care enough about them.
> TERRY: Ah, what are you kiddin' me?

Other conversations further illustrate their differences:

> EDIE: Shouldn't everybody care about everybody else?
> TERRY: Boy, what a fruitcake you are!
> EDIE: I mean, isn't everybody a part of everybody else?
> TERRY: And you really believe that drool?
> EDIE: Yes, I do.
> TERRY: . . . You wanna hear my philosophy of life? Do it to him before he does it to you.
> EDIE (complaining): I never met anyone like you. There's not a spark of sentiment or romance or human kindness in your whole body.
> TERRY: What good does it do ya besides get ya in trouble?
> EDIE: And when things and people get in your way, you just knock them aside, get rid of them, is that your idea? . . .
> TERRY: Listen, down here, it's every man for himself. It's keepin' alive. It's standin' in with the right people, so you got a little bit of change jinglin' in your pocket.
> EDIE: And if you don't?
> TERRY: And if you don't—right down.
> EDIE: That's living like an animal.
> TERRY: All right, I'd rather live like an animal than end up like—
> EDIE: Like Joey? Are you afraid to mention his name?

Joey, of course, is the main obstacle to their relationship, and Terry is torn between loyalty to Charley and Johnny Friendly and his desire to help Edie prosecute her brother's killer. When she pleads with him, "Help me if you can, for God's sake," he answers, "Edie, I'd like to help, I'd like to help, but there's nothing I can do."

After Terry receives a subpoena to testify before the Crime Commission Edie asks him:

> EDIE: What are you going to do?
>
> TERRY: I ain't gonna eat cheese for no cops, and that's for sure.
>
> EDIE: It was Johnny Friendly who killed Joey, wasn't it? Or he had him killed, or he had something to do with it, didn't he? He and your big brother Charley? You can't tell me, can you? Because you're part of it. Cause you're just as bad as the worst of them. Tell me the truth, Terry!
>
> TERRY: You'd better go back to that school out in daisyland. You're driving yourself nuts. You're driving me nuts. Quit worrying about the truth all the time. Worry about yourself.
>
> EDIE: I should've known you wouldn't help me. Pop said Johnny Friendly used to own you. Well, I think he still owns you.

Edie then calls him "a bum," which wounds him deeply because he is beginning to feel genuine love for her.

> TERRY: I'm only tryin' to help ya out. I'm tryin' to keep ya from gettin' hurt. What more do ya want me to do?
>
> EDIE: Much more!
>
> TERRY: Wait a minute.
>
> EDIE: Much, much, much more!

Perhaps Edie is asking too much of Terry, especially since self-preservation has prevailed throughout his life over his sense of justice. To name Friendly as the person responsible for Joey's murder would be to risk his livelihood and his life. Terry, in fact, only decides to expose Johnny Friendly when Father Barry receives a beating, which suggests that his action is precipitated by rage not outrage.

Terry and Edie do wind up together after he has done the right thing, and at that point he understands that the violence and injustice cannot go on. Terry rises to the challenge, a less than ordinary man acting in an extraordinary way. He testifies at a hearing and confronts the crime boss, and in this way regains his dignity. "They always said I was a bum," he declares, "Well, I ain't a bum, Edie."

Terry is at his most sensitive with Edie and in handling his pigeons. In one tender scene by the coop on the roof, she presses close to him when he says, "There was a hawk around here before." The two of them are obviously the vulnerable pigeons threatened by predators. When Terry does testify against the mob, all of his pigeons are killed, their necks wrung by a neighborhood friend, Tommy, who regards him as a traitor and a pariah. "A pigeon for a pigeon," Tommy says, tossing a dead bird at him.

Father Barry demands as much of Terry as he asks of himself as a priest, which means that he wants unusual courage. After another long-shoreman named Kayo Nolan is killed because he was cooperating with the Crime Commission, the priest delivers a sermon from the hold of the ship where the man was crushed to death. Seventy-five longshoreman look down from the hatch, dock and loft, including the shape up boss Big Mac and other supporters of Johnny Friendly—Truck, Sonny, and J.P. In something of a set-piece for the stage, Father Barry tells the men that Christ will be there with them if they fight the mobsters.

The screenplay by Schulberg is as follows:

INT HATCH DAY

CLOSE ON FATHER BARRY

He stands over the body of Kayo Nolan, which lies on the pallet and has been covered by a tarpaulin.

FATHER BARRY (aroused): I came down here to keep a promise. I gave Kayo my word that if he stood up to the mob I'd stand up with him all the way. Now Kayo Nolan is dead. He was one of those fellows who had the gift of getting up. But this time they fixed him good—unless it was an accident like Big Mac says.

Pop, Moose, and some of the others glare at Big Mac, who chews his tobacco sullenly. Some of the others snicker "accident."

FATHER BARRY: Some people think the Crucifixion only took place on Calvary. They better wise up. Taking Joey Doyle's life to stop him from testifying is a crucifixion—Dropping a sling on Kayo Nolan because he was ready to spill his guts tomorrow—that's a crucifixion. Every time the mob puts the crusher on a good man—tries to stop him from doing his duty as a citizen—it's a crucifixion.

CLOSE ON TERRY

Voice of Father Barry continues.

FATHER BARRY: And anybody who sits around and lets it happen, keeps silent about something he knows has happened—shares the guilt of it just as much as the Roman soldier who pierced the flesh of Our Lord to see if He was dead.

SHOT OF EDIE ON DOCK

Listening, moved. Terry has come up behind her and stands nearby. She notices him but barely reacts. He listens intently to the Father's words.

CLOSE ON TRUCK

TRUCK: Go back to your church, Father.

INT HATCH DAY

FATHER BARRY (looking up at Truck and pointing to the ship): Boys, this is my church. If you don't think Christ is here on the waterfront, you got another guess coming. And who do you think He lines up with—

CLOSE ON SONNY

SONNY: Get off the dock, Father.

Sonny reaches for a box of rotten bananas on the dock and flings one down into the hatch.

CLOSE ON FATHER BARRY

The banana splatters him, but he ignores it.

BACK TO SONNY ON DOCK

Terry turns to him. Edie notices this and watches with approval.

TERRY: Do that again and I'll flatten you.
SONNY: What're you doing. Joining them—
TERRY: Let him finish.
SONNY: Johnny ain't going to like that, Terry.
TERRY: Let him finish.

Edie looks at him amazed. Terry catches her eye, and then looks down, embarrassed at his good deed. They both turn to watch Father Barry.

CLOSE SHOT CHARLEY

Near Johnny, watching Terry and then looking at Johnny apprehensively.

INT HATCH DAY

FATHER BARRY: Every morning when the hiring boss blows his whistle, Jesus stands alongside you in the shape-up.

More missiles fly, some hitting the Father, but he continues:

He sees why some of you get picked and some of you get passed over. He sees the family men worrying about getting their rent and getting food in the house for the wife and kids. He sees them selling their souls to the mob for a day's pay.

CLOSE ON JOHNNY FRIENDLY

Nodding to Barney. Barney picks up an empty beer can and hurls it down into the hatch.

INT HATCH DAY

It strikes Father Barry and blood etches his forehead. Pop jumps forward and shakes his fist.

POP: By Christ, the next bum who throws something deals with me. I don't care if he's twice my size.

Some of the other longshoremen grumble approval.

FATHER BARRY: What does Christ think of the easy-money boys who do none of the work and take all of the gravy? What does He think of these fellows wearing hundred-and-fifty-dollar suits and diamond rings—on *your* union dues and *your* kickback money? How does He feel about bloodsuckers picking up a longshoreman's work tab and grabbing twenty percent interest at the end of a week?

CLOSE ON J.P.

J.P.: Never mind about that!

CLOSE OF SONNY ON DOCK
Scowling.

Terry, nearby, is increasingly moved by the Father's challenge.

FATHER BARRY: How does He, who spoke up without fear against evil, feel about your silence?
SONNY: Shut up about that!

He reaches for another rotten banana and is poised to throw it. Almost simultaneously, Terry throws a short hard right that flattens Sonny neatly. Edie is watching, a deeply felt gratitude in her eyes.

CLOSE ON JOHNNY FRIENDLY AND TRUCK
A little way off.

TRUCK: You see that?

Johnny presses his lips together but makes no sign.

CLOSE ON TERRY AND EDIE
She moves closer to him. He barely glances at her, then continues listening to Father Barry.

INT HATCH DAY

FATHER BARRY: You want to know what's wrong with our waterfront? It's love of a lousy buck. It's making love of a buck—the cushy job—more important than the love of man. It's forgetting that every fellow down here is your brother in Christ.

Father Barry's voice rises to a climax—

FATHER BARRY: But remember, fellows, Christ is always with you—Christ is in the shape-up, He's in the hatch—He's in the union hall—He's kneeling here beside Nolan—and He's saying with all of you—

CLOSE ON FATHER BARRY

FATHER BARRY: If you do it to the least of mine, you do it to me! What they did to Joey, what they did to Nolan, they're doing to you. And you. And YOU. And only you, with God's help, have the power to knock 'em off for good! (turns to Nolan's corpse) Okay, Kayo? (then looks up and says, harshly) Amen.

Kayo Dugan's body is then lifted out of the hold by a crane with Father Barry riding the pallet beside him. Perhaps the ascent from the depths of the ship is symbolic of the spirit rising from the body as well as the men elevated by a higher vision.

Shortly afterwards, Terry confesses to Father Barry that he'd set up Joey Doyle, saying, "Father, help me. I've got blood on my hands." But he also tells the priest that he cannot bring himself to inform on Friendly and his own brother.

TERRY: You know, if I spill, my life ain't worth a nickel.
FATHER BARRY: And how much is your soul worth if you don't.
TERRY: But it's my own brother they're asking me to finger . . .
FATHER BARRY: So you got a brother. Well, let me tell you something, you got some other brothers—and they're all getting the short end . . . Listen, if I were you, I would walk . . . Never mind. I'm not asking you to do anything. It's your own conscience that's got to do the asking.
TERRY: Conscience . . . I didn't even know I had one until I met you and Edie . . . this conscience stuff can drive you nuts.

Meanwhile Johnny Friendly is growing apprehensive that Terry might inform on him, so he sends Charley to give his brother a forceful warning. The most poignant, memorable, and celebrated scene in the film then follows, with the two brothers talking in the back seat of a taxi.

INT TAXICAB EVENING (N.Y. B.G)

Charley and Terry have just entered the cab.

TERRY: Gee, Charley, I'm sure glad you stopped by for me. I needed to talk to you. What's it they say about blood, it's— (falters)
CHARLEY (looking away coldly): Thicker than water.
DRIVER (gravel voice, without turning around): Where to?
CHARLEY: Four thirty-seven River Street.
TERRY: River Street? I thought we was going to the Garden.

CHARLEY: I've got to cover a bet there on the way over. Anyway, it gives us a chance to talk.

TERRY (good-naturedly): Nothing ever stops you from talking, Charley.

CHARLEY: The grapevine says you picked up a subpoena.

TERRY (noncommittal, sullen.): That's right. . . .

CHARLEY (watching for his reaction): Of course the boys know you too well to mark you down for a cheese-eater.

TERRY: Mm—hmm.

CHARLEY: You know, the boys are getting rather interested in your future.

TERRY: Mm—hmmm.

CHARLEY: They feel you've been sort of left out of things, Terry. They think it's time you had a few little things going for you on the docks.

TERRY: A steady job and a few bucks extra, that's all I wanted.

CHARLEY: Sure, that's all right when you're a kid, but you'll be pushing thirty pretty soon, slugger. It's time you got some ambition.

TERRY: I always figured I'd live longer without it.

CHARLEY: Maybe.

Terry looks at him.

CHARLEY: There's a slot for a boss loader on the new pier we're opening up.

TERRY (interested): Boss loader!

CHARLEY: Ten cents a hundred pounds on everything that moves in and out. And you don't have to lift a finger. It'll be three-four hundred a week just for openers.

TERRY: And for all that dough I don't do nothin'?

CHARLEY: Absolutely nothing. You do nothing and you say nothing. You understand, don't you, kid?

TERRY (struggling with an unfamiliar problem of conscience and loyalties): Yeah—yeah—I guess I do—but there's a lot more to this whole thing than I thought, Charley.

CHARLEY: You don't mean you're thinking of testifying against— (turns a thumb in toward himself)

TERRY: I don't know—I don't know! I tell you I ain't made up my mind yet. That's what I wanted to talk to you about.

CHARLEY (patiently, as to a stubborn child): Listen, Terry, these piers we handle through the local—you know what they're worth to us?

TERRY: I know. I know.

CHARLEY: Well, then, you know Cousin Johnny isn't going to jeopardize a setup like that for one rubber-lipped—

TERRY (simultaneous): Don't say that!

CHARLEY (continuing): —ex-tanker who's walking on his heels—?

TERRY: Don't say that!

CHARLEY: What the hell!!!

TERRY: I could have been better!

CHARLEY: Listen, that isn't the point.

TERRY: I could have been better!

CHARLEY: The point is—there isn't much time, kid.

There is a painful pause, as they appraise each other.

TERRY (desperately): I tell you, Charley, I haven't made up my mind!

CHARLEY: Make up your mind, kid, I beg you, before we get to four thirty-seven River. . . .

TERRY (stunned): Four thirty-seven—that isn't where Gerry G . . . ?

Charley nods solemnly. Terry grows more agitated.

TERRY: Charley . . . you wouldn't take me to Gerry G . . . ?

Charley continues looking at him. He does not deny it. They stare at each other for a moment. Then suddenly Terry starts out of the cab. Charley pulls a pistol. Terry is motionless, now, looking at Charley.

CHARLEY: Take the boss loading, kid. For God's sake. I don't want to hurt you.

TERRY (hushed, gently guiding the gun down toward Charley's lap): Charley . . . Charley . . . Wow. . . .

CHARLEY (genuinely): I wish I didn't have to do this, Terry.

Terry eyes him, beaten. Charley leans back and looks at Terry strangely. Terry raises his hands above his head, somewhat in the manner of a prizefighter mitting the crowd. The image nicks Charley's memory.

TERRY (an accusing sigh): Wow. . . .

CHARLEY (gently): What do you weigh these days, slugger?

TERRY (shrugs): —eighty-seven, eighty-eight. What's it to you?

CHARLEY (nostalgically): Gee, when you tipped one seventy-five you were beautiful. You should've been another Billy Conn. That skunk I got to manage you brought you along too fast.

TERRY: It wasn't him! (years of abuse crying out in him) It was you, Charley. You and Johnny. Like the night the two of youse come in the dressing room and says, 'Kid, this ain't your night— we're going for the price on Wilson.' *It ain't my night.* I'd of taken Wilson apart that night! I was ready—remember the early rounds throwing them combinations. So what happens—This bum Wilson he gets the title shot—outdoors in the ball park!—and what do I get—a couple of bucks and a one-way ticket to Palookaville. (more and more aroused as he relives it) It was you, Charley. You

was my brother. You should of looked out for me. Instead of making me take them dives for the short-end money.
CHARLEY (defensively): I always had a bet down for you. You saw some money.
TERRY (agonized): See! You don't understand!
CHARLEY: I tried to keep you in good with Johnny.
TERRY: You don't understand! I could've been a contender. I could've had class and been somebody. Real class. Instead of a bum, let's face it, which is what I am. It was you, Charley.

Charley takes a long, fond look at Terry. Then he glances quickly out the window.

MEDUIM SHOT WATERFRONT NIGHT

From Charley's angle. A gloomy light reflects the street numbers—433—435—

INT CLOSE CAB ON CHARLEY AND TERRY NIGHT

TERRY: It was you, Charley. . . .
CHARLEY (turning back to Terry, his tone suddenly changed): Okay—I'll tell him I couldn't bring you in. Ten to one they won't believe it, but—go ahead, blow. Jump out, quick, and keep going . . . and God help you from here on in . . .

Elia Kazan has commented on Brando's mesmerizing acting in this scene: ". . . what was extraordinary about his performance, I feel, is the contrast of the tough-guy front and the extreme delicacy and gentle cast of his behavior. What other actor, when his brother draws a pistol to force him to do something shameful, would put his hand on the gun and push it away with the gentleness of a caress? Who else could read 'Oh, Charley!' in a tone of reproach that is so loving and so melancholy and suggest the terrific depth of pain?"

Following the confrontation between the brothers in the taxi, Charley is murdered, presumably by Friendly's orders, and the gangsters even attempt to kill Edie; Terry saves her from being run down by a car. This finally galvanizes Terry to fight the union racketeers.

At first he wants to shoot Friendly, but Father Barry convinces him to use the force of law rather than violence. ". . . don't fight him like a hoodlum down here in the jungle because that's just what he wants. He'll hit you in the head and plead self-defense. You fight him in the court-room tomorrow, with the truth as you know the truth." In a symbolic gesture, Terry throws his gun at a picture of Friendly and his boss that is hanging above the bar.

The next day Terry testifies in court against the crooked union and the mobsters, and he remains resolved and determined despite ostracism from his friends and threats from Johnny Friendly. "You've just dug your own grave," Friendly screams at him in court. "You're dead on this waterfront and every waterfront from Boston to New Orleans. You don't drive a truck or a cab. You don't push a baggage rack. You don't work no place. YOU'RE DEAD."

Despite Friendly's warning, Terry puts on Joey Doyle's jacket in the morning and appears at the shape-up. Everyone is chosen except him, but rather than withdrawing he challenges Friendly at the union shack before a crowd of longshoremen.

EXT UNION LOCAL OFFICE WHARF DAY

Terry walks compulsively down the ramp to the office.

TERRY (shouts): Hey, Friendly! Johnny Friendly, come out here!

Johnny comes out of his office followed by his goons....

TERRY: You want to know something? Take the heater away and you're nothin'—take the good goods away, and the kickback and shakedown cabbage away and the pistoleros—(indicating the others)—away and you're a great big hunk of nothing—(takes a deep breath as if relieved) Your guts is all in your wallet and your trigger finger!

JOHNNY (with fury): Go on talkin'. You're talkin' yourself right into the river. Go on, go on. . . .

TERRY (voice rising defiantly): I'm glad what I done today, see? You give it to Joey, you give it to Nolan, you give it to Charley who was one of your own. You thought you was God Almighty instead of a cheap—conniving—good-for-nothing bum! So I'm glad what I done—you hear me?—glad what I done!

JOHNNY (coldly): You ratted on us, Terry.

TERRY (aware of fellow longshoremen anxiously watching the duel): From where you stand, maybe. But I'm standing over here now. I was rattin' on myself all them years and didn't know it, helpin' punks like you against people like Pop and Nolan.

A furious and brutal fight ensues which Terry wins, but Friendly's thugs then join in and he is kicked and punched nearly senseless. When Edie and Father Barry arrive Friendly gives them his battered body. "You want 'im. You can have 'im. The little rat's yours."

The rebellion might have ended there, but the longshoremen rally behind Terry and refuse to work unless he does. Friendly replies "Work! He can't even walk." When Friendly orders the men to load the ships,

Pop Doyle says, "All my life you pushed me around," and shoves him into the scummy water while the men cheer at his humiliation.

No one moves, waiting for a sign from Terry. He is bloody and barely conscious, but Father Barry helps him to his feet despite Edie's protests.

As the groggy Terry starts up the ramp, Edie reaches out to him. Father Barry holds her back.

FATHER BARRY: Leave him alone. Take your hands off him—Leave him alone.

Staggering, moving painfully forward, Terry starts up the ramp. Edie's instinct is to help him but Father Barry, knowing the stakes of this symbolic act, holds her back. Terry stumbles, but steadies himself and moves forward as if driven on by Father Barry's will.

TERRY APPROACHING PIER ENTRANCE

As he staggers forward as if blinded, the longshoremen form a line on either side of him, awed by his courage, waiting to see if he'll make it. Terry keeps going.

REVERSE ANGLE BOSS STEVEDORE TERRY'S POV

Waiting at pier entrance as Terry approaches. Shot out of focus as Terry would see him through bloody haze.

TERRY

As the men who have formed a path for him watch intently, Terry staggers up until he is face to face with the Stevedore. He gathers himself as if to say, "I'm ready. Let's go!"

STEVEDORE (calls officially): All right—let's go to work!

As Terry goes past him into the pier, the men with a sense of inevitability fall in behind him.

JOHNNY FRIENDLY

Hurrying forward in a last desperate effort to stop the men from following Terry in.

JOHNNY (screams): Where you guys goin'? Wait a minute!

As they stream past him.

I'll be back! I'll be back! And I'll remember every last one of ya!

He points at them accusingly. But they keep following Terry into the pier.

WIDER ANGLE PIER ENTRANCE

As Father Barry and Edie look on, Stevedore blows his whistle for work to begin. Longshoremen by the hundreds march into the pier behind Terry like a conquering army. In the B.G. a frenzied Johnny Friendly is still screaming, "I'll be back! I'll be back!"

The threat, real as it is, is lost in the forward progress of Terry and the ragtail army of dock workers he now leads.

FADE OUT

During this final scene Terry resembles paintings of Christ with blood streaming down his face and his eyes turned heavenward. He has, in fact, been transformed into a martyr, and the film has become a morality play in which good triumphs over evil. The longshoremen had adopted a relativistic ethic and felt they had to conform to the ethos of the waterfront, while Edie, Father Barry, and Terry had recognized more fundamental, humane values that made them fight the evil. At the end, the men, too, understand that corruption must be opposed, for their own good and because some principles such as fairness are basic to human dignity.

Study Questions

1. Do you have an ethical responsibility to inform on your friends if they are doing something wrong? Should you report someone in your class for cheating because it is unfair to those who prepared for the exam?

2. How does Father Barry show the connection between Christ and the situation on the docks?

3. What was the significance to Terry's life in his throwing the fight so the racketeers could win their bets?

4. Why were Terry and Edie attracted to each other? Was Terry's relationship with his brother good for him?

5. Does *On the Waterfront* endorse an ethical relativism or an objectivism? How, exactly?

B. Ideals in Living: Doing What's Right or Achieving the Good

Two principal and competing theories have emerged in philosophic history as to what would be an ideal human life: that pleasure or happiness constitutes the goal in living, or that we should live in accordance with moral principles and responsibilities. The first can be broadly categorized as *hedonism,* or in its social form *utilitarianism;* the second as a *duty ethic,* usually associated with the philosopher Immanuel Kant.

Secondary theories include the *religious ethic* and *self-realization,* both of which are discussed below, as well as such philosophies as naturalism, humanism, and Stoicism.

Hedonism, the theory that we should live for the sake of pleasure or happiness, is probably the most ancient, natural, and persuasive theory in ethics. Most people would agree that pleasure or happiness is the goal in life, which supports the idea that it is in fact the supreme value, "that at which all things aim." (The idea that popularity establishes truth is a doubtful assumption, but several ethicists have maintained it.)

Although people may differ in their views on the meaning of happiness, very few would want anything else. Some people define happiness as arising from honor, recognition, status, and prestige; others regard it as the satisfaction of our appetites, that is, sensuous pleasure and physical gratification; still others see it as the acquisition of wealth, property, and financial power; and philosophers sometimes identify it as contemplation of timeless realities.

Besides the prevalence of hedonism, several arguments have been offered as proof that happiness is the ideal. For example, it has been pointed out that happiness is self-sufficient. If we are happy we lack nothing, and if we lack something we are not truly happy. Another consideration is that happiness is always chosen for its own sake and never as a means to anything further; we do a number of things in order to be happy, but we do not seek happiness for any other goal. Like a mountain peak, it leads nowhere.

Hedonism proper originated with two ancient Greek philosophers, Aristippus (c. 435–356 B.C.) and Epicurus (342–270 B.C.). In their individual ways, both men affirmed pleasure or happiness as the good. Aristippus, the founder of a band called the Cyrenaics, emphasized bodily pleasure that is intense (i.e., strong), brief, and immediately available. He would have agreed with the twelfth-century Persian poet Omar Khayyam who wrote in the *Rubaiyat,* "Ah, make the most of what we yet may spend, / Before we too into the Dust descend; / Dust into Dust and under dust to lie / Sans wine, sans Song, sans Singer, and—sans End!"

The Cyrenaics are generally regarded as short-sighted, preferring to enjoy themselves today despite the pains that would follow tomorrow.

Drinking heavily may be fun now, but the more we drink the more we regret it in the morning. Also, the Cyrenaics were unwilling to endure any present discomfort for the sake of future pleasure. They argued that the future is only a hope just as the past is a dream, so we should never suffer for the sake of some enjoyment that might not come. According to one story, a Cyrenaic boy was carrying a bag of gold and, because it was heavy, he threw it away. However, if he had suffered the discomfort of carrying it, chances are he would have thanked himself later, so this approach to life seems rather foolish.

Epicurus developed hedonism in a more intelligent way, endorsing enjoyment that is serene, lasting, and pervasive in our lives overall. To be an Epicurean we do not, "Eat, drink, and be merry," but relish in a tranquil way the more subtle modes of enjoyment. Epicurus lived simply, and in his name today we become gourmets and connoisseurs, relishing the flavor of food and drink and nourishing our spirit. In one surviving fragment he wrote, "I know not how I can conceive the good if I withdraw the pleasure of taste, and withdraw the pleasures of love, and withdraw the pleasures of hearing, and withdraw the pleasurable emotions caused to sight by beautiful form." Epicurus expressed a joy and celebration of living that is hard to resist. It is reminiscent of the Greek poet Homer who said, "Dear to us ever is the banquet and the harp and the dance and changes of raiment and the warm bath and love and sleep."

Unfortunately Epicureanism became a negative philosophy that tried to avoid pain more than seek pleasure. The walled garden in which Epicurus taught became a fitting symbol of this outlook because it walled trouble out rather than walling enjoyment in.

The hedonism of both Aristippus and Epicurus was of an individualistic kind, solely concerned with maximizing enjoyment for the person. In the nineteenth century, hedonism underwent a major change when two English philosophers, Jeremy Bentham and John Stuart Mill, transformed it into a doctrine aimed at social welfare. That is, Bentham and Mill created a *Utilitarian* theory that interpreted the good as the greatest amount of happiness for the greatest number of people.

Bentham is usually credited as the founder of the Utilitarian philosophy, and his emphasis was on increasing the sum total of happiness for society. He wanted governments to enact legislation based on utilitarian principles, taking the maximization of pleasure as the goal. Bentham wrote "Pleasure is in itself a good—nay even, setting aside immunity from pain, the only good; pain is in itself an evil—and, indeed without exception, the only evil." There could be more or less pleasure but not better and worse, and Bentham created a "hedonic calculus" for assessing the amount of pleasure that any given action would yield. In this way, he hoped to determine precisely and scientifically which act would produce more pleasure for more people. The most ethical act is that with the highest pleasure quotient.

Mill also accepted utilitarianism but he rejected Bentham's formulation that only the amount of pleasure matters. He maintained that the quality of pleasure is more important than its quantity. According to Mill, pleasures can be higher or lower, better or worse, superior or inferior, and only an ethic that recommends pleasures of a higher kind is consistent with human dignity. We need to differentiate between the pleasures of a pig and that of a person, and only human pleasures can be considered as the good in life. "It is better to be a human being dissatisfied than a pig satisfied," Mill wrote, and better to be an unhappy Socrates than a happy fool.

Unfortunately for Mill, this corrective weakens rather than strengthens the hedonistic theory. For Mill is endorsing the qualitatively higher activity over the pleasurable one, the human experience over the animalistic, even if no pleasure is involved. Perhaps it is better to be human even if that means dissatisfaction, but such a position is contrary to the hedonistic idea that pleasure is most important.

All hedonists encounter this problem when they try to refine the doctrine by introducing qualitative distinctions. Yet without this refinement hedonism seems a vulgar philosophy, recommending animal pleasure as the human ideal.

One general problem with utilitarian hedonism should also be mentioned. Seeking the greatest happiness for the greatest number may seem highly moralistic, but suppose that the majority would be happiest if they hanged the minority; on utilitarian grounds that would be justified. Because atrocities could be committed in the name of utilitarianism, we can see that the theory has a fatal ethical flaw.

Some utilitarians try to meet this objection by adopting a *rule* rather than an *act* utilitarianism. According to the first, we should endorse rules that make people happy such as 'minority rights should be protected.' Whether that saves the moral character of utilitarianism is a matter of debate.

The *religious ethic* by contrast centers on the being of God, and advocates living in accordance with His will. Judaism, Christianity, Islam, Buddhism, Hinduism, Taoism, and so forth all tell their followers to lead a virtuous life in the spirit of God. Of course, the nature of that life has been variously painted depending on the particular scriptures and theological system that is followed. In whatever way the ideal life is defined, the common feature of religious ethics is that we exist to glorify God and carry out his will on earth.

To take Christian ethics as a prime example, the Christian believes in unconditional love that is expressed by the Greek term *agape*. In an agape type of love, we want what is best for the other person, regardless of whether it would be good for us. Our love for others even impels us to let them go if that would be the best thing for them, sacrificing our welfare for theirs. For we are in the relationship not for what we can get but for what we can give, and if we are hurting the other person or not meeting their needs, then we should leave, regardless of how painful we might find it.

According to Christian ethics, this kind of love should extend not just to personal relationships but to all humanity. We should treat our fellow human beings with selfless love, acting for their sake and not for what we will get in return. Our intention should be to dedicate ourselves to humankind just as Christ did, not because human beings have earned it but because they need our care and compassion; our love ought to be unconditional. This is how the best parents treat their children, loving them most when they deserve it least, if that is what they need.

One problem with this theory, of course, is that selfish people will take advantage of anyone who is generous; in fact, their selfish behavior will be encouraged by default. The abused wife who continually forgives her abusive husband out of agapeistic love is not helping him or herself. Furthermore, athletes cannot do what is best for the opposing team, any more than business people can meet the needs of their competitor. If a loan officer practiced the biblical precept, "Give to him who asketh of thee, and he who would borrow of thee turn not thou away," the bank would soon be out of business. In the same way, governments cannot act in the best interests of rival nations or their countries would be invaded and enslaved. Christian love is a beautiful ideal which can function between people who are equally committed to each other, but it becomes impractical in the wider world when people act out of self-interest.

A further problem has plagued all forms of religious ethics that are based on the word of God. Plato in the *Euthyphro* first raised the pivotal question as to whether an act is right because God wills it or whether God wills an act because it is right. That is, does the rightness of such things as honesty or faithfulness depend upon the fact that God commands them, or did God command them because of their (intrinsic) rightness?

It seems more defensible to argue that God tells us to act in a certain way, for example, to follow the Ten Commandments, because he knows it is right, otherwise he is making arbitrary rules, commanding actions for no good reason. What's more, even a God cannot turn values upside down, making the wrong right or the right wrong. Even if he changed his mind (which an omniscient God would not do), he could not make hating our neighbor a virtue and loving him a vice.

This means that ethics is independent of religion rather than being derived from it. If we believe we should love one another that is not because it is God's word but because it is the right thing to do. We are left with the question of what makes actions right, but at least we know it is not because God says so.

The *duty ethic* stands diametrically opposed to hedonism (while sharing some features in common with religious ethics). Rather than recommending pleasure or happiness as the goal in life, this ethical theory stresses our responsibilities and obligations to humanity. Immanuel Kant, the chief spokesman for this ethic, maintained that we should always act in terms of universal principles, respecting the moral law. The good life is not maximum enjoyment but doing our moral duty.

To determine our duty in any situation, Kant formulated what he calls the Categorical Imperative: "Act so that the maxim for our actions could become a universal law." That is, whenever we consider an action we must ask ourselves whether we could recommend it for all people at all times in all places. Genuine ethical conduct is universalizable to Kant, for if an action is right it is always right. Conversely, if we make an exception for ourselves, claiming that other people are obliged to act in a certain way but we are not, that is a sure sign of unethical conduct.

It is important to notice what Kant excludes from the circle of worthwhile conduct. The consequences of an action do not determine its rightness, including a hedonistic or Utilitarian outcome. To Kant, it is irrelevant whether pleasure or any other good is produced, for it is the inherent rightness of an action that makes it worthwhile not its consequences. Whatever can be supported by universalizable moral principles is justified, and whatever cannot be so justified should never be done, regardless of the benefits that might accrue from it.

Kant also rejects the idea that we should behave toward others with sympathy, warmth, concern, or even impulses of love, because emotional inclinations of any kind are an unreliable basis for morality. If an act is grounded in universal principles then we can be sure it is right, but feelings are too fluid and fickle; their ethical value cannot be tested. Actions based on principle, however, can always be verified by asking whether we would want everyone to behave in the same way.

Kant's theory seems very pure and admirable—a much higher ethic than a hedonistic desire for pleasure. At the same time, we wonder whether it is too strict and uncompromising. To take one aspect of his philosophy, Kant seems wrong in thinking that the consequences of actions are unimportant in deciding how to behave, for we would not want to do what is correct in principle but harmful in its effects. For example, we should not give someone with a weak heart very bad news, or tell a potential murderer where his victim is hiding, despite the fact that truth-telling is a virtue. To Kant, the ends do not justify the means, but then neither do the means justify the ends. As for the irrelevance of feelings, we would much rather be surrounded by people who are generous and loving by disposition than on principle. Kant seems far too ready to dismiss the emotions and to elevate reason as the acid test of morality.

Critics have pointed out other problems in the Kantian theory, particularly that of finding any principle that is universalizable. For example, the moral rule that we should keep promises has exceptions; for if a marriage breaks down to the point where the children are threatened, then the marriage vows should probably be broken. (Some promises should never have been made; others should not be kept when circumstances radically alter.) That we should not steal has exceptions in the case of spies acting for our nation, or if some tyrant denies people food (as in the case of Jean Valjean). That we should not kill has exceptions in situations of self-defense, to protect those we love, and perhaps for euthanasia, capital punishment, and just wars.

A principle may be right, but that does not mean it should always be done; sometimes it should be suspended for the larger good. Kant fails to differentiate between making exceptions for ourselves and qualifying a principle because of particular circumstances and overall human welfare. He has created a noble theory, extolling a life of duty, but he is so concerned with principles that he forgets about people.

Nevertheless, the idea of dutifully following principles is very appealing as a dignified and disciplined approach to life. It stands in major contrast to hedonism, and makes pleasure seem like a cheap alternative. If we could embrace both theories that would be ideal, but very often we cannot do our duty and achieve happiness at the same time. One or the other must be sacrificed, and in such cases we are forced to decide which is more important.

Self-realization is still another option in ethics. This theory has surfaced at various points in intellectual history, mainly in England and the United States although the Greek philosopher Aristotle and the German philosopher G. W. F. Hegel are often regarded as its founders. F. H. Bradley, T. H. Green, Josiah Royce, and W. C. Hocking are usually identified with self-realization as well as the psychologists Carl Rogers, Erich Fromm, and Abraham Maslow.

According to the self-realization theory, following principles or following God is too austere, and hedonism is shallow and deficient in moral fiber. (Something can be pleasurable but not good, and good but not pleasurable, therefore pleasure cannot be taken as the good in life.) As a more inclusive approach the self-realizationist recommends the complete development of our talents, capacities, and interests. We should actualize our potentialities and become all we are capable of becoming. To realize ourselves we should not only satisfy our physical need for food, sex, and shelter, in the most fulfilling way, but realize our higher tendencies as well. For example, our social part should be realized by joining together with others in a rich community; we are gregarious creatures by nature and need outlets for caring and nurture. Also included in human nature is an intellectual curiosity, which is expressed in the need to know, a spiritual sense of reverence and holiness that seeks union with God, and an aesthetic sensibility that enables us to appreciate beauty and create works of art. All of these individual and human capacities should be developed to the utmost.

Unfortunately, we are not sure that everyone's self should be realized. Mass murderers such as Charles Manson and Richard Speck, the Boston Strangler and Jack the Ripper, as well as tyrants such as Hitler and Mussolini, Attila the Hun and Genghis Khan, should suppress their tendencies rather than develop them. And if realizing oneself is not necessarily good, then the good cannot be defined as self-realization.

The preceding thumbnail sketch should convey some sense of the various ethical ideals. The selections that follow in Section B trace the two main alternatives: hedonism, specifically Mill's utilitarianism, and the ethic of duty of Immanuel Kant. *Antigone* by Jean Anouih dramatizes the clash of the two as does Steven Spielberg in *Saving Private Ryan*. Once the theories are elaborated in philosophic, literary, and cinematic form, the reader is in a position to decide which one is worth adopting as a personal ethic.

Utilitarianism (Chapter II)
John Stuart Mill

John Stuart Mill (1806–1873) was an English philosopher, economist, and political scientist who significantly affected nineteenth-century thought. His best known writing, "On Liberty," was influential in promoting individual freedom against social tyranny, and his book On the Subjection of Women *helped launch the women's suffrage movement. His other main writings include* A System of Logic, Principles of Political Economy, Three Essays on Religion, *and* Utilitarianism. *Although Mill lived part of his life in France, he did serve in the British Parliament where he supported such measures as birth control and compulsory education as well as equality for women; these stands made him a radical in his time.*

    Mill's book, Utilitarianism, *expounds the theory of the greatest happiness for the greatest number as previously described. As a disciple of his father, James Mill, and of Jeremy Bentham, Mill was a strong advocate of the utilitarian theory as well as both empiricism and rationalism. Although he preferred modes of happiness that are qualitatively higher, he thought we should maximize happiness or pleasure for all, and that there could be no higher aim for humanity. To Mill, this "principle of utility" is the standard for ethical conduct and the highest rendering of the golden rule.*

What Utilitarianism Is

A passing remark is all that needs be given to the ignorant blunder of supposing that those who stand up for utility as the test of right and wrong, use the term in that restricted and merely colloquial sense in which utility is opposed to pleasure. An apology is due to the philosophical opponents of utilitarianism, for even the momentary appearance of confounding them with any one capable of so absurd a misconception; which is the more extraordinary, inasmuch as the contrary accusation, of referring everything to pleasure, and that too in its grossest form, is another of the common charges against utilitarianism: and, as has been pointedly remarked by an able writer, the same sort of persons, and often the very same persons, denounce the theory "as impracticably dry when the word utility precedes the word pleasure, and as too practicably voluptuous when the word pleasure precedes the word utility." Those who know anything about the matter are aware that every writer, from Epicurus to Bentham, who maintained the theory of utility, meant by it, not something to be contradistinguished from pleasure, but pleasure itself, together with exemption from pain; and instead of opposing the useful to the agreeable or the ornamental, have always declared that the useful means these, among other things. Yet the common herd, including the herd of writers, not only in newspapers and periodicals, but in books of weight and pretension, are perpetually falling into this shallow mistake. Having caught up the word utilitarian, while knowing nothing whatever about it but its sound, they habitually express by it the rejection, or the neglect, of pleasure in some of its forms; of beauty, or ornament, or of amusement. Nor is the term thus ignorantly misapplied solely in disparagement, but occasionally in compliment; as though it implied superiority to frivolity and the mere pleasures of the moment. And this perverted use is the only one in which the word is popularly known, and the one from which the new generation are acquiring their sole notion of its meaning. Those who introduced the word, but who had for many years discontinued it as a distinctive appellation, may well feel themselves called upon to resume it, if by doing so they can hope to contribute anything towards rescuing it from this utter degradation.*

The creed which accepts as the foundation of morals, Utility, or the Greatest Happiness Principle, holds that actions are right in proportion as they tend to promote happiness, wrong as they tend to produce the reverse of happiness. By happiness is intended pleasure, and the absence of pain; by unhappiness, pain, and the privation of pleasure. To give a clear view of the moral standard set up by the theory, much more requires to be said; in particular, what things it includes in the ideas of pain and pleasure; and to what extent this is left an open question. But these supplementary explanations do not affect the theory of life on which this theory of morality is grounded—namely, that pleasure, and freedom from pain, are the only things desirable as ends; and that all desirable things (which are as numerous in the utilitarian as in any other scheme) are desirable either for the pleasure inherent in themselves, or as means to the promotion of pleasure and the prevention of pain.

Now, such a theory of life excites in many minds, and among them in some of the most estimable in feeling and purpose, inveterate dislike. To suppose that life has (as they express it) no higher end than pleasure—no better and nobler object of desire and pursuit—they designate as utterly mean and grovelling; as a doctrine worthy only of swine, to whom

---

*The author of this essay has reason for believing himself to be the first person who brought the word utilitarian into use. He did not invent it, but adopted it from a passing expression in Mr. Galt's *Annals of the Parish*. After using it as a designation for several years, he and others abandoned it from a growing dislike to anything resembling a badge or watchword of sectarian distinction. But as a name for one single opinion, not a set of opinions—to denote the recognition of utility as a standard, not any particular way of applying it—the term supplies a want in the language, and offers, in many cases, a convenient mode of avoiding tiresome circumlocution.

the followers of Epicurus were, at a very early period, contemptuously likened; and modern holders of the doctrine are occasionally made the subject of equally polite comparisons by its German, French, and English assailants.

When thus attacked, the Epicureans have always answered, that it is not they, but their accusers, who represent human nature in a degrading light; since the accusation supposes human beings to be capable of no pleasures except those of which swine are capable. If this supposition were true, the charge could not be gainsaid, but would then be no longer an imputation; for if the sources of pleasure were precisely the same to human beings and to swine, the rule of life which is good enough for the one would be good enough for the other. The comparison of the Epicurean life to that of beasts is felt as degrading, precisely because a beast's pleasures do not satisfy a human being's conceptions of happiness. Human beings have faculties more elevated than the animal appetites, and when once made conscious of them, do not regard anything as happiness which does not include their gratification. I do not, indeed, consider the Epicureans to have been by any means faultless in drawing out their scheme of consequences from the utilitarian principle. To do this in any sufficient manner, many Stoic, as well as Christian elements require to be included. But there is no known Epicurean theory of life which does not assign to the pleasures of the intellect, of the feelings and imagination, and of the moral sentiments, a much higher value as pleasures than to those of mere sensation. It must be admitted, however, that utilitarian writers in general have placed the superiority of mental over bodily pleasures chiefly in the greater permanency, safety, uncostliness, etc., of the former—that is, in their circumstantial advantages rather than in their intrinsic nature. And on all these points utilitarians have fully proved their case; but they might have taken the other, and, as it may be called, higher ground, with entire consistency. It is quite compatible with the principle of utility to recognize the fact, that some *kinds* of pleasure are more desirable and more valuable than others. It would be absurd that while, in estimating all other things, quality is considered as well as quantity, the estimation of pleasures should be supposed to depend on quantity alone.

If I am asked, what I mean by difference of quality in pleasures, or what makes one pleasure more valuable than another, merely as a pleasure, except its being greater in amount, there is but one possible answer. Of two pleasures, if there be one to which all or almost all who have experience of both give a decided preference, irrespective of any feeling of moral obligation to prefer it, that is the more desirable pleasure. If one of the two is, by those who are competently acquainted with both, placed so far above the other that they prefer it, even though knowing it to be attended with a greater amount of discontent, and would not resign it for any quantity, of the other pleasure which their nature is capable of, we are justified in ascribing to the preferred enjoyment a superiority in quality, so far outweighing quantity as to render it, in comparison, of small account.

Now it is an unquestionable fact that those who are equally acquainted with, and equally capable of appreciating and enjoying, both, do give a most marked preference to the manner of existence which employs their higher faculties. Few human creatures would consent to be changed into any of the lower animals, for a promise of the fullest allowance of a beast's pleasures; no intelligent human being would consent to be a fool, no instructed person would be an ignoramus, no person of feeling and conscience would be selfish and base, even though they should be persuaded that the fool, the dunce, or the rascal is better satisfied with his lot than they are with theirs. They would not resign what they possess more than he for the most complete satisfaction of all the desires which they have in common with him. If they ever fancy they would, it is only in cases of unhappiness so extreme, that to escape from it they would exchange their lot for almost any other, however undesirable in their own eyes. A being of higher faculties requires more to make him happy, is capable probably of more acute suffering, and certainly accessible to it at more points, than one of an inferior type; but in spite of these liabilities, he can never really wish to sink into what he feels to be a lower grade of existence. We may give what explanation we please of this unwillingness; we may attribute it to pride, a name which is given indiscriminately to some of the most and to some of the least estimable feelings of which mankind are capable: we may refer it to the love of liberty and personal independence, an appeal to which was with the Stoics one of the most effective means for the inculcation of it; to the love of power, or to the love of excitement, both of which do really enter into and contribute to it: but its most appropriate appellation is a sense of dignity, which all human beings possess in one form or other, and in some, though by no means in exact, proportion to their higher faculties, and which is so essential a part of the happiness of those in whom it is strong, that nothing which conflicts with it could be, otherwise than momentarily, an object of desire to them. Whoever supposes that this preference takes place at a sacrifice of happiness—that the superior being, in anything like equal circumstances, is not happier than the inferior—confounds the two very different ideas, of happiness, and content. It is indisputable that the being whose capacities of enjoyment are low, has the greatest chance of having them fully satisfied; and a highly endowed being will always feel that any happiness which he can look for, as the world is constituted, is imperfect. But he can learn to bear its imperfections, if they are at all bearable; and they will not make him envy the being who is indeed unconscious of the imperfections, but only because he feels not at all the good which those imperfections qualify. It is better to be a human being dissatisfied than a pig satisfied; better to be Socrates dissatisfied than a fool satisfied. And if the fool, or the pig, are of a different opinion, it is because they only know their own side of the question. The other party to the comparison knows both sides.

It may be objected, that many who are capable of the higher pleasures, occasionally, under the influence of temptation, postpone them to the lower. But this is quite compatible with a full appreciation of the intrinsic superiority of the higher. Men often, from infirmity of character, make their election for the nearer good, though they know it to be the less valuable; and this no less when the choice is between two bodily pleasures, than when it is between bodily and mental. They pursue sensual indulgences to the injury of health, though perfectly aware that health is the greater good. It may be further objected, that many who begin with youthful enthusiasm for everything noble, as they advance in years sink into indolence and selfishness. But I do not believe that those who undergo this very common change, voluntarily choose the lower description of pleasures in preference to the higher. I believe that before they devote themselves exclusively to the one, they have already become incapable of the other. Capacity for the nobler feelings is in most natures a very tender plant, easily killed, not only by hostile influences, but by mere want of sustenance; and in the majority of young persons it speedily dies away if the occupations to which their position in life has devoted them, and the society into which it has thrown them, are not favourable to keeping that higher capacity in exercise. Men lose their high aspirations as they lose their intellectual tastes, because they have not time or opportunity for indulging them; and they addict themselves to inferior pleasures, not because they deliberately prefer them, but because they are either the only ones to which they have access, or the only ones which they are any longer capable of enjoying. It may be questioned whether any one who has remained equally susceptible to both classes of pleasures, ever knowingly and calmly preferred the lower; though many, in all ages, have broken down in an ineffectual attempt to combine both.

From this verdict of the only competent judges, I apprehend there can be no appeal. On a question which is the best worth having of two pleasures, or which of two modes of existence is the most grateful to the feelings, apart from its moral attributes and from its consequences, the judgment of those who are qualified by knowledge of both, or, if they differ, that of the majority among them, must be admitted as final. And there needs be the less hesitation to accept this judgment respecting the quality of pleasures, since there is no other tribunal to be referred to even on the question of quantity. What means are there of determining which is the acutest of two pains, or the intensest of two pleasurable sensations, except the general suffrage of those who are familiar with both? Neither pains nor pleasures are homogeneous, and pain is always heterogeneous with pleasure. What is there to decide whether a particular pleasure is worth purchasing at the cost of a particular pain, except the feelings and judgment of the experienced? When, therefore, those feelings and judgment declare the pleasures derived from the higher faculties to be preferable *in kind,* apart from the question of intensity, to those of which the animal nature, disjoined from the higher faculties, is susceptible, they are entitled on this subject to the same regard.

I have dwelt on this point, as being a necessary part of a perfectly just conception of Utility or Happiness, considered as the directive rule of human conduct. But it is by no means an indispensable condition to the acceptance of the utilitarian standard; for that standard is not the agent's own greatest happiness, but the greatest amount of happiness altogether; and if it may possibly be doubted whether a noble character is always the happier for its nobleness, there can be no doubt that it makes other people happier, and that the world in general is immensely a gainer by it. Utilitarianism, therefore, could only attain its end by the general cultivation of nobleness of character, even if each individual were only benefited by the nobleness of others, and his own, so far as happiness is concerned, were a sheer deduction from the benefit. But the bare enunciation of such an absurdity as this last, renders refutation superfluous.

According to the Greatest Happiness Principle, as above explained, the ultimate end, with reference to and for the sake of which all other things are desirable (whether we are considering our own good or that of other people), is an existence exempt as far as possible from pain, and as rich as possible in enjoyments, both in point of quantity and quality; the test of quality, and the rule for measuring it against quantity, being the preference felt by those who in their opportunities of experience, to which must be added their habits of self-consciousness and self-observation, are best furnished with the means of comparison. This, being, according to the utilitarian opinion, the end of human action, is necessarily also the standard of morality; which may accordingly be defined, the rules and precepts for human conduct, by the observance of which an existence such as has been described might be, to the greatest extent possible, secured to all mankind; and not to them only, but, so far as the nature of things admits, to the whole sentient creation.

Against this doctrine, however, arises another class of objectors, who say that happiness, in any form, cannot be the rational purpose of human life and action; because, in the first place, it is unattainable: and they contemptuously ask, what right hast thou to be happy? a question which Mr. Carlyle clenches by the addition, What right, a short time ago, hadst thou even *to be?* Next, they say, that men can do *without* happiness; that all noble human beings have felt this, and could not have become noble but by learning the lesson of Entsagen, or renunciation; which lesson, thoroughly learnt and submitted to, they affirm to be the beginning and necessary condition of all virtue.

The first of these objections would go to the root of the matter were it well founded; for if no happiness is to be had at all by human beings, the attainment of it cannot be the end of morality, or of any rational conduct. Though, even in that case, something might still be said for the utilitarian theory; since utility includes not solely the pursuit of happiness, but the prevention or mitigation of unhappiness; and if the former aim be chimerical, there will be all the greater scope and more imperative need for the latter, so long at least as mankind think fit to live, and do not take refuge in the simultaneous act of suicide recommended under certain conditions by Novalis. When, however, it is thus positively asserted to be impossible that human life should be happy, the assertion, if not something like a verbal quibble, is at least an exaggeration. If by happiness be meant a continuity of highly pleasurable excitement, it is evident enough that this is impossible. A state of exalted pleasure lasts only moments, or in some cases, and with some intermissions, hours or days, and is the occasional brilliant flash of enjoyment, not its permanent and steady flame. Of this the philosophers who have taught that happiness is the end of life were as fully aware as those who taunt them. The happiness which they meant was not a life of rapture; but moments of such, in an existence made up of few and transitory pains, many and various pleasures, with a decided predominance of the active over the passive, and having as the foundation of the whole, not to expect more from life than it is capable of bestowing. A life thus composed, to those who have been fortunate enough to obtain it, has always appeared worthy of the name of happiness. And such an existence is even now the lot of many, during some considerable portion of their lives. The present wretched education, and wretched social arrangements, are the only real hindrance to its being attainable by almost all.

The objectors perhaps may doubt whether human beings, if taught to consider happiness as the end of life, would be satisfied with such a moderate share of it. But great numbers of mankind have been satisfied with much less. The main constituents of a satisfied life appear to be two, either of which by itself is often found sufficient for the purpose: tranquillity, and excitement. With much tranquillity, many find that they can be content with very little pleasure: with much excitement, many can reconcile themselves to a considerable quantity of pain. There is assuredly no inherent impossibility in enabling even the mass of mankind to unite both; since the two are so far from being incompatible that they are in natural alliance, the prolongation of either being a preparation for, and exciting a wish for, the other. It is only those in whom indolence amounts to a vice, that do not desire excitement after an interval of repose: it is only those in whom the need of excitement is a disease, that feel the tranquility which follows excitement dull and insipid, instead of pleasurable in direct proportion to the excitement which preceded it. When people who are tolerably fortunate in their outward lot do not find in life sufficient enjoyment to make it valuable to them, the cause generally is, caring for nobody but themselves. To those who have neither public nor private affections, the excitements of life are much curtailed, and in any case dwindle in value as the time approaches when all selfish interests must be terminated by death: while those who leave after them objects of personal affection, and especially those who have also cultivated a fellow-feeling with the collective interests of mankind, retain as lively an interest in life on the eve of death as in the vigor of youth and health. Next to selfishness, the principal cause which makes life unsatisfactory is want of mental cultivation. A cultivated mind—I do not mean that of a philosopher, but any mind to which the fountains of knowledge have been opened, and which has been taught, in any tolerable degree, to exercise its faculties—finds sources of inexhaustible interest in all that surrounds it; in the objects of nature, the achievements of art, the imaginations of poetry, the incidents of history, the ways of mankind, past and present, and their prospects in the future. It is possible, indeed, to become indifferent to all this, and that too without having exhausted a thousandth part of it; but only when one has had from the beginning no moral or human interest in these things, and has sought in them only the gratification of curiosity . . .

I must again repeat, what the assailants of utilitarianism seldom have the justice to acknowledge, that the happiness which forms the utilitarian standard of what is right in conduct, is not the agent's own happiness, but that of all concerned. As between his own happiness and that of others, utilitarianism requires him to be as strictly impartial as a disinterested and benevolent spectator. In the golden rule of Jesus of Nazareth, we read the complete spirit of the ethics of utility. To do as you would be done by, and to love your neighbor as yourself, constitute the ideal perfection of utilitarian morality. As the means of making the nearest approach to this ideal, utility would enjoin, first, that laws and social arrangements should place the happiness, or (as speaking practically it may be called) the interest, of every individual, as nearly as possible in harmony with the interest of the whole; and secondly, that education and opinion, which have so vast a power over human character, should so use that power as to establish in the mind of every individual an indissoluble association between his own happiness and the good of the whole; especially between his own happiness and the practice of such modes of conduct, negative and positive, as regard for the universal happiness prescribes; so that not only he may be unable to conceive the possibility of happiness to himself, consistently with conduct opposed to the general good, but also that a direct impulse to promote the general good may be in every individual one of the habitual motives of action, and the sentiments connected there with may fill a large and prominent place in every human being's sentient existence.

Study Questions

1. What is the principle of Utility, and how can it be applied in moral decision making?
2. How does Mill define happiness?
3. What is Mill's criterion for differentiating between more and less desirable pleasures?
4. According to Mill, under what circumstances do people find insufficient enjoyment in life?
5. Suppose that it would bring happiness to the majority to remove the minority, as happened in Yugoslavia during "ethnic cleansing." Would that be justified? Why or why not?

Groundwork of the Metaphysic of Morals (Chapter 1)

Immanuel Kant

Immanuel Kant (1724–1804) was a German philosopher who is generally regarded as one of the greatest minds in the history of philosophy. Kant was principally concerned with epistemology, metaphysics, ethics, and religion, in that order. His central work, the Critique of Pure Reason, *deals with theory of knowledge, and attempts a synthesis of sense perception and reason. The* Critique of Practical Reason *explains Kant's concept of the freedom of the individual, and his* General Natural History *and* Theory of the Heavens *contains various scientific views.*

In the Groundwork of the Metaphysic of Morals, *an excerpt from which appears below, Kant presents a foundation for ethical conduct. Instead of the happiness principle of Bentham and Mill, he offers his Categorical Imperative: "I ought never to act except in such a way that I can also will that my maxim should become a universal law." Kant also maintains that a good will is critically important in ethical behavior because we should only will actions that are right for all. Everyone is required to do his or her duty by willing those acts that are right in themselves and therefore universal obligations; whether happiness is produced is irrelevant.*

Passage from Ordinary Rational Knowledge of Morality to Philosophical

The good will

It is impossible to conceive anything at all in the world, or even out of it, which can be taken as good without qualification, except a *good will*. Intelligence, wit, judgement, and any other *talents* of the mind we may care to name, or courage, resolution, and constancy of purpose, as qualities of *temperament*, are without doubt good and desirable in many respects; but they can also be extremely bad and hurtful when the will is not good which has to make use of these gifts of nature, and which for this reason has the term *'character'* applied to its peculiar quality. It is exactly the same with *gifts of fortune*. Power, wealth, honor, even health and that complete well-being and contentment with one's state which goes by the name of *'happiness'*, produce boldness, and as a consequence often over-boldness as well, unless a good will is present by which their influence on the mind—and so too the whole principle of action—may be corrected and adjusted to universal ends; not to mention that a rational and impartial spectator can never feel approval in contemplating the uninterrupted prosperity of a being graced by no touch of a pure and good will, and that consequently a good will seems to constitute the indispensable condition of our very worthiness to be happy.

Some qualities are even helpful to this good will itself and can make its task very much easier. They have none the less no inner unconditioned worth, but rather presuppose a good will which sets a limit to the esteem in which they are rightly held and does not permit us to regard them as absolutely good. Moderation in affections and passions, self-control, and sober reflection are not only good in many respects: they may even seem to constitute part of the *inner* worth of a person. Yet they are far from being properly described as good without qualification (however unconditionally they have been commended by the ancients). For without the principles of a good will they may become exceedingly bad; and the very coolness of a scoundrel makes him, not merely more dangerous, but also immediately more abominable in our eyes than we should have taken him to be without it.

The good will and its results

A good will is not good because of what it effects or accomplishes—because of its fitness for attaining some proposed end: it is good through its willing alone—that is, good in itself. Considered in itself it is to be esteemed beyond comparison as far higher than anything it could ever bring about merely in order to favour some inclination or, if you like, the sum total of inclinations. Even if, by some special disfavour of destiny or by the niggardly endowment of step-motherly nature, this will is entirely lacking in power to carry out its intentions; if by its utmost effort it still accomplishes nothing, and only good will is left (not, admittedly, as a mere wish, but as the straining of every means so far as they are in our control); even then it would still shine like a jewel for its own sake as something which has its full value in itself. Its usefulness or fruitfulness can neither add to, nor subtract from, this value. Its usefulness would be merely, as it were, the setting which enables us to handle it better in our ordinary dealings or to attract the attention of those not yet sufficiently expert, but not to commend it to experts or to determine its value.

The function of reason

Yet in this Idea of the absolute value of a mere will, all useful results being left out of account in its assessment, there is something so strange that, in spite of all the agreement it receives even from ordinary reason, there must arise the suspicion that perhaps its secret basis is merely some high-flown fantasticality, and that we may have misunderstood the purpose of nature in attaching reason to our will as its governor. We will therefore submit our Idea to an examination from this point of view.

In the natural constitution of an organic being—that is, of one contrived for the purpose of life—let us take it as a principle that in it no organ is to be found for any end unless it is also the most appropriate to that end and the best fitted for it. Suppose now that for a being possessed of reason and a will the real purpose of nature were his *preservation*, his *welfare*, or in a word his *happiness*. In that case nature would have hit on a very bad arrangement by choosing reason in the creature to carry out this purpose. For all the actions he has to perform with this end in view, and the whole rule of his behavior, would have been mapped out for him far more accurately by instinct; and the end in question could have been maintained far more surely by instinct than it ever can be by reason. If reason should have been imparted to this favoured creature as well, it would have had to serve him only for contemplating the happy disposition of his nature, for admiring it, for enjoying it, and for being grateful to its beneficent Cause—not for subjecting his power of appetition to such feeble and defective guidance or for meddling incompetently with the purposes of nature. In a word, nature would have prevented reason from striking out into a *practical use* and from presuming, with its feeble vision, to think out for itself a plan for happiness and for the means to its attainment. Nature would herself have taken over the choice, not only of ends, but also of means, and would with wise precaution have entrusted both to instinct alone.

In actual fact too we find that the more a cultivated reason concerns itself with the aim of enjoying life and happiness, the farther does man get away from true contentment. This is why there arises in many, and that too in those who have made most trial of this use of reason, if they are only candid enough to admit it, a certain degree of *misology*—that is, a hatred of reason; for when they balance all the advantage they draw, I will not say from thinking out all the arts of ordinary indulgence, but even from science (which in the last resort seems to them to be also an indulgence of the mind), they discover that they have in fact only brought more trouble on their heads than they have gained in the way of happiness. On this account they come to envy, rather than to despise, the more common run of men, who are closer to the guidance of mere natural instinct, and who do not allow their reason to have much influence on their conduct. So far we must admit that the judgement of those who seek to moderate—and even to reduce below zero—the conceited glorification of such advantages as reason is supposed to provide in the way of happiness and contentment with life is in no way soured or ungrateful to the goodness with which the world is governed. These judgements rather have as their hidden ground the Idea of another and much more worthy purpose of existence, for which, and not for happiness, reason is quite properly designed, and to which, therefore, as a supreme condition the private purposes of man must for the most part be subordinated.

For since reason is not sufficiently serviceable for guiding the will safely as regards its objects and the satisfaction of all our needs (which it in part even multiplies)—a purpose for which an implanted natural instinct would have led us much more surely; and since none the less reason as been imparted to us as a practical power—that is, as one which is to have influence on the *will*; its true function must be to produce a *will* which is *good*, not as a *means* to some further end, but *in itself*; and for this function reason was absolutely necessary in a world where nature, in distributing her aptitudes, has everywhere else gone to work in a purposive manner. Such a will need not on this account be the sole and complete good, but it must be the highest good and the condition of all the rest, even of all our demands for happiness. In that case we can easily reconcile with the wisdom of nature our observation that the cultivation of reason which is required for the first and unconditioned purpose may in many ways, at least in this life, restrict the attainment of the second purpose—namely, happiness—which is always conditioned; and indeed that it can even reduce happiness to less than zero without nature proceeding contrary to its purpose; for reason, which recognises as its highest practical function the establishment of a good will, in attaining this end is capable only of its own peculiar kind of contentment—contentment in fulfilling a purpose which in turn is determined by reason alone, even if this fulfillment should often involve interference with the purposes of inclination.

The good will and duty

We have now to elucidate the concept of a will estimable in itself and good apart from any further end. This concept, which is already present in a sound natural understanding and requires not so much to be taught as merely to be clarified, always holds the highest place in estimating the total worth of our actions and constitutes the condition of all the rest. We will therefore take up the concept of *duty*, which includes that of a good will, exposed, however, to certain subjective limitations and obstacles. These, so far from hiding a good will or disguising it, rather bring it out by contrast and make it shine forth more brightly.

I will here pass over all actions already recognized as contrary to duty, however useful they may be with a view to this or that end; for about these the question does not even arise whether they could have been done *for the sake of duty* inasmuch as they are directly opposed to it. I will also set aside actions which in fact accord with duty, yet for which men have *no immediate inclination*, but perform them because impelled to do so by some other inclination. For there it is easy to decide whether the action which accords with duty has been done *from duty* or from some purpose of self-interest. This distinction is far more difficult to perceive when the action accords with duty and the subject has in addition an *immediate* inclination to the action. For example, it certainly accords with duty that a grocer should not overcharge his inexperienced customer; and where there is much competition a sensible shopkeeper refrains from so doing and keeps to a fixed and general price for everybody so that a child can buy from him just as well as anyone else. Thus people are served *honestly*; but this is not nearly enough to justify us in believing that the shopkeeper has acted in this way from duty or from principles of fair dealing; his interest required him to do so. We cannot assume him to have in addition an immediate inclination towards his customers, leading him, as it were out of love, to give no man preference over another in the matter of price. Thus the action was done neither from duty nor from immediate inclination, but solely from purposes of self-interest.

On the other hand, to preserve one's life is a duty, and besides this every one has also an immediate inclination to do so. But on account of this the often anxious precautions taken by the greater part of mankind for this purpose have no inner worth, and the maxim of their action is without moral content. They do protect their lives *in conformity with duty*, but not *from the motive of duty*. When on the contrary, disappointments and hopeless misery have quite taken away the taste for life; when a wretched man, strong in soul and more angered at his fate than faint-hearted or cast down, longs for death and still preserves his life without loving it—not from inclination or fear but from duty; then indeed his maxim has a moral content . . .

It is doubtless in this sense that we should understand too the passages from Scripture in which we are commanded to love our neighbor and even our enemy. For love out of inclination cannot be commanded; but kindness done from duty—although no inclination impels us, and even although natural and unconquerable disinclination stands in our way—is *practical*, and not *pathological*, love, residing in the will and not in the propensions of feeling, in principles of action and not of melting compassion; and it is this practical love alone which can be an object of command.

The formal principle of duty

Our second proposition is this: An action done from duty has its moral worth, *not in the purpose* to be attained by it, but in the maxim according with which it is decided upon; it depends therefore, not on the realization of the object of the action, but solely on the *principle of volition* in accordance with which, irrespective of all objects of the faculty of desire, the action has been performed. That the purposes we may have in our actions, and also their effects considered as ends and motives of the will, can give to actions no unconditioned and moral worth is clear from what has gone before. Where then can this worth be found if we are not to find it in the will's relation to the effect hoped for from the action? It can be found nowhere but *in the principle of the will,* irrespective of the ends which can be brought about by such an action; for between its *a priori* principle, which is formal, and its *a posteriori* motive, which is material, the will stands, so to speak, at a parting of the ways; and since it must be determined by some principle, it will have to be determined by the formal principle of volition when an action is done from duty, where, as we have seen, every material principle is taken away from it.

Reverence for the law

Our third proposition, as an inference from the two preceding, I would express thus: *Duty is the necessity to act out of reverence for the law.* For an object as the effect of my proposed action I can have an *inclination,* but *never reverence,* precisely because it is merely the effect, and not the activity, of a will. Similarly for inclination as such, whether my own or that of another, I cannot have reverence: I can at most in the first case approve, and in the second case sometimes even love—that is, regard it as favourable to my own advantage. Only something which is conjoined with my will solely as a ground and never as an effect—something which does not serve my inclination, but outweighs it or at least leaves it entirely out of account in my choice—and therefore only bare law for its own sake, can be an object of reverence and therewith a command. Now an action done from duty has to set aside altogether the influence of inclination, and along with inclination every object of the will; so there is nothing left able to determine the will except objectively the *law* and subjectively *pure reverence* for this practical law, and therefore the maxim* of obeying this law even to the detriment of all my inclinations.

Thus the moral worth of an action does not depend on the result expected from it, and so too does not depend on any principle of action that needs to borrow its motive from this expected result. For all these results (agreeable states and even the promotion of happiness in others) could have been brought about by other causes as well, and consequently their production did not require the will of a rational being, in which, however, the highest and unconditioned good can alone be found. Therefore nothing but the *idea of the law* in itself, *which admittedly is present only in a rational being*—so far as it, and not an expected result, is the ground determining the will—can constitute that pre-eminent good which we call

---

*A *maxim* is the subjective principle of a volition: an objective principle (that is, one which would also serve subjectively as a practical principle for all rational beings if reason had full control over the faculty of desire) is a practical *law.*—Trans.

moral, a good which is already present in the person acting on this idea and has not to be awaited merely from the result.[†]

The categorical imperative

But what kind of law can this be the thought of which, even without regard to the results expected from it, has to determine the will if this is to be called good absolutely and without qualification? Since I have robbed the will of every inducement that might arise for it as a consequence of obeying any particular law, nothing is left but the conformity of actions to universal law as such, and this alone must serve the will as its principle. That is to say, I ought never to act except in such a way *that I can also will that my maxim should become a universal law.* Here bare conformity to universal law as such (without having as its base any law prescribing particular actions) is what serves the will as its principle, and must so serve it if duty is not to be everywhere an empty delusion and a chimerical concept. The ordinary reason of mankind also agrees with this completely in its practical judgements and always has the aforesaid principle before its eyes.

Take this question, for example. May I not, when I am hard pressed, make a promise with the intention of not keeping it? Here I readily distinguish the two senses which the question can have—Is it prudent, or is it right, to make a false promise? The first no doubt can often be the case. I do indeed see that it is not enough for me to extricate myself from present embarrassment by this subterfuge: I have to consider whether from

---

[†]It might be urged against me that I have merely tried, under cover of the word 'reverence', to take refuge in an obscure feeling instead of giving a clearly articulated answer to the question by means of a concept of reason. Yet although reverence is a feeling, it is not a feeling *received* through outside influence, but one *self-produced* by a rational concept, and therefore specifically distinct from feelings of the first kind, all of which can be reduced to inclination or fear. What I recognise immediately as law for me, I recognise with reverence, which means merely consciousness of the *subordination* of my will to a law without the mediation of external influences on my senses. Immediate determination of the will by the law and consciousness of this determination is called 'reverence', so that reverence is regarded as the *effect* of the law on the subject and not as the *cause* of the law. Reverence is properly awareness of a value which demolishes my self-love. Hence there is something which is regarded neither as an object of inclination nor as an object of fear, though it has at the same time analogy with both. The *object* of reverence is the *law* alone—that law which we impose *on ourselves* but yet as necessary in itself. Considered as a law, we are subject to it without any consultation of self-love; considered as self-imposed it is a consequence of our will. In the first respect it is analogous to fear, in the second to inclination. All reverence for a person is properly only reverence for the law (of honesty and so on) of which that person gives us an example. Because we regard the developments of our talents as a duty, we see too in a man of talent a sort of *example of the law* (the law of becoming like him by practice), and this is what constitutes our reverence for him. All moral *interest*, so-called, consists solely in *reverence* for the law.—TRANS.

this lie there may not subsequently accrue to me much greater inconvenience than that from which I now escape, and also—since, with all my supposed *astuteness*, to foresee the consequences is not so easy that I can be sure there is no chance, once confidence in me is lost, of this proving far more disadvantageous than all the ills I now think to avoid—whether it may not be a *more prudent* action to proceed here on a general maxim and make it my habit not to give a promise except with the intention of keeping it. Yet it becomes clear to me at once that such a maxim is always founded solely on fear of consequences. To tell the truth for the sake of duty is something entirely different from doing so out of concern for inconvenient results; for in the first case the concept of the action already contains in itself a law for me, while in the second case I have first of all to look around elsewhere in order to see what effects may be bound up with it for me. When I deviate from the principle of duty, this is quite certainly bad; but if I desert my prudential maxim, this can often be greatly to my advantage, though it is admittedly safer to stick to it. Suppose I seek, however, to learn in the quickest way and yet unerringly how to solve the problem 'Does a lying promise accord with duty?' I have then to ask myself 'Should I really be content that my maxim (the maxim of getting out of a difficulty by a false promise) should hold as a universal law (one valid both for myself and others)? And could I really say to myself that every one may make a false promise if he finds himself in a difficulty from which he can extricate himself in no other way?' I then become aware at once that I can indeed will to lie, but I can by no means will a universal law of lying; for by such a law there could properly be no promises at all, since it would be futile to profess a will for future action to others who would not believe my profession or who, if they did so overhastily, would pay me back in like coin; and consequently my maxim, as soon as it was made a universal law, would be bound to annul itself.

Thus I need no far-reaching ingenuity to find out what I have to do in order to possess a good will. Inexperienced in the course of world affairs and incapable of being prepared for all the chances that happen in it, I ask myself only 'Can you also will that your maxim should become a universal law?' Where you cannot, it is to be rejected, and that not because of a prospective loss to you or even to others, but because it cannot fit as a principle into a possible enactment of universal law. For such an enactment reason compels my immediate reverence, into whose grounds (which the philosopher may investigate) I have as yet no *insight*, although I do at least understand this much: reverence is the assessment of a worth which far outweighs all the worth of what is commended by inclination, and the necessity for me to act out of *pure* reverence for the practical law is what constitutes duty, to which every other motive must give way because it is the condition of a will good *in itself*, whose value is above all else.

Study Questions

1. What does Kant mean by a "good will"?
2. Does Kant believe that reason is the best way to attain happiness?
3. Why does Kant think that we should not act out of inclination but out of duty? Would you rather live next to someone who is kind by disposition or on principle?
4. Explain the meaning of the categorical imperative. How can it be criticized?
5. In what way(s) does Kant's formalistic ethic differ from Mill's teleological approach?

Antigone
Jean Anouilh
(trans. by Lewis Galantiére)

Jean Anouilh (1910–1987) was a French playwright first celebrated for his Antigone, *which was interpreted as both a parable of the German Occupation and a statement of existentialism. Anouilh's other works, notably* Point of Departure, Becket, *and* Waltz of the Toreadors, *range from historical to surrealistic to comic, but the common element in all of his plays is a political pessimism and a pervasive metaphysical despair.*

The conflict between happiness and duty, previously described, provides the dramatic force in Jean Anouilh's Antigone. *For Creon the king is committed to securing the maximum good for his country despite the violence done to decency, justice, honesty, and family love, whereas Antigone, his niece, is primarily motivated by personal integrity and pure principles despite the futility of her stand and the threat of death. The moral conflict that occurs is much more subtle than a mere clash between altruism and egoism because both characters appear altruistic in their behavior. Antigone does what she feels she must do, uncompromisingly and courageously, and Creon takes the necessary steps to promote the well-being of the society when, initially, he never wished to be king.*

Despite the fact that they are equally unselfish, the two characters operate on fundamentally different levels and cannot communicate. Creon presents arguments showing the fruitlessness of Antigone's conduct, which is of course irrelevant to her righteousness and Antigone criticizes Creon's lies and self-betrayal, which is beside the point when one is working for the happiness of society. Since Creon cannot yield in the direction of right any more than Antigone can modify her position relative to the good, the outcome is decided by power and Antigone is killed. However, the moral dilemma remains unresolved.

In the following section of the play Antigone's views clash with Creon's specifically when she attempts to bury the body of her brother Polynices. Creon had decreed that the body was to remain exposed upon a hill because Polynices had died a traitor. He had led a revolt against his brother Eteocles, thus precipitating a bloody civil war in which the two brothers had killed one another. When Creon ascended to the throne he declared Eteocles a national hero and Polynices anathema; his body was to be left above ground to decay as a gesture of detestation and an awful warning to potential revolutionaries.

CREON: Why did you try to bury your brother?

ANTIGONE: I owed it to him.

CREON: I had forbidden it.

ANTIGONE: I owed it to him. Those who are not buried wander eternally and find no rest. If my brother were alive, and he came home weary after a long day's hunting, I should kneel down and unlace his boots, I should fetch him food and drink, I should see that his bed was ready for him. Polynices is home from the hunt. I owe it to him to unlock the house of the dead in which my father and my mother are waiting to welcome him. Polynices has earned his rest.

CREON: Polynices was a rebel and a traitor, and you know it.

ANTIGONE: He was my brother.

CREON: You heard my edict. It was proclaimed throughout Thebes. You read my edict. It was posted up on the city walls.

ANTIGONE: Of course I did.

CREON: You knew the punishment I decreed for any person who attempted to give him burial.

ANTIGONE: Yes, I knew the punishment.

CREON: Did you by any chance act on the assumption that a daughter of Oedipus, a daughter of Oedipus' stubborn pride, was above the law?

ANTIGONE: No, I did not act on that assumption.

CREON: Because if you had acted on that assumption, Antigone, you would have been deeply wrong. Nobody has a more sacred obligation to obey the law than those who make the law. You are a daughter of law-makers, a daughter of kings, Antigone. You must observe the law.

ANTIGONE: Had I been a scullery maid washing my dishes when that law was read aloud to me, I should have scrubbed the greasy water from my arms and gone out in my apron to bury my brother.

CREON: What nonsense! If you had been a scullery maid, there would have been no doubt in your mind about the seriousness of that edict. You would have known that it meant death; and you would have been satisfied to weep for your brother in your kitchen. But you! You thought that because you come of the royal line, because you were my niece and were going to marry my son, I shouldn't dare have you killed.

ANTIGONE: You are mistaken. Quite the contrary. I never doubted for an instant that you would have me put to death.

(A pause, as CREON stares fixedly at her)

CREON: The pride of Oedipus! Oedipus and his headstrong pride all over again. I can see your father in you—and I believe you. Of course you thought that I should have you killed! Proud as you are, it seemed to you a natural climax in your existence. Your father was like that. For him as for you human happiness was meaningless; and mere human misery was not enough to satisfy his passion for torment. *(He sits on a stool behind the table)* You come of people for whom the human vestment is a kind of strait jacket: it cracks at the seams. You spend your lives wriggling to get out of it. Nothing less than a cosy tea party with death and destiny will quench your thirst. The happiest hour of your father's life came when he listened greedily to the story of how, unknown to himself, he had killed his own father and dishonored the bed of his own mother. Drop by drop, word by word, he drank in the dark story that the gods had destined him, first to live and then to hear. How avidly men and women drink the brew of such a tale when their names are Oedipus—and Antigone! And it is so simple, afterward, to do what your father did, to put out one's eyes and take one's daughter begging on the highways.

Let me tell you, Antigone: those days are over for Thebes. Thebes has a right to a king without a past. My name, thank God, is only Creon. I stand here with both feet firm on the ground; with both hands in my pockets; and I have decided that so long as I am king—being less ambitious than your father was—I shall merely devote myself to introducing a little order into this absurd kingdom; if that is possible.

Don't think that being a king seems to me romantic. It is my trade; a trade a man has to work at every day; and like every other trade, it isn't all beer and skittles. But since it is my trade, I take it seriously. And if, tomorrow, some wild and bearded messenger walks in from some wild and distant valley—which is what happened to your dad—and tells me that he's not quite sure who my parents were, but thinks that my wife Eurydice is actually my mother, I shall ask him to do me the kindness to go back where he came from; and I shan't let a little matter like that persuade me to order my wife to take a blood test and the police to let me know whether or not my birth certificate was forged. Kings, my girl, have other things to do than to surrender themselves to their private feelings. *(He looks at her and smiles)* Hand you over to be killed! *(He rises, moves to end of table and sits on the top of table)* I have other plans for you. You're going to marry Haemon; and I want you to fatten up a bit so that you can give him a sturdy boy. Let me assure you that Thebes needs that boy a good deal more than it needs your death. You will go to your room, now, and do as you have been told; and you won't say a word about this to anybody. Don't fret about the guards: I'll see that their mouths are shut. And don't annihilate me with those eyes. I know that you think I am a brute, and I'm sure you must consider me very prosaic. But the fact is, I have always been fond of you, stubborn though you always were. Don't forget that the first doll you ever had came from me. (*A pause.* ANTIGONE *says nothing, rises and crosses slowly below the table toward the arch.* CREON *turns and watches her; then*) Where are you going?

ANTIGONE (*Stops downstage. Without any show of rebellion*): You know very well where I am going.

CREON (*After a pause*): What sort of game are you playing?

ANTIGONE: I am not playing games.

CREON: Antigone, do you realize that if, apart from those three guards, a single soul finds out what you have tried to do, it will be impossible for me to avoid putting you to death? There is still a chance that I can save you; but only if you keep this to yourself and give up your crazy purpose. Five minutes more, and it will be too late. You understand that?

ANTIGONE: I must go and bury my brother. Those men uncovered him.

CREON: What good will it do? You know that there are other men standing guard over Polynices. And even if you did cover him over with earth again, the earth would again be removed.

ANTIGONE: I know all that. I know it. But that much, at least, I can do. And what a person can do, a person ought to do.

(Pause)

CREON: Tell me, Antigone, do you believe all that flummery about religious burial? Do you really believe that a so-called shade of your brother is condemned to wander for ever homeless if a little earth is not flung on his corpse to the accompaniment of some priestly abracadabra? Have you ever listened to the priests of Thebes when they were mumbling their formula? Have you ever watched those dreary bureaucrats while they were preparing the dead for burial—skipping half the gestures required by the ritual, swallowing half their words, hustling the dead into their graves out of fear that they might be late for lunch?

ANTIGONE: Yes, I have seen all that.

CREON: And did you never say to yourself as you watched them, that if someone you really loved lay dead under the shuffling, mumbling ministrations of the priests, you would scream aloud and beg the priests to leave the dead in peace?

ANTIGONE: Yes, I've thought all that.

CREON: And you still insist upon being put to death—merely because I refuse to let your brother go out with that grotesque passport; because I refuse his body the wretched consolation of that mass-production jibber-jabber, which you would have been the first to be embarrassed by if I had allowed it. The whole thing is absurd!

ANTIGONE: Yes, it's absurd.

CREON: Then why, Antigone, why? For whose sake? For the sake of them that believe in it? To raise them against me?

ANTIGONE: No.

CREON: For whom then if not for them and not for Polynices either?

ANTIGONE: For nobody. For myself.

(A pause as they stand looking at one another)

CREON: You must want very much to die. You look like a trapped animal.

ANTIGONE: Stop feeling sorry for me. Do as I do. Do your job. But if you are a human being, do it quickly. That is all I ask of you. I'm not going to be able to hold out for ever.

CREON (*Takes a step toward her*): I want to save you, Antigone.

ANTIGONE: You are the king, and you are all-powerful. But that you cannot do.

CREON: You think not?

ANTIGONE: Neither save me nor stop me.

CREON: Prideful Antigone! Little Oedipus!

ANTIGONE: Only this can you do: have me put to death.

CREON: Have you tortured, perhaps?

ANTIGONE: Why would you do that? To see me cry? To hear me beg for mercy? Or swear whatever you wish, and then begin over again?

(A pause)

CREON: You listen to me. You have cast me for the villain in this little play of yours, and yourself for the heroine. And you know it, you damned little mischief-marker! But don't you drive me too far! If I were one of your preposterous little tyrants that Greece is full of, you would be lying in a ditch this minute with your tongue pulled out and your body drawn and quartered. But you can see something in my face that makes me hesitate to send for the guards and turn you over to them. Instead, I let you go on arguing; and you taunt me, you take the offensive. (*He grasps her left wrist*) What are you driving at, you she-devil?

ANTIGONE: Let me go. You are hurting my arm.

CREON (*Gripping her tighter*): I will not let you go.

ANTIGONE (*Moans*): Oh!

CREON: I was a fool to waste words. I should have done this from the beginning. (*He looks at her*) I may be your uncle—but we are not a particularly affectionate family. Are we, eh? (*Through his teeth, as he twists)* Are we? (CREON *propels* ANTIGONE *round below him to his side)* What fun for you, eh? To be able to spit in the face of a king who has all the power in the world; a man who has done his own killing in his day; who has killed people just as pitiable as you are—and who is still soft enough to go to all this trouble in order to keep you from being killed.

(A pause)

ANTIGONE: Now you are squeezing my arm too tightly. It doesn't hurt any more.

(CREON stares at her, then drops her arm)

CREON: I shall save you yet. *(He goes below the table to the chair at end of table, takes off his coat and places it on the chair)* God knows, I have things enough to do today without wasting my time on an insect like you. There's plenty to do, I assure you, when you've just put down a revolution. But urgent things can wait. I am not going to let politics be the cause of your death. For it is a fact that this whole business is nothing but politics: the mournful shade of Polynices, the decomposing corpse, the sentimental weeping and the hysteria that you mistake for heroism—nothing but politics.

Look here. I may not be soft, but I'm fastidious. I like things clean, ship-shape, well scrubbed. Don't think that I am not just as offended as you are by the thought of that meat rotting in the sun. In the evening, when the breeze comes in off the sea, you can smell it in the palace, and it nauseates me. But I refuse even to shut my window. It's vile; and I can tell you what I wouldn't tell anybody else: it's stupid, monstrously stupid. But the people of Thebes have got to have their noses rubbed into it a little longer. My God! If it was up to me, I should have had them bury your brother long ago as a mere matter of public hygiene. I admit that what I am doing is childish. But if the featherheaded rabble I govern are to understand what's what, that stench has got to fill the town for a month!

ANTIGONE *(Turns to him):* You are a loathsome man!

CREON: I agree. My trade forces me to be. We could argue whether I ought or ought not to follow my trade; but once I take on the job, I must do it properly.

ANTIGONE: Why do you do it at all?

CREON: My dear, I woke up one morning and found myself King of Thebes. God knows, there were other things I loved in life more than power.

ANTIGONE: Then you should have said no.

CREON: Yes, I could have done that. Only, I felt that it would have been cowardly. I should have been like a workman who turns down a job that has to be done. So I said yes.

ANTIGONE: So much the worse for you, then. I didn't say yes. I can say no to anything I think vile, and I don't have to count the cost. But because you said yes, all that you can do, for all your crown and your trappings, and your guards—all that you can do is to have me killed.

CREON: Listen to me.

ANTIGONE: If I want to. I don't have to listen to you if I don't want to. You've said your *yes*. There is nothing more you can tell me that I don't know. You stand there, drinking in my words. *(She moves behind chair)* Why is it that you don't call your guards? I'll tell you why. You want to hear me out to the end; that's why.

CREON: You amuse me.

ANTIGONE: Oh, no, I don't. I frighten you. That is why you talk about saving me. Everything would be so much easier if you had a docile, tongue-tied little Antigone living in the palace. I'll tell you something, Uncle Creon: I'll give you back one of your own words. You are too fastidious to make a good tyrant. But you are going to have to put me to death today, and you know it. And that's what frightens you. God! Is there anything uglier than a frightened man!

CREON: Very well. I am afraid, then. Does that satisfy you? I am afraid that if you insist upon it, I shall have to have you killed. And I don't want to.

ANTIGONE: I don't have to do things that I think are wrong. If it comes to that, you didn't really want to leave my brother's body unburied, did you? Say it! Admit that you didn't.

CREON: I have said it already.

ANTIGONE: But you did it just the same. And now, though you don't want to do it, you are going to have me killed. And you call that being a king!

CREON: Yes, I call that being a king.

ANTIGONE: Poor Creon! My nails are broken, my fingers are bleeding, my arms are covered with the welts left by the paws of your guards—but I am a queen!

CREON: Then why not have pity on me, and live? Isn't your brother's corpse, rotting there under my windows, payment enough for peace and order in Thebes? My son loves you. Don't make me add your life to the payment. I've paid enough.

ANTIGONE: No, Creon! You said yes, and made yourself king. Now you will never stop paying.

CREON: But God in Heaven! Won't you try to understand me! I'm trying hard enough to understand you! There had to be one man who said yes. Somebody had to agree to captain the ship. She had sprung a hundred leaks; she was loaded to the water-line with crime, ignorance, poverty. The wheel was swinging with the wind. The crew refused to work and were looting the cargo. The officers were building a raft, ready to slip overboard and desert the ship. The mast was splitting, the wind was howling, the sails were beginning to rip. Every man jack on board was about to drown—and only because the only thing they thought of was their own skins and their cheap little day-to-day traffic. Was that a time, do you think, for playing with words like yes and no? Was that a time for a man to be weighing the pros and cons, wondering if he wasn't going to pay too dearly later on; if he wasn't going to lose his life, or his family, or his touch with other men? You grab the wheel, you right the ship in the face of a mountain of water. You shout an order, and if one man refuses to obey, you shoot straight into the mob. Into the mob, I say! The beast as nameless as the wave that crashes down upon your deck; as nameless as the whipping wind. The thing that drops when you shoot may be someone who poured you a drink the night before; but it has no name. And you, braced at the wheel, you have no name, either. Nothing has a name—except the ship, and the storm. (*A pause as he looks at her*) Now do you understand?

ANTIGONE: I am not here to understand. That's all very well for you. I am here to say no to you, and die.

CREON: It is easy to say no.

ANTIGONE: Not always.

CREON: It is easy to say no. To say yes, you have to sweat and roll up your sleeves and plunge both hands into life up to the elbows. It is easy to say no, even if saying no means death. All you have to do is to sit still and wait. Wait to go on living; wait to be killed. That is the coward's part. *No* is one of your man-made words. Can you imagine a world in which trees say *no* to the sap? In which beasts say *no* to hunger or to propagation? Animals are good, simple, tough. They move in droves, nudging one another onward, all traveling the same road. Some of them keel over; but the rest go on; and no matter how many may fall by the wayside, there are always those few left which go on bringing their young into the world, traveling the same road with the same obstinate will, unchanged from those who went before.

ANTIGONE: Animals, eh, Creon! What a king you could be if only men were animals!

(A pause. CREON turns and looks at her)

CREON: You despise me, don't you? (ANTIGONE *is silent.* CREON *goes on, as if to himself*) Strange. Again and again, I have imagined myself holding this conversation with a pale young man I have never seen in the flesh. He would have come to assassinate me, and would have failed. I would be trying to find out from him why he wanted to kill me. But with all my logic and all my powers of debate, the only thing I could get out of him would be that he despised me. Who would have thought that the white-faced boy would turn out to be you? And that the debate would arise out of something so meaningless as the burial of your brother?

ANTIGONE *(Repeats contemptuously):* Meaningless!

CREON *(Earnestly, almost desperately):* And yet, you must hear me out. My part is not an heroic one, but I shall play my part. I shall have you put to death. Only, before I do, I want to make one last appeal. I want to be sure that you know what you are doing as well as I know what I am doing. Antigone, do you know what you are dying for? Do you know the sordid story to which you are going to sign your name in blood, for all time to come?

ANTIGONE: What story?

CREON: The story of Eteocles and Polynices, the story of your brothers. You think you know it, but you don't. Nobody in Thebes knows that story but me. And it seems to me, this afternoon, that you have a right to know it too. *(A pause as* ANTIGONE *moves to chair and sits)* It's not a pretty story. *(He turns, get stool from behind the table and places it between the table and the chair)* You'll see. *(He looks at her for a moment)* Tell me, first. What do you remember about your brothers? They were older than you, so they must have looked down on you. And I imagine that they tormented you—pulled your pigtails, broke your dolls, whispered secrets to each other to put you in a rage.

ANTIGONE: They were big and I was little.

CREON: And later on, when they came home wearing evening clothes, smoking cigarettes, they would have nothing to do with you; and you thought they were wonderful.

ANTIGONE: They were boys and I was a girl.

CREON: You didn't know why, exactly, but you knew that they were making your mother unhappy. You saw her in tears over them; and your father would fly into a rage because of them. You heard them come in, slamming doors, laughing noisily in the corridors—insolent, spineless, unruly, smelling of drink.

ANTIGONE *(Staring outward):* Once, it was very early and we had just got up. I saw them coming home, and hid behind a door. Polynices was very pale and his eyes were shining. He was so handsome in his evening clothes. He saw me, and said: "Here, this is for you"; and he gave me a big paper flower that he had brought home from his night out.

CREON: And of course you still have that flower. Last night, before you crept out, you opened a drawer and looked at it for a time, to give yourself courage.

ANTIGONE: Who told you so?

CREON: Poor Antigone! With her night-club flower. Do you know what your brother was?

ANTIGONE: Whatever he was, I know that you will say vile things about him.

CREON: A cheap, idiotic bounder, that is what he was. A cruel, vicious little voluptuary. A little beast with just wit enough to drive a car faster and throw more money away than any of his pals. I was with your father one day when Polynices, having lost a lot of money gambling, asked him to settle the debt; and when your father refused, the boy raised his hand against him and called him a vile name.

ANTIGONE: That's a lie!

CREON: He struck your father in the face with his fist. It was pitiful. Your father sat at his desk with his head in his hands. His nose was bleeding. He was weeping with anguish. And in a corner of your father's study, Polynices stood sneering and lighting a cigarette.

ANTIGONE: That's a lie.

(A pause)

CREON: When did you last see Polynices alive? When you were twelve years old. *That's* true, isn't it?

ANTIGONE: Yes, that's true.

CREON: Now you know why. Oedipus was too chicken-hearted to have the boy locked up. Polynices was allowed to go off and join the Argive army. And as soon as he reached Argos, the attempts upon your father's life began—upon the life of an old man who couldn't make up his mind to die, couldn't bear to be parted from his kingship. One after another, men slipped into Thebes from Argos for the purpose of assassinating him, and every killer we caught always ended by confessing who had put him up to it, who had paid him to try it. And it wasn't only Polynices. That is really what I am trying to tell you. I want you to know what went on in the back room, in the kitchen of politics; I want you to know what took place in the wings of this drama in which you are burning to play a part.

Yesterday, I gave Eteocles a State funeral, with pomp and honors. Today, Eteocles is a saint and a hero in the eyes of all Thebes. The whole city turned out to bury him. The schoolchildren emptied their savings boxes to buy wreaths for him. Old men, orating in quavering, hypocritical voices, glorified the virtues of the great-hearted brother, the devoted son, the loyal prince. I made a speech myself; and every temple priest was present with an appropriate show of sorrow and solemnity in his stupid face. And military honors were accorded the dead hero.

Well, what else could I have done? People had taken sides in the civil war. Both sides couldn't be wrong; that would be too much. I couldn't have made them swallow the truth. Two gangsters was more of a luxury than I could afford. *(He pauses for a moment)* And this is the whole point of my story. Eteocles, that virtuous brother, was just as rotten as Polynices. That greathearted son had done his best, too, to procure the assassination of his father. That loyal prince had also offered to sell out Thebes to the highest bidder. Funny, isn't it? Polynices lies rotting in the sun while Eteocles is given a hero's funeral and will be housed in a marble vault. Yet I have absolute proof that everything that Polynices did, Eteocles had plotted to do. They were a pair of blackguards—both engaged in selling out Thebes, and both engaged in selling out each other; and they died like the cheap gangsters they were, over a division of the spoils.

But, as I told you a moment ago, I had to make a martyr of one of them. I sent out to the holocaust for their bodies; they were found clasped in one another's arms—for the first time in their lives, I imagine. Each had been spitted on the other's sword, and the Argive cavalry had trampled them down. They were mashed to a pulp, Antigone. I had the prettier of the two carcasses brought in, and gave it a State funeral; and I left the other to rot. I don't know which was which. And I assure you, I don't care.
(Long silence, neither looking at the other)
ANTIGONE *(In a mild voice):* Why do you tell me all this?
CREON: Would it have been better to let you die a victim to that obscene story?
ANTIGONE: It might have been. I had my faith.
CREON: What are you going to do now?
ANTIGONE *(Rises to her feet in a daze):* I shall go up to my room.
CREON: Don't stay alone. Go and find Haemon. And get married quickly.
ANTIGONE *(In a whisper):* Yes.
CREON: All this is really beside the point. You have your whole life ahead of you—and life is a treasure.
ANTIGONE: Yes.
CREON: And you were about to throw it away. Don't think me fatuous if I say that I understand you; and that at your age I should have done the same thing. A moment ago, when we were quarreling, you said I was drinking in your words. I was. But it wasn't you I was listening to; it was a lad named Creon who lived here in Thebes many years ago. He was thin and pale, as you are. His mind, too, was filled with thoughts of self-sacrifice. Go and find Haemon. And get married quickly, Antigone. Be happy. Life flows like water, and you young people let it run

away through your fingers. Shut your hands; hold on to it, Antigone. Life is not what you think it is. Life is a child playing round your feet, a tool you hold firmly in your grip, a bench you sit down upon in the evening, in your garden. People will tell you that that's not life, that life is something else. They will tell you that because they need your strength and your fire, and they will want to make use of you. Don't listen to them. Believe me, the only poor consolation that we have in our old age is to discover that what I have said to you is true. Life is nothing more than the happiness that you get out of it.

ANTIGONE *(Murmurs, lost in thought)*: Happiness . . .

CREON *(Suddenly a little self-conscious)*: Not much of a word, is it?

ANTIGONE *(Quietly)*: What kind of happiness do you foresee for me? Paint me the picture of your happy Antigone. What are the unimportant little sins that I shall have to commit before I am allowed to sink my teeth into life and tear happiness from it? Tell me: to whom shall I have to lie? Upon whom shall I have to fawn? To whom must I sell myself? Whom do you want me to leave dying, while I turn away my eyes?

CREON: Antigone, be quiet.

ANTIGONE: Why do you tell me to be quiet when all I want to know is what I have to do to be happy? This minute; since it is this very minute that I must make my choice. You tell me that life is so wonderful. I want to know what I have to do in order to be able to say that myself.

CREON: Do you love Haemon?

ANTIGONE: Yes, I love Haemon. The Haemon I love is hard and young, faithful and difficult to satisfy, just as I am. But if what I love in Haemon is to be worn away like a stone step by the tread of the thing you call life, the thing you call happiness; if Haemon reaches the point where he stops growing pale with fear when I grow pale, stops thinking that I must have been killed in an accident when I am five minutes late, stops feeling that he is alone on earth when I laugh and he doesn't know why—if he too has to learn to say yes to everything—why, no, then, no! I do not love Haemon!

CREON: You don't know what you are talking about!

ANTIGONE: I do know what I am talking about! Now it is you who have stopped understanding. I am too far away from you now, talking to you from a kingdom you can't get into, with your quick tongue and your hollow heart. *(Laughs)* I laugh, Creon, because I see you suddenly as you must have been at fifteen: the same look of impotence in your face and the same inner conviction that there was nothing you couldn't do. What has life added to you, except those lines in your face, and that fat on your stomach?

CREON: Be quiet, I tell you!

ANTIGONE: Why do you want me to be quiet? Because you know that I am right? Do you think I can't see in your face that what I am saying is true? You can't admit it, of course; you have to go on growling and defending the bone you call happiness.

CREON: It is your happiness, too, you little fool!

ANTIGONE: I spit on your happiness! I spit on your idea of life—that life that must go on, come what may. You are all like dogs that lick everything they smell. You with your promise of a hum-drum happiness—provided a person doesn't ask too much of life. I want everything of life, I do; and I want it now! I want it total, complete: otherwise I reject it! I will *not* be moderate. I will *not* be satisfied with the bite of cake you offer me if I promise to be a good little girl. I want to be sure of everything this very day; sure that everything will be as beautiful as when I was a little girl. If not, I want to die!

Study Questions

1. Explain how Antigone exemplifies principles and Creon happiness.
2. Why does the burial of Polynices generate such strong conflict?
3. Is Antigone ultimately motivated by her religious belief that a shade of Polynices will wander forever unless his body is buried?
4. Did Creon decide to become king because of the power and wealth it would bring?
5. Why is saying "no" treated by Antigone as her greatest strength and by Creon as the easy way out?

Saving Private Ryan

Director: Steven Spielberg

Screenplay: Robert Rodat

Steven Spielberg (1946–) is one of America's most prolific and celebrated film directors. He has twenty-six feature films to his credit, most notably Saving Private Ryan, Jurassic Park, Amistad, Schindler's List, Poltergeist, Jaws, Close Encounters of the Third Kind, Artificial Intelligence, *and the* Indiana Jones *trilogy. Spielberg also produced and/or wrote several of his films, as well as numerous episodes in several television series. He has been honored with Academy Awards as Best Director for* Saving Private Ryan *and* Schindler's List, *along with receiving awards from the Director's Guild of America and several Golden Globes and Emmys.*

Synopsis

Spielberg's intention in *Saving Private Ryan* was to create a monument to the brave men who fought and died in World War II, especially on D-Day. The star of the film, Tom Hanks, reinforced this purpose when he stated in an interview, "We are trying to communicate to [the audience] that mere mortals, people who are the same age as themselves, had to be called upon to make the hard sacrifice in service to mankind." However, Spielberg has also woven into his film an inner moral theme, and the film as a whole presents a humanistic motive for pursuing the war. The plot, the action, and the conversations between Captain Miller (Tom Hanks) and his squad gradually refine the reason for their particular mission. Initially, it seems the height of absurdity to risk the lives of several soldiers in order to save one man.

After a brief Prologue, the beginning sequences of the film plunge the viewer into the carnage at Omaha Beach, Normandy, in 1944 at the start of the Allied invasion of Europe. This twenty-five-minute segment is often regarded as the most realistic, gruesome, and compelling depiction of warfare ever filmed. The battle is neither sensationalized nor glorified but simply shown as it must have been, and for that reason the wounding and killing is almost too life-like for the audience to bear.

The viewer experiences the action directly rather than merely observing it. The air is thick with machine gun and mortar fire, tracer bullets, and artillery shells from the moment the landing craft open until the beach is taken. Bullets whiz past the sick and panicky soldiers, even penetrating the water and sending up clouds of crimson. Men are shown drowning before their feet can touch land, dragged down by the weight of their equipment. We see half a torso being dragged up the beach, a soldier dazed and wandering in shock, picking up his severed arm, another with an open stomach wound trying to hold in his intestines and calling for his mother. The ironies are also depicted: a man who is killed just after the medics have treated him; another shot in the head while examining the bullet hole in his helmet. The viewer feels in the presence of both absurdity and death.

Other graphic battle scenes are shown in the film, especially the concluding episode, but none are as vivid or harrowing. Here the impact is hallucinatory, suggesting an allegory of hell. In one surreal sequence, the camera scans across the many bodies bobbing in the water.

The sound is of real guns, the actual kind used in World War II, and the hand-held camera of Janusz Kaminski makes no sense of the action; it only augments the chaos. The camera shakes when Tiger tanks rumble up, and blood sometimes spatters the lens, as though both the audience and the cameraman are there. "I wanted the audience in the arena, not sitting off to one side," Spielberg has written. "I didn't want something it was easy to look away from."

John Williams's film score remains in the background, eloquent but never romanticizing the scenes, and during the battles it ceases altogether. His "Hymn to the Fallen" at the beginning and end of the film is subdued and moving, but for the most part he lets the action speak for itself. At times the mix of sounds becomes muffled, perhaps to show how the explosions numb both the ears and the mind.

As a historical note, the carnage that occurred on June 6, 1944 is quite accurate because, contrary to plan, the German defenses were not eliminated by aerial bombardment. The night before the landing the Allied bombers were supposed to destroy the heavy German fortifications on the cliffs above Omaha Beach. However, because of heavy cloud cover the planes missed almost all of their targets, and the landing troops were nearly all slaughtered.

The second phase of the film sets up the moral question when General George Marshall (Harve Presnell) is informed by his staff that Mrs. Ryan, an Iowa farm wife, has lost three of her four sons in the war. The general resolves that the surviving son, James Ryan (Matt Damon), must be found and returned home safely. His decision is probably based on both politics and compassion. A Colonel Dye objects to the plan saying "If we send a patrol flat-hatting around, through swarms of German reinforcements, all along our axis of advance...we'll be sending out death notifications to all of their mothers." In reply General Marshall quotes a letter from Abraham Lincoln to a Mrs. Bixby in Boston.

Dear Madam,

I have been shown in the files of the War Department a statement of the Adjutant General of Massachusetts that you are the mother of five sons who have died gloriously on the field of battle. I feel how weak and fruitless must be any words of mine which should attempt to beguile you from the grief of a loss so overwhelming. But I cannot refrain from tendering to you the consolation that may be found in the thanks of the Republic they have died to save.

I pray that our Heavenly Father may assuage the anguish of your bereavement, and leave you only the cherished memory of the loved and lost, and the solemn pride that must be yours to have laid so costly a sacrifice upon the altar of freedom.

Yours very sincerely,
Abraham Lincoln

Marshall concludes by saying, "If that boy is alive, we're going to send someone to find him . . . and get him the hell out of there."

Captain Miller of Charlie Company, Second Ranger Battalion, is ordered to carry out this special mission, so he assembles the remains of his platoon plus a French/German interpreter. The men are a mixed bag and almost caricatures of characters in war films. That is, they are near clichés of the griping men from disparate backgrounds who gradually bond and become willing to risk their lives for each other. Private Reiben (Edward Burns) represents the stock Brooklyn tough-guy, sarcastic and street-smart; Sergeant Michael Horvath (Tom Sizemore) from Minneapolis is battle-scarred, dependable, and courageous; Private Jackson (Barry Pepper) is a prayerful southern sharpshooter; Anthony Caparzo (Vin Diesel) from Chicago is a good-natured grunt; Stanley Mellish (Adam Goldberg) from Yonkers portrays a sarcastic Jewish complainer; Corporal Upham (Jeremy Davies) is the terrified combat rookie, a clerk-typist who intends to write a book; and Wade (Giovanni Ribisi) portrays the altruistic medic.

When the men learn of their mission they are naturally incredulous, unable to believe that a squad of men is being sent into a war zone in order to return one individual to his mother. "What about your mother?" Reiben says to Wade. "We all got mothers, you, me, Sarge, even Corporal Upchuck. Captain, I'll bet even you have a mother." To them it seems a "public relations" mission, another incident of the army's "foobar," fucked up beyond all recognition. They wonder whether James Ryan is anyone special, which would justify the risks they are taking:

"Captain, where's this Ryan from anyway?"
"Iowa, Private Caparzo. The great Middle West."
"Iowa? Oh, well, that's different. Who wouldn't mind riskin' his ass to save some fuckin' farmer? The world couldn't get along with one less

sodbuster, it's not like it's rainin' fuckin' sodbusters back home or anything. Western civilization would cease."

In an ironic exchange, underscoring that Ryan is very ordinary not
"Eisenhower or Patton or something," Captain Miller tells Reiben,

> "I got a look at Ryan's service record, which is exemplary."
> "Oh, that changes everything."
> "But it also includes his high school report cards—he got an A-plus in
> civics and won the school's Good Citizenship Award . . . two years in a
> row. Now—isn't that worth risking your asses over?"
> "Was he an Eagle Scout, sir?"
> "Youngest in the history of the state of Iowa. Forty-eight merit badges."

Tom Hanks as Captain Miller is "everyman" risen to heroic proportions, an incarnation of James Stewart. He also wonders privately why a
dangerous mission should be launched to save one man, although he
tells his men "orders are orders." This is echoed by Upham who quotes
Tennyson "Theirs is not to reason why / Theirs but to do and die." But
that reasoning (or lack of reasoning) never satisfies Miller, and a justification in terms of risks and benefits certainly does not work in this situation either. In one conversation while the squad is marching through the
French countryside Reiben expresses Miller's own reservations:

> "You know, Captain, this little expedition goes against everything the
> army taught me."
> "How so?"
> "I mean, it doesn't make any sense."
> "What doesn't make any sense, Reiben."
> "The math, sir, the sheer fuckin' math of it. Maybe you could explain it
> to me."
> "Sure. That's what I'm here for. To make you boys feel everything we do
> is logical."
> "Gimme a break, Cap."
> "So what do you want to know?"
> "Well, sir, strictly just talkin' arithmetic here, what's the sense, the strat-
> egy, in risking eight lives to save one?"

In a later conversation Miller raises the same question with
Sergeant Horvath, except here he questions his previous morality
whereby he calculated numbers saved and lost in order to justify his actions. Thinking more deeply, he wonders whether such a calculus is the
correct approach. Miller says,

> "Every time you get one of your boys killed you tell yourself you just
> saved the lives of two, three, ten, maybe a hundred other men and
> boys."
> "Not a bad way to look at it."

"You know how many men I've lost under my command?"

"Not offhand."

"Caparzo made ninety-four. So hell, that means I probably saved the lives of ten times that many. Maybe twenty times. See, it's simple. Just do the math—it lets you choose the mission over the men, every time."

Horvath replies, "Except this time the mission is the man," thereby articulating the central principle of the film. That is, although Miller reverts to weighing the numbers periodically, and even tries to justify the mission in terms of Ryan's special worth, he comes to understand that something more fundamental is at stake. He does say "This Private Ryan better . . . cure cancer or invent a light bulb that never fuckin' burns out, or a car that runs on water," but such thinking is superficial. It is not enough to sacrifice lives just to save a larger number of lives, or to save a life only if that life benefits society enormously. The men who gave up their lives in the war were as valuable as those whose lives were saved.

In effect, the mission forces Miller to realize the more ultimate reasons behind his actions and for the war. That is, certain values are fundamental and transcend a pragmatic, cost/benefit analysis. The war is being fought to safeguard ethical values, which include comradeship, integrity, loyalty, and honor, as well as liberty and freedom. In the case of this mission, the humane value is sparing a mother the tragedy of losing all her sons.

In philosophic terms, Spielberg chooses the ethical position of formalism that treats values as supreme over the more utilitarian approach that champions the greater good. He places Kantianism over Utilitarianism. Just as we should respect the rules of justice even though it might lead to the acquittal of a guilty person, we should try to bring home a remaining son even though the lives of several soldiers are put in danger. Principles matter more than consequences. Our conscience dictates that we do what's right even if it does no good, because we have a responsibility to honor moral values. Our self-respect depends on the respect we accord to individual human life.

As the film progresses the squad advances to the front lines searching for Private Ryan, and are suddenly bombarded by 88-mm. shells, landing the men in a drainage ditch and shattering their jeep. They then enter the town of Ste.-Mère-Église and find themselves in the midst of a firefight. The presence of civilians complicates the situation, and a sniper in a bell-tower kills Caparzo as he hands a little girl back to her parents. The sniper is killed in turn by Jackson, the sharpshooter.

The squad then encounters a machine-gun nest manned by *Falshirmjager*, elite German paratroopers who are responsible for the corpses of American soldiers littering the ground. Dissension occurs over whether to attack the site or bypass it, skirting around the woods. Miller commands his troops to attack, and in the battle the medic Wade is hit. In a poignant scene, Wade dies while his comrades ask, "Tell us what to do. Tell us how to fix you." This incident causes dissension over whether the attack (and the entire mission) was warranted.

In this situation, neither we nor Miller know whether he made the right choice. The same question arises in a subsequent incident where Miller releases a German prisoner who ironically turns out to be the S.S. soldier responsible for Miller's death. Is a right decision one based on good reasons or one that turns out well? Can we only judge the wisdom of our choices retrospectively?

The final scene of the film takes place in Neuville-au-Plain where Private Ryan is finally found. Ryan is informed that his brothers have been killed and that he is going home, but oddly enough he refuses to leave his comrades.

> RYAN: "I can't leave them, sir. At least not until reinforcements arrive . . . there's barely enough of us as it is."
> MILLER: "Private . . . you've got five [minutes] to grab your gear and report back to me."
> RYAN: "Captain, if I go, what are they gonna . . ."
> REIBEN: "Hey, asshole! Two of us died, buyin' you this ticket home! Fuckin' *take* it! I would."
> RYAN: "What . . . were their names?"
> MELLISH: "Wade and Caparzo."
> RYAN: "Wade . . . and . . ."
> MELLISH: "Caparzo."
> RYAN: "Sir, this doesn't make any sense. What have I done to deserve special treatment?"
> REIBEN: "Give that man a cigar."
> MILLER: "This isn't about you. It's about politics . . . and your mother."
> RYAN: "I mean, for Christ's sake, my life isn't worth the lives of two others. Hell, these guys deserve to go home as much as I do, as much as anybody. They've fought just as long, just as hard."
> MILLER: "Should I tell your mother that? That she can look forward to another flag in her window?"
> RYAN: "My mother didn't raise any of us to be cowards."
> MILLER: "She didn't raise you to lose you."
> RYAN: "Well, then, you just tell her when you found me, I was with the only brothers I had left. Tell her that there was no way I was going to desert those brothers. You tell her that . . . and she'll understand."

Miller does not force the issue, and his squad then fights with Ryan's company to hold a bridge against a German counter-offensive. This battle too is rendered in harrowing detail, and it becomes more personal because we have come to relate to each of the men just as they have with each other. Even though they are vastly outnumbered and outgunned, the small force manages to hold the bridge until reinforcements arrive. They are remarkably courageous and resourceful but the price they pay is enormous. Captain Miller dies, and of the original squad only Upham and Reiben survive. Ryan lives as well, and toward the end of the film Miller's last words to him are: "Earn this. Earn it."

These words seem to suggest that the sacrifice of six men in the squad is only justified if the person then leads an outstanding life. However, we do not protect people only when they deserve it, and Ryan was saved for humanitarian reasons not because he would contribute to society. As the prologue and epilogue show, Ryan apparently did lead a worthwhile life afterwards, but if he hadn't, that would not negate the sacrifice. We see him as a grandfather at the St. Laurent military graveyard, talking to Miller's grave, wondering whether he had been a good enough man. By all indications, he was thoroughly decent, not exceptional but he worked with his hands, raised a family—did the best he knew how.

Perhaps the definitive word is uttered earlier by Sergeant Horvath: "Someday we might look back on this and decide that saving Private Ryan was the only decent thing we were able to pull out of this whole godawful mess."

Respect for the worth of the individual is the type of value that justified the war altogether.

Study Questions

1. Why is Captain Miller and his squad sent to rescue Private Ryan? Does the mission make sense?

2. What is the moral rationale behind risking eight lives to save one? How does this relate to the Kantian and Utilitarian ethic?

3. Do you think the mission would only be justified if Private Ryan subsequently contributed something outstanding to humanity?

4. Should the squad have attacked the machine-gun nest or bypassed it in order to carry out their primary mission?

5. When Private Ryan was found, should he have been forced to leave with Miller and his men or were they right to remain and try to stop the German advance?

Bibliography of Philosophy, Literature, and Films

III. Judging the Value of Conduct: Ethics

Philosophy

Beyond Good and Evil, The Joyful Wisdom	Friedrich Nietzsche
The Data of Ethics	Herbert Spencer
The Emotive Theory of Ethics	J. O. Urmson
Ethical Studies	F. H. Bradley
Ethics	G. E. Moore
Ethics	N. Hartman
Ethics	P. H. Nowell-Smith
Ethics	Baruch Spinoza
Ethics and Language	Charles Stevenson
Ethics Since 1900	Mary Warnock
Five Types of Ethical Theory	C. D. Broad
The Foundation of Ethics	W. D. Ross
Gorgias, Meno, Republic	Plato
Groundwork of the Metaphysic of Morals	Immanuel Kant
Human Nature and Conduct	John Dewey
"The Humanism of Existentialism"	Jean-Paul Sartre
In a Different Voice	Carol Gilligan
The Language of Morals	R. M. Hare
Methods of Ethics	Henry Sidgwick
"The Myth of Sisyphus"	Albert Camus
The Nicomachean Ethics	Aristotle
The Philosophy of Humanism	Corliss Lamont
The Philosophy of Right	G. W. F. Hegel
Principles of Morals & Legislation	Jeremy Bentham
Problems of Ethics	Moritz Schlick
Prolegomena to Ethics	T. H. Green
Situation Ethics	Joseph Fletcher
The Souls of Black Folk	W. E. B. DuBois
Theories of Ethics	Philippa Foot
A Theory of Justice	John Rawls
Utilitarianism	John Stuart Mill
The Varieties of Goodness	G. H. von Wright
A Vindication of the Rights of Women	Mary Wollstonecraft
World of Color	W. E. B. DuBois

Literature

The Ambassadors	William James
Anna Karenina	Leo Tolstoy

Antigone	Jean Anouilh
The Bell Jar	Sylvia Plath
Baal	Bertolt Brecht
Billy Budd	Joseph Conrad
Beloved	Toni Morrison
Caligula, The Plague	Albert Camus
The Catcher in the Rye	J. D. Salinger
Cry the Beloved Country	Alan Paton
The Color Purple	Alice Walker
The Cherry Orchard	Anton Chekhov
Crime and Punishment	Fedor Dostoevski
Dead Souls	Nikolai Gogol
Everything That Rises Must Converge	Flannery O'Connor
Everyman	Hugo Hofmannsthal
The Fall	Albert Camus
The Good Woman of Setzuan	Bertolt Brecht
Gulliver's Travels	Jonathan Swift
Heart of Darkness	Joseph Conrad
The Immoralist	Andre Gide
Justice	John Galsworthy
King Lear	William Shakespeare
A Lost Lady	Willa Cather
"The Lottery"	Shirley Jackson
Macbeth	William Shakespeare
Madame Bovary	Gustave Flaubert
Marius the Epicurean	Walter Pater
The Master of Santiago	Henry de Montherlant
The Misanthrope	Jean Baptiste Moliere
Native Son	Richard Wright
No Exit	Jean Paul Sartre
The Ogre	Henri de Montherlant
A Passage to India	E. M. Forester
The Plague	Albert Camus
Portrait of a Lady	William James
The Quest of the Absolute	Honore de Balzac
Romola	George Eliot
The Scarlet Letter	Nathaniel Hawthorne
A Ship of Fools	Kathryn Ann Porter
Silas Marner	George Eliot
Song of Solomon	Toni Morrison
Steppenwolf	Herman Hesse
A Tale of Two Cities	Charles Dickens
Tartuffe	Jean Baptiste Moliere
The Visit	Friedrich Durrenmatt

Vanity Fair	William Thackeray
"The Wall"	Jean-Paul Sartre

Films

Abandon Ship	Richard Sale
Alfie	Lewis Gilbert
All About Eve	Joseph Mankiewicz
All My Sons	Irving Reis
American Beauty	Sam Mendes
Amistad	Steven Spielberg
The Bicycle Thief	Vittorio de Sica
The Blue Angel	Josef von Sternberg
Blue Velvet	David Lynch
Bread and Chocolate	Franco Brusati
Breathless	Jean-Luc Godard
The Bridges of Madison County	Clint Eastwood
The Browning Version	Anthony Asquith
Central Statiom	Walter Sales
Chloe in the Afternoon	Eric Rohmer
City Lights	Charles Chaplin
A Civil Action	Steven Zaillian
A Clockwork Orange	Stanley Kubrick
Compulsion	Richard Fleischer
Do the Right Thing	Spike Lee
La Dolce Vita	Federico Fellini
Extreme Measures	Michael Apted
The Godfather	Francis Ford Coppola
The Grifters	Steven Frears
Ikuru	Akira Kurosawa
It's a Wonderful Life	Frank Capra
Jules and Jim	Francois Truffaut
Jurassic Park	Steven Spielberg
La Dolce Vita	Federico Fellini
La Strada	Federico Fellini
L'Avventura	Michaelangelo Antonioni
Last Tango in Paris	Bernardo Betalucci
Law of Desire	Pedro Almodovar
Los Olvidados	Luis Bunuel
Malcolm X	Spike Lee
Night and Fog	Alain Resnais
On the Waterfront	Elia Kazan
Philadelphia	Jonathan Demme
Pulp Fiction	Quentin Tarantino
The Rules of the Game	Jean Renoir
Roma	Federico Fellini

Room at the Top	Jack Clayton
Saving Private Ryan	Steven Spielberg
Tokyo Story	Yasujiro Ozu
Twelve Angry Men	Sidney Lumet
Wild Strawberries	Ingmar Bergman
Woman in the Dunes	Hiroshi Teshigahara
Zorba the Greek	Michael Cacoyannis

IV. Foundations of Belief: The Philosophy of Religion

The philosophy of religion is philosophic thinking about religion. It attempts to probe the underlying assumptions of personal faith and organized religion to determine whether good reasons exist for belief in a supernatural realm. It examines the nature of that realm, the character of the God who is supreme within it, and the relation of that God to the world—most particularly, to human life. It asks why a loving and almighty God would allow human beings, including innocent children, to suffer; whether prayer makes a difference and how one can tell; what life after death might mean, the survival of the soul after the disintegration of the body; and what role reason plays in judging matters of faith, what Athens has to do with Jerusalem.

Philosophers who explore such questions are sympathetic to the spirit of religion and the remarkably rich traditions, institutions, and forms of worship that have persisted from the beginning of civilization itself. They are also moved by the human yearning for order and purpose in the world, the need for things to make sense in terms of a divine being who controls and orders all events to some meaningful end. At the same time, they are as critical of spiritual claims as any other claims, demanding evidence and reasoned argument to prove that religious statements are true and not just emotionally comforting. They recognize that the desire to believe in a divine being is very great and could induce people to accept ideas they would otherwise dismiss as farfetched, and that religious convictions are often acquired during childhood and, for that reason, assimilated without question.

The task in philosophic thinking about religion, then, is to be receptive to religious belief in light of the significant role it has played in human history and in the human heart, while at the same time maintaining a certain critical awareness in evaluating religious assertions. We must not, of course, be so alert to the possibility of error that we fail to recognize the truth when we come across it. Rather, we should bring a sympathetic intelligence to bear on religion as an important phenomenon in human existence.

Philosophers, unlike theologians, are not necessarily believers, and, *qua* philosophers, they strive to operate with minimum assumptions and maximum objectivity, attempting to determine whether the system of beliefs does, in fact, diagram reality. The philosopher begins with questions rather than certainty, wondering above all whether *God* is the name of an actual being or simply an imaginative construct that personifies our hunger for direction, comfort, and immortality. Theologians, on the other hand, are already committed to the worship of God and look for the structure of support that lies within; they seek to comprehend, interpret, elaborate, and refine that religious system. The difference, in short, is that the theologian cries, "Dear God in heaven," while the philosopher says, "Dear God, if there be a God, in heaven, if there be a heaven." Both look for the justifying structure, but only one assumes that it is there.

A. The Existence of God: Examining the Arguments

The central question in the philosophy of religion is the existence of God, and in Judeo-Christian thought this means the personal being, omnipotent, omniscient, and omni-good, holy, eternal, and infinite, the creator of all life. Is such a being real or only an imaginative construct, arising from human needs and fears? Voltaire once wrote: "If there were no God, it would be necessary to invent him." Are there good reasons for believing that God is an existent being and not a human invention? The Bible states God created man in his own image; did man return the compliment?

Some believers refuse to address the question, claiming that faith, not reason, brings us to the truth. But not only is this a rational argument against the use of reason (and therefore self-contradictory) but it offers no protection against mistakes. If we argued this way, we would have no reliable method of separating one person's true beliefs from another person's false ones; each individual could claim that his or her views are based on faith and are beyond all reasoning. Furthermore, we would have a welter of different beliefs, many inconsistent with one another, with each claiming to be the final truth. Each would be immune from rational examination, yet they could not all be true. Clearly, this would be an impossible situation.

Although the relation between faith and reason is very complex, many theologians and philosophers have maintained that reason has a legitimate role in religion. They have offered rational arguments as proofs for the religious reality, and although they may not have been willing to abandon their faith when their arguments were criticized as untenable, they did attempt a logical justification for believing in God's existence.

The medieval theologian Saint Anselm presented one of these justifications, called the *ontological argument*.* He reasoned that if he had the idea of a being "than which none greater can be conceived," then that being had to exist. He means by such a being God, of course, and so he is claiming that God necessarily exists.

Saint Anselm argues specifically that if he has the idea of a being than which none greater can be conceived, this being must possess all positive attributes. Such a being must be almighty, perfectly wise, wholly loving, and so forth, otherwise Anselm could conceive of a greater entity, one that includes the attributes that are lacking. In addition, if this is truly a being than which none greater can be conceived, Anselm argues, he would have to possess the essential element of existence or, otherwise, not be a supreme being. The conclusion, then, is that the being Anselm is considering must possess existence, in other words, that God must be acknowledged to exist.

At first reading, Anselm's argument seems bewildering, and he appears to be saying that whatever he thinks of must exist. This was the criticism of a medieval monk named Gaunilon who argued that his ability to imagine a unicorn did not mean there are real unicorns.

However, Anselm's point is more subtle than that. He is not claiming that everything we reflect upon, including centaurs, gremlins, and Santa Claus, must be real, but that in this one unique case existence must be present. For we are thinking of a being than which none greater can be conceived, and here existence is a necessary part of such a being. In more modern terms, if we reflect on what a perfect God would be, we would have to include existence. We may not know everything that perfection entails, but we do know that existence is a necessary part, and that a being without existence could not be called perfect. This means that God, the perfect being, must exist.

If we still feel that something is wrong, that we cannot prove the existence of God just from the thought of God, perhaps our reaction is correct. In fact, those philosophers who criticize Anselm's argument identify this shift as the basic flaw.

Anselm's mistake seems to be that he confuses an *idea* with the reality the idea refers to. Although the idea of a perfect God must include existence as part of the idea, that does not prove there is an actually existent God behind the idea. Or differently put, the idea of a being than which none greater can be conceived must contain the notion of existence, but that does not imply that an actual being exists that the idea represents.

---

*St. Thomas Aquinas also formulated a version of this argument; see selection.

More technically put, existence is not an attribute to be added to others in describing a perfect being. It is the positing of a being with its various attributes. As the philosopher Immanuel Kant said, you cannot add to the value of a hundred imaginary dollars by taking a real one out of your pocket.

Because of some of these problems, another version of the ontological argument was proposed by the seventeenth-century French philosopher René Descartes. Sometimes this "Cartesian" argument is classified as causal, but since it does attempt to prove that God exists from the very thought of such a being, it seems basically ontological in character.

Descartes begins his argument with the principle that the greater can produce the lesser, but the lesser cannot produce the greater; that is, you can get less from more, but not more from less. This being so, if we have an idea that is greater than ourselves, then we could not have produced it. God is such an idea, for we as finite beings could not have conceived of the infinite; imperfect man could never have thought of the idea of a perfect God.

Descartes goes on to argue that the only being capable of producing the idea of God in our minds is God himself. He concludes therefore that God must exist. From the fact that we know of God, yet could not have conceived of that being by ourselves, we must admit the existence of a God who implanted the idea of himself within us.

Unfortunately, this argument has serious flaws as well. Perhaps the lesser can produce the greater, as in an avalanche caused by a snowball, an acorn that produces an oak tree, or a nuclear explosion that results from a split atom. Here, however, the effect is produced by the combination of causes, for example, the snowball plus additional snow, rocks, and trees. But whether or not less can produce more in the physical realm, human beings seem able to conceive of things far greater than themselves. Through the power of our imagination we can envision creatures with much greater strength, intelligence, or perception than our own, yet these creatures do not necessarily exist. Using Descartes's argument, we could even "prove" the existence of devils and supermen.

A second classic argument, which is generally attributed to Saint Thomas Aquinas, concerns the idea of cause and effect, and in its more sophisticated versions, change and unchangingness, and contingency and necessity. The *cosmological argument* proceeds as follows:

The world is arranged in a network of cause-and-effect relations such that every event has a cause which is itself the effect of a prior cause. Whatever occurs, we can legitimately ask what caused it. The tree crashed against the house because it was blown down by the wind; the old man died because his heart failed; the glass shattered because it fell on the stone floor. We can even trace a series of causes and effects backwards in time to see the causal factors that precipitated earlier and still earlier events. The flower grew because of the rich soil, but the soil was deposited by the weathering of rock, and the rock weathered because of the action of wind, water, and ice, which was caused by a changing climate, which in turn was due to . . . and so on.

However, the proponents of the cosmological argument say, this process of finding more and more ultimate causes cannot go on indefinitely; we cannot have an "infinite regress." Something must be shown to be the first cause, responsible for all succeeding links in the chain. There must be a beginning to the series, a *primum mobile* behind everything that occurs, and this first cause can only be God.

This argument seems natural and plausible, and it occurs even to children wondering where things first came from. However, it has been criticized on various grounds by numerous thinkers. First, no logical reason exists for claiming that an infinite regress is impossible. Just as there may not be a last effect (or a last number), there may not be a first cause; in a circular system, for example, the final event becomes the initial one (which is why the ring is a symbol of eternity).

Second, even if a first cause is necessary, that cause may not be God. A natural rather than a supernatural force may be responsible. For instance, the creation of the universe may be due to the explosion of the primal atom, something that astronomers refer to as the "big bang" theory. The background noise of that explosion has, in fact, been detected, as well as an unevenness in the radiation which would have allowed energy to form into clusters of stars and planets.

Third, if the argument takes as its premise that everything has a cause, then presumably God has a cause as well and cannot be regarded as an uncaused cause. If, on the other hand, God is an exception to the rule, then there might well be other exceptions. The universe itself might be uncaused, in which case there would be no necessity for postulating a God who caused it.

Many times the advocates of the cosmological argument find themselves arguing in a circle. They claim that everything must have a beginning and that God is that beginning; but when asked how God began, they assert that God did not begin at all, but has always been. When the logical point is made that perhaps the universe also has always been, they object that everything must have a beginning.

The more sophisticated versions, also presented by Saint Thomas, state that the fact of change in the world implies the existence of that which is unchanging, and that the contingency of all things implies that something must exist necessarily. By *contingent* is meant "dependent upon something else for its existence," as distinct from that which is self-existent, or carrying the reason for its existence within itself. These iterations, however, suffer from the same problems as the simple version in terms of cause and effect.

The *teleological argument* is a third justification that has traditionally been offered for belief in God; and, like the cosmological argument, it is part of Saint Thomas's Five Ways. This argument turns on the fact of order and harmony in nature, and it claims that if the world shows evidence of design, there must be a cosmic designer. The argument runs that when one examines the natural world, the regularity, balance, and arrangement of objects and events are immediately apparent. Instead of encountering randomness, we see orderliness everywhere.

The temperature and chemical composition of the earth's atmosphere is ideal for maintaining life; if the chemical mixture changed, or the earth were closer or father away from the sun, life would be impossible. In addition, there is a perfect symbiotic relationship between insects, plants, and animals, so that the organisms within the biosphere are mutually supportive.

Furthermore, each species has exactly what it requires in order to survive: the porcupine has been equipped with quills, the bird with wings, the tiger with sharp teeth and claws, the turtle with an armored shell, the zebra with camouflage, the snake with venom, and so forth. Every class of creature, in fact has been given the perfect characteristics to meet the needs of the environment—including human beings who have been given a superior brain. At the anatomical and physiological level, animals and people have exactly the muscles, organs, and skeletal structure and the circulatory, digestive, reproductive, nervous, and respiratory systems that they require. Even the eye and the heart are marvelous mechanisms, perfectly suited to their functions, as are the fin, the paw, and the hand.

In short, nature provides ample evidence of rational organization in all of its manifestations, which means a cosmic intelligence must exist. For there to be order, there must be an orderer, a plan requires a planner, and if an overall design is apparent, then a divine designer is responsible. God therefore exists as the only being capable of designing this intelligible world.

The teleological argument is extremely persuasive also, and even when philosophers criticize it, they respect its power and commonsense appeal. However, it does have serious weaknesses that make it problematic as a proof of God's existence.

For one thing, the design of the world is far from perfect and the imperfections that abound raise questions about the goodness of a God who created such a system. Not only is there chaos as well as order, but parts of the design involve pain and suffering for the creatures on earth, including human beings. Natural catastrophes (e.g., floods, earthquakes), genetic defects (e.g., blindness, Down syndrome), illnesses and disabilities (e.g., leukemia, cerebral palsy), savage animals (e.g., tigers, crocodiles), inhospitable environments (e.g., jungles, deserts), and the overwhelming fact of death, leave us in a state of doubt as to the beneficence of the plan. We wonder why a benevolent, almighty God would adopt a design of this kind, or whether the world might simply be the result of natural forces and not designed at all.

This leads to a second criticism, namely, that the order that exists could have come about naturally, not supernaturally. That is, another explanation for the regularity and orderliness in nature, besides that of an intelligent designer, is the scientific one offered by Darwin. According to the theory of evolution, those creatures that had the characteristics called for by the environment were able to survive; they then produced offspring with those same characteristics. Those that did not have the requisite skills, features, or capabilities perished in the struggle for survival, and their genetic line died out. Through this process of natural selection, only the fittest species survived, so it is not at all surprising that the species that exist on earth are fit for survival; if they weren't, they would not exist.

To be surprised that animals are well adapted to their environment would be like finding it uncanny that all Olympic winners are good athletes; obviously, if they weren't good athletes, they would not have won the Olympics. Or to use another parallel, one should not be amazed that so many major cities have navigable rivers; if the rivers had not been navigable, these cities would never have become major ones.

A third criticism that has been offered is that even if the teleological argument were valid, it would not prove a *creator* of the universe but only a cosmic architect who arranged the materials. Both the cosmological and the teleological arguments would have to be sound in order to establish a God who both created and organized the world. What's more, by analogy with human constructions, a number of designers would have been involved in the project. Polytheism, then, might be established, but not monotheism.

After confronting these three classic arguments, the result is rather disappointing. Not all philosophers accept the criticisms, of course, and some champion one or another of the arguments today, but most find them logically flawed for the reasons given.

Now if the ontological, cosmological, and teleological arguments are invalid, does that prove that God does not exist? Clearly not. To disprove an argument for the existence of God is not to disprove God's existence. Rather, we are left with an open question and must seek further for our answer.

In the first set of selections, St. Thomas Aquinas presents several of the classic arguments for the existence of God, and Leo Tolstoy describes the conversion to faith of Ivan Ilyitch on his deathbed. The film *Contact* is then summarized, emphasizing the power of a direct religious experience.

Summa Theologica
St. Thomas Aquinas

St. Thomas Aquinas (1225–1274), the Italian philosopher and theologian, is considered to be the most important figure in the development of Christian thought. He produced some eighty works during his lifetime, most notably Summa Contra Gentiles *(On the Truth of the Catholic Faith) and* Summa Theologica *(Summary Treatise of Theology). His fellow students labeled him the Dumb Ox, but during the Middle Ages he became more influential than any other theologian and was subsequently referred to as the Prince of Scholastics.*

Historically, Aquinas is important for reconciling the conflict between Greek and Arab thought, and between the Augustinians and Averroists. These doctrinal disputes are not important for our purposes. What is significant is that Aquinas championed the ability of reason to support faith and achieve genuine knowledge of God. To Aquinas, faith and reason were in harmony, and unity existed between philosophy and religion.

In the following excerpt from Summa Theologica, *sometimes known as the "Five Ways," Aquinas presents rational arguments for the existence of God. To his mind, these demonstrations showed that the head as well as the heart could prove God's reality.*

First Article: Whether the Existence of God Is Self-Evident?

We proceed thus to the First Article:—

Objection 1. It seems that the existence of God is self-evident. For those things are said to be self-evident to us the knowledge of which exists naturally in us, as we can see in regard to first principles. But as Damascene says, *the knowledge of God is naturally implanted in all.* Therefore the existence of God is self-evident.

Obj. 2. Further, those things are said to be self-evident which are known as soon as the terms are known, which the Philosopher says is true of the first principles of demonstration. Thus, when the nature of a whole and of a part is known, it is at once recognized that every whole is greater than its part. But as soon as the signification of the name *God* is understood, it is at once seen that God exists. For by this name is signified that thing than which nothing greater can be conceived. But that which exists actually and mentally is greater than that which exists only mentally. Therefore, since as soon as the name *God* is understood it exists mentally, it also follows that it exists actually. Therefore the proposition *God exists* is self-evident.

Obj. 3. Further, the existence of truth is self-evident. For whoever denies the existence of truth grants that truth does not exist: and, if truth does not exist, then the proposition *Truth does not exist* is true: and if there is anything true, there must be truth. But God is truth itself: *I am the way, the truth, and the life* (*Jo.* xiv. 6). Therefore *God exists* is self-evident.

On the contrary, No one can mentally admit the opposite of what is self-evident, as the Philosopher states concerning the first principles of demonstration. But the opposite of the proposition *God is* can be mentally admitted: *The fool said in his heart, There is no God* (Ps. lii. 1). Therefore, that God exists is not self-evident.

I answer that, A thing can be self-evident in either of two ways: on the one hand, self-evident in itself, though not to us; on the other, self-evident in itself, and to us. A proposition is self-evident because the predicate is included in the essence of the subject: *e.g., Man is an animal*, for animal is contained in the essence of man. If, therefore, the essence of the predicate and subject be known to all, the proposition will be self-evident to all; as is clear with regard to the first principles of demonstration, the terms of which are certain common notions that no one is ignorant of, such as being and non-being, whole and part, and the like. If, however, there are some to whom the essence of the predicate and subject is unknown, the proposition will be self-evident in itself, but not to those who do not know the meaning of the predicate and subject of the proposition. Therefore, it happens, as Boethius says, that there are some notions of the mind which are common and self-evident only to the learned, as that incorporeal substances are not in space. Therefore I say that this proposition, *God exists,* of itself is self-evident, for the predicate is the same as the subject, because God is His own existence as will be hereafter shown. Now because we do not know the essence of God, the proposition is not self-evident to us, but needs to be demonstrated by things that are more known to us, though less known in their nature—namely, by His effects.

Reply Obj. 1. To know that God exists in a general and confused way is implanted in us by nature, inasmuch as God is man's beatitude. For man naturally desires happiness, and what is naturally desired by man is naturally known by him. This, however, is not to know absolutely that God exists; just as to know that someone is approaching is not the same as to know that Peter is approaching, even though it is Peter who is approaching; for there are many who imagine that man's perfect good, which is happiness, consists in riches, and others in pleasures, and others in something else.

Reply Obj. 2. Perhaps not everyone who hears this name *God* understands it to signify something than which nothing greater can be thought, seeing that some have believed God to be a body. Yet, granted that everyone understands that by this name *God* is signified something than which nothing greater can be thought, nevertheless, it does not therefore follow that he understands that what the name signifies exists actually, but only that it exists mentally. Nor can it be argued that it actually exists, unless it be admitted that there actually exists something than which nothing greater can be thought; and this precisely is not admitted by those who hold that God does not exist.

Reply Obj. 3. The existence of truth in general is self-evident, but the existence of a Primal Truth is not self-evident to us.

Second Article: Whether It Can Be Demonstrated that God Exists

We proceed thus to the Second Article:—

Objection 1. It seems that the existence of God cannot be demonstrated. For it is an article of faith that God exists. But what is of faith cannot be demonstrated, because a demonstration produces scientific knowledge, whereas faith is of the unseen, as is clear from the Apostle (*Heb.* xi. 1). Therefore it cannot be demonstrated that God exists.

Obj. 2. Further, essence is the middle term of demonstration. But we cannot know in what God's essence consists, but solely in what it does not consist, as Damascene says. Therefore we cannot demonstrate that God exists.

Obj. 3. Further, if the existence of God were demonstrated, this could only be from His effects. But His effects are not proportioned to Him, since He is infinite and His effects are finite, and between the finite and infinite there is no proportion. Therefore, since a cause cannot be demonstrated by an effect not proportioned to it, it seems that the existence of God cannot be demonstrated.

On the contrary, The Apostle says: *The invisible things of Him are clearly seen, being understood by the things that are made* (*Rom.* i. 20). But this would not be unless the existence of God could be demonstrated through the things that are made; for the first thing we must know of anything is, whether it exists.

I answer that, Demonstration can be made in two ways: One is through the cause, and is called *propter quid,* and this is to argue from what is prior absolutely. The other is through the effect, and is called a demonstration *quia;* this is to argue from what is prior relatively only to us. When an effect is better known to us than its cause, from the effect we proceed to the knowledge of the cause. And from every effect the existence of its proper cause can be demonstrated, so long as its effects are better known to us; because, since every effect depends upon its cause, if the effect exists, the cause must pre-exist. Hence the existence of God, in so far as it is not self-evident to us, can be demonstrated from those of His effects which are known to us.

Reply Obj. 1. The existence of God and other like truths about God, which can be known by natural reason, are not articles of faith, but are preambles to the articles; for faith presupposes natural knowledge, even as grace presupposes nature and perfection the perfectible. Nevertheless, there is nothing to prevent a man, who cannot grasp a proof, from accepting, as a matter of faith, something which in itself is capable of being scientifically known and demonstrated.

Reply Obj. 2. When the existence of a cause is demonstrated from an effect, this effect takes the place of the definition of the cause in proving the cause's existence. This is especially the case in regard to God, because, in order to prove the existence of anything, it is necessary to accept as a middle term the meaning of the name, and not its essence, for the question of its essence follows on the question of its existence. Now the names given to God are derived from His effects. . . . Consequently, in demonstrating the existence of God from His effects, we may take for the middle term the meaning of the name *God*.

Reply Obj. 3. From effects not proportioned to the cause no perfect knowledge of that cause can be obtained. Yet from every effect the existence of the cause can be clearly demonstrated, and so we can demonstrate the existence of God from His effects; though from them we cannot know God perfectly as He is in His essence.

Third Article: Whether God Exists?

We proceed thus to the Third Article:—

Objection 1. It seems that God does not exist; because if one of two contraries be infinite, the other would be altogether destroyed. But the name *God* means that He is infinite goodness. If, therefore, God existed, there would be no evil discoverable; but there is evil in the world. Therefore God does not exist.

Obj. 2. Further, it is superfluous to suppose that what can be accounted for by a few principles has been produced by many. But it seems that everything we see in the world can be accounted for by other principles, supposing God did not exist. For all natural things can be reduced to one principle, which is nature; and all voluntary things can be reduced to one principle, which is human reason, or will. Therefore there is no need to suppose God's existence.

On the contrary, It is said in the person of God: *I am Who am* (*Exod.* iii. 14).

I answer that, The existence of God can be proved in five ways.

The first and more manifest way is the argument from motion. It is certain, and evident to our senses, that in the world some things are in motion. Now whatever is moved is moved by another, for nothing can be moved except it is in potentiality to that towards which it is moved; whereas a thing moves inasmuch as it is in act. For motion is nothing else than the reduction of something from potentiality to actuality. But nothing can be reduced from potentiality to actuality, except by something in a state of actuality. Thus that which is actually hot, as fire, makes wood, which is potentially hot, to be actually hot, and thereby moves and changes it. Now it is not possible that the same thing should be at once in actuality and potentiality in the same respect, but only in different respects. For what is actually hot cannot simultaneously be potentially hot; but it is simultaneously potentially cold. It is therefore impossible that in the same respect and in the same way a thing should be both mover and moved, *i.e.*, that it should move itself. Therefore, whatever is moved must be moved by another. If that by which it is moved be itself moved, then this also must needs be moved by another, and that by another again. But this cannot go on to infinity, because then there would be no first mover, and, consequently, no other mover, seeing that subsequent movers move only inasmuch as they are moved by the first mover; as the staff moves only because it is moved by the hand. Therefore it is necessary to arrive at a first mover, moved by no other; and this everyone understands to be God.

The second way is from the nature of efficient cause. In the world of sensible things we find there is an order of efficient causes. There is no case known (neither is it, indeed, possible) in which a thing is found to be the efficient cause of itself; for so it would be prior to itself, which is impossible. Now in efficient causes it is not possible to go on to infinity, because in all efficient causes following in order, the first is the cause of the intermediate cause, and the intermediate is the cause of the ultimate cause, whether the intermediate cause be several, or one only. Now to take away the cause is to take away the effect. Therefore, if there be no first cause among efficient causes, there will be no ultimate, nor any intermediate, cause. But if in efficient causes it is possible to go on to infinity, there will be no first efficient cause, neither will there be an ultimate effect, nor any intermediate efficient causes; all of which is plainly false. Therefore it is necessary to admit a first efficient cause, to which everyone gives the name of God.

The third way is taken from possibility and necessity, and runs thus We find in nature things that are possible to be and not to be, since they are found to be generated, and to be corrupted, and consequently, it is possible for them to be and not to be. But it is impossible for these always to exist for that which can not-be at some time is not. Therefore, if everything can not-be, then at one time there was nothing in existence. Now if this were true, even now there would be nothing in existence, because that which does not exist begins to exist only through something already existing. Therefore, if at one time nothing was in existence, it would have been impossible for anything to have begun to exist and thus even now nothing would be in existence—which is absurd. Therefore, not all beings are merely possible, but there must exist something the existence of which is necessary. But every necessary thing either has its necessity caused by another, or not. Now it is impossible to go on to infinity in necessary things which have their necessity caused by another, as has been already proved in regard to efficient causes. Therefore we cannot but admit the existence of some being having of itself its own necessity, and not receiving it from another, but rather causing in others their necessity. This all men speak of as God.

The fourth way is taken from the gradation to be found in things. Among beings there are some more and some less good, true, noble, and the like. But *more* and *less* are predicated of different things according as they resemble in their different ways something which is the maximum, as a thing is said to be hotter according as it more nearly resembles that which is hottest; so that there is something which is truest, something best, something noblest, and, consequently, something which is most being, for those things that are greatest in truth are greatest in being, as it is written in *Metaph.* ii. Now the maximum in any genus is the cause of all in that genus, as fire, which is the maximum of heat, is the cause of all hot things, as is said in the same book. Therefore there must also be something which is to all beings the cause of their being, goodness, and every other perfection; and this we call God.

The fifth way is taken from the governance of the world. We see that things which lack knowledge, such as natural bodies, act for an end, and this is evident from their acting always, or nearly always, in the same way, so as to obtain the best result. Hence it is plain that they achieve their end, not fortuitously, but designedly. Now whatever lacks knowledge cannot move towards an end, unless it be directed by some being endowed with knowledge and intelligence; as the arrow is directed by the archer. Therefore some intelligent being exists by whom all natural things are directed to their end; and this being we call God.

Reply Obj. 1. As Augustine says: *Since God is the highest good, He would not allow any evil to exist in His works, unless His omnipotence and goodness were such as to bring good even out of evil.* This is part of the infinite goodness of God, that He should allow evil to exist, and out of it produce good.

Reply Obj. 2. Since nature works for a determinate end under the direction of a higher agent, whatever is done by nature must be traced back to God as to its first cause. So likewise whatever is done voluntarily must be traced back to some higher cause other than human reason and will, since these can change and fail; for all things that are changeable and capable of defect must be traced back to an immovable and self-necessary first principle, as has been shown.

Study Questions

1. What does Aquinas mean when he says that the existence of God is self-evident?
2. Does Aquinas believe that the existence of God can be proven ("demonstrated"), or does he think it is a matter of faith not reason?

3. Explain the argument from motion which says "whatever is moved is moved by another . . . but this cannot go on to infinity . . . Therefore it is necessary to arrive at a first mover . . . this everyone understands to be God."

4. Explain Aquinas's argument from possibility and necessity.

5. Can you detect any flaws in any of the "Five Ways" of establishing God's existence?

The Death of Ivan Ilyitch
Leo Tolstoy

Leo Tolstoy (1828–1910) is one of the three great Russian writers, the other two being Ivan Turgenev and Fedor Dostoevsky. His most acclaimed works are War and Peace, *a grand epic of five aristocratic Russian families in the turbulent early nineteenth century, and* Ana Karenina, *a realistic tale of adultery and ultimate suffering. Ana transgressed moral laws and, to Tolstoy's mind, deserved punishment.*

Tolstoy's other novels as well as his short stories present a rich pageant of Russian life, always viewed in spiritual dimension. They include The Cossacks, Sevastopol Stories, Stories for the People, *and the autobiographical novels* Childhood, Boyhood, *and* Youth. *He also wrote a number of didactic essays and religious tracts, most notably* What Is Art?, A Confession, *and* The Kingdom of God Is Within You. *In all of his works, Tolstoy tries to demonstrate that God's hand is at work behind the scenes, both in human history and in our individual lives.*

Tolstoy's short story The Death of Ivan Ilyitch *deals with an individual's experience of dying, but it does not treat the phenomenon as an irredeemable evil. Rather, Tolstoy shows how dying can be a time for profound reflection on the significance of one's life, on whether one has lived well or badly, and where one stands in relation to God and one's fellow human beings. Through suffering and isolation in his suffering, Ivan Ilyitch comes to certain realizations about the sham, hypocrisy, and empty conventionality of the society of which he had been a part, and at the last moment repents and asks forgiveness of God. Tolstoy is demonstrating that even death has a place in the grand cosmic scheme, bringing people to an awareness of fundamental values and the purpose of life on earth, which is to serve God through love for all humankind.*

Chapter II

The past history of Ivan Ilyitch's life was most simple and uneventful, and yet most terrible.

Ivan Ilyitch died at the age of forty-five, a member of the Court of Justice. He was the son of a functionary who had followed, in various ministries and departments at Petersburg, a career such as brings men into a position from which, on account of their long service and their rank, they are never turned adrift, even though it is plainly manifest that their actual usefulness is at an end; and consequently they obtain imaginary, fictitious places, and from six to ten thousand that are not fictitious, on which they live till a good old age.

Such had been Ilya Yefimovitch Golovin, privy councilor, a useless member of various useless commissions.

He had three sons; Ivan Ilyitch was the second. The eldest had followed the same career as his father's, but in a different ministry, and was already nearing that period of his service in which inertia carries a man into emoluments. The third son had been a failure. He had completely gone to pieces in several positions, and he was now connected with railways; and his father and his brothers and especially their wives not only disliked to meet him, but, except when it was absolutely necessary, even forgot that he existed.

A sister was married to Baron Gref, who, like his father-in-law, was a Petersburg chinovnik. Ivan Ilyitch had been *le phénix de la famille,* as they used to say. He was neither so chilling and formal as the eldest brother, nor so unpromising as the youngest. He was the mean between them,—an intelligent, lively, agreeable, and polished man. He had studied at the law school with his younger brother, who did not graduate but was expelled from the fifth class; Ivan Ilyitch, however, finished his course creditably. At the law-school he showed the same characteristics by which he was afterward distinguished all his life: he was capable, good-natured even to gayety, and sociable, but strictly fulfilling all that he considered to be his duty; duty, in his opinion, was all that is considered to be such by men in the highest station. He was not one to curry favor, either as a boy, or afterward in manhood; but from his earliest years he had been attracted by men in the highest station in society, just as a fly is by the light; he adopted their ways, their views of life, and entered into relations of friendship with them. All the passions of childhood and youth had passed away, not leaving serious traces. He had yielded to sensuality and vanity, and, toward the last of his life, to the higher forms of liberalism, but all within certain limits which his nature faithfully prescribed for him.

While at the law-school, he had done some things which hitherto had seemed to him very shameful, and which while he was engaged in them aroused in him deep scorn for himself. But afterward, finding that these things were also done by men of high position, and were not considered by them disgraceful, he came to regard them, not indeed as worthy, but as something to put entirely out of his mind, and he was not in the least troubled by the recollection of them.

When Ivan Ilyitch had graduated from the law-school with the tenth rank, and received from his father some money for his uniform, he ordered a suit of Scharmer, added to his trinkets the little medal with the legend *respice finem,* bade the prince and principal farewell, ate a dinner with his classmates at Donon's and, furnished with new and stylish trunk, linen, uniform, razors, and toilet articles, and a plaid, ordered or

*the paragon of the family

bought at the very best shops, he departed for the province, as chinovnik and private secretary to the governor—a place which his father procured for him.

In the province, Ivan Ilyitch at once got himself into the same sort of easy and agreeable position as his position in the law-school had been. He attended to his duties, pressed forward in his career, and at the same time enjoyed life in a cheerful and circumspect manner. From time to time, delegated by his chief, he visited the districts, bore himself with dignity toward both his superiors and subordinates, and, without overweening conceit, fulfilled with punctuality and incorruptible integrity the duties imposed upon him, preëminently in the affair of the dissenters.

Notwithstanding his youth, and his tendency to be gay and easygoing, he was, in matters of State, thoroughly discreet, and carried his official reserve even to sternness. But in society he was often merry and witty, and always good-natured, polite, and *bon enfant,* as he was called by his chief and his chief's wife, at whose house he was intimate.

While he was in the province, he had maintained relations with one of those ladies who are ready to fling themselves into the arms of an elegant young lawyer. There was also a dressmaker; and there were occasional sprees with visiting flügel-adjutants, and visits to some out-of-the-way street after supper; he had also the favor of his chief and even of his chief's wife, but everything of this sort was attended with such a high tone of good-breeding that it could not be qualified by hard names; it all squared with the rubric of the French expression, *Il faut que jeunesse se passe.**

All was done with clean hands, with clean linen, with French words, and, above all, in company with the very highest society, and therefore with the approbation of those high in rank.

In this way Ivan Ilyitch served five years, and a change was instituted in the service. The new tribunals were established; new men were needed.

And Ivan Ilyitch was chosen as one of the new men.

He was offered the position of examining magistrate; and accepted it, notwithstanding the fact that this place was in another government, and that he would be obliged to give up the connections he had formed, and form new ones.

Ivan Ilyitch's friends saw him off. They were photographed in a group, they presented him a silver cigarette-case, and he departed for his new post.

As an examining magistrate, Ivan Ilyitch was just as *comme il faut,*** just as circumspect, and careful to sunder the obligations of his office from his private life, and as successful in winning universal

*A man must sow his wild oats.
**proper; correct

consideration, as when he was a chinovnik with special functions. The office of magistrate itself was vastly more interesting and attractive to Ivan Ilyitch than his former position had been.

To be sure, it used to be agreeable to him, in his former position, to pass with free and easy gait, in his Scharmer-made uniform, in front of trembling petitioners and petty officials, waiting for an interview, and envying him, as he went without hesitation into his chief's private room, and sat down with him to drink a cup of tea, and smoke a cigarette; but the men who had been directly dependent on his pleasure were few,— merely police captains and dissenters, if he were sent out with special instructions. And he liked to meet these men, dependent on him, not only politely, but even on terms of comradeship; he liked to make them feel that he, who had the power to crush them, treated them simply, and like friends. Such men at that time were few.

But now, as examining magistrate, Ivan Ilyitch felt that all, all without exception, even men of importance, of distinction, all were in his hands, and that all he had to do was to write such and such words on a piece of paper and a heading, and this important, distinguished man would be brought to him in the capacity of accused or witness, and, unless he wished to ask him to sit down, he would have to stand in his presence, and submit to his questions. Ivan Ilyitch never took undue advantage of this power; on the contrary, he tried to temper the expression of it. But the consciousness of this power, and the possibility of tempering it, furnished for him the chief interest and attractiveness of his new office.

In the office itself, especially in investigations, Ivan Ilyitch was very quick to master the process of eliminating all circumstances extraneous to the case, and of disentangling the most complicated details in such a manner that the case would be presented on paper only in its essentials, and absolutely shorn of his own personal opinion, and, last and not least, that every necessary formality would be fulfilled. This was a new mode of doing things. And he was one of the first to be engaged in putting into operation the code of 1864.

When he took up his residence in the new city, as examining magistrate, Ivan Ilyitch made new acquaintances and ties; he put himself on a new footing, and adopted a somewhat different tone. He held himself rather aloof from the provincial authorities, and took up with a better circle among the judges and wealthy nobles living in the city; and he adopted a tone of easy-going criticism of the government, together with a moderate form of liberalism and "civilized citizenship." At the same time, though Ivan Ilyitch in no wise diminished the elegance of his toilet, yet he ceased to shave his chin, and allowed his beard to grow as it would.

Ivan Ilyitch's life in the new city also passed very agreeably. The society which *fronded* against the government was good and friendly; his salary was larger than before; and, while he had no less zest in life, he had the additional pleasure of playing whist, a game in which, as he enjoyed playing cards, he quickly learned to excel, so that he was always on the winning side.

After two years of service in the new city Ivan Ilyitch met the lady who became his wife. Praskovia Feodorovna Mikhel was the most fascinating, witty, brilliant young girl in the circle where Ivan Ilyitch moved. In the multitude of other recreations, and as a solace from the labors of his office, Ivan Ilyitch established sportive, easy-going relations with Praskovia Feodorovna.

At the time when Ivan Ilyitch was a chinovnik with special functions, he had been a passionate lover of dancing; but now that he was examining magistrate, he danced only as an occasional exception. He now danced with the idea that, "though I am an advocate of the new order of things, and belong to the fifth class, still, as far as the question of dancing goes, I can at least show that in this respect I am better than the rest."

Thus, it frequently happened that, toward the end of a party, he danced with Praskovia Feodorovna; and it was principally at the time of these dances, that he made the conquest of Praskovia Feodorovna. She fell in love with him. Ivan Ilyitch had no clearly decided intention of getting married; but when the girl fell in love with him, he asked himself this question: "In fact, why should I not get married?" said he to himself.

The young lady, Praskovia Feodorovna, came of a good family belonging to the nobility, far from ill-favored, had a small fortune. Ivan Ilyitch might have aspired to a more brilliant match, but this was an excellent one. Ivan Ilyitch had his salary; she, he hoped, would have as much more. She was of good family; she was sweet, pretty, and a thoroughly well-bred woman. To say that Ivan Ilyitch got married because he was in love with his betrothed, and found in her sympathy with his views of life, would be just as incorrect as to say that he got married because the men of his set approved of the match.

Ivan Ilyitch took a wife for two reasons: he gave himself a pleasure in taking such a wife; and, at the same time, the people of the highest rank considered such an act proper.

And so Ivan Ilyitch got married.

The wedding ceremony itself, and the first few days of their married life with its connubial caresses, their new furniture, their new plate, their new linen, everything, even the prospects of an increasing family, were all that could be desired. So that Ivan Ilyitch began to think that marriage not only was not going to disturb his easy-going, pleasant, gay, and always respectable life, so approved by society, and which Ivan Ilyitch considered a perfectly natural characteristic of life in general, but was also going to add to it. But from the first months of his wife's pregnancy, there appeared something new, unexpected, disagreeable, hard, and trying, which he could not have foreseen, and from which it was impossible to escape.

His wife, without any motive, as it seemed to Ivan Ilyitch, *de gaité de cœur,** as he said to himself, began to interfere with the pleasant and decent current of his life; without any cause she grew jealous of him, demanded attentions from him, found fault with everything, and caused him disagreeable and stormy scenes.

At first Ivan Ilyitch hoped to free himself from this unpleasant state of things by the same easy-going and respectable acceptation of life which had helped him in days gone by. He tried to ignore his wife's disposition, and continued to live as before in an easy and pleasant way. He invited his friends, he gave card-parties, he attempted to make his visits to the club or to friends; but his wife began one time to abuse him with rough and energetic language, and continued persistently to scold him each time that he failed to fulfil her demands, having evidently made up her mind not to cease berating him until he was completely subjected to her authority,—in other words, until he would stay at home, and be just as deeply in the dumps as she herself,—a thing which Ivan Ilyitch dreaded above all.

He learned that married life, at least as far as his wife was concerned, did not always add to the pleasantness and decency of existence, but, on the contrary, disturbed it, and that, therefore, it was necessary to protect himself from such interference. And Ivan Ilyitch tried to devise means to this end. His official duties were the only thing that had an imposing effect upon Praskovia Feodorovna; and Ivan Ilyitch, by means of his office, and the duties arising from it, began the struggle with his wife, for the defense of his independent life.

When the child was born, and in consequence of the various attempts and failures to have it properly nursed, and the illnesses, real and imaginary, of both mother and child, wherein Ivan Ilyitch's sympathy was demanded, but which were absolutely foreign to him, the necessity for him to secure a life outside of his family became still more imperative.

According as his wife grew more irritable and exacting, so Ivan Ilyitch transferred the center of his life's burdens more and more into his office. He began to love his office more and more, and became more ambitious than he had ever been.

Very soon, not longer than a year after his marriage, Ivan Ilyitch came to the conclusion that married life, while affording certain advantages, was in reality a very complicated and burdensome thing, in relation to which, if one would fulfil his duty, that is, live respectably and

*frivolously; gratuitously; out of sheer wantonness

with the approbation of society, one must work out a certain system, just as in public office.

And such a system Ivan Ilyitch secured in his matrimonial life. He demanded of family life only such conveniences in the way of home dinners, a housekeeper, a bed, as it could furnish him, and, above all, that respectability in external forms which was in accordance with the opinions of society. As for the rest, he was anxious for pleasant amenities; and if he found them, he was very grateful. On the other hand, if he met with opposition and complaint, then he immediately took refuge in the far-off world of his official duties, which alone offered him delight.

Ivan Ilyitch was regarded as an excellent magistrate, and at the end of three years he was appointed deputy-prokuror. His new functions, their importance, the power vested in him of arresting and imprisoning any one, the publicity of his speeches, his success obtained in this field,— all this still more attached him to the service.

Children came; his wife kept growing more irritable and ill-tempered; but the relations which Ivan Ilyitch maintained toward family life made him almost proof against her temper.

After seven years of service in one city, Ivan Ilyitch was promoted to the office of prokuror in another government. They moved; they had not much money, and the place where they went did not suit his wife. Although his salary was larger than before, yet living was more expensive; moreover, two of their children died; and thus family life became still more distasteful to Ivan Ilyitch.

Praskovia Feodorovna blamed her husband for all the misfortunes that came on them in their new place of abode. Most of the subjects of conversation between husband and wife, especially the education of their children, led to questions which were productive of quarrels, so that quarrels were always ready to break out. Only at rare intervals came those periods of affection which distinguish married life, but they were not of long duration. These were little islands in which they rested for a time; but then again they pushed out into the sea of secret animosity, which expressed itself by driving them farther and farther apart.

This alienation might have irritated Ivan Ilyitch, if he had not considered that it was inevitable; but he now began to look on this situation not merely as normal, but even as the goal of his activity in the family. This goal consisted in withdrawing as far as possible from these unpleasantnesses, or of giving them a character of innocence and respectability; and he attained this end by spending less and less time with his family; but when he was to do so, then he endeavored to guarantee his position by the presence of strangers.

But Ivan Ilyitch's chief resource was his office. In the world of his duties was concentrated all his interest in life. And this interest wholly absorbed him. The consciousness of his power of ruining any one whom he might wish to ruin; the importance of his position manifested outwardly when he came into court or met his subordinates; his success with superiors and subordinates; and, above all, his skill in the conduct of affairs,—and he was perfectly conscious of it,—all this delighted him, and, together with conversations with his colleagues, dinners and whist, filled all his life. Thus, for the most part, Ivan Ilyitch's life continued to flow in its even tenor as he considered that it ought to flow,—pleasantly and respectably.

Thus he lived seven years longer. His eldest daughter was already sixteen years old; still another little child had died; and there remained a lad, the one who was in school, the object of their wrangling. Ivan Ilyitch wanted to send him to the lawschool; but Praskovia, out of spite toward him, selected the gymnasium. The daughter studied at home, and made good progress; the lad also was not at all backward in his studies.

(Ivan Ilyitch receives an advance in rank and a consequent increase in salary which enables him to live on an even grander scale. By all social standards he is an extremely successful man and he himself looks upon his life as a fortunate one, but a shadow falls over his happiness. One day while climbing a ladder he slips and injures his side. The bruise seems minor, but gradually he begins to feel pain internally, and his suffering increases to a point where he realizes that the injury is a serious one. The doctors differ in their diagnoses and ultimately cannot offer any help; Ivan Ilyitch slowly accepts the fact that he is dying.)

* * *

Chapter VII

It was morning.

It was morning merely because Gerasim had gone, and Piotr, the lackey, had come. He put out the candles, opened one curtain, and began noiselessly to put things to rights. Whether it were morning, whether it were evening, Friday or Sunday, all was a matter of indifference to him, all was one and the same thing. The agonizing, shooting pain, never for an instant appeased; the consciousness of a life hopelessly wasting away, but not yet departed; the same terrible, cursed death coming nearer and nearer, the one reality, and always the same lie,—what matter, then, here, of days, weeks, and hours of the day?

"Will you not have me bring the tea?"

"He must follow form, and that requires masters to take tea in the morning," he thought; and he said merely:—

"No."

"Wouldn't you like to go over to the divan?"

"He has to put the room in order, and I hinder him; I am uncleanness, disorder!" he thought to himself, and said merely:—

"No; leave me!"

The lackey still bustled about a little. Ivan Ilyitch put out his hand. Piotr officiously hastened to him:—

"What do you wish?"

"My watch."

Piotr got the watch, which lay near by, and gave it to him.

"Half-past eight. They aren't up yet?"

"No one at all. Vasili Ivanovitch"—that was his son—"has gone to school, and Praskovia Feodorovna gave orders to wake her up if you asked for her. Do you wish it?"

"No, it is not necessary.—Shall I not try the tea?" he asked himself. "Yes...tea...bring me some."

Piotr started to go out. Ivan Ilyitch felt terror-stricken at being left alone. "How can I keep him? Yes, my medicine. Piotr, give me my medicine.—Why not? perhaps the medicine may help me yet."

He took the spoon, sipped it.

"No, there is no help. All this is nonsense and delusion," he said, as he immediately felt the familiar, mawkish, hopeless taste.

"No, I cannot have any faith in it. But this pain, . . . why this pain? Would that it might cease for a minute!"

And he began to groan. Piotr came back.

"Nothing . . . go! Bring the tea."

Piotr went out. Ivan Ilyitch, left alone, began to groan, not so much from the pain, although it was horrible, as from mental anguish.

"Always the same thing, and the same thing; all these endless days and nights. Would it might come very soon! What very soon? Death, blackness? No, no! Anything rather than death!"

When Piotr came back with the tea on a tray, Ivan Ilyitch stared long at him in bewilderment, not comprehending who he was, what he was. Piotr was abashed at this gaze; and when Piotr showed his confusion, Ivan Ilyitch came to himself.

"Oh, yes," said he, "the tea; very well, set it down. Only help me to wash, and to put on a clean shirt."

And Ivan Ilyitch began to perform his toilet. With resting spells he washed his hands and face, cleaned his teeth, began to comb his hair, and looked into the mirror. It seemed frightful, perfectly frightful, to him, to see how his hair lay flat upon his pale brow.

While he was changing his shirt, he knew that it would be still more frightful if he gazed at his body; and so he did not look at himself. But now it was done. He put on his khalat, wrapped himself in his plaid, and sat down in his easy-chair to take his tea. For a single moment he felt refreshed; but as soon as he began to drink the tea, again that same taste, that same pain. He compelled himself to drink it all, and lay down, stretching out his legs. He lay down, and let Piotr go.

Always the same thing. Now a drop of hope gleaming, then a sea of despair rising up, and always pain, always melancholy, and always the same monotony. It was terribly melancholy to the lonely man; he longed to call in some one, but he knew in advance that it is still worse when others are present.

"Even morphine again . . . to get a little sleep! . . . I will tell him, tell the doctor, to find something else. It is impossible, impossible so."

One hour, two hours, would pass in this way. But there! the bell in the corridor. Perhaps it is the doctor. Exactly: it is the doctor, fresh, hearty, portly, jovial, with an expression as if he said, "You may feel apprehension of something or other, but we will immediately straighten things out for you."

The doctor knows that this expression is not appropriate here; but he has already put it on once for all, and he cannot rid himself of it—like a man who has put on his dress-coat in the morning, and gone to make calls.

The doctor rubs his hands with an air of hearty assurance.

"I am cold. A healthy frost Let me get warm a little," says he, with just the expression that signifies that all he needs is to wait until he gets warmed a little, and, when he is warmed, then he will straighten things out.

"Well, now, how goes it?"

Ivan Ilyitch feels that the doctor wants to say, "How go your little affairs?" but that he feels that it is impossible to say so; and he says, "What sort of a night did you have?"

Ivan Ilyitch would look at the doctor with an expression which seemed to ask the question, "Are you never ashamed of lying?"

But the doctor has no desire to understand his question.

And Ivan Ilyitch *says:*—

"It was just horrible! The pain does not cease, does not disappear. If you could only give me something for it!"

"That is always the way with you sick folks! Well, now, it seems to me I am warm enough; even the most particular Praskovia Feodorovna would not find anything to take exception to in my temperature. Well, now, how are you really?"

And the doctor shakes hands with him.

And, laying aside his former jocularity, the doctor begins with serious mien to examine the sick man, his pulse and temperature, and he renews the tappings and the auscultation.

Ivan Ilyitch knew for a certainty, and beyond peradventure, that all this was nonsense and foolish deception; but when the doctor, on his knees, leaned over toward him, applying his ear, now higher up, now lower down, and with most sapient mien performed various gymnastic evolutions on him, Ivan Ilyitch succumbed to him, as once he succumbed to the discourses of the lawyers, even when he knew perfectly well that they were deceiving him, and why they were deceiving him.

The doctor, still on his knees on the divan, was still performing the auscultation, when at the door were heard the rustle of Praskovia Feodorovna's silk dress, and her words of blame to Piotr because he had not informed her of the doctor's visit.

She came in, kissed her husband, and immediately began to explain that she had been up a long time; and only through a misunderstanding she had not been there when the doctor came.

Ivan Ilyitch looked at her, observed her from head to foot, and felt a secret indignation at her fairness and her plumpness, and the cleanliness of her hands, her neck, her glossy hair, and the brilliancy of her eyes, brimming with life. He hated her with all the strength of his soul, and her touch made him suffer an actual paroxysm of hatred of her.

Her attitude toward him and his malady was the same as before. Just as the doctor had formulated his treatment of his patient and could not change it, so she had formulated her treatment of him, making him feel that he was not doing what he ought to do, and was himself to blame; and she liked to reproach him for this, and she could not change her attitude toward him.

"Now, just see! he does not heed, he does not take his medicine regularly; and, above all, he lies in a position that is surely bad for him—his feet up."

She related how he made Gerasim hold his legs.

The doctor listened with a disdainfully good-natured smile, as much as to say:—

"What is to be done about it, pray? These sick folks are always conceiving some such foolishness. But you must let it go."

When the examination was over, the doctor looked at his watch; and then Praskovia Feodorovna declared to Ivan Ilyitch that, whether he was willing or not, she was going that very day to call in the celebrated doctor to come and have an examination and consultation with Mikhaïl Danilovitch—that was the name of their ordinary doctor.

"Now, don't oppose it, please. I am doing this for my own self," she said ironically, giving him to understand that she did it all for him, and only on this account did not allow him the right to oppose her.

He said nothing, and frowned. He felt that this lie surrounding him was so complicated that it was now hard to escape from it.

She did all this for him, only in her own interest; and she said that she was doing it for him, while she was in reality doing it for herself, as some incredible thing, so that he was forced to take it in its opposite sense.

The celebrated doctor, in fact, came about half-past eleven. Once more they had auscultations; and learned discussions took place before him, or in the next room, about his kidney, about the blind intestine, and questions and answers in such a learned form that again the place of the real question of life and death, which now alone faced him, was driven away by the question of the kidney and the blind intestine, which were not acting as became them, and on which Mikhaïl Danilovitch and the celebrity were to fall instantly and compel to attend to their duties.

The famous doctor took leave with a serious but not hopeless expression. And in reply to the timid question which Ivan Ilyitch's eyes, shining with fear and hope, asked of him, whether there was a possibility of his getting well, it replied that it could not vouch for it, but there was a possibility.

The look of hope with which Ivan Ilyitch followed the doctor was so pathetic that Praskovia Feodorovna, seeing it, even wept, as she went out of the library door in order to give the celebrated doctor his honorarium.

The raising of his spirits, caused by the doctor's hopefulness, was but temporary. Again the same room, the same pictures, curtains, wall-paper, vials, and his aching, pain-broken body. And Ivan Ilyitch began to groan. They gave him a subcutaneous injection, and he fell asleep.

When he woke up it was beginning to grow dusky. They brought him his dinner. He forced himself to eat a little *bouillon*. And again the same monotony, and again the advancing night.

About seven o'clock, after dinner, Praskovia Feodorovna came into his room, dressed as for a party, with her exuberant bosom swelling in her stays, and with traces of powder on her face. She had already that morning told him that they were going to the theater. Sarah Bernhardt had come to town, and they had a box which he had insisted on their taking.

Now he had forgotten about that, and her toilet offended him. But he concealed his vexation when he recollected that he himself had insisted on their taking a box, and going, on the ground that it would be an instructive, esthetic enjoyment for the children.

Praskovia Feodorovna came in self-satisfied, but, as it were, feeling a little to blame. She sat down, asked after his health, as he saw, only for the sake of asking, and not so as to learn, knowing that there was nothing to learn, and began to say what was incumbent on her to say,—that she would not have gone for anything, but that they had taken the box; and that Elen and her daughter and Petrishchef—the examining magistrate, her daughter's betrothed—were going, and it was impossible to let them go alone, but that it would have been more agreeable to her to stay at home with him. Only he should be sure to follow the doctor's prescriptions in her absence.

"Yes—and Feodor Petrovitch"—the betrothed—"wanted to come in. May he? And Liza!"

"Let them come."

The daughter came in, in evening dress, with her fair young body,—her body that made his anguish more keen. But she paraded it before him, strong, healthy, evidently in love, and irritated against the disease, the suffering, and death which stood in the way of her happiness.

Feodor Petrovitch also entered, in his dress-coat, with curly hair *à la Capoul*, with long, sinewy neck tightly incased in a white standing collar, with a huge white bosom, and his long, muscular legs in tight black trousers, with a white glove on one hand, and with an opera hat.

Immediately behind him, almost unnoticed, came the gymnasium scholar, in his new uniform, poor little fellow, with gloves on, and with that terrible blue circle under the eyes, the meaning of which Ivan Ilyitch understood.

He always felt a pity for his son. And terrible was his timid and compassionate glance. With the exception of Gerasim, Vasya alone, it seemed to Ivan Ilyitch, understood and pitied him.

All sat down; again they asked after his health. Silence ensued. Liza asked her mother if she had the opera-glasses. A dispute arose between mother and daughter as to who had mislaid them. It was a disagreeable episode.

Feodor Petrovitch asked Ivan Ilyitch if he had seen Sarah Bernhardt. Ivan Ilyitch did not at first understand his question, but in a moment he said:—

"No . . . why, have you seen her yet?"

"Yes, in 'Adrienne Lecouvreur.'"

Praskovia Feodorovna said that she was especially good in that. The daughter disagreed with her. A conversation arose about the grace and realism of her acting,—the same conversation, which is always and forever one and the same thing.

In the midst of the conversation, Feodor Petrovitch glanced at Ivan Ilyitch, and grew silent. The others glanced at him, and grew silent. Ivan Ilyitch was looking straight ahead with gleaming eyes, evidently indignant at them. Some one had to extricate them from their embarrassment, but there seemed to be no way out of it. No one spoke; and a panic seized them all, lest suddenly this ceremonial lie should somehow be shattered, and the absolute truth become manifest to all.

Liza was the first to speak. She broke the silence. She wished to hide what all felt, but she betrayed it.

"One thing is certain,—*if we are going*, it is time," she said, glancing at her watch, her father's gift; and giving the young man a sign, scarcely perceptible, and yet understood by him, she smiled, and arose in her rustling dress.

All arose, said good-by, and went.

When they had gone, Ivan Ilyitch thought that he felt easier: the lying was at an end; it had gone with them; but the pain remained. Always this same pain, always this same terror, made it hard as hard could be. There was no easing of it. It grew ever worse, always worse.

Again minute after minute dragged by, hour after hour, forever the same monotony, and forever endless, and forever more terrible—the inevitable end.

"Yes, send me Gerasim," was his reply to Piotr's question.

Chapter IX

Late at night his wife returned. She came in on her tiptoes, but he heard her; he opened his eyes, and quickly closed them again. She wanted to send Gerasim away, and sit with him herself. He opened his eyes, and said:—

"No, go away."

"You suffer very much."

"It makes no difference."

"Take some opium."

He consented, and drank it. She went.

Until three o'clock he was in a painful sleep. It seemed to him that they were forcing him cruelly into a narrow sack, black and deep; and they kept crowding him down, but could not force him in. And this performance, horrible for him, was accompanied with anguish. And he was afraid, and yet wished to get in, and struggled against it, and yet tried to help.

And here suddenly he broke through, and fell . . . and awoke.

There was Gerasim still sitting at his feet on the bed, dozing peacefully, patiently.

But he was lying there with his emaciated legs in stockings resting on his shoulders, the same candle with its shade, and the same never ending pain.

"Go away, Gerasim," he whispered.

"It's nothing; I will sit here a little while."

"No, go away."

He took down his legs, lay on his side on his arm, and began to pity himself. He waited only until Gerasim had gone into the next room, and then he no longer tried to control himself, but wept like a child. He wept over his helplessness, over his terrible loneliness, over the cruelty of men, over the cruelty of God, over the absence of God.

"Why hast Thou done this? Why didst Thou place me here? Why, why dost Thou torture me so horribly?"

He expected no reply; and he wept because there was none, and could be none. The pain seized him again; but he did not stir, did not call. He said to himself:—

"There, now again, now strike! But why? What have I done to Thee? Why is it?"

Then he became silent; ceased not only to weep, ceased to breathe, and became all attention: as it were, he heard, not a voice speaking with sounds, but the voice of his soul, the tide of his thoughts, arising in him.

"What dost thou need?" was the first clear concept possible to be expressed in words which he heard.

"'What dost thou need? What dost thou need?'" he said to himself.

"What? Freedom from suffering. To live," he replied.

And again he gave his attention, with such effort that already he did not even notice his pain.

"To live? how live?" asked the voice of his soul.

"Yes, to live as I used to live—well, pleasantly."

"How didst thou live before when thou didst live well and pleasantly?" asked the voice.

And he began to call up in his imagination the best moments of his pleasant life. But, strangely enough, all these best moments of his pleasant life seemed to him absolutely different from what they had seemed then,—all, except the earliest remembrances of his childhood. There, in childhood, was something really pleasant, which would give new zest to life if it were to return. But the person who had enjoyed that pleasant existence was no more; it was as if it were the remembrance of some one else.

As soon as the period began which had produced the present *he,* Ivan Ilyitch, all the pleasures which seemed such then, now in his eyes dwindled away, and changed into something of no account, and even disgusting.

And the farther he departed from infancy, and the nearer he came to the present, so much the more unimportant and dubious were the pleasures.

This began in the law-school. There was still something even then which was truly good; then there was gayety, there was friendship, there were hopes. But in the upper classes these good moments became rarer.

Then, in the time of his first service at the governor's, again appeared good moments; these were the recollections of love for a woman. Then all this became confused, and the happy time grew less. The nearer he came to the present, the worse it grew, and still worse and worse it grew.

"My marriage . . . so unexpected, and disillusionment and my wife's breath, and sensuality, hypocrisy! And this dead service, and these labors for money; and thus one year, and two, and ten, and twenty,—and always the same thing. And the longer it went, the more dead it became.

"It is as if all the time I were going down the mountain, while thinking that I was climbing it. So it was. According to public opinion, I was climbing the mountain; and all the time my life was gliding away from under my feet. . . . And here it is already . . . die!

"What is this? Why? It cannot be! It cannot be that life has been so irrational, so disgusting. But even if it is so disgusting and irrational, still, why die, and die in such agony? There is no reason."

"Can it be that I did not live as I ought?" suddenly came into his head. "But how can that be, when I have done all that it was my duty to do?" he asked himself. And immediately he put away this sole explanation of the enigma of life and death as something absolutely impossible.

"What dost thou wish now?—To live? To live how? To live as thou livest in court when the usher proclaims, 'The court is coming! the court is coming'?

"The court is coming—the court," he repeated to himself. "Here it is, the court. Yes; but I am not guilty," he cried with indignation. "What for?"

And he ceased to weep; and, turning his face to the wall, he began to think about that one thing, and that alone. "Why, wherefore, all this horror?"

But, in spite of all his thoughts, he received no answer. And when the thought occurred to him, as it had often occurred to him, that all this came from the fact that he had not lived as he should, he instantly remembered all the correctness of his life, and he drove away this strange thought.

Chapter X

Thus two weeks longer passed. Ivan Ilyitch no longer got up from the divan. He did not wish to lie in bed, and he lay on the divan. And, lying almost all the time with his face to the wall, he still suffered in solitude the same inexplicable sufferings, and still thought in solitude the same inexplicable thought.

"What is this? Is it true that this is death?"

And an inward voice responded:—

"Yes, it is true."

"Why these torments?"

And the voice responded:—

"But it is so. There is no why."

Farther and beyond this, there was nothing.

From the very beginning of his malady, from the time when Ivan Ilyitch for the first time went to the doctor, his life was divided into two conflicting tendencies, alternately succeeding each other. Now it was despair, and the expectation of an incomprehensible and frightful death; now it was hope, and the observation of the functional activity of his body, so full of interest for him. Now before his eyes was the kidney, or the intestine, which, for the time being, failed to fulfil its duty. Then it was that incomprehensible, horrible death, from which it was impossible for any one to escape.

These two mental states, from the very beginning of his illness, kept alternating with one another. But the farther the illness progressed, the more dubious and fantastical became his ideas about the kidney, and the more real his consciousness of approaching death.

He had but to call to mind what he had been three months before, and what he was now, to call to mind with what regularity he had been descending the mountain; and that was sufficient for all possibility of hope to be dispelled.

During the last period of this solitude through which he was passing, as he lay with his face turned to the back of the divan,—a solitude amid a populous city, and amid his numerous circle of friends and family,—a solitude deeper than which could not be found anywhere, either in the depths of the sea, or in the earth,—during the last period of this terrible solitude, Ivan Ilyitch lived only by imagination in the past.

One after another, the pictures of his past life arose before him. They always began with the time nearest to the present, and went back to the very remotest,—to his childhood, and there they rested.

If Ivan Ilyitch remembered the stewed prunes which they had given him to eat that very day, then he remembered the raw, puckery French prunes of his childhood, their peculiar taste, and the abundant flow of saliva caused by the stone. And in connection with these recollections of taste, started a whole series of recollections of that time,—his nurse, his brother, his toys.

"I must not think about these things; it is too painful," said Ivan Ilyitch to himself. And again he transported himself to the present,—the button on the back of the divan, and the wrinkles of the morocco. "Morocco is costly, not durable. There was a quarrel about it. But there was some other morocco, and some other quarrel, when we tore father's portfolio and got punished, and mamma brought us some tarts."

And again his thoughts reverted to childhood; and again it was painful to Ivan Ilyitch, and he tried to avoid it, and think of something else.

And again, together with this current of recollections, there passed through his mind another current of recollections about the progress and rise of his disease. Here, also, according as he went back, there was more and more of life. There was more, also, of excellence in life, and more of life itself. And the two were confounded.

"Just as this agony goes from worse to worse, so also all my life has gone from worse to worse," he thought. "One shining point, there back in the distance, at the beginning of life; and then all growing blacker and blacker, swifter and swifter, in inverse proportion to the square of the distance from death," thought Ivan Ilyitch.

And the comparison of a stone falling with accelerating rapidity occurred to his mind. Life, a series of increasing tortures, always speeding swifter and swifter to the end,—the most horrible torture.

"I am falling." . . .

He shuddered, he tossed, he wished to resist it. But he already knew that it was impossible to resist; and again, with eyes weary of looking, but still not able to resist looking at what was before him, he stared at the back of the divan, and waited, waited for this frightful fall, shock, and destruction.

"It is impossible to resist," he said to himself. "But can I not know the wherefore of it? Even that is impossible. It might be explained by saying that I had not lived as I ought. But it is impossible to acknowledge that," he said to himself, recollecting all the legality, the uprightness, the propriety of his life.

"It is impossible to admit that," he said to himself, with a smile on his lips, as if some one were to see that smile of his, and be deceived by it.

"No explanation! torture, death. . . . why?"

Chapter XI

Thus passed two weeks. In these weeks, there occurred an event desired by Ivan Ilyitch and his wife. Petrishchef made a formal proposal. This took place in the evening. On the next day, Praskovia Feodorovna went to her husband, meditating in what way to explain to him Feodor Petrovitch's proposition; but that very same night, a change for the worse had taken place in Ivan Ilyitch's condition. Praskovia Feodorovna found him on the same divan, but in a new position. He was lying on his back; he was groaning, and looking straight up with a fixed stare.

She began to speak about medicines. He turned his eyes on her. She did not finish saying what she had begun, so great was the hatred against her expressed in that look.

"For Christ's sake, let me die in peace!" said he.

She was about to go out; but just at this instant the daughter came in, and came near to wish him good-morning. He looked at his daughter as he had looked at his wife, and, in reply to her questions about his health, told her dryly that he would quickly relieve them all of his presence. Neither mother nor daughter said anything more; but they sat for a few moments longer, and then went out.

"What are we to blame for?" said Liza to her mother. "As if we had made him so! I am sorry for papa, but why should he torment us?"

At the usual time the doctor came. Ivan Ilyitch answered "yes," "no," not taking his angry eyes from him; and at last he said:—

"Now see here, you know that you don't help any, so leave me!"

"We can appease your sufferings," said the doctor.

"You cannot even do that; leave me!"

The doctor went into the drawing-room, and advised Praskovia Feodorovna that it was very serious, and that there was only one means—opium—of appeasing his sufferings, which must be terrible.

The doctor said that his physical sufferings were terrible, and this was true; but more terrible than his physical sufferings were his moral sufferings, and in this was his chief torment.

His moral sufferings consisted in the fact that that very night, as he looked at Gerasim's sleepy, good-natured face, with its high cheek-bones, it had suddenly come into his head:—

"But how is it if in reality my whole life, my conscious life, has been wrong?"

It came into his head that what had shortly before presented itself to him as an absolute impossibility—that he had not lived his life as he ought—might be true. It came into his head that the scarcely recognizable desires to struggle against what men highest in position considered good,—desires scarcely recognizable, which he had immediately banished,—might be true, and all the rest might be wrong. And his service, and his course of life, and his family, and these interests of society and office—all this might be wrong.

He endeavored to defend all this before himself. And suddenly he realized all the weakness of what he was defending. And there was nothing to defend.

"But if this is so," he said to himself, "and I am departing from life with the consciousness that I have wasted all that was given me, and that it is impossible to rectify it, what then?"

He lay flat on his back, and began entirely anew to examine his whole life.

When in the morning he saw the lackey, then his wife, then his daughter, then the doctor, each one of their motions, each one of their words, confirmed for him the terrible truth which had been disclosed to him that night. He saw in them himself, all that for which he had lived; and he saw clearly that all this was wrong, all this was a terrible, monstrous lie, concealing both life and death.

This consciousness increased his physical sufferings, added tenfold to them. He groaned and tossed, and threw off the clothes. It seemed to him that they choked him, and loaded him down.

And that was why he detested them.

They gave him a great dose of opium; he became unconscious, but at dinner-time the same thing began again. He drove them from him, and threw himself from place to place.

His wife came to him, and said:—

"Jean, darling, do this for me (*for me!*). It cannot do any harm, and sometimes it helps. Why, it is a mere nothing. And often well people try it."

He opened his eyes wide.

"What? Take the sacrament? Why? It's not necessary. But, however . . ."

She burst into tears.

"Will you, my dear? I will get our priest. He is so sweet!"

"Excellent! very good," he continued.

When the priest came, and confessed him, he became calmer, felt, as it were, an alleviation of his doubts, and consequently of his sufferings; and there came a moment of hope. He again began to think about the blind intestine and the possibility of curing it. He took the sacrament with tears in his eyes.

When they put him to bed after the sacrament, he felt comfortable for the moment, and once more hope of life appeared. He began to think of the operation which they had proposed.

"I want to live, to live," he said to himself.

His wife came to congratulate him. She said the customary words, and added:—

"You feel better, don't you?"

Without looking at her, he said:—

"Yes."

Her hope, her temperament, the expression of her face, the sound of her voice, all said to him one thing:—

"Wrong! all that for which thou hast lived, and thou livest, is falsehood, deception, hiding from thee life and death."

And as soon as he expressed this thought, his exasperation returned, and, together with his exasperation, the physical, tormenting agony; and, with the agony, the consciousness of inevitable death close at hand. Something new took place: a screw seemed to turn in him, twinging pain to show through him, and his breathing was constricted.

The expression of his face, when he said "yes," was terrible. After he had said that "yes," he looked straight into her face, and then, with extraordinary quickness for one so weak, he threw himself on his face and cried:—

"Go away! go away! leave me!"

Chapter XII

From that moment began that shriek that did not cease for three days, and was so terrible that, when it was heard two rooms away, it was impossible to hear it without terror. At the moment that he answered his wife, he felt that he was lost, and there was no return, that the end had come, absolutely the end, and the question was not settled, but remained a question.

"U! uu! u!" he cried in varying intonations. He began to shriek, "*N'ye khotchu*—I won't;" and thus he kept up the cry on the letter *u*.

Three whole days, during which for him there was no time, he struggled in that black sack into which an invisible, invincible power was thrusting him. He fought as one condemned to death fights in the hands of the hangman, knowing that he cannot save himself, and at every moment he felt that, notwithstanding all the violence of his struggle, he was nearer and nearer to that which terrified him. He felt that his suffering consisted, both in the fact that he was being thrust into that black hole, and still more that he could not make his way through into it. What hindered him from making his way through was the confession that his life had been good. This justification of his life caught him and did not let him advance, and more than all else tormented him.

Suddenly some force knocked him in the breast, in the side, still more forcibly compressed his breath; he was hurled through the hole, and there at the bottom of the hole some light seemed to shine on him. It happened to him as it sometimes does on a railway carriage when you think that you are going forward, but are really going backward, and suddenly recognize the true direction.

"Yes, all was wrong," he said to himself; "but that is nothing. I might, I might have done right. What is right?" he asked himself, and suddenly stopped.

This was at the end of the third day, two hours before his death. At this very same time the little student noiselessly stole into his father's room, and approached his bed. The moribund was continually shrieking desperately, and tossing his arms. His hand struck upon the little student's head. The little student seized it, pressed it to his lips, and burst into tears.

It was at this very same time that Ivan Ilyitch fell through, saw the light, and it was revealed to him that his life had not been as it ought, but that still it was possible to repair it. He was just asking himself, "What is right?" and stopped to listen.

Then he felt that some one was kissing his hand. He opened his eyes, and looked at his son. He felt sorry for him. His wife came to him. He looked at her. With open mouth, and with her nose and cheeks wet with tears, with an expression of despair, she was looking at him. He felt sorry for her.

"Yes, I am a torment to them," he thought. "I am sorry for them, but they will be better off when I am dead."

He wanted to express this, but he had not the strength to say it.

"However, why should I say it? I must do it."

He pointed out his son to his wife by a glance, and said:—

"Take him away . . . I am sorry . . . and for thee."

He wanted to say also, "*Prosti*—Forgive," but he said, "*Propusti*—Let it pass;" and, not having the strength to correct himself, he waved his hand, knowing that he would comprehend who had the right.

And suddenly it became clear to him that what oppressed him, and was hidden from him, suddenly was lighted up for him all at once, and on two sides, on ten sides, on all sides.

He felt sorry for them; he felt that he must do something to make it less painful for them. To free them, and free himself, from these torments, "How good and simple," he thought.

"But the pain," he asked himself, "where is it?—Here, now, where art thou, pain?"

He began to listen.

"Yes, here it is! Well, then, do your worst pain!"

"And death? Where is it?"

He tried to find his former customary fear of death, and could not.

"Where is death? What is it?"

There was no fear, because there was no death.

In place of death was light!

"Here is something like!" he suddenly said aloud. "What joy!"

For him all this passed in a single instant, and the significance of this instant did not change.

For those who stood by his side, his death agony was prolonged two hours more. In his breast something bubbled up, his emaciated body shuddered. Then more and more rarely came the bubbling and the rattling.

"It is all over," said someone above him.

He heard those words, and repeated them in his soul.

"It is over! Death!" he said to himself. "It does not exist more."

He drew in one more breath, stopped in the midst of it, stretched himself, and died.

Study Questions

1. Has Ivan Ilyitch lived well according to society's standards? Has he lived a life that people respect?

2. What pleasant moments of his life does Ivan recall? Does he remember his family with love?

3. Why is Gerasim a comfort while the doctor is not?

4. What realizations does Ivan reach on his death bed? Can death be an opportunity to discover truths?

5. What Christian message is Tolstoy sending the reader? How should Ivan Ilyitch have lived?

Contact

Director: Robert Zemeckis

Screenplay: Jim Hart, Michael Goldenberg, Carl Sagan, Ann Druyan, et al.

Robert Zemeckis (1952–), a preeminent, contemporary filmmaker, has directed, produced, or written screenplays for some sixteen films to date. His best known works are Romancing the Stone, *about a female novelist trying to rescue her sister in South America;* Back To the Future *(I,II, and III) that portrays the adventures of a teenager who travels back in time;* Who Framed Roger Rabbit *a groundbreaking popular hit combining live action and animation;* Forrest Gump, *a film dealing with a retarded man's involvement in world events; and* Cast Away, *the story of a castaway's suffering, both on his deserted island and when he tries to resume his former relationship. He also directed* I Wanna Hold Your Hand *(his debut film),* Death Becomes Her, *and* Used Cars, *and he acted as executive producer for* The Frighteners, The Public Eye, *and* Trespass. *His films have grossed over two billion dollars worldwide.*

Zemeckis won an Oscar as best director for Forrest Gump, *which was also named Best Picture, and several of his films have won Academy Awards for visual effects, sound effects, editing, and screenplay. In his film* Contact, *based on the book by Carl Sagan, his theme is the search for extraterrestrial intelligence in the universe.*

Synopsis

The search for intelligent life on other planets is not just the stuff of science fiction but of serious scientific interest as well. Beginning in 1960, astronomers have been searching for alien signals using arrays of telescopes at various places on Earth. These SETI projects (Search for Extraterrestrial Intelligence) have ranged from the pioneering Project Ozma in West Virginia, to the mammoth Arecebo dish in Puerto Rico, to the Allen Telescope under construction in California and due for completion in 2005.

In addition, the spacecrafts Pioneer 10 and 11, the first to leave the solar system, both carried six- by nine-inch plaques with drawings of human beings and the location of Earth in the cosmos; Carl Sagan and Frank Drake co-designed the plaque. Pioneer 10 is still transmitting signals from 6.6 billion miles away, but no response has been received from any civilizations in deep space. A further message was sent from the Arecibo Observatory describing our chemical makeup, our planetary system, and so forth; it will reach its destination in M13 globular cluster in twenty-five thousand years. What's more, the spacecrafts Voyager I and II carried a gold-plated phonograph record with information about our planet and its life forms. The Interstellar Recording contains animal noises, including the sounds of humpback whales, music from a variety of human cultures, and the electrical activity of a person's body over a one-hour period. The recording will last for one billion years.

The scientific community supports these projects because of the high probability that intelligent life does exist on other planets. An estimated 400 billion stars make up our Milky Way galaxy alone, half of which have orbiting planets that might sustain life, and there are approximately 100 billion galaxies in the universe. Astronomers can calculate the odds of receiving signals from an alien civilization using a formula called the "Drake Equation":

$$N = R^* \cdot f_p \cdot n_e \cdot f_l \cdot f_i \cdot f_c \cdot L$$

Where,

N = The number of civilizations in The Milky Way Galaxy whose radio emissions are detectable.

R^* = The rate of formation of stars suitable for the development of intelligent life.

f_p = The fraction of those stars with planetary systems.

n_e = The number of planets, per solar system, with an environment suitable for life.

f_l = The fraction of suitable planets on which life actually appears.

f_j = The fraction of life bearing planets on which intelligent life emerges.

f_c = The fraction of civilizations that develop a technology that releases detectable signs of their existence into space.

L = The length of time such civilizations release detectable signals into space.

Using this formula, the astronomers involved in SETI support the possibility of communication with some form of extraterrestrial intelligence, however they dismiss the idea of UFO sightings and abductions by alien creatures. Such reports, coming mainly from the rural southwest, are treated as misinterpretations of ordinary events or as signs of emotional problems. The reason for the skepticism is that no scientific proof exists that we have ever been visited by extraterrestrials. Personal accounts abound, but verifiable evidence is lacking.

Furthermore, the enormous dimensions of space and time make interstellar travel impractical. Astronomers measure cosmic distances in light years, which is the space traversed by a ray of light over one year traveling at a rate of 486,281 miles per second. Aside from the sun, our nearest star is over 4 light years away or about 24 trillion (24,000,000,000,000) miles. Given the capabilities of rocketry and the absolute limit of the speed of light, that means it would take 300,000 years for aliens from the closest star system to reach the Earth. Any travel from a further star among the billions in the Milky Way would take millions of years.*

Nevertheless, the likelihood is that we are not alone. As Frank Drake has stated, "Everything we've learned about the universe has pointed in one direction: we are not so very special. Planets are commonplace, and . . . life is not a rare occurrence at all, but is as natural throughout the universe as the formation of planets and stars . . . It seems only reasonable to conclude that intelligent life will also be widespread." Carl Sagan also remarked, "There may be millions of worlds in the Milky Way Galaxy which are at this moment inhabited by other intelligent beings."

Although we may never be able to meet these beings, one of our radio telescopes may someday receive a signal from space, either as incidental sound waves released into space or as a message deliberately beamed to Earth. If and when that day happens, we will have to reassess our place in the universe and our religious beliefs about the relation between God and man. If we were not unique, would that make our species less valuable? Would it raise doubts about God's existence or, on the contrary, show his creation as even grander than we imagined?

Within this context, the film *Contact* portrays the search for extraterrestrial intelligence and the implications, religious, political, and social, when an alien signal is received. Furthermore, it deals with the role played by faith and revelation and by science and rationality in our understanding. As a personal dimension, the film also contains a love story between an astronomer, Ellie Arroway (Jodie Foster) and a theologian, Palmer Joss (Matthew McConaughey), who manage to transcend the differences in their outlook.† Their passionate discussions on how truth is revealed form the philosophic structure of the plot.

The film begins with a visual tour of the stars and planets, beginning on Earth and taking us to the edge of the universe, 8 billion light years away. The camera then zooms back from the macrocosm to the microcosm so that the blackness of space resolves itself into the eye of a young Ellie Arroway.

We see Ellie turning the dial of a short-wave radio under the gentle guidance of her father, Ted Arroway (David Morse), and tuning in

---

*This is the answer given to Fermi's Paradox, which is usually stated as follows: Most of the stars in the galaxy are more than a billion years older than the sun. If intelligent life and civilizations exist throughout the galaxy, then they should have colonized other planets long ago. Where are they? The answer of most astronomers is not that aliens are here in flying saucers but that physical limitations make interstellar space travel impossible.
†The "arrow way" could represent the direct way to a target; a "joss" is an idol or cult image.

Pensacola, Florida. She is enthralled at hearing a voice materialize out of the air from miles away, and draws a scene of a Florida beach. She asks her father "Could we hear to China? . . . Could we hear to the moon?" Her father answers quietly "Big enough radio, I don't see why not." She then asks "Could we hear God?" to which her father replies "Hmm, that's a good one. Maybe his echo . . ." Conceivably, this is an allusion to the sound of Big Bang, the explosion of the primal atom that produced our universe. If God lies behind it, we would be hearing his reverberations.

When Ellie asks whether he thinks there are people on other planets her father answers "Well let's see . . . the Universe is a pretty big place . . . And the one thing I know about nature is it hates to waste anything. So I guess I'd say if it is just us, seems like an awful waste of space."

Ted Arroway dies of a heart attack when Ellie is nine years old, leaving her orphaned and with an acute feeling of loss and abandonment. The film suggests that this trauma may be driving her subsequent search for brothers and sisters in space, and her receptivity to a father in the universe. In fact, one of her professors asks, "What is it that makes you so lonely, Miss Arroway? What is it that compels you to search the heavens for life . . . ?"

Ellie subsequently studies astronomy at Cal Tech, receiving her degree magna cum laude. In graduate school she receives financial support through her mentor, Professor Drumlin (Tom Skerrit), for a research project at the Arecibo dish in Puerto Rico. She remains at Arecibo for some time, trying to detect radio signals from space. However, when Drumlin becomes head of the National Science Foundation, he withdraws her funds, deciding that taxpayer's money should be spent on more practical and profitable projects. He calls her quest "professional suicide," and Ellie herself wonders whether she ought to be jeopardizing her chances at publishing and, in effect, risking her entire career by searching for "little green men."

Before Ellie leaves Arecibo she begins a relationship with the religious scholar Palmer Joss, who later becomes a significant figure in her life. They spend one night together, and although Ellie feels drawn to him, she inexplicably throws his telephone number away. Perhaps she fears the conflict that their differences will generate. In one significant conversation, Palmer describes a mystical experience that is the source of his faith.

> PALMER: [I was] looking at the sky and then I felt something. All I know is that I wasn't alone, and for the first time in my life I wasn't afraid of nothing, not even dying. It was God.
> ELLIE: There's no chance that you had this experience because some part of you needed to have it?
> PALMER: I mean. I'm a reasonably intelligent guy, but this, no this . . . My intellect, it couldn't even touch this.

Eventually Ellie obtains private backing from a philanthropist, S. R. Hadden (John Hurt) that enables her to rent time at the Very Large Array (VLA) telescope in New Mexico—thirty-one linked dishes that allow more of the sky to be searched in a day than she could formerly do in a year.*

Ellie works at the facility for four years, listening almost continuously at the radio telescope and living in a painted cinderblock room; her team refer to her as the High Priestess of the Desert. However, her search proves fruitless, yielding no appreciable results, so once again her funding is cancelled.

At this point the whole enterprise seems lost, but just before the deadline on the grant expires, Ellie hears a deep pulsing signal that her team traces to the star Vega, 26 light years away. The signal takes the form of prime numbers—59, 61, 67, 71, and so forth, indicating a deliberate transmission from an intelligent source. She quickly informs David Drumlin who is now Science Advisor to the President, and sends out a request to telescope facilities around the world to corroborate her findings; forty-four stations confirm the signal.

After a brief meeting with officials at White Sands AFB, a command center is set up at the VLA to pursue the communication. The periodic frequency of the signal appears to be a complex code, so a cryptographer is brought in to decipher the message. As the team watches transfixed, the prime numbers are translated into images—moving pictures of Hitler at the 1936 Olympic Games. This seems bizarre until David Drumlin explains, "this was the first television transmission of any power that went into space. That they recorded it and sent it back is simply a way of saying 'Hello, we heard you.'" However, Michael Kitz (James Wood), the National Security Advisor who is present, warns that it could mean "*Sieg Heil!* You're our kind of people."

During the succeeding months Kitz continuously presses for the project to be "militarized," citing national security interests. Kitz, along with Drumlin, functions as the villain of the piece. He suspects the "Vĕgans" of having hostile intentions, and he fears that such an advanced civilization will have alarming destructive power. This theme persists throughout the film, often supported by religious leaders who view the aliens as spawn of the devil and science as his cat's paw.

Soon after the discovery President Clinton calls a press conference, announcing to the world that American scientists have detected a radio

---

*Ellie's methodology follows that of Project Phoenix in New South Wales, Australia, a targeted search of individual stars. However, rather than listening with earphones as Ellie Arroway does, computers scan for signals, examining twenty-eight million channels simultaneously, and when unusual sounds appear they alert the astronomers. Interestingly, Project Phoenix has a blind researcher like Kent Clark (William Fichtner) in the film, and a woman astronomer, Jill Tarter, heads it. She is a leading astronomer in the search for extraterrestrial life. Dr. Tarter declared in an interview, however, that although Ellie does what she does, the film is not based on her.

signal from space. Ellie Arroway should then have presented an explanation of the SETI project and the significance of the results, but she is upstaged by Drumlin. In effect, he takes credit for the achievement, leaving Ellie shaken and hurt. Through his political manipulation, she is here marginalized and almost loses control of her project.

Now that the extraterrestrial contact is public knowledge, vans, buses, cars, and recreation vehicles jam the roads to the New Mexico facility. A tent city is set up with campfires and barbeques. Elvis impersonators appear, Indians perform tribal dances, and con men sell abduction insurance. News reporters gather in a media frenzy, and New Age gurus preach to crowds of people in an atmosphere resembling Woodstock. One memorable preacher named Joseph declares, "The millennium is upon us. God has fulfilled his promise, sending us this herald to warn the faithless—the scientists who tell us He doesn't even exist—and to promise us, the faithful, we will be saved."

Meanwhile, additional data has been received, encrypted pages of text interlaced in frames of Hitler's image. Page after page of complex geometric patterns begin to appear on the screen, and these "hieroglyphics" amount to sixty-three thousand pages of data before the transmission ends. Furthermore, the message starts to repeat itself with no key or "primer" at the end. Ellie begins to work on the code herself, when suddenly someone hacks into the secured system, inviting her to see him. He promises to reveal a secret, presumably about the hieroglyphics.

The man is her benefactor, S. R. Hadden, and Ellie meets with him aboard a transport plane that is his home, outfitted as a high-tech laboratory with state-of-the art computers and banks of monitors. Hadden had access to the VLA data and has cracked the code. Using the primer, he shows Ellie that the signal contains a set of instructions for building a highly sophisticated transport that presumably can travel to Vega. He offers Ellie a deal: He wants to construct the machine in exchange for which he will disclose the decryption primer. He understands the politics and knows "the powers that be are falling all over themselves to play the game of the millennium. Maybe I can help deal you back in the game."

Ellie accepts, agreeing to promote his cause as long as it remains consistent with the best interests of science. Hadden then shows her how, when viewed three-dimensionally, the hieroglyphics emerge as engineering schematics for a machine—a transporter designed to carry a single human occupant into space.

Following their discussion, Ellie meets Palmer Joss again, first seeing him at a high-level meeting as spiritual advisor to the President, then at a Washington cocktail party. Their conversation invariably turns to religion and science.

Ellie quotes from Joss's book in which he depreciates science: "Ironically, the thing that people are most hungry for, meaning, is the one thing science has not been able to give them." She then refers to Occam's

Razor, the rule of thought that says the simplest explanation is best, implying that the God hypothesis is complicated and therefore dubious.

> ELLIE: So what's more likely, an all-powerful, mysterious God created the universe and decided not to give any proof of his existence, or that he simply does not exist at all and we created him so we wouldn't have to feel so small and alone?
> PALMER: I don't know. I couldn't imagine living in a world in which God didn't exist. I wouldn't want to.
> ELLIE: How do you know you aren't deluding yourself?

The theme of possible self-delusion recurs throughout the film.

When the world governments learn that the signal contains plans for a transporter, they decide to build it with the United States providing most of the quarter-trillion-dollar cost and with Hadden as chief contractor. Gradually the machine takes shape as a gigantic crucible powered by crystals in unearthly fractal patterns. Three concentric rings rotate in different directions at enormous speed, with a metal ball at the center that can encapsulate a person—a compartment referred to as an IPV.

A group of international dignitaries is assembled including Palmer Joss to determine who should be that emissary from Earth, and Ellie and Drumlin are among the ten candidates the panel considers, probing their political, philosophical, and religious views. Ellie is especially anxious to be chosen, despite the obvious danger, for as she tells Palmer, "For as long as I can remember I've been searching for something, some reason why we're here. What are we doing, who are we? If this is a chance to find out even a little part of that answer, I think that's worth a human life." Palmer embraces her, realizing they are both on a quest for truth in their separate ways.

At the hearing it looks as though Ellie will be selected because the panel is most impressed with her replies. For example, when asked what questions she might ask the Vegans she answers, "How did you evolve, how did you survive this technological adolescence without destroying yourselves." However just as her confirmation seems assured, Palmer Joss asks whether she believes in God, and when it becomes clear that she is an atheist, David Drumlin is chosen over her. Drumlin claims to be a believer, which is what the group wants to hear, and that prevails over honesty. Ellie, of course, views Palmer's question as sabotage, but as he explains, the person should represent the mainstream views of humanity. His deeper reason, as he later confesses, is that he was afraid of losing her.

As it turns out, Drumlin is killed when the religious fanatic Joseph blows up the transporter in a suicide bombing, and Ellie is given the chance to travel into space in a duplicate machine that Hadden has constructed.

At this point, the story becomes ambiguous. When the transporter is fired Ellie experiences herself being propelled into space, traveling through translucent, electromagnetic fields. She sees explosions, whorls of light, and feels herself shot through wormholes in space. When the motion stops, she floats down to a beautiful beach like the one she drew of Florida as a child and, mysteriously, her father is there. He tells her that the beach and perhaps his form had been created to make it easier for her, but he offers no proof of the reality of this realm because "that's the way it has always been done." He also says, "The only thing we've found that makes the emptiness bearable is each other."

Immediately afterwards Ellie finds herself back at the launch site where people tell her she did not go anywhere. The IPV had dropped straight through the rings, and she had been rescued. Only a few seconds had elapsed.

At a subsequent investigation headed by Michael Kitz, her experience is treated as a hallucination, and the entire episode, from receipt of the signal to the space machine, as an elaborate hoax by S. R. Hadden. Kitz challenges Ellie to offer any evidence of her space travel since all that the monitors recorded was static. Using her own weapons against her, he reasons that according to Occam's Razor, the simplest explanation is that she was deluded.

Ellie cannot refute the logic but she declares,

> I had an experience. I can't prove it, I can't even explain it, but everything that I know as a human being, everything I am tells me it was real. I was given something wonderful, something that changed me forever, a vision of the universe that tells me undeniably how tiny and insignificant and how rare and precious we all are, a vision that tells us we belong to something that is greater than ourselves, that we are not, that none of us are alone.

Her speech is a parallel to that of Palmer Joss when he described his religious experience at their first meeting. The implication is that faith is a matter of individual, private revelation. It transcends the bounds of evidence and reason, utterly convincing the people who experience the presence of God and transforming their lives.

This might be the ultimate message of the film, except for a scene toward the end of the film that makes the conclusion muddy. The government official, Rachel Constantine, points out to Michael Kitz that the video did record only static but there were eighteen hours of it whereas Ellie had been in the module a few minutes. Hard evidence therefore seems to verify Ellie's account, and we need not trust in faith alone to authenticate one's personal experience.

Contact obviously poses the question of whether intelligent life exists on other planets, but it also explores the question of God's existence and how belief is proven. Palmer Joss functions as a counterpoint to Ellie

Arroway's scientific viewpoint, balancing her demand for proof with the perspective of faith, and her strict rationality with personal feelings. In the end, the two manage to find common ground in a mystical experience so that their ideologies no longer divide them. Nevertheless, we are left uncertain as to whether Ellie really passed through a spiritual doorway to another dimension. If there had not been eighteen hours of static as scientific proof, would a subjective impression be enough to support religious belief? Don't people make mistakes all the time about what they think they've seen or heard, especially when placed in extraordinary conditions?

Religion and science seem to clash on numerous points and, philosophically, the relation between the fields can be viewed in one of three ways: 1.) Religion and science can be found to be *compatible.* For example, it is sometimes argued that *Genesis* and *The Origin of Species* tell the same story, but scripture uses metaphorical language whereas science is more literal. We have to understand, we are told, that a day in the life of God is millions of years to man, so the six days of creation are comparable to the millions of years of evolution that Darwin described. 2.) Religion and science *contradict* each other, offering alternative explanations of events. For example, religious people have interpreted lightning as a sign of God's wrath, rainbows as benedictions, illness as evil spirits, and children as a divine miracle. Science, however, views the same events in terms of electrical discharges, the refraction of light, bacteria and viruses, and the union of ovum and sperm, respectively. 3.) Religion and science operate in *different* spheres, science describing the features of the world, religion understanding its meaning. For example, the biologist knows how the brain and nervous system function, but the theologian tries to explain why human beings were made this way.

With regard to the existence of God, we are not sure whether the ideas of religion and science are compatible, contradictory, or just different. *Contact* suggests that, beginning from opposite starting points, there is compatibility and harmony in the end, that both support belief in God. However, the film contains enough uncertainty to leave the matter a mystery for the viewer to pursue.

Study Questions

1. Is it probable or improbable that intelligent life exists elsewhere in the universe? If such life exists, would that indicate the presence of a God who created it?
2. In what ways do Ellie and Palmer represent the approaches of science and religion?

3. What drives Ellie to explore the possibility of extraterrestrial life? Is her quest in any way religious?

4. Do you think Ellie contacted some supernatural dimension or imagined the entire episode?

5. In what way do you think religious belief can be established? What would have to happen for people to reject belief in God?

B. THE PROBLEM OF EVIL: IF GOD IS GOOD WHY DO PEOPLE SUFFER?

According to the Judeo-Christian concept, God is a personal being who is infinitely loving, wise, and powerful, a deity who has existed for all eternity, and who created man and the world out of the void. Given this description of God, however, certain logical questions arise as to why he introduced or permitted natural evil as part of his creation. If God is wholly good, supremely intelligent, and almighty, why are there natural evils such as hurricanes, volcanic eruptions, avalanches, tidal waves, earthquakes, and floods? Why should there be lions, sharks, and cobras, arctic wastes and barren deserts, disease, sickness, and death? In short, if God is good, why is man's earthly home filled with so many sources of pain and suffering?

This is the problem of evil that has puzzled philosophers and plagued theologians for several hundred years. Why should a benevolent father permit harm to come to his children? The suffering that people inflict upon each other in wars or violent crimes might be explained within a theological system, but the suffering that human beings experience because of the natural environment is more difficult to justify. With regard to man's inhumanity to man, it can be argued that God wants human beings to possess free will and that entails the ability to perform good or evil actions. Since free will is an important element in human life (and a necessary ingredient for moral responsibility), a good God would want people to have freedom of choice even though they could choose cruelty and destructiveness. Therefore man was created "sufficient to have stood, though free to fall" as Milton writes in *Paradise Lost*. But why would a God of perfect love permit natural disasters to occur and, above all, allow children to suffer the pain of terrible genetic defects and diseases?

If one does not believe in God's existence, of course, the problem of evil does not arise. For then all natural events, whether helpful or harmful to man, are thought to happen accidentally, without any reason or ultimate purpose behind them. Although explanations may be offered in terms of physical laws governing the behavior of energy and matter, there can be no meaning to events and no possible account can be given of their purpose. Catastrophes are not meant to occur; they simply happen as part of the natural order of the world and no one is responsible for the human misery that occurs as a result.

In the same way, if God is thought to exist but to be limited with regard to attributes of power, wisdom, and love, then the problem of evil is easily resolved. For God could then be viewed as lacking the ability to prevent evil from occurring, the knowledge that it is occurring (he cannot know everything), or to be less than wholly loving toward humanity.

Both alternatives, however, have been unacceptable to most theologians who view omnipotence and absolute love as essential characteristics of God. Hence the existence of evil remains a problem for the believer. As the philosopher David Hume writes, paraphrasing Epicurus, "Is [God] willing to prevent evil, but not able? then he is impotent. Is he able, but not willing? then is he malevolent. Is he both able and willing? whence then is evil?"

Various answers have been offered to this question within the field of *theodicy*—an area of theology devoted to a defense of God's treatment of man in the light of natural evil. One recurring explanation is the claim that evil functions to punish people for their sins. In order for the universe to operate fairly, it is argued, people must be punished for their transgressions just as they must be rewarded for their virtues. For the sake of justice, therefore, God makes the wicked suffer by visiting natural evils upon them, not only in hell but on earth as well. This is the explanation offered in scripture for the Fall of Adam and Eve, the destruction of Sodom and Gomorrah, and for the Flood that drowned everyone on earth except for the virtuous Noah and his family. It is also the explanation that is often invoked when disasters occur in everyday life, for people frequently ask themselves what they have done to deserve such punishment, thereby assuming that all suffering is caused by wrongdoing.

Although this kind of "retributive" thinking may be natural and prevalent, a moment's reflection will show that it cannot be a valid explanation for natural evil. For good people seem to experience as many natural calamities as awful people; sinners alone are not singled out for suffering. When an earthquake devastates a city, good and bad alike are buried beneath the wreckage, and when ships capsize in hurricanes, it is not just the wicked who are drowned. Patients in hospitals are not all depraved, and people with fine characters are not spared the misery of excruciating illnesses. In short, the human misery that exists as a result of natural evil cannot be correlated with the sinfulness of the individuals. Not only is the distribution of evils askew, but the degree of suffering is often grossly out of proportion to the guilt or innocence of the sufferer. This is most evident in the case of children who may barely have had time to sin before they are afflicted with poliomyelitis or leukemia.

Quite obviously, then, this explanation for natural evil is not justified by the facts. Most theologians find it as unacceptable as Job did in the Old Testament when he protested against the suffering he underwent even though he was "blameless and upright." Job finally declared, "I call aloud, but there is no justice."

Another solution that has been proposed to the problem of evil centers around the idea that contrasts are necessary for appreciation. That is, unless we experienced evil we would be unable to value the good. God therefore allows a variety of negative events to occur so that we can appreciate the positive blessings in life. The discomfort of sickness enables us to enjoy good health; storms and cold temperatures make us value fine weather; and hunger enables us to relish the joy of eating well. In other words, God permits natural evil in order to provide human beings with a base for comparison so they can thereby appreciate the pleasures of the earth. It is sometimes added to this argument that unless the world were somewhat hellish, people would lack the incentive to strive for heaven.

Upon analysis, however, the logic of this proposal is also found to be questionable. It is not at all certain that contrasts are necessary for appreciation; an infant seems to like milk immediately and a child might well enjoy the taste of strawberries without ever having eaten sour or bitter foods. Furthermore, even if contrasts should be necessary, *opposites* certainly would not be. That is, we may need partly sunny days to appreciate brilliantly sunny ones, but we do not need blizzards or torrential rains that precipitate floods. More precisely, contrasts can occur between various shades of good; there is no necessity for having the bad; just the presence of good might help us appreciate the better and best. The natural evils that occur, therefore, are hardly needed to accomplish the end of appreciation.*

Still another alleged solution claims that both good and evil must exist so that we can have genuine choice. If good were the only available option in the world, our freedom would be rendered meaningless. If real choice is to occur, then the alternatives of good and evil must be present.

But the argument is something of a straw man. Not only are natural evils compounded far beyond what is required to ensure the existence of options, but in most cases, natural evils do not permit any choices to be made. The avalanche or tidal wave, shark or poisonous snake strikes down its victim without providing alternatives. The survivors, admittedly, may have the option of deciding whether or not to combat the destructive forces in nature, but surely we cannot applaud a scheme that secures freedom of choice for some by the suffering and death of others. God, with all possibilities at his disposal, could devise a more humane system.

A somewhat more persuasive claim is that natural evil is justified as a catalyst to the development of fine character. The argument asserts that people who undergo severe or prolonged suffering develop dimensions to their personalities that individuals living in continual comfort can never hope to attain. Pain is purifying and disciplining, tempering people through fire. It refines the individual's emotional capacities, orders

---

*It has been argued that our blessings are appreciated more when disasters have been experienced, but this argument stresses only the greater degree of appreciation and tacitly assumes that opposites are not needed for appreciation *per se*. Furthermore, most people would happily settle for less appreciation if the sufferings due to natural evil could be eliminated.

his or her will, and encourages a more reflective attitude of mind. Soft conditions, on the other hand, tend to produce soft people who are complacent and self-satisfied. The race as a whole has progressed by overcoming natural adversities—winter cold, predatory animals, plagues—and throughout history civilization has thrived in environments that were somewhat harsh. Languishing in Tennyson's "Land of the Lotus Eaters" we would never have developed our potentialities, individually or collectively. Just as athletes and artists can only achieve success by prolonged and painful effort, human achievement as a whole must always be preceded by struggle. God, in his wisdom, has provided us with the necessary challenges in our environment so that by surmounting obstacles, we can refine our characters and the species as a whole can continually improve.

However, many victims of hurricanes, tornadoes, volcanic eruptions, and so on, never survive to have their characters improved; babies that die of disease have no chance to develop any character. Furthermore, even though some individuals may find severe hardship a stimulus to development and creativity, most people are demeaned by suffering. For every Helen Keller, there are hundreds of similarly afflicted individuals who lead miserable lives. A final consideration is that many great people in history seem to have developed outstanding characters without having endured great suffering, which implies that experiencing natural evil is not a necessary condition for building character.

Faced with all of these difficulties, some theologians have declared that we simply must have faith in God's goodness despite appearances. Perhaps the evil we see is only apparent, not real; in the overall scheme of the universe it may well be good. With our finite understanding we are not able to comprehend the true purpose of human suffering, but in the infinitude of God's wisdom it may have a necessary place.

But if we as finite beings cannot know, then we cannot know that evil is justified and God is good. If we are unable to judge these matters, then we are unable to judge, and no conclusion is possible.

Furthermore, blind faith is a poor substitute for lucid reasons, and the appeal to faith cannot simply ignore damaging arguments. That would be like kicking over the chess board when one's opponent says "check mate." Genuine faith carries the believer beyond the point where the logical evidence leaves off; it does not fly in the face of reason. The world does contain suffering from natural causes, and the believer must either reconcile this fact with God's goodness or change his or her belief system. Robert Browning wrote that when "God's in His heaven, all's right with the world," which suggests that when all's not right with the world, God's not in His heaven. At least before we accept the claims of religion we can expect to be given some justification for human suffering in a world governed by an allegedly loving God.

In the selections in Part B, C. S. Lewis argues that the earth is a place of soul-making, that suffering builds character. This solution is questionable as we have seen but Lewis makes a very persuasive case for it. Then Fedor Dostoevsky brings an indictment against God because of the suffering of children, although he vitiates his own argument in the end.

To conclude this section, Taylor Hackford shows the temptations of Satan in his film *The Devil's Advocate*. From the standpoint of the philosophy of religion, the question is why a loving, almighty God would allow the devil to operate, tempting human beings.

The Problem of Pain

C. S. Lewis

C. S. Lewis (1898–1963) was a medieval scholar and critic who taught at both Oxford and Cambridge University as well as being a popular novelist, poet, and a writer of children's literature. All of his writings are infused with a commitment to Christianity following his conversion experience that he describes in Surprised by Joy *and his other autobiographical work* Pilgrim's Regress.

Lewis's most important works of literary criticism include The Discarded Image, *and* Allegory of Love, *but he is best known for his literary works, especially the Perelandra trilogy that includes* Out of the Silent Planet. *His didactic works in defense of faith include* Beyond Personality, Miracles, Mere Christianity, The Four Loves, *and his celebrated* Screwtape Letters. *Lewis is also well known for a series of children's books called the Chronicles of Narnia, especially* The Lion, the Witch and the Wardrobe.

In The Problem of Pain *Lewis addresses the question of why a benevolent God would allow humankind to suffer. His answer is that a loving father would not want his son just to have a good time but would "use his authority to make the son into the sort of human being he . . . wants him to be." The earth is a place where character is formed through overcoming adversity, and it is therefore compatible with God's goodness toward man. God wants the best for us, and that is only possible by creating conditions that ennoble our souls.*

I. Introductory

Not many years ago when I was an atheist, if anyone had asked me, "Why do you not believe in God?" my reply would have run something like this: "Look at the universe we live in. By far the greatest part of it consists of empty space, completely dark and unimaginably cold. The bodies which move in this space are so few and so small in comparison with the space itself that even if every one of them were known to be crowded as full as it could hold with perfectly happy creatures, it would still be difficult to believe that life and happiness were more than a byeproduct to the power that made the universe. As it is, however, the scientists think it likely that very few of the suns of space—perhaps none of them except our own—have any planets[1]; and in our own system it is

---

[1] Astronomers now know that in our Milky Way galaxy alone billions of planets are orbiting other stars. Furthermore, traces of life have been discovered on the moon (Ed.).

improbable that any planet except the Earth sustains life. And Earth herself existed without life for millions of years and may exist for millions more when life has left her. And what is it like while it lasts? It is so arranged that all the forms of it can live only by preying upon one another. In the lower forms this process entails only death, but in the higher there appears a new quality called consciousness which enables it to be attended with pain. The creatures cause pain by being born, and live by inflicting pain, and in pain they mostly die. In the most complex of all the creatures, Man, yet another quality appears, which we call reason, whereby he is enabled to foresee his own pain which henceforth is preceded with acute mental suffering, and to foresee his own death while keenly desiring permanence. It also enables men by a hundred ingenious contrivances to inflict a great deal more pain than they otherwise could have done on one another and on the irrational creatures. This power they have exploited to the full. Their history is largely a record of crime, war, disease, and terror, with just sufficient happiness interposed to give them, while it lasts, an agonised apprehension of losing it, and, when it is lost, the poignant misery of remembering. Every now and then they improve their condition a little and what we call a civilisation appears. But all civilisations pass away and, even while they remain, inflict peculiar sufferings of their own probably sufficient to outweigh what alleviations they may have brought to the normal pains of man. That our own civilisation has done so, no one will dispute; that it will pass away like all its predecessors is surely probable. Even if it should not, what then? The race is doomed. Every race that comes into being in any part of the universe is doomed; for the universe, they tell us, is running down, and will sometime be a uniform infinity of homogeneous matter at a low temperature. All stories will come to nothing: all life will turn out in the end to have been a transitory and senseless contortion upon the idiotic face of infinite matter. If you ask me to believe that this is the work of a benevolent and omnipotent spirit, I reply that all the evidence points in the opposite direction. Either there is no spirit behind the universe, or else a spirit indifferent to good and evil, or else an evil spirit."

There was one question which I never dreamed of raising. I never noticed that the very strength and facility of the pessimists' case at once poses us a problem. If the universe is so bad, or even half so bad, how on earth did human beings ever come to attribute it to the activity of a wise and good Creator? Men are fools, perhaps; but hardly so foolish as that. The direct inference from black to white, from evil flower to virtuous root, from senseless work to a workman infinitely wise, staggers belief. The spectacle of the universe as revealed by experience can never have been the ground of religion: it must always have been something in spite of which religion, acquired from a different source, was held.

It would be an error to reply that our ancestors were ignorant and therefore entertained pleasing illusions about nature which the progress of science has since dispelled. For centuries, during which all men believed, the nightmare size and emptiness of the universe was already known. You will read in some books that the men of the Middle Ages thought the Earth flat and the stars near, but that is a lie. Ptolemy had told them that the Earth was a mathematical point without size in relation to the distance of the fixed stars—a distance which one mediæval popular text estimates as a hundred and seventeen million miles. And in times yet earlier, even from the beginnings, men must have got the same sense of hostile immensity from a more obvious source. To prehistoric man the neighbouring forest must have been infinite enough, and the utterly alien and infest which we have to fetch from the thought of cosmic rays and cooling suns, came snuffing and howling nightly to his very doors. Certainly at all periods the pain and waste of human life was equally obvious. Our own religion begins among the Jews, a people squeezed between great warlike empires, continually defeated and led captive, familiar as Poland or Armenia with the tragic story of the conquered. It is mere nonsense to put pain among the discoveries of science. Lay down this book and reflect for five minutes on the fact that all the great religions were first preached, and long practised, in a world without chloroform.

At all times, then, an inference from the course of events in this world to the goodness and wisdom of the Creator would have been equally preposterous; and it was never made.[1] Religion has a different origin.

II. Divine Omnipotence

"IF God were good, He would wish to make His creatures perfectly happy, and if God were almighty He would be able to do what He wished. But the creatures are not happy. Therefore God lacks either goodness, or power, or both." This is the problem of pain, in its simplest form. The possibility of answering it depends on showing that the terms "good" and "almighty", and perhaps also the term "happy" are equivocal: for it must be admitted from the outset that if the popular meanings attached to these words are the best, or the only possible, meanings, then the argument is unanswerable. In this chapter I shall make some comments on the idea of Omnipotence, and, in the following, some on the idea of Goodness.

Omnipotence means "power to do all, or everything".[2] And we are told in Scripture that "with God all things are possible". It is common

[1]Lewis speculates on the origin of religion, in such sources as a sense of the holy, then returns to a discussion of pain as an empediment to faith (Ed.).
[2]The original meaning in Latin may have been "power *over* or *in* all". I give what I take to be current sense.

enough, in argument with an unbeliever, to be told that God, if He existed and were good, would do this or that; and then, if we point out that the proposed action is impossible, to be met with the retort, "But I thought God was supposed to be able to do anything". This raises the whole question of impossibility.

In ordinary usage the word *impossible* generally implies a suppressed clause beginning with the word *unless*. Thus it is impossible for me to see the street from where I sit writing at this moment; that is, it is impossible to see the street *unless* I go up to the top floor where I shall be high enough to overlook the intervening building. If I had broken my leg I should say "But it is impossible to go up to the top floor"—meaning, however, that it is impossible *unless* some friends turn up who will carry me. Now let us advance to a different plane of impossibility, by saying "It is, at any rate, impossible to see the street *so long as* I remain where I am and the intervening building remains where it is." Someone might add "unless the nature of space, or of vision, were different from what it is". I do not know what the best philosophers and scientists would say to this, but I should have to reply "I don't know whether space and vision *could possibly* have been of such a nature as you suggest". Now it is clear that the words *could possibly* here refer to some absolute kind of possibility or impossibility which is different from the relative possibilities and impossibilities we have been considering. I cannot say whether seeing round corners is, in this new sense, possible or not, because I do not know whether it is self-contradictory or not. But I know very well that if it is self-contradictory it is absolutely impossible. The absolutely impossible may also be called the intrinsically impossible because it carries its impossibility within itself, instead of borrowing it from other impossibilities which in their turn depend upon others. It has no *unless* clause attached to it. It is impossible under all conditions and in all worlds and for all agents.

"All agents" here includes God Himself. His Omnipotence means power to do all that is intrinsically possible, not to do the intrinsically impossible. You may attribute miracles to Him, but not nonsense. This is no limit to His power. If you choose to say "God can give a creature free-will and at the same time withhold free-will from it," you have not succeeded in saying *anything* about God: meaningless combinations of words do not suddenly acquire meaning simply because we prefix to them the two other words "God can". It remains true that all *things* are possible with God: the intrinsic impossibilities are not things but nonentities. It is no more possible for God than for the weakest of His creatures to carry out both of two mutually exclusive alternatives; not because His power meets an obstacle, but because nonsense remains nonsense even when we talk it about God . . .

By the goodness of God we mean nowadays almost exclusively His lovingness; and in this we may be right. And by Love, in this context, most of us mean kindness—the desire to see others than the self happy; not happy in this way or in that, but just happy. What would really satisfy us would be a God who said of anything we happened to like doing, "What does it matter so long as they are contented?" We want, in fact, not so much a Father in Heaven as a grandfather in heaven—a senile benevolence who, as they say, "liked to see young people enjoying themselves" and whose plan for the universe was simply that it might be truly said at the end of each day, "a good time was had by all". Not many people, I admit, would formulate a theology in precisely those terms: but a conception not very different lurks at the back of many minds. I do not claim to be an exception: I should very much like to live in a universe which was governed on such lines. But since it is abundantly clear that I don't, and since I have reason to believe, nevertheless, that God is Love, I conclude that my conception of love needs correction.

I might, indeed, have learned, even from the poets, that Love is something more stern and splendid than mere kindness: that even the love between the sexes is, as in Dante, "a lord of terrible aspect". There is kindness in Love: but Love and kindness are not coterminous, and when kindness (in the sense given above) is separated from the other elements of Love, it involves a certain fundamental indifference to its object, and even something like contempt of it. Kindness consents very readily to the removal of its object—we have all met people whose kindness to animals is constantly leading them to kill animals lest they should suffer. Kindness, merely as such, cares not whether its object becomes good or bad, provided only that it escapes suffering. As Scripture points out, it is bastards who are spoiled: the legitimate sons, who are to carry on the family tradition, are punished.[1] It is for people whom we care nothing about that we demand happiness on any terms: with our friends, our lovers, our children, we are exacting and would rather see them suffer much than be happy in contemptible and estranging modes. If God is Love, He is, by definition, something more than mere kindness. And it appears, from all the records, that though He has often rebuked us and condemned us, He has never regarded us with contempt. He has paid us the intolerable compliment of loving us, in the deepest, most tragic, most inexorable sense.

The relation between Creator and creature is, of course, unique, and cannot be paralleled by any relations between one creature and another. God is both further from us, and nearer to us, than any other being. He is further from us because the sheer difference between that which has Its principle of being in Itself and that to which being is communicated, is one compared with which the difference between an archangel and a worm is quite insignificant. He makes, we are made: He is original, we

---

[1]Heb, xii, 8.

derivative. But at the same time, and for the same reason, the intimacy between God and even the meanest creature is closer than any that creatures can attain with one another. Our life is, at every moment, supplied by Him: our tiny, miraculous power of free will only operates on bodies which His continual energy keeps in existence—our very power to think is His power communicated to us. Such a unique relation can be apprehended only by analogies: from the various types of love known among creatures we reach an inadequate, but useful, conception of God's love for man.

The lowest type, and one which is "love" at all only by an extension of the word, is that which an artist feels for an artefact. God's relation to man is pictured thus in Jeremiah's vision of the potter and the clay,[2] or when St. Peter speaks of the whole Church as a building on which God is at work, and of the individual members as stones.[3] The limitation of such an analogy is, of course, that in the symbol the patient is not sentient, and that certain questions of justice and mercy which arise when the "stones" are really "living" therefore remain unrepresented. But it is an important analogy so far as it goes. We are, not metaphorically but in very truth, a Divine work of art, something that God is making, and therefore something with which He will not be satisfied until it has a certain character. Here again we come up against what I have called the "intolerable compliment". Over a sketch made idly to amuse a child, an artist may not take much trouble: he may be content to let it go even though it is not exactly as he meant it to be. But over the great picture of his life—the work which he loves, though in a different fashion, as intensely as a man loves a woman or a mother a child—he will take endless trouble—and would, doubtless, thereby *give* endless trouble to the picture if it were sentient. One can imagine a sentient picture, after being rubbed and scraped and re-commenced for the tenth time, wishing that it were only a thumb-nail sketch whose making was over in a minute. In the same way, it is natural for us to wish that God had designed for us a less glorious and less arduous destiny; but then we are wishing not for more love but for less.

Another type is the love of a man for a beast—a relation constantly used in Scripture to symbolise the relation between God and men; "we are his people and the sheep of his pasture". This is in some ways a better analogy than the preceding, because the inferior party is sentient, and yet unmistakably inferior: but it is less good in so far as man has not made the beast and does not fully understand it. Its great merit lies in the fact that the association of (say) man and dog is primarily for the man's sake: he tames the dog primarily that he may love it, not that it may love him, and that it may serve him, not that he may serve it. Yet at

[2]Jer. xviii.
[3]x Pet. ii, 5.

the same time, the dog's interests are not sacrificed to the man's. The one end (that he may love it) cannot be fully attained unless it also, in its fashion, loves him, nor can it serve him unless he, in a different fashion, serves it. Now just because the dog is by human standards one of the "best" of irrational creatures, and a proper object for a man to love—of course, with that degree and kind of love which is proper to such an object, and not with silly anthropomorphic exaggerations—man interferes with the dog and makes it more lovable than it was in mere nature. In its state of nature it has a smell, and habits, which frustrate man's love: he washes it, house-trains it, teaches it not to steal, and is so enabled to love it completely. To the puppy the whole proceeding would seem, if it were a theologian, to cast grave doubts on the "goodness" of man: but the full-grown and full-trained dog, larger, healthier, and longer-lived than the wild dog, and admitted, as it were by Grace, to a whole world of affections, loyalties, interests, and comforts entirely beyond its animal destiny, would have no such doubts. It will be noted that the man (I am speaking throughout of the good man) takes all these pains with the dog, and gives all these pains to the dog, only because it is an animal high in the scale—because it is so nearly lovable that it is worth his while to make it fully lovable. He does not house-train the earwig or give baths to centipedes. We may wish, indeed, that we were of so little account to God that He left us alone to follow our natural impulses— that He would give over trying to train us into something so unlike our natural selves: but once again, we are asking not for more Love, but for less.

A nobler analogy, sanctioned by the constant tenor of Our Lord's teaching, is that between God's love for man and a father's love for a son. Whenever this is used, however (that is, whenever we pray the Lord's Prayer), it must be remembered that the Saviour used it in a time and place where paternal authority stood much higher than it does in modern England. A father half apologetic for having brought his son into the world, afraid to restrain him lest he should create inhibitions or even to instruct him lest he should interfere with his independence of mind, is a most misleading symbol of the Divine Fatherhood. I am not here discussing whether the authority of fathers, in its ancient extent, was a good thing or a bad thing: I am only explaining what the conception of Fatherhood would have meant to Our Lord's first hearers, and indeed to their successors for many centuries. And it will become even plainer if we consider how Our Lord (though, in our belief, one with His Father and co-eternal with Him as no earthly son is with an earthly father) regards His own Sonship, surrendering His will wholly to the paternal will and not even allowing Himself to be called "good" because Good is the name of the Father. Love between father and son, in this symbol, means essentially authoritative love on the one side, and obedient love on the other. The father uses his authority to make the son into the sort of human being he, rightly, and in his superior wisdom, wants him to be. Even in our own days, though a man might say, he could mean nothing by saying, "I love my son but don't care how great a blackguard he is provided he has a good time." . . .

The problem of reconciling human suffering with the existence of a God who loves, is only insoluble so long as we attach a trivial meaning to the word "love", and look on things as if man were the centre of them. Man is not the centre. God does not exist for the sake of man. Man does not exist for his own sake. "Thou hast created all things, and for thy pleasure they are and were created."[2] We were made not primarily that we may love God (though we were made for that too) but that God may love us, that we may become objects in which the Divine love may rest "well pleased". To ask that God's love should be content with us as we are is to ask that God should cease to be God: because He is what He is, His love must, in the nature of things, be impeded and repelled, by certain stains in our present character, and because He already loves us He must labour to make us lovable. We cannot even wish, in our better moments, that He could reconcile Himself to our present impurities—no more than the beggar maid could wish that King Cophetua should be content with her rags and dirt, or a dog, once having learned to love man, could wish that man were such as to tolerate in his house the snapping, verminous, polluting creature of the wild pack. What we would here and now call our "happiness" is not the end God chiefly has in view: but when we are such as He can love without impediment, we shall in fact be happy.

Study Questions

1. On what grounds did C. S. Lewis formerly reject the existence of God?

2. How would you answer Lewis's question: "If the universe is so bad . . . how on earth did human beings ever come to attribute it to the activity of a wise and good Creator?"

3. What is the distinction Lewis makes between the intrinsically possible (which God can do) and the intrinsically impossible (which God cannot do)?

4. What is Lewis's solution to the problem of evil, that is, reconciling God's love with human suffering?

5. Evaluate the soundness of Lewis's answer. What is your own reasoned conclusion?

[2]Rev. iv, II.

The Brothers Karamazov
("The Grand Inquisitor")

Fedor Dostoevsky
(trans. by Constance Garnett)

Fedor Dostoevsky (1821–1881) was a Russian novelist who, as the author of works such as Crime and Punishment, The Idiot, The Possessed, *and* The Brothers Karamazov, *is universally acknowledged to be one of the world's most profound writers. In all of his novels, Dostoevsky stresses man's inherent sinfulness, perversity, and passional will, which make it impossible to have a utopia of rationality and benevolence on earth.*

In the following section from The Brothers Karamazov, *Dostoevsky depicts Ivan Karamazov as rebelling against a God who permits the innocent to suffer—particularly innocent children. Even if the harmony of the universe in some incomprehensible way requires earthly pain, Ivan cannot accept the scheme; too high a price is asked. Ivan would rather return his passport to heaven than condone an inhumane system. When his brother Alyosha counters in an indirect way by claiming that Christ has the power to forgive the torturers of the innocent, Ivan introduces his parable of The Grand Inquisitor. The parable apparently condemns Christ for bringing men freedom rather than happiness, but Ivan actually feels that freedom is of greater importance, and as this becomes apparent his opposition to Christ loses its point. However, Ivan does succeed in exploring the problem of evil with great dramatic force in passages that have become classic expositions of the problem of evil.*

At this point in the narrative, Ivan expresses his outrage at the unjust suffering in the world, and cites several cases in which innocent children were cruelly treated while God apparently remained indifferent.

"Listen! I took the case of children only to make my case clearer. Of the other tears of humanity with which the earth is soaked from its crust to its centre, I will say nothing. I have narrowed my subject on purpose. I am a bug, and I recognise in all humility that I cannot understand why the world is arranged as it is. Men are themselves to blame, I suppose; they were given paradise, they wanted freedom, and stole fire from heaven, though they knew they would become unhappy, so there is no need to pity them. With my pitiful, earthly, Euclidian understanding, all I know is that there is suffering and that there are none guilty; that cause follows effect, simply and directly; that everything flows and finds its level—but that's only Euclidian nonsense, I know that, and I can't consent to live by it! What comfort is it to me that there are none guilty and that cause follows effect simply and directly, and that I know it—I must have justice, or I will destroy myself. And not justice in some remote infinite time and space, but here on earth, and that I could see myself. I have believed in it. I want to see it, and if I am dead by then, let me rise again, for if it all happens without me, it will be too unfair. Surely I haven't suffered, simply that I, my crimes and my sufferings, may manure the soil of the future harmony for somebody else. I want to see with my own eyes the hind lie down with the lion and the victim rise up and embrace his murderer. I want to be there when every one suddenly understands what it has all been for. All the religions of the world are built on this longing, and I am a believer. But then there are the children, and what am I to do about them? That's a question I can't answer. For the hundredth time I repeat, there are numbers of questions, but I've only taken the children, because in their case what I mean is so unanswerably clear. Listen! If all must suffer to pay for the eternal harmony, what have children to do with it, tell me, please? It's beyond all comprehension why they should suffer, and why they should pay for the harmony. Why should they, too, furnish material to enrich the soil for the harmony of the future? I understand solidarity in sin among men. I understand solidarity in retribution, too; but there can be no such solidarity with children. And if it is really true that they must share responsibility for all their fathers' crimes, such a truth is not of this world and is beyond my comprehension. Some jester will say, perhaps, that the child would have grown up and have sinned, but you see he didn't grow up, he was torn to pieces by the dogs, at eight years old. Oh, Alyosha, I am not blaspheming! I understand, of course, what an upheaval of the universe it will be, when everything in heaven and earth blends in one hymn of praise and everything that lives and has lived cries aloud: 'Thou art just, O Lord, for Thy ways are revealed.' When the mother embraces the fiend who threw her child to the dogs, and all three cry aloud with tears, 'Thou art just, O Lord!' then, of course, the crown of knowledge will be reached and all will be made clear. But what pulls me up here is that I can't accept that harmony. And while I am on earth, I make haste to take my own measures. You see, Alyosha, perhaps it really may happen that if I live to that moment, or rise again to see it, I, too, perhaps, may cry aloud with the rest, looking at the mother embracing the child's torturer, 'Thou art just, O Lord!' but I don't want to cry aloud then. While there is still time, I hasten to protect myself and so I renounce the higher harmony altogether. It's not worth the tears of that one tortured child who beat itself on the breast with its little fist and prayed in its stinking outhouse, with its unexpiated tears to 'dear, kind God'! It's not worth it, because those tears are unatoned for. They must be atoned for, or there can be no harmony. But how? How are you going to atone for them? Is it possible? By their being avenged? But what do I care for avenging them? What do I care for a hell for oppressors? What good can hell do, since those children have already been tortured? And what becomes of harmony, if there is hell? I want to forgive. I want to embrace. I don't want more suffering. And if the sufferings of children go to swell the sum of sufferings which was necessary to pay for truth, then I protest that the truth is not worth such a price. I don't want the mother to embrace the oppressor who threw her son to the dogs! She dare not forgive him! Let her forgive him for herself, if she will, let her forgive the torturer for the immeasurable suffering of her mother's heart. But the sufferings of her tortured child she has no right to forgive; she dare not forgive the torturer, even if the child were to forgive him! And if that is so, if they dare not forgive, what becomes of harmony? Is there in the whole world a being who would have the right to forgive and could forgive? I don't want harmony. From love for humanity I don't want it. I would rather be left with the unavenged suffering. I would rather remain with my unavenged suffering and unsatisfied indignation, *even if I were wrong.* Besides, too high a price is asked for harmony; it's beyond our means to pay so much to enter on it. And so I hasten to give back my entrance ticket, and if I am an honest man I am bound to give it back as soon as possible. And that I am doing. It's not God that I don't accept, Alyosha, only I most respectfully return Him the ticket."

"That's rebellion," murmured Alyosha, looking down.

"Rebellion? I am sorry you call it that," said Ivan earnestly. "One can hardly live in rebellion, and I want to live. Tell me yourself, I challenge you—answer. Imagine that you are creating a fabric of human destiny with the object of making men happy in the end, giving them peace and rest at last, but that it was essential and inevitable to torture to death only one tiny creature—that baby beating its breast with its fist, for instance—and to found that edifice on its unavenged tears, would you consent to be the architect on those conditions? Tell me, and tell the truth."

"No, I wouldn't consent," said Alyosha softly.

"And can you admit the idea that men for whom you are building it would agree to accept their happiness on the foundation of the unexpiated blood of a little victim? And accepting it would remain happy for ever?"

"No, I can't admit it. Brother," said Alyosha suddenly, with flashing eyes, "you said just now, is there a being in the whole world who would have the right to forgive and could forgive? But there is a Being and He can forgive everything, all and for all, because He gave His innocent blood for all and everything. You have forgotten Him, and on Him is built the edifice, and it is to Him they cry aloud, 'Thou art just, O Lord, for Thy ways are revealed!' "

"Ah! the One without sin and His blood! No, I have not forgotten Him; on the contrary I've been wondering all the time how it was you did not bring Him in before, for usually all arguments on your side put Him in the foreground. Do you know, Alyosha—don't laugh! I made a poem about a year ago. If you can waste another ten minutes on me, I'll tell it to you."

"You wrote a poem?"

"Oh, no, I didn't write it," laughed Ivan, "and I've never written two lines of poetry in my life. But I made up this poem in prose and I remembered it. I was carried away when I made it up. You will be my first reader—that is, listener. Why should an author forego even one listener?" smiled Ivan. "Shall I tell it to you?"

"I am all attention," said Alyosha.

"My poem is called 'The Grand Inquisitor'; it's a ridiculous thing, but I want to tell it to you."

The Grand Inquisitor

* * *

"My story is laid in Spain, in Seville, in the most terrible time of the Inquisition, when fires were lighted every day to the glory of God, and 'in the splendid *auto da fé* the wicked heretics were burnt.' Oh, of course, this was not the coming in which He will appear according to His promise at the end of time in all His heavenly glory, and which will be sudden 'as lightning flashing from east to west.' No, He visited His children only for a moment, and there where the flames were crackling round the heretics. In His infinite mercy He came once more among men in that human shape in which He walked among men for three years fifteen centuries ago. He came down to the 'hot pavement' of the southern town in which on the day before almost a hundred heretics had, *ad majorem gloriam Dei,* been burnt by the cardinal, the Grand Inquisitor, in a magnificent *auto da fé,* in the presence of the king, the court, the knights, the cardinals, the most charming ladies of the court, and the whole population of Seville.

"He came softly, unobserved, and yet, strange to say, every one recognised Him. That might be one of the best passages in the poem. I mean, why they recognised Him. The people are irresistibly drawn to Him, they surround Him, they flock about Him, follow Him. He moves silently in their midst with a gentle smile of infinite compassion. The sun of love burns in His heart, light and power shine from His eyes, and their radiance, shed on the people, stirs their hearts with responsive love. He holds out His hands to them, blesses them, and a healing virtue comes from contact with Him, even with His garments. An old man in the crowd, blind from childhood, cries out, 'O Lord, heal me and I shall see Thee!' and, as it were, scales fall from his eyes and the blind man sees Him. The crowd weeps and kisses the earth under His feet. Children throw flowers before Him, sing, and cry hosannah. 'It is He—it is He!' all repeat 'It must be He, it can be no one but Him!' He stops at the steps of the Seville cathedral at the moment when the weeping mourners are bringing in a little open white coffin. In it lies a child of seven, the only daughter of a prominent citizen. The dead child lies hidden in flowers. 'He will raise your child,' the crowd shouts to the weeping mother. The priest, coming to meet the coffin, looks perplexed, and frowns, but the mother of the dead child throws herself at His feet with a wail. 'If it is Thou, raise my child!' she cries, holding out her hands to Him. The procession halts, the coffin is laid on the steps at His feet. He looks with compassion, and His lips once more softly pronounce, 'Maiden, arise!' and the maiden arises. The little girl sits up in the coffin and looks round, smiling with wide-open wondering eyes, holding a bunch of white roses they had put in her hand.

"There are cries, sobs, confusion among the people, and at that moment the cardinal himself, the Grand Inquisitor, passes by the cathedral. He is an old man, almost ninety, tall and erect, with a withered face and sunken eyes, in which there is still a gleam of light. He is not dressed in his gorgeous cardinal's robes, as he was the day before, when he was burning the enemies of the Roman Church—at that moment he was wearing his coarse, old, monk's cassock. At a distance behind him come his gloomy assistants and slaves and the 'holy guard.' He stops at the sight of the crowd and watches it from a distance. He sees everything; he sees them set the coffin down at His feet, sees the child rise up, and his face darkens. He knits his thick grey brows and his eyes gleam with a sinister fire. He holds out his finger and bids the guards take Him. And such is his power, so completely are the people cowed into submission and trembling obedience to him, that the crowd immediately make way for the guards, and in the midst of deathlike silence they lay hands on Him and lead Him away. The crowd instantly bows down to the earth, like one man, before the old inquisitor. He blesses the people in silence and passes on. The guards lead their prisoner to the close, gloomy vaulted prison in the ancient palace of the Holy Inquisition and shut Him in it. The day passes and is followed by the dark, burning 'breathless' night of Seville. The air is 'fragrant with laurel and lemon.' In the pitch darkness the iron door of the prison is suddenly opened and the Grand Inquisitor himself comes in with a light in his hand. He is alone; the door is closed at once behind him. He stands in the doorway and for a minute or two gazes into His face. At last he goes up slowly, sets the light on the table and speaks.

" 'Is it Thou? Thou?' but receiving no answer, he adds at once, 'Don't answer, be silent. What canst Thou say, indeed? I know too well what Thou wouldst say. And Thou hast no right to add anything to what Thou hadst said of old. Why, then, art Thou come to hinder us? For Thou hast come to hinder us, and Thou knowest that. But dost Thou know what will be to-morrow? I know not who Thou art and care not to know whether it is Thou or only a semblance of Him, but to-morrow I shall condemn Thee and burn Thee at the stake as the worst of heretics. And the very people who have today kissed Thy feet, to-morrow at the faintest sign from me will rush to heap up the embers of Thy fire. Knowest Thou that? Yes, maybe Thou knowest it,' he added with thoughtful penetration, never for a moment taking his eyes off the Prisoner."

"I don't quite understand, Ivan. What does it mean?" Alyosha, who had been listening in silence, said with a smile. "Is it simply a wild fantasy, or a mistake on the part of the old man—some impossible *quiproquo?*"

"Take it as the last," said Ivan, laughing, "if you are so corrupted by modern realism and can't stand anything fantastic. If you like it to be a case of mistaken identity, let it be so. It is true," he went on, laughing, "the old man was ninety, and he might well be crazy over his set idea. He might have been struck by the appearance of the Prisoner. It might, in fact, be simply his ravings, the delusion of an old man of ninety, overexcited by the *auto da fé* of a hundred heretics the day before. But does it matter to us after all whether it was a mistake of identity or a wild fantasy? All that matters is that the old man should speak out, should speak openly of what he has thought in silence for ninety years."

"And the Prisoner too is silent? Does He look at him and not say a word?"

"That's inevitable in any case," Ivan laughed again. "The old man has told Him He hasn't the right to add anything to what He has said of old. One may say it is the most fundamental feature of Roman Catholicism, in my opinion at least. 'All has been given by Thee to the Pope,' they say, 'and all, therefore, is still in the Pope's hands, and there is no need for Thee to come now at all. Thou must not meddle for the time, at least.' That's how they speak and write too—the Jesuits, at any rate. I have read it myself in the works of their theologians. 'Hast Thou the right to reveal to us one of the mysteries of that world from which Thou hast come?' my old man asks Him, and answers the question for Him. 'No, Thou hast not; that Thou mayest not add to what has been said of old and mayest not take from men the freedom which Thou didst exalt when Thou wast on earth. Whatsoever Thou revealest anew will encroach on men's freedom of faith; for it will be manifest as a miracle, and the freedom of their faith was dearer to Thee than anything in those days fifteen hundred years ago. Didst Thou not often say then, "I will make you free"? But now Thou hast seen "free" men,' the old man adds suddenly, with a pensive smile. 'Yes, we've paid dearly for it,' he goes on, looking sternly at Him, 'but at last we have completed that work in Thy name. For fifteen centuries we have been wrestling with Thy freedom, but now it is ended and over for good. Dost Thou not believe that it's over for good? Thou lookest meekly at me and deignest not even to be wroth with me. But let me tell Thee that now, today, people are more persuaded than ever that they have perfect freedom, yet they have brought their freedom to us and laid it humbly at our feet. But that has been our doing. Was this what Thou didst? Was this Thy freedom?"'

"I don't understand again," Alyosha broke in. "Is he ironical, is he jesting?"

"Not a bit of it! He claims it as a merit for himself and his Church that at last they have vanquished freedom and have done so to make men happy. 'For now' (he is speaking of the Inquisition, of course) 'for the first time it has become possible to think of the happiness of men. Man was created a rebel; and how can rebels be happy? Thou wast warned,' he says to Him. 'Thou hast had no lack of admonitions and warnings, but Thou didst not listen to those warnings; Thou didst reject the only way by which men might be made happy. But, fortunately, departing Thou didst hand on the work to us. Thou hast promised, Thou hast established by Thy word, Thou hast given to us the right to bind and to unbind, and now, of course, Thou canst not think of taking it away. Why, then, hast Thou come to hinder us?"'

"And what's the meaning of 'no lack of admonitions and warnings?"' asked Alyosha.

"Why, that's the chief part of what the old man must say."

"'The wise and dread spirit, the spirit of self-destruction and nonexistence,' the old man goes on, 'the great spirit talked with Thee in the wilderness, and we are told in the books that he "tempted" Thee. Is that so? And could anything truer be said than what he revealed to Thee in three questions and what Thou didst reject, and what in the books is called "the temptation"? And yet if there has ever been on earth a real stupendous miracle, it took place on that day, on the day of the three temptations. The statement of those three questions was itself the miracle. If it were possible to imagine simply for the sake of argument that those three questions of the dread spirit had perished utterly from the books, and that we had to restore them and to invent them anew, and to do so had gathered together all the wise men of the earth—rulers, chief priests, learned men, philosophers, poets—and had set them the task to invent three questions, such as would not only fit the occasion, but express in three words, three human phrases, the whole future history of the world and of humanity—dost Thou believe that all the wisdom of the earth united could have invented anything in depth and force equal to the three questions which were actually put to Thee then by the wise and mighty spirit in the wilderness? From those questions alone, from the miracle of their statement, we can see that we have here to do not with the fleeting human intelligence, but with the absolute and eternal. For in those three questions the whole subsequent history of mankind is, as it were, brought together into one whole, and foretold, and in them are united all the unsolved historical contradictions of human nature. At the time it could not be so clear, since the future was unknown; but now that fifteen hundred years have passed, we see that everything in those three questions was so justly divined and foretold, and has been so truly fulfilled, that nothing can be added to them or taken from them.

"'Judge Thyself who was right—Thou or he who questioned Thee then? Remember the first question; its meaning, in other words, was this: "Thou wouldst go into the world, and art going with empty hands, with some promise of freedom which men in their simplicity and their natural unruliness cannot even understand, which they fear and dread—for nothing has ever been more insupportable for a man and a human society than freedom. But seest Thou these stones in this parched and barren wilderness? Turn them into bread, and mankind will run after Thee like a flock of sheep, grateful and obedient, though for ever trembling, lest Thou withdraw Thy hand and deny them Thy bread." But Thou wouldst not deprive man of freedom and didst reject the offer, thinking, what is that freedom worth, if obedience is bought with bread? Thou didst reply that man lives not by bread alone. But dost Thou know that for the sake of that earthly bread the spirit of the earth will rise up against Thee and will strive with Thee and overcome Thee, and all will follow him, crying, "Who can compare with this beast? He has given us fire from heaven!" Dost Thou know that the ages will pass, and humanity will proclaim by the lips of their sages that there is no crime, and therefore no sin; there is only hunger? "Feed men, and then ask of them virtue!" that's what they'll write on the banner, which they will raise against Thee, and with which they will destroy Thy temple. Where Thy temple stood will rise a new building; the terrible tower of Babel will be built again, and though, like the one of old, it will not be finished, yet Thou mightest have prevented that new tower and have cut short the sufferings of men for a thousand years; for they will come back to us after a thousand years of agony with their tower. They will seek us again, hidden underground in the catacombs, for we shall be again persecuted and tortured. They will find us and cry to us, "Feed us, for those who have promised us fire from heaven haven't given it!" And then we shall finish building their tower, for he finishes the building who feeds them. And we alone shall feed them in Thy name, declaring falsely that it is in Thy name. Oh, never, never can they feed themselves without us! No science will give them bread so long as they remain free. In the end they will lay their freedom at our feet, and say to us, "Make us your slaves, but feed us." They will understand themselves, at last, that freedom and bread enough for all are inconceivable together, for never, never will they be able to share between them! They will be convinced, too, that they can never be free, for they are weak, vicious, worthless and rebellious. Thou didst promise them the bread of Heaven, but, I repeat again, can it compare with earthly bread in the eyes of the weak, ever sinful and ignoble race of man? And if for the sake of the bread of Heaven thousands and tens of thousands shall follow Thee, what is to become of the millions and tens of thousands of millions of creatures who will not have the strength to forego the earthly bread for the sake of the heavenly? Or dost Thou care only for the tens of thousands of the great and strong, while the millions, numerous as the sands of the sea, who are weak but love Thee, must exist only for the sake of the great and strong? No, we care for the weak too. They are sinful and rebellious, but in the end they too will become obedient. They will marvel at us and look on us as gods, because we are ready to endure the freedom which they have found so dreadful and to rule over them—so awful it will seem to them to be free. But we shall tell them that we are Thy servants and rule them in Thy name. We shall deceive them again, for we will not let Thee come to us again. That deception will be our suffering, for we shall be forced to lie.

"'This is the significance of the first question in the wilderness, and this is what Thou hast rejected for the sake of that freedom which Thou hast exalted above everything. Yet in this question lies hid the great secret of this world. Choosing "bread," Thou wouldst have satisfied the universal and everlasting craving of humanity—to find some one to worship. So long as man remains free he strives for nothing so incessantly and so painfully as to find some one to worship. But man seeks to worship what is established beyond dispute, so that all men would agree at once to worship it. For these pitiful creatures are concerned not only to find what one or the other can worship, but to find something that all would believe in and worship; what is essential is that all may be *together* in it. This craving for *community* of worship is the chief misery of every man individually and of all humanity from the beginning of time. For the sake of common worship they've slain each other with the sword. They have set up gods and challenged one another, "Put away your gods and come and worship ours, or we will kill you and your gods!" And so it will be to the end of the world, even when gods disappear from the earth; they will fall down before idols just the same. Thou didst know, Thou couldst not but have known, this fundamental secret of human nature, but Thou didst reject the one infallible banner which was offered Thee to make all men bow down to Thee alone—the banner of earthly bread; and Thou hast rejected it for the sake of freedom and the bread of Heaven. Behold what Thou didst further. And all again in the name of freedom! I tell Thee that man is tormented by no greater anxiety than to find some one quickly to whom he can hand over that gift of freedom with which the ill-fated creature is born. But only one who can appease their conscience can take over their freedom. In bread there was offered Thee an invincible banner; give bread, and man will worship Thee, for nothing is more certain than bread. But if some one else gains possession of his conscience—oh! then he will cast away Thy bread and follow after him who has ensnared his conscience. In that Thou wast right. For the secret of man's being is not only to live but to have something to live for. Without a stable conception of the object of life, man would not consent to go on living, and would rather destroy himself than remain on earth, though he had bread in abundance. That is true. But what happened? Instead of taking men's freedom from them, Thou didst make it greater than ever! Didst Thou forget that man prefers peace, and even death, to freedom of choice in the knowledge of good and evil? Nothing is more seductive for man than his freedom of conscience, but nothing is a greater cause of suffering. And behold, instead of giving a firm foundation for setting the conscience of man at rest for ever, Thou didst choose all that is exceptional, vague and enigmatic; Thou didst choose what was utterly beyond the strength of men, acting as though Thou didst not love them at all—Thou who didst come to give Thy life for them! Instead of taking possession of men's freedom, Thou didst increase it, and burdened the spiritual kingdom of mankind with its sufferings for ever. Thou didst desire man's free love, that he should follow Thee freely, enticed and taken captive by Thee. In place of the rigid ancient law, man must hereafter with free heart decide for himself what is good and what is evil, having only Thy image before him as his guide. But didst Thou not know he would at last reject even Thy image and Thy truth, if he is weighed down with the fearful burden of free choice? They will cry aloud at last that the truth is not in Thee, for they could not have been left in greater confusion and suffering than Thou hast caused, laying upon them so many cares and unanswerable problems.

"'So that, in truth, Thou didst Thyself lay the foundation for the destruction of Thy kingdom, and no one is more to blame for it. Yet what was offered Thee? There are three powers, three powers alone, able to conquer and to hold captive for ever the conscience of these impotent rebels for their happiness—those forces are miracle, mystery and authority. Thou hast rejected all three and hast set the example for doing so. When the wise and dead spirit set Thee on the pinnacle of the temple and said to Thee, "If Thou wouldst know whether Thou art the Son of God then cast Thyself down, for it is written: the angels shall hold him up lest he fall and bruise himself, and Thou shalt know then whether Thou art the Son of God and shalt prove then how great is Thy faith in Thy Father." But Thou didst refuse and wouldst not cast Thyself down. Oh! of course, Thou didst proudly and well, like God; but the weak, unruly race of men, are they gods? Oh, Thou didst know then that in taking one step, in making one movement to cast Thyself down, Thou wouldst be tempting God and have lost all Thy faith in Him, and wouldst have been dashed to pieces against that earth which Thou didst come to save. And the wise spirit that tempted Thee would have rejoiced. But I ask again, are there many like Thee? And couldst Thou believe for one moment that men, too, could face such a temptation? Is the nature of men such, that they can reject miracle, and at the great moments of their life, the moments of their deepest, most agonising spiritual difficulties, cling only to the free verdict of the heart? Oh, Thou didst know that Thy deed would be recorded in books, would be handed down to remote times and the utmost ends of the earth, and Thou didst hope that man, following Thee, would cling to God and not ask for a miracle. But Thou didst not know that when man rejects miracle he rejects God too; for man seeks not so much God as the miraculous. And as man cannot bear to be without the miraculous, he will create new miracles of his own for himself, and will worship deeds of sorcery and witchcraft, though he might be a hundred times over a rebel, heretic and infidel. Thou didst not come down from the Cross when they shouted to Thee, mocking and reviling Thee, "Come down from the cross and we will believe that Thou art He." Thou didst not come down, for again Thou wouldst not enslave man by a miracle, and didst crave faith given freely, not based on miracle. Thou didst crave for free love and not the base raptures of the slave before the might that has overawed him for ever. But Thou didst think too highly of men therein, for they are slaves, of course, though rebellious by nature. Look round and judge; fifteen centuries have passed, look upon them. Whom hast Thou raised up to Thyself? I swear, man is weaker and baser by nature than Thou hast believed him! Can he, can he do what Thou didst? By showing him so much respect, Thou didst, as it were, cease to feel for him, for Thou didst ask far too much from him—Thou who hast loved him more than Thyself! Respecting him less, Thou wouldst have asked less of him. That would have been more like love, for his burden would have been lighter. He is weak and vile. What though he is everywhere now rebelling against our power, and proud of his rebellion? It is the pride of a child and a schoolboy. They are little children rioting and barring out the teacher at school. But their childish delight will end; it will cost them dear. They will cast down temples and drench the earth with blood. But they will see at last, the foolish children, that, though they are rebels, they are impotent rebels, unable to keep up their own rebellion. Bathed in their foolish tears, they will recognise at last that He who created them rebels must have meant to mock at them. They will say this in despair, and their utterance will be a blasphemy which will make them more unhappy still, for man's nature cannot bear blasphemy, and in the end always avenges it on itself. And so unrest, confusion and unhappiness—that is the present lot of man after Thou didst bear so much for their freedom! Thy great prophet tells in vision and in image, that he saw all those who took part in the first resurrection and that there were of each tribe twelve thousand. But if there were so many of them, they must have been not men but gods. They had borne Thy cross, they had endured scores of years in the barren, hungry wilderness, living upon locusts and roots—and Thou mayest indeed point with pride at those children of freedom, of free love, of free and splendid sacrifice for Thy name. But remember that they were only some thousands; and what of the rest? And how are the other weak ones to blame, because they could not endure what the strong have endured? How is the weak soul to blame that it is unable to receive such terrible gifts? Canst Thou have simply come to the elect and for the elect? But if so, it is a mystery and we cannot understand it. And if it is a mystery, we too have a right to preach a mystery, and to teach them that it's not the free judgment of their hearts, not love that matters, but a mystery which they must follow blindly, even against their conscience. So we have done. We have corrected Thy work and have founded it upon *miracle, mystery* and *authority.* And men rejoiced that they were again led like sheep, and that the terrible gift that had brought them such suffering, was, at last, lifted from their hearts. Were we right teaching them this? Speak! Did we not love mankind, so meekly acknowledging their feebleness, lovingly lightening their burden, and permitting their weak nature even sin with our sanction? Why hast Thou come now to hinder us? And why dost Thou look silently and searchingly at me with Thy mild eyes? Be angry. I don't want Thy love, for I love Thee not. And what use is it for me to hide anything from Thee? Don't I know to Whom I am speaking? All that I can say is known to Thee already. And is it for me to conceal from Thee our mystery? Perhaps it is Thy will to hear it from my lips. Listen, then. We are not working with Thee, but with *him*—that is our mystery. It's long— eight centuries—since we have been on *his* side and not on Thine. Just eight centuries ago, we took from him what Thou didst reject with scorn, that last gift he offered Thee, showing Thee all the kingdoms of the earth. We took from him Rome and the sword of Caesar, and proclaimed ourselves sole rulers of the earth, though hitherto we have not been able to complete our work. But whose fault is that? Oh, the work is only beginning, but it has begun. It has long to await completion and the earth has yet much to suffer, but we shall triumph and shall be Caesars, and then we shall plan the universal happiness of man. But Thou mightest have taken even then the sword of Caesar. Why didst Thou reject that last gift? Hadst Thou accepted that last counsel of the mighty spirit, Thou wouldst have accomplished all that man seeks on earth—that is, some one to worship, some one to keep his conscience, and some means of uniting all in one unanimous and harmonious ant-heap, for the craving for universal unity is the third and last anguish of men. Mankind as a whole has always striven to organise a universal state. There have been many great nations with great histories, but the more highly they were developed the more unhappy they were, for they felt more acutely than other people the craving for worldwide union. The great conquerors, Timours and Ghenghis-Khans, whirled like hurricanes over the face of the earth striving to subdue its people, and they too were but the unconscious expression of the same craving for universal unity. Hadst Thou taken the world and Caesar's purple, Thou wouldst have founded the universal state and have given universal peace. For who can rule men if not he who holds their conscience and their bread in his hands? We have taken the sword of Caesar, and in taking it, of course, have rejected Thee and followed *him*. Oh, ages are yet to come of the confusion of free thought, of their science and cannibalism. For having begun to build their tower of Babel without us, they will end, of course with cannibalism. But then the beast will crawl to us and lick our feet and spatter them with tears of blood. And we shall sit upon the beast and raise the cup, and on it will be written, "Mystery." But then, and only then, the reign of peace and happiness will come for men. Thou art proud of Thine elect, but Thou hast only the elect, while we give rest to all. And besides, how many of those elect, those mighty ones who could become elect, have grown weary waiting for Thee, and have transferred and will transfer the powers of their spirit and the warmth of their heart to the other camp, and end by raising their *free* banner against Thee. Thou didst Thyself lift up that banner. But with us all will be happy and will no more rebel nor destroy one another as under Thy freedom. Oh, we shall persuade them that they will only become free when they renounce their freedom to us and submit to us. And shall we be right or shall we be lying? They will be convinced that we are right, for they will remember the horrors of slavery and confusion to which Thy freedom brought them. Freedom, free thought and science, will lead them into such straits and will bring them face to face with such marvels and insoluble mysteries, that some of them, the fierce and rebellious, will destroy themselves, others, rebellious but weak, will destroy one another, while the rest, weak and unhappy, will crawl fawning to our feet and whine to us: "Yes, you were right, you alone possess His mystery, and we come back to you, save us from ourselves!"

"'Receiving bread from us, they will see clearly that we take the bread made by their hands from them, to give it to them, without any miracle. They will see that we do not change the stones to bread, but in truth they will be more thankful for taking it from our hands than for the bread itself! For they will remember only too well that in old days, without our help, even the bread they made turned to stones in their hands, while since they have come back to us, the very stones have turned to bread in their hands. Too, too well they know the value of complete submission! And until men know that, they will be unhappy. Who is most to blame for their not knowing it, speak? Who scattered the flock and sent it astray on unknown paths? But the flock will come together again and will submit once more, and then it will be once for all. Then we shall give them the quiet humble happiness of weak creatures such as they are by nature. Oh, we shall persuade them at last not to be proud, for Thou didst lift them up and thereby taught them to be proud. We shall show them that they are weak, that they are only pitiful children, but that childlike happiness is the sweetest of all. They will become timid and will look to us and huddle close to us in fear, as chicks to the hen. They will marvel at us and will be awestricken before us, and will be proud at our being so powerful and clever, that we have been able to subdue such a turbulent flock of thousands of millions. They will tremble impotently before our wrath, their minds will grow fearful, they will be quick to shed tears like women and children, but they will be just as ready at a sign from us to pass to laughter and rejoicing, to happy mirth and childish song. Yes, we shall set them to work, but in their leisure hours we shall make their life like a child's game, with children's songs and innocent dance. Oh, we shall allow them even sin, they are weak and helpless, and they will love us like children because we allow them to sin. We shall tell them that every sin will be expiated, if it is done with our permission, that we allow them to sin because we love them, and the punishment for these sins we take upon ourselves. And we shall take it upon ourselves, and they will adore us as their saviours who have taken on themselves their sins before God. And they will have no secrets from us. We shall allow or forbid them to live with their wives and mistresses, to have or not to have children—according to whether they have been obedient or disobedient—and they will submit to us gladly and cheerfully. The most painful secrets of their conscience, all, all they will bring to us, and we shall have an answer for all. And they will be glad to believe our answer, for it will save them from the great anxiety and terrible agony they endure at present in making a free decision for themselves. And all will be happy, all the millions of creatures except the hundred thousand who rule over them. For only we, we who guard the mystery, shall be unhappy. There will be thousands of millions of happy babes, and a hundred thousand sufferers who have taken upon themselves the curse of the knowledge of good and evil. Peacefully they will die, peacefully they will expire in Thy name, and beyond the grave they will find nothing but death. But we shall keep the secret, and for their happiness we shall allure them with the reward of heaven and eternity. Though if there were anything in the other world, it certainly would not be for such as they. It is prophesied that Thou wilt come again in victory, Thou wilt come with Thy chosen, the proud and strong, but we will say that they have only saved themselves, but we have saved all. We are told that the harlot who sits upon the beast, and holds in her hands the *mystery*, shall be put to shame, that the weak will rise up again, and will rend her royal purple and will strip naked her loathsome body. But then I will stand up and point out to Thee the thousand millions of happy children who have known no sin. And we who have taken their sins upon us for their happiness will stand up before Thee and say: "Judge us if Thou canst and darest." Know that I fear Thee not. Know that I too have been in the wilderness, I too have lived on roots and locusts, I too prized the freedom with which Thou hast blessed men, and I too was striving to stand among Thy elect, among the strong and powerful, thirsting "to make up the number." But I awakened and would not serve madness. I turned back and joined the ranks of those *who have corrected Thy work*. I left the proud and went back to the humble, for the happiness of the humble. What I say to Thee will come to pass, and our dominion will be built up. I repeat, to-morrow Thou shalt see that obedient flock who at a sign from me will hasten to heap up the hot cinders about the pile on which I shall burn Thee for coming to hinder us. For if any one has ever deserved our fires, it is Thou. To-morrow I shall burn Thee. Dixi.'"

Ivan stopped. He was carried away as he talked and spoke with excitement; when he had finished, he suddenly smiled.

Alyosha had listened in silence; towards the end he was greatly moved and seemed several times on the point of interrupting, but restrained himself. Now his words came with a rush.

"But . . . that's absurd!" he cried, flushing. "Your poem is in praise of Jesus, not in blame of Him—as you meant it to be. And who will believe you about freedom? Is that the way to understand it? That's not the idea of it in the Orthodox Church . . . That's Rome, and not even the whole of Rome, it's false—those are the worst of the Catholics, the Inquisitors, the Jesuits! . . . And there could not be such a fantastic creature as your Inquisitor. What are these sins of mankind they take on themselves? Who are these keepers of the mystery who have taken some curse upon themselves for the happiness of mankind? When have they been seen? We know the Jesuits, they are spoken ill of, but surely they are not what you describe? They are not that at all, not at all. . . . They are simply the Romish army for the earthly sovereignty of the world in the future, with the Pontiff of Rome for Emperor . . . that's their ideal, but there's no sort of mystery or lofty melancholy about it. . . . It's simple lust of power, of filthy earthly gain, of domination—something like a universal serfdom with them as masters—that's all they stand for. They don't even believe in God perhaps. Your suffering inquisitor is a mere fantasy."

"Stay, stay," laughed Ivan, "how hot you are! A fantasy you say, let it be so! Of course it's a fantasy. But allow me to say: do you really think that the Roman Catholic movement of the last centuries is actually nothing but the lust of power, of filthy earthly gain? Is that Father Païssy's teaching?"

"No, no, on the contrary, Father Païssy did once say something rather the same as you . . . but of course it's not the same, not a bit the same," Alyosha hastily corrected himself.

"A precious admission, in spite of your 'not a bit the same.' I ask you why your Jesuits and Inquisitors have united simply for vile material gain? Why can there not be among them one martyr oppressed by great sorrow and loving humanity? You see, only suppose that there was one such man among all those who desire nothing but filthy material gain—if there's only one like my old inquisitor, who had himself eaten roots in the desert and made frenzied efforts to subdue his flesh to make himself free and perfect. But yet all his life he loved humanity, and suddenly his eyes were opened, and he saw that it is no great moral blessedness to attain perfection and freedom, if at the same time one gains the conviction that millions of God's creatures have been created as a mockery, that they will never be capable of using their freedom, that these poor rebels can never turn into giants to complete the tower, that it was not for such geese that the great idealist dreamt his dream of harmony. Seeing all that he turned back and joined—the clever people. Surely that could have happened?"

"Joined whom, what clever people?" cried Alyosha, completely carried away. "They have no such great cleverness and no mysteries and secrets. . . . Perhaps nothing but Atheism, that's all their secret. Your inquisitor does not believe in God, that's his secret!"

"What if it is so! At last you have guessed it. It's perfectly true that that's the whole secret, but isn't that suffering, at least for a man like that, who has wasted his whole life in the desert and yet could not shake off his incurable love of humanity? In his old age he reached the clear conviction that nothing but the advice of the great dread spirit could build up any tolerable sort of life for the feeble, unruly, 'incomplete, empirical creatures created in jest.' And so, convinced of this, he sees that he must follow the counsel of the wise spirit, the dread spirit of death and destruction, and therefore accept lying and deception, and lead men consciously to death and destruction, and yet deceive them all the way so that they may not notice where they are being led, that the poor blind creatures may at least on the way think themselves happy. And note, the deception is in the name of Him in Whose ideal the old man had so fervently believed all his life long. Is not that tragic? And if only one such stood at the head of the whole army 'filled with the lust of power only for the sake of filthy gain'—would not one such be enough to make a tragedy? More than that, one such standing at the head is enough to create the actual leading idea of the Roman Church with all its armies and Jesuits, its highest idea. I tell you frankly that I firmly believe that there has always been such a man among those who stood at the head of the movement. Who knows, there may have been some such even among the Roman Popes. Who knows, perhaps the spirit of that accursed old man who loves mankind so obstinately in his own way, is to be found even now in a whole multitude of such old men, existing not by chance but by agreement, as a secret league formed long ago for the guarding of the mystery, to guard it from the weak and the unhappy, so as to make them happy. No doubt it is so, and so it must be indeed. I fancy that even among the Masons there's something of the same mystery at the bottom, and that that's why the Catholics so detest the Masons as their rivals breaking up the unity of the idea, while it is so essential that there should be one flock and one shepherd. . . . But from the way I defend my idea I might be an author impatient of your criticism. Enough of it."

"You are perhaps a Mason yourself!" broke suddenly from Alyosha. "You don't believe in God," he added, speaking this time very sorrowfully. He fancied besides that his brother was looking at him ironically. "How does your poem end?" he asked, suddenly looking down. "Or was it the end?"

"I meant to end it like this. When the Inquisitor ceased speaking he waited some time for his Prisoner to answer him. His silence weighed down upon him. He saw that the Prisoner had listened intently all the time, looking gently in his face and evidently not wishing to reply. The old man longed for Him to say something, however bitter and terrible. But He suddenly approached the old man in silence and softly kissed him on his bloodless aged lips. That was all his answer. The old man shuddered. His lips moved. He went to the door, opened it, and said to Him: 'Go, and come no more . . . come not at all, never, never!' And he let Him out into the dark alleys of the town. The Prisoner went away."

"And the old man?"

"The kiss glows in his heart, but the old man adheres to his idea."

Study Questions

1. Ivan Karamazov's dilemma is that if God forgives evil people, especially the torturers of children, then there is no justice in the universe, and if he punishes them, then there is no absolute forgiveness, love, and harmony. Do you think this dilemma can be resolved?

2. What accusations does the Grand Inquisitor make against Christ?

3. Do you think that the church has used "miracle, mystery, and authority" to coerce people into faith? If so, is it justified?

4. Do you think freedom is more important than happiness, as Ivan seems to contend?

5. In what way do Ivan and Alyosha Karamazov address the problem of evil? Whose position do you think is stronger?

The Devil's Advocate

Director: Taylor Hackford

Screenplay: Jonathan Lemkin and Tony Gilroy

Based on the book by Andrew Neiderman

Taylor Hackford (1945–), an American director and producer, is known for his fast-paced, high-energy films charged with sexuality. His critically acclaimed The Idolmakers *about rock and roll, was followed by the box office success* An Officer and a Gentleman, *a love story set at a naval flight school. He then directed* Against All Odds, *a remake of a film noir classic, and* White Nights, *a cold war drama about dancers in Moscow. This was followed by the documentary* Chuck Berry Hail! Hail! Rock 'n' Roll. *More recently he has directed and/or produced* Bound By Honor, Dolores Claiborne, *and* Proof of Life, *all of which have enhanced his reputation as a filmmaker.*

In The Devil's Advocate, *Hackford presents a supernatural thriller about a lawyer who is seduced into serving the devil. Choosing a law firm as the setting for a morality play is an astute choice, for attorneys can become easy prey for "Satan" if they emphasize winning over the pursuit of justice.*

In terms of the problem of evil, the reader must ask why God would allow the devil to tempt people to sin, dangling the forbidden fruit. Furthermore, the outcome must be known by God since he is all-knowing, which includes foreknowledge, so it is hardly a test of faith.

The Devil's Advocate *does not depict natural evil, that is, the suffering people undergo from natural causes, but the evil perpetrated by Satan. The underlying question, then, is why God would allow the devil to operate, bringing pain to human beings. In his omnipotence, he could have prevented it, so why doesn't he do so? The same question can be asked with regard to the suffering caused by wars and other forms of violence, including the terrorist attacks of September 11th. Should we thank God for those who were saved or wonder why he allowed so many to be lost?*

Synopsis

The theme of a devil's bargain has been presented in numerous literary works, most notably the Dr. Faust tales of Johann Wolfgang von Goethe, Christopher Marlowe, and to a lesser extent, Stephen Vincent Benet. A man makes a pact with the devil in order to get something he desperately desires—so desperately that he is willing to forfeit his soul to obtain it. In the Faust legends it is unearthly knowledge that is sought, reminiscent of the forbidden fruit in the Garden of Eden. (Adam succumbed to the temptations of the serpent [and the woman], thereby losing paradise for himself and all his descendants.) In the literary versions, Faust is ultimately saved, for despite the fact that he violates the realm of sacred knowledge, he does so as a seeker after truth. In Goethe's tale, Faust's soul is borne upwards by angels chanting "Lo! Rescued is this noble one / From evil machinations; / "Who e'er aspiring struggles on, / For him there is salvation."

The Devil's Advocate explores this same terrain but updated to the contemporary practice of law. In our adversarial system, defense attorneys mount the strongest possible case for their clients, including those they believe are guilty, just as prosecuting attorneys will try cases even when they are convinced the accused is innocent. Furthermore, the trial lawyers' reputation, wealth, power, and status depend on their victories in court. Such circumstances can tempt attorneys to use deceitful practices, rhetorical devices, legal technicalities, and so forth to win the case. They remain within the law but outside ethics. In this way, the lawyer may become the instrument of the devil, selling his soul for the rewards of success.

Kevin Lomax (Keanu Reeves) practices law in Gainesville, Florida, and his win/loss record is unblemished, which is uncanny: sixty-four convictions as county prosecutor, no losses as a defense attorney. When the film begins he is defending a schoolteacher named Geddes who is accused of molesting a young student. Although Lomax thinks the man is guilty as sin, he plants a doubt in the jury's mind about the girl's truthfulness, and the teacher is subsequently acquitted. He has a minor crisis of conscience in the washroom, but his pride induces him to continue the defense, aided by the (diabolical) prompting of a reporter.

At the celebration party Lomax is offered a position in the prestigious New York law firm of Milton, Chadwick, and Waters, initially to help in jury selection—something he seems able to do with unnatural skill. The terms are so generous and the career prospects so promising, that he accepts the offer despite the objections of his mother Alice Lomax (Judith Ivey). As a Bible-thumping, fundamentalist Christian, his mother, has "bad feelings" about the move, regarding New York as "Babylon . . . the dwelling place of demons." However, his wife, Mary Ann (Charlize Theron), supports his decision, remarking that the mother just needs grandkids.

After successfully assisting in jury selection at a New York trial (the jury deliberated only thirty-eight minutes before finding the defendant not guilty), Lomax is invited to meet the senior partner of the firm, John Milton (Al Pacino). The name is an obvious reference to the English poet Milton who wrote *Paradise Lost*, a poem in which Mephistopheles (inadvertently?) becomes the hero. Milton's famous line "Better to rule in hell than serve in heaven" is actually incorporated into the ending of the film. The viewer is thus given a hint at the outset that Satan heads the law firm.

Lomax confesses during the interview that he used to listen to juries deliberate through a hole in the wall, which of course pleases Milton; it shows a vulnerability to corruption. Milton asks him whether he can summon his powers at will, whether he can sleep well at night, which sound more like theological questions than legal ones. Tellingly, the meeting between Milton and Lomax takes place on a penthouse roof with all of Manhattan at their feet. The two men talk on a perilous walkway, suggesting the possibility of a fall, and a thin layer of water spills over the edges of the building creating a sense of a deep descent. Perhaps this is a modern setting for the temptations in the wilderness.

Lomax is subsequently given a luxurious condominium in uptown Manhattan with paneled walls and inlaid floors; it even has an extra bedroom for the baby his wife wants. He is also assigned a court case as a test of his abilities. A man named Moyez (Delroy Lindo) is charged with violating public health codes because he slaughtered a goat in a voodoo ceremony. In a clever defense, Lomax refers to other religious practices that are accepted even though they are bizarre: the circumcision of infants, water being transformed into blood during communion, fakirs who walk on burning coals, cults that handle poisonous snakes. By citing such precedents, which is standard procedure in law, sacrificing a goat is made to appear reasonable. In a comic note, Moyez causes the prosecutor to have a coughing fit, presumably by invoking demonic powers.

By winning this case Lomax becomes further enmeshed in the life of the law office, riding on his success and feeling a part of the wealth and power surrounding him; his time is billed at four hundred dollars an hour. He is also responsive to the attractive Christabella Andreoli (Connie Nielsen), a femme fatale at the firm, who eagerly leads him astray through his vanity; as the plot unfolds, she turns out to be his half-sister. Milton orchestrates her moves, including the invitation to a bisexual orgy, because she is critical to his master plan. Christabella does not actually seduce Lomax, but when he makes love to his wife Mary Ann, trying to conceive a child, her images appear in his mind. In this way he sins in thought, which in scripture is equivalent to the deed, and their lovemaking to conceive a child is subverted into sexual lust.

Christianity has always viewed sex with suspicion mixed with fear, regarding it as one of the devil's principal snares. Woman may be regarded as the epitome of purity like Mary but usually she is thought of as the temptress Eve, Jezebel, Mary Magdalen. According to Catholic doctrine, the function of sex is procreation not pleasure or even the expression of love, and virginity and celibacy are highly prized. To subdue the desires of the body, monks will lash themselves with knouts, seeking the humiliation of the flesh for the purification of the soul. It would be natural, therefore, for sex to play a prominent role in Lomax's fall.

At one point Milton does warn Lomax to remain discrete and unobtrusive in all that he does. This is his own approach, so that he has been "underestimated from day one." He tells Lomax, "They don't see me coming," and wouldn't think "I was the master of the universe." This would be Satan's way of functioning, just as we can understand his comment: "Subways—the only way I travel."

In another significant speech, delivered after Milton arranges the murder of Eddie Barzoon (Jeffrey Jones), an associate at the firm, he discourses about man saying:

"God's creature, God's special creature . . . You sharpen the human appetite to the point where it can split atoms with its desire. You build egos the size of cathedrals, fiber optically connect the world to every eager impulse, grease even the dullest dream with these dollar green, gold plated fantasies until every human becomes an aspiring emperor, his own God. And where can you go from there? And as for scrabbling from one deal to the next, who's got his eye on the planet as the air thickens, the water sours, even the bee's honey takes on the metallic taste of radioactivity. And it just keeps on coming faster and faster. There's no chance to think or prepare to buy futures or sell futures when there is no future. We got a runaway train." Al Pacino received high praise for his performance as John Milton/Satan, and this scene and the climax of the film show him at his gleeful, boorish, wicked, lusty best.

As the firm consumes more and more of Lomax's time, Mary Ann is increasingly neglected. She becomes second to his career, even an impediment, especially when he is assigned a high-profile case. He is asked to defend Alexander Cullen (Craig T. Nelson), a major real estate developer accused of murdering his wife, stepson, and maid. The evidence against Cullen looks damning: His fingerprints are on the murder weapon, blood was splattered on the wall and on his clothes, and he was the one who telephoned the police saying he had discovered the crime.

Despite the difficulties and Lomax's relative inexperience, Milton insists that he handle the defense. In retrospect we see that Milton hopes this case will alienate Lomax from his wife, and that he will persuade a jury once more to acquit a guilty man. Perhaps then, when love is destroyed and evil triumphs, he will belong to Satan completely.

Milton succeeds in his first aim. The love relationship is destroyed, not only because Mary Ann is neglected but because she is driven insane. She begins to hear voices, to see faces reverting to ghoulish forms, and she wakes up one day to find a baby playing with human tissue. She realizes it is her own ovaries, and that she will never have children. Her breakdown is ultimately precipitated when she is seduced then slashed and raped by Milton.

The events are real, of course, not visions, and she truly recognizes that Milton and the firm are responsible for the horrors perpetrated on her. However, in our age we do not accept the reality of evil but only violence; we believe in guilt perhaps but not shame or sin. Therefore, Lomax thinks she is hallucinating and has her sent to the psychiatric unit of a hospital. Here she commits suicide, declaring her love for Lomax with her last breath.

As for the court case, Cullen's main defense is that at the time of the murder he was having an affair with his assistant Melissa Black (Laura Harrington). At first the woman verifies the alibi, but it quickly becomes clear that she is lying. Lomax faces the critical decision of whether to put her on the stand, knowing she will lie and that a guilty client might be acquitted. He calls her as a witness, thereby choosing to win the case rather than affirm his integrity.

The action proceeds quickly from this point. A member of the Justice Department, Mitch Weaver (Vyto Ruginis), warns Lomax that the law firm is involved in arms brokering, the illegal disposal of chemical waste, and money laundering. Just before being killed by a car, he also informs him that the schoolteacher Geddes, whom Lomax successfully defended in Gainesville, was found with the body of a ten-year-old girl in the trunk of his car. In a further devastating disclosure, his mother reveals the identity of his father. Thirty years previously she had come to New York with the Baptist Endeavor Youth Crusade and, out of loneliness, she had made love with a waiter. When she saw Milton, she recognized him as that man. The devil took advantage of her neediness just as he did Mary Ann, and Kevin was produced from that sordidness, the child of Satan.

The remainder of the film and its denouement consists of the confrontation between Milton and Lomax, the devil and his progeny. Throughout the scene a fire blazes in the fireplace (appropriately), and the figures in the low-relief sculptures come alive as the background begins to swirl. The supernatural effects form a fitting background to the metaphysical debate that follows.

In this climactic scene Lomax accuses Milton of causing Mary Ann's insanity and suicide, and even tries to shoot him, but the devil remains unharmed and unimpressed.

> MILTON: I'm no puppeteer, Kevin. I don't make things happen. It doesn't work like that. Free will. I only set the stage, you pull the strings . . . Never lost a case. Why? Because you're so fucking good? But why?
> LOMAX: Because you're my father?
> MILTON: I'm a little more than that Kevin. Awfully hot in the courtroom, wasn't it? What's the game plan, Kevin? Was a nice run kid. Had to close out someday. Nobody wins them all.
> LOMAX: What are you?
> MILTON: Oh I have so many names.
> LOMAX: Satan?
> MILTON: Call me dad.
> LOMAX: Mary Ann, she knew it. She knew it. She knew it so you destroyed her.

MILTON: You blaming me for Mary Ann. Oh I hope you're kidding. You could have saved her any time you liked. All she wanted was love. Heh, you were too busy.

LOMAX: That's a lie.

MILTON: Mary Ann in New York? Face it, you started looking to better-deal her the minute you got here.

LOMAX: That's not true. You don't know what we had. You're a liar. You don't know anything about it.

MILTON: Hey, I'm on your side. Kevin there's nothing out there for you. Don't be such a fucking chump. Stop deluding yourself. I told you to take care of your wife. What did I say? The world would understand. Didn't I say that? What did you do? [In Kevin's voice] 'You know what scares me John? I leave the case, she gets better, then I hate her for it.' Remember?

LOMAX: I know what you did. You set me up.

MILTON: Who told you to pull out all the stops on Mr. Geddes? Who made that choice?

LOMAX: It's entrapment. You set me up.

MILTON: And more yet, the direction you took popes, swamis, snake handlers, all feeding at the same trough. Whose ideas were those?

LOMAX: You played me. It was a test, your test.

MILTON: And Cullen, knowing he was guilty, seeing those pictures, what did you do? You put that lying bitch on the stand.

LOMAX: You brought me in. You put me there. You made her lie.

MILTON: I don't do that Kevin. That day on the subway, what did I say to you? What were my words to you? Maybe it was your time to lose. You didn't think so.

LOMAX: Lose? I don't lose. I win! I win! I'm a lawyer, that's my job, that's what I do.

MILTON: I rest my case. Vanity is definitely my favorite sin. Kevin, it's so basic, self-love, the all-natural opiate. You know it's not that you didn't care for Mary Ann, Kevin, it's just that you were a little more involved with someone else, yourself.

LOMAX: You're right. I did it all. I let her go.

MILTON: Ah, don't be too hard on yourself, Kevin. You wanted something more, believe me.

LOMAX: I left her behind and just kept going.

MILTON: You can't keep punishing yourself, Kevin. It's awesome how far you've come. I didn't make it easy. Couldn't. Not for you, or your sister. Half-sister to be exact.

[Christabella Andreoli appears] Surprise.

MILTON: Some scene, eh Kevin?

CHRISTABELLA: Don't let him scare you.

MILTON: I've had so many children. I've had so many disappointments. Mistake after mistake. And then there's you, the two of you.

LOMAX: What do you want from me?

MILTON: I want you to be yourself. You know, I tell you boy, guilt is like a bag of fucking bricks. All you have to do is set it down.

CHRISTABELLA: Heh, I know what you're going through. I've been there. Just come here. Let it go.

LOMAX: I can't do that.

MILTON: Who are you carrying all those bricks for anyway? For God? Is that it, God? Well, I'll tell you. Let me give you some inside information. God is a prankster. He likes to watch. He gives man instincts, he gives you this extraordinary gift and then what does he do? I swear, for his own amusement, for his own private, cosmic gag-reel, he sets the rules in opposition. It's the goof of all time. Look but don't touch. Touch but don't taste. Taste, don't swallow. And while you're jumping from one foot to the next, what's he doing? He's laughing his sick fucking ass off. He's a tight-ass, he's a sadist, he's an absentee landlord. Worship that? Never!

LOMAX: Better to reign in hell than serve in heaven, is that it?

MILTON: Why not? I'm here on the ground with my nose in it since the whole thing began. I've nurtured every sensation man has been inspired to have. I've cared about what he wanted and I never judged him. Why? Because I never rejected him. In spite of all his imperfections, I'm a fan of man. I'm a humanist, maybe the last humanist. Who in his right mind could possibly deny the 20th century was entirely mine. All of it, Kevin. All of it. Mine. I'm peaking, Kevin. It's my time now, it's our time.

CHRISTABELLA: Anybody want a drink? I'm having a drink.

LOMAX: Is this some pitch? You must need me pretty bad. What do you want?

MILTON: I want you to take over the firm [sic]. You and your sister.

LOMAX: Is that it?

MILTON: No. She's ovulating, right now.

LOMAX: What?

MILTON: Your vanity is justified, Kevin. Your seed is the key to the new future. Your son is going to sit at the head of all tables, my boy. He's going to set this whole thing free.

LOMAX: You want a child.

MILTON: I want a family.

LOMAX: The Antichrist.

MILTON: Whatever.

LOMAX: But I have to volunteer.

MILTON: Free will. It's a bitch. Kevin, I need a family. I need help. I'm busy. Millennium's coming soon, title fight, round 20. I'm ready to work. What do you say, kid?

LOMAX: What are you offering?

MILTON: We negotiating?

LOMAX: Always.

MILTON: Yes!

LOMAX: What are you offering?

MILTON: Everything, anything. What about bliss for a start, instant bliss, bliss on tap, bliss any way you want it. How about that first line of cocaine. That walk into a strange girl's bedroom. Familiar?

LOMAX: You're going to have to do a lot better than that.

MILTON: I know. I'm just getting warmed up. You want more, don't you? You deserve more. How about the thing you love the most, a smile from a jury. Oh, that cold courtroom just giving itself over, bending to your strength.

LOMAX: I get that on my own.

MILTON: Not like this. I take the bricks out of the briefcase. I give you pleasure, no strings. Freedom, baby, is never having to say you're sorry. This is revolution, Kevin.

[A Frank Sinatra song begins playing in the background; Christabella and Kevin begin to dance.]

CHRISTABELLA: Forget about him, this is about us, Kevin. You don't know how hard it has been for me to wait for you.

LOMAX [to Milton]: Why the law? Cut the shit, dad. Why lawyers, why the law?

MILTON: Because the law, my boy, puts us into everything. It is the ultimate backstage pass, it's the new priesthood, baby. Did you know there are more students in law school than there are lawyers walking the earth? We're coming out, guns blazing. The two of you, all of us, acquittal after acquittal, after acquittal, until the stench of it reaches so high, far into heaven, it chokes the whole fucking lot of them.

LOMAX: In the Bible you lose. We're destined to lose, dad.

MILTON: Consider the source, son. Besides, we're going to write our own Book, chapter 1, right here, this altar, this moment.

CHRISTABELLA: Will you stop talking. You talk too much, both of you. Kevin, look at me, just look at me. [She undresses.]

MILTON: Oh, she really is stunning.

CHRISTABELLA: Who am I? [They kiss.] I've wanted you from the moment we met.

MILTON [chanting]: *Diaboli virtus in lumbus est.* The virtue of the devil is in his loins.

LOMAX: What about love?

MILTON: Overrated. Biochemical. No different than eating large quantities of chocolate.

CHRISTABELLA: Heh, in two minutes you won't be thinking about Mary Ann ever again. Come here. [They begin to make love.]

MILTON: She's right, my son . . . It's time to step up and take what's yours.

LOMAX: You're right, it's time. Free will, right? [He shoots himself.]

By opting out of the devil's bargain Lomax saves his soul, but the scene suddenly shifts back to the courthouse in Gainesville when Lomax made his fateful decision to defend Geddes. This time, however, he chooses the high road and withdraws from the case, even though he could ruin his career by doing so.

The film might have ended there when Lomax's wife is returned to him and his integrity is restored, but the devil never sleeps. A reporter asks to interview Lomax for a news story about his honesty, and he agrees. After Lomax leaves the courthouse the reporter's face changes to that of Milton who says "Vanity. Definitely my favorite sin."

In essence, *The Devil's Advocate* is a cautionary tale, a Christian allegory complete with the seven deadly sins of pride, avarice, lust, anger, gluttony, envy, and sloth, and some opposing virtues of prudence, fortitude, temperance, and justice. It shows in superb dramatic form the way in which otherwise decent people can be lured by worldly success into betraying their principles and those they love. The devil here does not use crude instruments such as pitchforks, fire and brimstone but operates through the more subtle and insidious method of temptation. The problem of evil, of course, is why would a benevolent God allow the devil that much power and not offer his children greater protection.

Study Questions

1. What lures does Satan use to entice Kevin Lomax to do the devil's work?

2. Is a lawyer the devil's advocate if he or she defends a client believed to be guilty? On the other hand, does a lawyer have the right to prejudge guilt or innocence or is that for the courts to decide?

3. To what extent is Kevin responsible for Mary Ann's disintegration, insanity, and suicide?

4. Do you think people are free to be saints or sinners as Milton argues, or does the devil compel people to do evil things?

5. Why would a wholly loving God allow the devil to entice people to hell and not protect them more from him and from themselves?

Bibliography of Philosophy, Literature, and Films

IV. Foundations of Belief: The Philosophy of Religion

Philosophy

African Religions and Philosophy	John Mbiti
The City of God	St. Augustine
The Courage to Be, Dynamics of Faith	Paul Tillich
Dialogues Concerning Natural Religion	David Hume
The Divine and the Human	Nicholas Berdyaev
Does God Exist?	A. E. Taylor
Euthyphro, Phaedo	Plato
Evil and the Christian Faith	Nels Ferre
The Concept of Dread	Soren Kierkegaard
The Cosmological Argument, The Existence of God	Richard Swinburne
God Has Many Names	John Hick
Faith and Logic	Basil Mitchell
Fear and Trembling	Soren Kierkegaard
The Female Nature of God	Rosemary R. Reuther
The Ontological Argument	Alvin Plantinga
Good and Evil	Martin Buber
Guide for the Perplexed	Moses Maimonides
I and Thou	Martin Buber
The Immortality of the Soul	Jacques Maritain
Lectures on the Philosophy of Religion	G. W. F. Hegel
Miracles	C. S. Lewis
Moral Man and Immoral Society	Reinhold Niebuhr
Mysticism and Logic	Bertrand Russell
Natural Theology	William Paley
Nature, Man, and God	William Temple
The Nature of God	Edward Wierenga
New Essays in Philosophical Theology	Anthony Flew
Philosophical Theology	F. R. Tenant
The Problem of Pain	C. S. Lewis
Proslogion	St. Anselm
Religion Within the Boundaries of Pure Reason	Immanuel Kant
The Religious Aspect of Philosophy	Josiah Royce
Saints and Postmodernism	Edith Wyschogrod
Summa Theologica	St. Thomas Aquinas
The Theodicy	G. W. Leibniz
Thoughts	Blaise Pascal
Three Essays on Religion	John Stuart Mill

Why Women Need the Goddess	Carol Christ
The Will to Believe	William James

Literature

Anna Karenina, War and Peace	Leo Tolstoy
Adam the Creator	Karel and Josef Capek
The Betrothal	Alessandro Manzoni
The Bridge of San Luis Rey	Thornton Wilder
The Brothers Karamazov	Fedor Dostoevski
Canterbury Tales	Geoffrey Chaucer
Faust	Wolfgang von Goethe
Doctor Faustus	Thomas Mann
The Father, The Spook Sonata	August Strindberg
Growth of the Soil	Knut Hamsun
The Hunchback of Notre Dame	Victor Hugo
The Idiot	Fedor Dostoevski
Joy	George Bernanos
The Lower Depths	Maxim Gorky
The Man Who Was Thursday	G. K. Chesterton
"The Masque of Reason"	Robert Frost
The Metamorphoses	Ovid
Moby Dick	Herman Melville
The Plumed Serpent	D. H. Lawrence
Saint Joan	George Bernard Shaw
The Screwtape Letters	C. S. Lewis
Siddhartha	Herman Hesse
The Tragical History of Dr. Faustus	Christopher Marlowe

Films

Agnes of God	Norman Jewison
Aguirre, The Wrath of God	Werner Herzog
The Apostle	Robert Duvall
Babette's Feast	Gabriel Axel
Ben-Hur	Fred Niblo (silent)
	William Wyler (sound)
Black Robe	Bruce Beresford
Christ Confounds His Critics	Herbert Dawley
The Communicants	Ingmar Bergman
Contact	Robert Zemeckis
Day of Wrath	Carl Dreyer
Dead Man Walking	Tim Robbins
Der Apfel Ist Ab	Helmut Kautner
The Devil's Advocate	Taylor Hackford
Diary of a Country Priest	Robert Bresson
The Exterminating Angel	Luis Bunuel
The Flowers of St. Francis	Roberto Rosselini

Gandhi	Richard Attenborough
The Garden of Allah	Richard Boleslawski
The Gospel According to St. Matthew	Pier Paolo Pasolini
The Gospel According to Vic	Charles Gormley
Green Pastures	William Keighley
Hail Mary	Jean-Luc Godard
Haxan	Benjamin Christensen
Jacob's Ladder	Adrian Lyne
Joan of Arc	Victor Fleming
Keys of the Kingdom	John Stahl
The King of Kings	Cecil de Mille
L'Age d'Or	Luis Bunuel
The Last Temptation of Christ	Martin Scorsese
The Life of Brian	Terry Gillian
The Meaning of Life	Terry Gillian
The Messiah	Roberto Rosselini
The Miracle	Roberto Rosselini
Monty Python and the Holy Grail	Terry Gilliam
Nazarin	Luis Bunuel
Oh God	Carl Reiner
Ordet	Carl Dreyer
The Passion of Joan of Arc	Carl Dreyer
The Rapture	Michael Tolkin
The Robe	Henry Koster
The Seventh Seal	Ingmar Bergman
The Shoes of the Fisherman	Michael Anderson
The Silence	Ingmar Bergman
Simon of the Desert	Luis Bunuel
The Song of Bernadette	Henry King
Stigmata	Rupert Wainwright
The Ten Commandments	Cecil de Mille
Therese	Alain Cavalier
Through a Glass Darkly	Ingmar Bergman
Ticket to Heaven	Ralph Thomas
Viridiana	Luis Bunuel
What Dreams May Come	Vincent Ward
Wings of Desire	Wim Wenders
Winter Light	Ingmar Bergman

V. Establishing the Social Order: Political Philosophy

Just as the philosophy of religion is critical thinking about religion, political philosophy is concerned with fundamental issues within the field of politics. Having studied the nature of philosophy, we are in a position to understand what those issues might be.

Specifically, the political philosopher looks at the foundation of the state, meaning by "state" the political organization of society that includes the government, legal system, and social institutions. The political philosopher wants to determine the basis for the state, the relation of its power and authority to individual freedom, rights, and social justice. What control can the state legitimately exercise over its citizens, and what allegiance does the individual owe to the state? For example, what gives the government the right to compel men to risk their lives in war? Does the state have the authority to incarcerate people or execute them for committing crimes, taking away their freedom or their lives? Do people possess property rights, and can one's property be legitimately taxed or appropriated? Can the state limit a woman's reproductive freedom by prohibiting abortion (protecting the fetus), or by requiring that couples have only one child as in China (for the social good)?

The answer to such questions depends in turn upon one's view of the nature of the state. That is, some political philosophers argue that an implicit *social contract* exists whereby the citizens agree to obey the laws in return for benefits that will accrue from membership in the society. Having derived the benefits, they have incurred the obligations. Others argue that the state is an *organic* entity with the people existing as limbs or even cells within the organism. On this view, citizens are not free and independent beings but parts of the body politic, members of the family or community. The individual can no more refuse the rules imposed by the state than the hand can rebel against the body.

The political philosopher also tries to evaluate the worth of various types of states, governments, and political structures to determine the conditions under which people will flourish. In trying to reach some conclusion, he or she will analyze the different views of human nature and relate them to the various ideals of the state. For instance, if human beings are considered bad, cursed with original sin or naturally depraved, violent, or selfish, then a strong central government is needed to ensure that everyone is protected from everyone else. On the other hand, if human beings are considered good at heart, then they can be trusted to behave decently without strict government control.

A. THE INDIVIDUAL AND SOCIETY: FREEDOM AND EQUALITY

An important part of political philosophy, therefore, concerns the relation between the citizen and the state, especially with regard to conflicts between personal independence and the welfare of society. How can we achieve freedom and equality in a way consistent with justice?

To begin with *freedom*, this has been a dominant value in our society since its inception, although the meaning has changed from time to time. Most societies, in fact, treat freedom as a social value, but differences arise over what that freedom implies. One distinction that is often made is between "freedom from" and "freedom to," and both are considered important for citizens of a state.

If people are oppressed by war, disease, poverty, insecurity, and so forth they want the freedom to escape from it, so that "freedom from" means protection against things undesirable. For example, as Americans we do not want taxation without representation, imprisonment without a trial, or unreasonable searches and seizures, any more than we want polluted environments, unsafe neighborhoods, or discrimination of any kind. In war-torn countries people want freedom from the threat of death, from hunger, displacement, and terror.

In terms of "freedom to," here the emphasis is on having a choice between alternatives that are positive in nature. In the United States and other democratic countries, we want to raise our children as we see fit, to vote for representatives to our government, to have access to work, housing, and education, and to enjoy the civil liberties of assembly, press, religion, movement, speech, and so forth. We want freedom from fear and the freedom to be happy.

But once we have made this important distinction we still need to justify the worth of freedom altogether. On what basis can we call it an important political value?

In the history of political philosophy, two principal theories have been offered. One school of thought declares freedom to be one of the *natural rights* to which people are entitled. According to this doctrine, which originated in ancient Greece and flourished in the eighteenth century, there are certain universal rights that are valid for all people. As Aristotle put it, referring to justice, "A rule of justice is natural that has the same validity everywhere, and does not depend on our accepting it or not." Natural rights are often considered part of a "higher law" that is embodied in human nature. According to religious views, these natural rights are provided by God and transmitted through revelation, while a secular interpretation sees them as grounded in the universe itself. Whatever the source, natural rights are thought to be guaranteed to citizens of a state.

In a characteristic expression of this concept, Thomas Jefferson wrote in the Declaration of Independence, "We hold these truths to be self-evident; that all men are created equal, that they are endowed by their Creator with certain *inalienable* rights; that among these are life, liberty, and the pursuit of happiness [italics added]." To Jefferson, rights inhere in persons, and no state can deprive its citizens of them. In arguing this way, Jefferson was endorsing the ideas of the seventeenth-century English philosopher John Locke, and this belief found its way into our founding documents as well as our national psyche. Americans believe we have a natural right to freedom.

The natural rights doctrine has had a stormy history, mainly because people disagree over which rights should be included, or even whether there are any rights apparent to everyone; the phrase "self-evident" might only mean "evident to oneself." Arguments have been made for slave-owning as a natural right and for wives as the natural property of their husbands. Furthermore, natural rights were identified with St. Thomas Aquinas who maintained that God's rational guidance gave us the Eternal law, and as society grew increasingly secular this became unconvincing. In the end, many philosophers judge natural rights to be neither provable nor useful.

In the nineteenth century, an alternative theory arose of *utilitarianism*—a theory we have already encountered in ethics. It claimed that rights such as freedom are not innate but conferred by the state for the purpose of maximizing the well being of its citizens. If a right has social utility then it is justified, but if it ceases to function for the public good then it must be abandoned.

Values such as freedom, therefore, are only contingent not absolute, and are wholly dependent on their utility. Society alone judges whether something is valuable in terms of its needs at the time. This implies that if freedom is a hindrance rather than a help in meeting social goals, the state should curtail the freedom of its citizens. As we have seen, this was done extensively by various regimes, especially the fascists and the communists.

Nevertheless, the assumption that values are not absolute, does not mean they can be easily dismissed. John Stuart Mill, for example, presented a very strong case for freedom on utilitarian grounds. In his famous essay "On Liberty," he argued that freedom enhances human happiness, and society is justified in interfering with citizens only to keep them from harming one another, not from harming themselves. In our context, this means we should make murder illegal but not suicide, stealing but not drug addiction, assault but not driving without a seatbelt.

With regard to freedom of speech, Mill argued that society should not suppress any opinion no matter how unpopular, sacrilegious, offensive, or unpatriotic. For the opinion that is expressed could be true, and by suppressing it we lose the chance to exchange error for truth. Furthermore, the opinion we want to suppress may contain a portion of the truth, and if we prohibit it that would be lost to us. Finally, even if an opinion is completely false, by suppressing it we are denied the opportunity to refine our own truth through the collision with error. On utilitarian grounds, therefore, freedom of speech can be justified for the well-being of society.

Mill, of course, asserts an extreme liberal position, and we wonder today whether, for example, hate speech and acts should be allowed such as anti-gay demonstrations, parades in Jewish neighborhoods by Nazi organizations, or rallies by the Klu Klux Klan against blacks. Speech must be curtailed if it incites riots, endangers the health of minors, discloses national secrets to an enemy power, and so forth, but we are not sure where the line should be drawn. According to the utilitarian view, the exercise of our freedom depends on the circumstances rather than being a natural right of citizens.

In recent years both theories have been further developed, the utilitarian theory through John Austin's positivist view of law, and the natural rights theory in Catholic writings on natural law. In war crimes tribunals such as that in the Hague following World War II and more recently to try Serbian and Cambodian leaders, a higher law has been cited as legitimizing the authority of the court. The Universal Declaration of Human Rights by the United Nations is certainly based on basic values that apply to all peoples, regardless of national boundaries.

Our decisions on questions of *equality* also depend on whether we accept a natural rights or utilitarian viewpoint, but the issues here are different and usually turn on matters of economics. We could discuss equal opportunity, equal treatment under the law, equal pay for equal work, and so forth, but political philosophers tend to focus on the fair distribution of wealth, especially property. What would be a just basis for the allocation of wealth? How should we divide our resources so that we achieve equality in society?

Our first thought might be that wealth should be distributed evenly so that everyone has an equal share. For one human being to have more than another seems unjust since everyone has an equal right to the earth's goods. If we level wealth that would respect the "equal worth" doctrine, or in religious terms, the view that all souls are equally precious.

This notion is consistent with the principle of "declining marginal utility" in economics. If a man owns a house, that usually brings him pleasure, but if he should purchase a second home that may increase his pleasure but not double it. On the other hand, if two men each own houses, that will double the sum total of pleasure in society as a whole since each man enjoys it fully. In other words, successive additions to one's wealth produce progressively less pleasure, so to maximize social well-being wealth should be distributed evenly.

But what if leveling wealth means that no one would have a decent standard of living, or worse, that all people would be below the poverty line? That is the force of lifeboat examples where if all those in the water were taken on board, the lifeboat would be swamped and everyone would drown. This might be the case in the world today. Two-thirds of the world's population is malnourished, mainly in the Third World where the birth rate is twice that of developed nations. Therefore, distributing wealth equally to everyone on earth could mean mass starvation. If only some can survive, what criterion should be used in deciding who to save? This is the dilemma we also face in allocating scarce medical resources such as drugs, equipment, specialists, and facilities. Who shall live when not everyone can live?

A second possibility is to leave matters to chance. We could say "first come, first served" or draw straws, and those with long straws would have greater wealth than those with short straws. This partly explains the present situation in the world where some nations happened to develop first or have greater resources and therefore enjoy a larger share of the earth's goods. Within nations some people are born into wealth and others not; it is just the luck of the draw.

But is it fair for those who got there first or have greater capabilities at the start to receive a larger share? Should an accident of birth determine the distribution of wealth? Why not prohibit all personal inheritances so people can start even?

Besides, aren't some people more deserving than others? Those who inherit a fortune may not be admirable people, while those who are deserving may have to struggle to survive because they were not born rich. This last consideration leads to distribution theories based on merit and to the rejection of both the leveling-of-wealth and the good-luck criteria. Perhaps wealth should not be distributed evenly or randomly but equitably according to worth.

Suppose we were to say, then, that the most deserving people should be the wealthiest, the least deserving the poorest. People would be distributed along the scale strictly according to merit, with nothing for the *un*deserving; they might fall by the wayside because people should be expected to earn a living for themselves.

Merit could be determined according to such factors as contribution to society, natural ability, education, industriousness, or character. In business organizations, for example, whether someone is hired or fired, promoted or given an increment depends on his or her qualifications and performance. The company does not reward everyone equally or haphazardly but in terms of their ability, industry, and contribution to the success of the business. In the same way, shouldn't society distribute wealth according to merit? No one could complain that the system is unjust since all would receive what they deserve.

This is the assumption underlying capitalism: those who are bright, work hard, obtain the necessary education, and are productive and successful in the marketplace, receive the highest salaries. The poorly paid workers do not have the intelligence or drive to succeed, so they deserve their lower income.

But conflicts can arise within those criteria. Should we allocate the greatest wealth to those who work the hardest even though they contribute little; to those who contribute the most even though they do not expend much effort; or to those who have the best qualifications in terms of education, skills, or degrees? Those we reward on a merit system may have come from privileged backgrounds with access to fine schools, health care, travel, and contacts, so that it was easier for them to succeed than for someone from the slum. And should those who are naturally more capable be given a larger slice of the pie while we allow the incapacitated to die because they are undeserving? As for capitalism, sometimes the marketplace rewards those who do not deserve it in terms of the social benefit they provide. We question the appropriateness of million-dollar salaries for athletes and celebrities while nurses and teachers can hardly make a living.

Still another option for bringing about economic justice is to distribute wealth not according to merit but in terms of need. Regardless of how undeserving a person might be, his or her needs may be great, and to ignore that would be inhumane. For example, a physically handicapped person such as a paraplegic should receive considerable assistance, and a family of six should be allocated more money than a bachelor—irrespective of whether their contribution to society merits the assistance. Everyone should work as much as they can, but their income should not depend upon their productivity. Thus the Marxist principle: from each according to his ability; to each according to his needs.

But wouldn't this encourage laziness and inefficiency? What incentive would people have to work hard if their income depended only on their needs? These are some of the problems that plagued the communist system and contributed to its collapse.

As this brief survey shows, the question of economic justice is not easily answered, and we agonize over specific issues in society today that depend upon the conclusions we reach. For example, should an unwed mother of six addicted to crack cocaine be given welfare to the extent of her needs? In case of a military draft, should we use a lottery system, giving everyone an equal chance of being chosen, or should we establish criteria for selection and give certain groups of people exemptions? Should student loans and scholarships be merit-based or, as is usually the case today, need-based? Should we have taxes that affect everyone equally, like a state sales tax, or a graduated tax that exacts more from the wealthy, like the federal income tax? (As the courts have ruled, the power to tax is the power to redistribute wealth.)

The issue of equality is therefore quite complex, but at this point we must leave the matter unresolved. However, we do know some of the considerations that apply, and with that understanding we can begin to reach some sound conclusions.

In the selections that follow, John Locke argues that in a "state of Nature" people are free, equal, and independent. However, since the natural state is an insecure one they join in civil society for the mutual preservation of their lives and property. Locke regards a person's property as "The 'labor' of his body and the 'work' of his hands," and people are entitled to as much as they can use. If a government violates the trust of its citizens, then power reverts to society.

Chinua Achebe in *Things Fall Apart* presents two instances of injustice within the framework of tribal custom and colonial rule. The injustice is not economic but social. The oracle of the village of Umuofia sentences a boy named Ikemefuna to death for obscure and superstitious reasons. Even though his surrogate father Okonkwo loves the boy, he kills him with his machete rather than be considered weak.

In a subsequent series of events, the warriors resist the white missionaries by destroying a church they had erected, and six tribal leaders are seized by the colonial government. While in captivity they are deeply humiliated, and this provokes further violence as the structure of the tribal society is undermined by British justice.

The final selection in this section, the film *Schindler's List*, shows the complete denial of freedom to Jews in Nazi occupied Poland. The Jews are rounded up, deported, imprisoned, or sent to concentration camps for extermination. Oskar Schindler, an enterprising businessman, uses the slave labor of Jews for his own profit, but later acts to help many Jews survive. Questions arise as to whether a state is required to extend freedom and equality to all citizens within a country.

Second Treatise of Government
John Locke

John Locke (1632–1704) was an English philosopher who is usually credited with founding the school of empiricism. He began his career as an academic at Oxford but then held a series of government posts, moving between England, France, and Holland as the political climate dictated. Most of his writing was done toward the latter part of his life, including his most important works. These include Essay Concerning Human Understanding *in which he expounds his epistemology, and* Two Treatises of Government *which contains his political philosophy. Among his other books are* Some Thoughts Concerning Education *and* The Reasonableness of Christianity.

In Locke's Two Treatises of Government, *he attacked the political philosophy of his contemporary Thomas Hobbes, especially the doctrine of the divine right of kings. Locke maintained that the sovereignty of a king is not the same as the authority of a father over his children. Rather, the people had ultimate political control, provided it was exercised within the bounds of civil and natural law. The state held power in trust for the good of society, and if that trust is violated then revolution is justified.*

Like most political philosophers of the time, Locke begins by speculating on the state of nature—that original condition of humankind before the organization of civil society. He then describes the "social contract" with the state, and he concludes by specifying the conditions under which power could revert to society. Political theory in the United States embodies many of Locke's ideas, particularly his views on property, the right of revolt, and natural rights that are based on universally valid, higher laws.

Of the State of Nature

4. To understand political power aright, and derive it from its original, we must consider what estate all men are naturally in, and that is, a state of perfect freedom to order their actions, and dispose of their possessions and persons as they think fit, within the bounds of the law of Nature, without asking leave or depending upon the will of any other man.

A state also of equality, wherein all the power and jurisdiction is reciprocal, no one have more than another, there being nothing more evident than that creatures of the same species and rank, promiscuously born to all the same advantages of Nature, and the use of the same faculties, should also be equal one amongst another, without subordination or subjection, unless the lord and master of them all should, by any manifest declaration of his will, set one above another, and confer on him, by an evident and clear appointment, an undoubted right to dominion and sovereignty.

* * *

6. But though this be a state of liberty, yet it is not a state of license; though man in that state have an uncontrollable liberty to dispose of his person or possessions, yet he has not liberty to destroy himself, or so much as any creature in his possession, but where some nobler use than its bare preservation calls for it. The state of Nature has a law of Nature to govern it, which obliges everyone, and reason, which is that law, teaches all mankind who will but consult it, that being all equal and independent, no one ought to harm another in his life, health, liberty or possessions; for men being all the workmanship of one omnipotent and infinitely wise Maker; all the servants of one sovereign Master, sent into the world by His order and about His business; they are His property, whose workmanship they are made to last during His, not one another's pleasure. And, being furnished with like faculties, sharing all in one community of Nature, there cannot be supposed any such subordination among us that may authorize us to destroy one another, as if we were made for one another's uses, as the inferior ranks of creatures are for ours. Everyone as he is bound to preserve himself, and not to quit his station willfully, so by the like reason, when his own preservation comes not in competition, ought he as much as he can to preserve the rest of mankind, and not unless it be to do justice on an offender, take away or impair the life, or what tends to the preservation of the life, the liberty, health, limb, or goods of another.

7. And that all men may be restrained from invading others' rights, and from doing hurt to one another, and the law of Nature be observed, which willeth the peace and preservation of all mankind, the execution of the law of Nature is in that state put into every man's hands, whereby everyone has a right to punish the transgressors of that law to such a degree as may hinder its violation. For the law of Nature would, as all other laws that concern men in this world, be in vain if there were nobody that in the state of Nature had a power to execute that law, and thereby preserve the innocent and restrain offenders; and if anyone in the state of Nature may punish another for any evil he has done, everyone may do so. For in that state of perfect equality, where naturally there is no superiority or jurisdiction of one over another, what any may do in prosecution of that law, everyone must needs have a right to do.

8. And thus, in the state of Nature, one man comes by a power over another, but yet no absolute or arbitrary power to use a criminal, when he has got him in his hands, according to the passionate heats of boundless extravagancy of his own will, but only to retribute to him so far as calm reason and conscience dictate, what is proportionate to his

transgression, which is so much as may serve for reparation and restraint. For these two are the only reasons why one man may lawfully do harm to another, which is that we call punishment. In transgressing the law of Nature, the offender declares himself to live by another rule than that of reason and common equity, which is that measure God has set to the actions of men for their mutual security, and so he becomes dangerous to mankind; the tie which is to secure them from injury and violence being slighted and broken by him, which being a trespass against the whole species, and the peace and safety of it, provided for by the law of Nature, every man upon this score, by the right he hath to preserve mankind in general, may restrain, or where it is necessary, destroy things noxious to them, and so may bring such evil on anyone who hath transgressed that law, as may make him repent the doing of it, and thereby deter him, and, by his example, others from doing the like mischief. And in this case, and upon this ground, every man hath a right to punish the offender, and be executioner of the law of Nature.

* * *

10. Besides the crime which consists in violating the laws, and varying from the right rule of reason, whereby a man so far becomes degenerate, and declares himself to quit the principles of human nature and to be a noxious creature, there is commonly injury done, and some person or other, some other man, receives damage by his transgression; in which case, he who hath received any damage has (besides the right of punishment common to him, with other men) a particular right to seek reparation from him that hath done it. And any other person who finds it just may also join with him that is injured, and assist him in recovering from the offender so much as may make satisfaction for the harm he hath suffered.

* * *

13. To this strange doctrine—viz., That in the state of Nature everyone has the executive power to the law of Nature—I doubt not but it will be objected that it is unreasonable for men to be judges in their own cases, that self-love will make men partial to themselves and their friends; and, on the other side, ill-nature, passion, and revenge will carry them too far in punishing others, and hence nothing but confusion and disorder will follow, and that therefore God hath certainly appointed government to restrain the partiality and violence of men. I easily grant that civil government is the proper remedy for the inconveniences of the state of Nature, which must certainly be great where men may be judges in their own case, since it is easy to be imagined that he who was so unjust as to do his brother an injury will scarce be so just as to condemn himself for it. But I shall desire those who make this objection to remember that absolute monarchs are but men; and if government is to be the remedy of those evils which necessarily follow from men being judges in their own cases, and the state of Nature is therefore not to be endured, I desire to know

what kind of government that is, and how much better it is than the state of Nature, where one man commanding a multitude has the liberty to be judge in his own case, and may do to all his subjects whatever he pleases without the least question or control of those who execute his pleasure? and in whatsoever he doth, whether led by reason, mistake, or passion, must be submitted to? which men in the state of Nature are not bound to do one to another. And if he that judges, judges amiss in his own or any other case, he is answerable for it to the rest of mankind.

14. It is often asked as a mighty objection, where are, or ever were, there any men in such a state of Nature? To which it may suffice as an answer at present, that since all princes and rulers of "independent" governments all through the world are in a state of Nature, it is plain the world never was, nor never will be, without numbers of men in that state. I have named all govenors of "independent" communities, whether they are, or are not, in league with others; for it is not every compact that puts an end to the state of Nature between men, but only this one of agreeing together mutually to enter into one community, and make one body politic; other promises and compacts men may make one with another, and yet still be in the state of Nature. The promises and bargains for truck, etc., between the two men in Soldania, in or between a Swiss and an Indian, in the woods of America, are binding to them, though they are perfectly in a state of Nature in reference to one another for truth, and keeping of faith belongs to men as men, and not as members of society.

* * *

Of Property

* * *

25. God, who hath given the world to men in common, hath also given them reason to make use of it to the best advantage of life and convenience. The earth and all that is therein is given to men for the support and comfort of their being. And though all the fruits it naturally produces, and beasts it feeds, belong to mankind in common, as they are produced by the spontaneous hand of Nature, and nobody has originally a private dominion exclusive of the rest of mankind in any of them, as they are thus in their natural state, yet being given for the use of men, there must of necessity be a means to appropriate them some way or other before they can be of any use, or at all beneficial, to any particular men. The fruit or venison which nourishes the wild Indian, who knows no enclosure, and is still a tenant in common, must be his, and so his— i.e., a part of him, that another can no longer have any right to it before it can do him any good for the support of his life.

26. Though the earth and all inferior creatures be common to all men, yet every man has a "property" in his own "person." This nobody

has any right to but himself. The "labor" of his body and the "work" of his hands, we may say, are properly his. Whatsoever, then, he removes out of the state that Nature hath provided and left it in, he hath mixed his labor with it, and joined to it something that is his own, and thereby makes it his property. It being by him removed from the common state Nature placed it in, it hath by this labor something annexed to it that excludes the common right of other men. For this "labor" being the unquestionable property of the laborer, no man but he can have a right to what that is once joined to, at least where there is enough, and as good left in common for others.

27. He that is nourished by the acorns he picked up under an oak, or the apples he gathered from the trees in the wood, has certainly appropriated them to himself. Nobody can deny but the nourishment is his. I ask, then, when did they begin to be his? when he digested? or when he ate? or when he boiled? or when he brought them home? or when he picked them up? And it is plain, if the first gathering made them not his, nothing else could. . . .

30. It will, perhaps, be objected to this, that if gathering the acorns or other fruits of the earth, etc., makes a right to them, then anyone may engross as much as he will. To which I answer, Not so. The same law of Nature that does by this means give us property, does also bound that property too. "God has given us all things richly." Is the voice of reason confirmed by inspiration? But how far has He given it us "to enjoy"? As much as anyone can make use of to any advantage of life before it spoils, so much he may by his labor fix a property in. Whatever is beyond this is more than his share, and belongs to others. Nothing was made by God for man to spoil or destroy. And thus considering the plenty of natural provisions there was a long time in the world, and the few spenders, and to how small a part of that provision the industry of one man could extend itself and engross it to the prejudice of others, especially keeping within the bounds set by reason of what might serve for his use, there could be then little room for quarrels or contentions about property so established.

31. But the chief matter of property being now not the fruits of the earth and the beasts that subsist on it, but the earth itself, as that which takes in and carries with it all the rest, I think it is plain that property in that too is acquired as the former. As much land as a man tills, plants, improves, cultivates, and can use the product of, so much is his property. He by his labor does, as it were, enclose it from the common. . . .

32. Nor was this appropriation of any parcel of land, by improving it, any prejudice to any other man, since there was still enough and as good left, and more than the yet unprovided could use. So that, in effect, there was never the less left for others because of his enclosure for himself. For he that leaves as much as another can make use of does as good as take nothing at all. Nobody could think himself injured by the

drinking of another man, though he took a good draught, who had a whole river of the same water left him to quench his thirst. And the case of land and water, where there is enough of both, is perfectly the same.

* * *

40. Nor is it so strange as, perhaps, before consideration, it may appear, that the property of labor should be able to overbalance the community of land, for it is labor indeed that puts the difference of value on everything; and let anyone consider what the difference is between an acre of land planted with tobacco or sugar, sown with wheat or barley, and an acre of the same land lying in common without any husbandry upon it, and he will find that the improvement of labor makes the far greater part of the value. I think it will be but a very modest computation to say, that of the produts of the earth useful to the life of man, nine-tenths are the effects of labor. Nay, if we will rightly estimate things as they come to our use, and cast up the several expenses about them—what in them is purely owing to Nature and what to labor—we shall find that in most of them ninety-nine hundredths are wholly to be put on the account of labor.

* * *

46. The greatest part of things really useful to the life of man, and such as the necessity of subsisting made the first commoners of the world look after—as it doth the Americans now—are generally things of short duration, such as—if they are not consumed by use—will decay and perish of themselves. Gold, silver, and diamonds are things that fancy or agreement hath put the value on, more than real use and the necessary support of life. Now of those good things which Nature hath provided in common, everyone has a right (as has been said) to as much as he could use, and had a property in all he could effect with his labor; all that his industry could extend to, to alter from the state Nature had put it in, was his. He that gathered a hundred bushels of acorns or apples had thereby a property in them; they were his goods as soon as gathered. He was only to look that he used them before they spoiled, else he took more than his share, and robbed others. And, indeed, it was a foolish thing, as well as dishonest, to hoard up more than he could make use of. If he gave away a part to anybody else, so that it perished not uselessly in his possession, these he also made use of. And if he also bartered away plums that would have rotted in a week, for nuts that would last good for his eating a whole year, he did no injury; he wasted not the common stock; destroyed no part of the portion of good that belonged to others, so long as nothing perished uselessly in his hands. Again, if he would give his nuts for a piece of metal, pleased with its color, or exchange his sheep for shells, or wool for a sparkling pebble or a diamond, and keep those by him all his life, he invaded not the right of others; he might heap up as much of these durable things as he pleased; the exceeding of the bounds of his just property not lying in the largeness of his possession, but the perishing of anything uselessly in it.

47. And thus came in the use of money; some lasting thing that men might keep without spoiling, and that, by mutual consent, men would take in exchange for the truly useful but perishable supports of life.

48. And as different degrees of industry were apt to give men possessions in different proportions, so this invention of money gave them the opportunity to continue and enlarge them. For supposing an island, separate from all possible commerce with the rest of the world, wherein there were but a hundred families, but there were sheep, horses, and cows, with other useful animals, wholesome fruits, and land enough for corn for a hundred thousand times as many, but nothing in the island, either because of its commonness or perishableness, fit to supply the place of money. What reason could anyone have there to enlarge his possessions beyond the use of his family, and a plentiful supply to its consumption, either in what their own industry produced, or they could barter for like perishable, useful commodities with others? Where there is not something both lasting and scarce, and so valuable to be hoarded up, there men will not be apt to enlarge their possessions of land, were it never so rich, never so free for them to take. For I ask, what would a man value ten thousand or a hundred thousand acres of excellent land, ready cultivated and well stocked, too, with cattle, in the middle of the inland parts of America, where he had no hopes of commerce with other parts of the world, to draw money to him by the sale of the product? It would not be worth the enclosing, and we should see him give up again to the wild common of Nature whatever was more than would supply the conveniences of life, to be had there for him and his family.

* * *

Of the Beginning of Political Societies

95. Men being, as has been said, by nature all free, equal, and independent, no one can be put out of this estate and subjected to the political power of another without his own consent, which is done by agreeing with other men, to join and unite into a community for their comfortable, safe, and peaceable living, one amongst another, in a secure enjoyment of their properties, and a greater security against any that are not of it. This any number of men may do, because it injures not the freedom of the rest; they are left, as they were, in the liberty of the state of Nature. When any number of men have so consented to make one community or government, they are thereby presently incorporated, and make one body politic, wherein the majority have a right to act and conclude the rest.

96. For, when any number of men have, by the consent of every individual, made a community, they have thereby made that community one body, with a power to act as one body, which is only by the will and

determination of the majority. For that which acts any community, being only the consent of the individuals of it, and it being one body, must move one way, it is necessary the body should move that way wither the greater force carries it, which is the consent of the majority, or else it is impossible it should act or continue one body, one community, which the consent of every individual that united into it agreed that it should; and so everyone is bound by that consent to be concluded by the majority. And therefore we see that in assemblies empowered to act by positive laws where no number is set by that positive law which empowers them, the act of the majority passes for the act of the whole, and of course determines as having, by the law of Nature and reason, the power of the whole.

* * *

98. For if the consent of the majority shall not in reason be received as the act of the whole, and conclude every individual, nothing but the consent of every individual can make anything to be the act of the whole, which, considering the infirmities of health and avocations of business, which in a number though much less than that of a commonwealth, will necessarily keep many away from the public assembly; and the variety of opinions and contrariety of interests which unavoidably happen in all collections of men, it is next impossible ever to be had. And, therefore, if coming into society be upon such terms, it will be only like Cato's coming into the theater, *tantum ut exiret*.* Such a constitution as this would make the mighty leviathan of a shorter duration than the feeblest creatures, and not let it outlast the day it was born in, which cannot be supposed till we can think that rational creatures should desire and constitute societies only to be dissolved. For where the majority cannot conclude the rest, there they cannot act as one body, and consequently will be immediately dissolved again.

* * *

119. Every man being, as has been showed, naturally free, and nothing being able to put him into subjection to any earthly power, but only his own consent, it is to be considered what shall be understood to be a sufficient declaration of a man's consent to make him subject to the laws of any government. There is a common distinction of an express and a tacit consent, which will concern our present case. Nobody doubts but an express consent of any man, entering into any society, makes him a perfect member of that society, a subject of that government. The difficulty is, what ought to be looked upon as a tacit consent, and how far it binds—i.e., how far anyone shall be looked on to have consented, and thereby submitted to any government, where he has made no expressions of it at all. And to this I say, that every man that hath any possession

---

*only to go out again; Cato (234–140 B.C.), the Roman statesman, disapproved of the theater.

or enjoyment of any part of the dominions of any government doth hereby give his tacit consent, and is as far forth obliged to obedience to the laws of that government, during such enjoyment, as anyone under it, whether this his possession be of land to him and his heirs forever, or a lodging only for a week; or whether it be barely traveling freely on the highway; and, in effect, it reaches as far as the very being of anyone within the territories of that government.

* * *

122. But submitting to the laws of any country, living quietly and enjoying privileges and protection under them, makes not a man a member of that society; it is only a local protection and homage due to and from all those who, not being in a state of war, come within the territories belonging to any government, to all parts whereof the force of its law extends. But this no more makes a man a member of that society, a perpetual subject of that commonwealth, than it would make a man a subject to another in whose family he found it convenient to abide for some time, though, whilst he continued in it, he were obliged to comply with the laws and submit to the government he found there. And thus we see that foreigners, by living all their lives under another government, and enjoying the privileges and protection of it, though they are bound, even in conscience, to submit to its administration as far forth as any denizen, yet do not thereby come to be subjects or members of that commonwealth. Nothing can make any man so but his actually entering into it by positive engagement and express promise and compact. This is that which, I think, concerning the beginning of political societies, and that consent which makes anyone a member of any commonwealth.

Of the Ends of Political Society and Government

123. If man in the state of Nature be so free as has been said, if he be absolute lord of his own person and possessions, equal to the greatest and subject to nobody, why will he part with his freedom, this empire, and subject himself to the dominion and control of any other power? To which it is obvious to answer, that though in the state of Nature he has such a right, yet the enjoyment of it is very uncertain and constantly exposed to the invasion of others; for all being kings as much as he, every man his equal, and the greater part no strict observers of equity and justice, the enjoyment of the property he has in this state is very unsafe, very insecure. This makes him willing to quit this condition which, however free, is full of fears and continual dangers; and it is not without reason that he seeks out and is willing to join in society with others who are already united, or have a mind to unite for the mutual preservation of their lives, liberties and estates, which I call by the general name—property.

124. The great and chief end, therefore, of men uniting into commonwealths, and putting themselves under government, is the preservation of their property; to which in the state of Nature there are many things wanting.

Firstly, there wants an established, settled, known law, received and allowed by common consent to be the standard of right and wrong, and the common measure to decide all controversies between them. For though the law of Nature be plain and intelligible to all rational creatures, yet men, being biased by their interest, as well as ignorant for want of study of it, are not apt to allow of it as a law binding to them in the application of it to their particular cases.

125. Secondly, in the state of Nature there wants a known and indifferent judge, with authority to determine all differences according to the established law. For everyone in that state being both judge and executioner of the law of Nature, men being partial to themselves, passion and revenge is very apt to carry them too far, and with too much heat in their own cases, as well as negligence and unconcernedness, make them too remiss in other men's.

126. Thirdly, in the state of Nature there often wants power to back and support the sentence when right, and to give it due execution. They who by any injustice offended will seldom fail where they are able by force to make good their injustice. Such resistance many times makes the punishment dangerous, and frequently destructive to those who attempt it.

243. To conclude. The power that every individual gave the society when he entered into it can never revert to the individuals again, as long as the society lasts, but will always remain in the community; because without this there can be no community—no commonwealth, which is contrary to the original agreement; so also when the society hath placed the legislative in any assembly of men, to continue in them and their successors, with direction and authority for providing such successors, the legislative can never revert to the people whilst that government lasts; because, having provided a legislative with power to continue forever, they have given up their political power to the legislative, and cannot resume it. But if they have set limits to the duration of their legislative, and made this supreme power in any person or assembly only temporary; or else when, by the miscarriages of those in authority, it is forfeited; upon the forfeiture of their rulers, or at the determination of the time set, it reverts to the society, and the people have a right to act as supreme, and continue the legislative in themselves or place it in a new form, or new hands, as they think good.

Study Questions

1. According to Locke, what is the "state of nature" and "the law of nature"?

2. On what grounds are people entitled to property?
3. According to Locke, do governments require the consent of the governed?
4. Can power revert to the individual once he or she has surrendered it to the community?
5. How much of a person's freedom is the state entitled to take?

Things Fall Apart
Chinua Achebe

*Chinua Achebe was born in 1930 in the village of Ogidi in Eastern
Nigeria. After studying medicine and literature at the University of Ibadan,
he went to work for the Nigerian broadcasting company in Lagos. Things
Fall Apart, his first novel, was published in 1958. It has sold over
2,000,000 copies, and has been translated into 30 languages. It was followed by No Longer at Ease, then Arrow of God (which won the first
New Statesman Jock Campbell Prize), then A Man of the People (a novel
dealing with post-independence Nigeria). Achebe has also written short
stories and children's books, and Beware Soul Brother, a book of his poetry, won the Commonwealth Poetry Prize in 1972.*

*In the following selection from Things Fall Apart, Achebe describes
the disparity between tribal and colonial customs, especially the differing
versions of justice. Achebe does not extoll the Nigerians and demonize the
British, or blindly endorse the native practices against the white laws. He
shows excesses and injustices on both sides, presenting a balanced portrait
of misunderstanding and needless violence.*

Principal Characters

Ezeudu	an important elder, the oldest man in Okonkwo's village
Ezinma	Okonkwo's favorite daughter
Ikemefuna	the boy from Mbaino given to Umuofia as compensation for murder
Mr. Smith	the zealous white missionary who replaced Mr. Brown
Nwoye	Okonkwo's oldest son, who converts to Christianity and adopts the name Isaac
Obierika	Okonkwo's good friend and confidant
Okonkwo	the main character, a strong, proud man

Chapter Seven

For three years Ikemefuna lived in Okonkwo's household and the elders
of Umuofia seemed to have forgotten about him. He grew rapidly like a
yam tendril in the rainy season, and was full of the sap of life. He had become wholly absorbed into his new family. He was like an elder brother

to Nwoye, and from the very first seemed to have kindled a new fire in the younger boy. He made him feel grown-up; and they no longer spent the evenings in mother's hut while she cooked, but now sat with Okonkwo in his *obi*, or watched him as he tapped his palm tree for the evening wine. Nothing pleased Nwoye now more than to be sent for by his mother or another of his father's wives to do one of those difficult and masculine tasks in the home, like splitting wood, or pounding food. On receiving such a message through a younger brother or sister, Nwoye would feign annoyance and grumble aloud about women and their troubles.

Okonkwo was inwardly pleased at his son's development, and he knew it was due to Ikemefuna. He wanted Nwoye to grow into a tough young man capable of ruling his father's household when he was dead and gone to join the ancestors. He wanted him to be a prosperous man, having enough in his barn to feed the ancestors with regular sacrifices. And so he was always happy when he heard him grumbling about women. That showed that in time he would be able to control his women-folk. No matter how prosperous a man was, if he was unable to rule his women and his children (and especially his women) he was not really a man. He was like the man in the song who had ten and one wives and not enough soup for his foo-foo.

So Okonkwo encouraged the boys to sit with him in his *obi*, and he told them stories of the land—masculine stories of violence and blood-shed. Nwoye knew that it was right to be masculine and to be violent, but somehow he still preferred the stories that his mother used to tell, and which she no doubt still told to her younger children—stories of the tortoise and his wily ways, and of the bird *eneke-nti-oba* who challenged the whole world to a wrestling contest and was finally thrown by the cat. He remembered the story she often told of the quarrel between Earth and Sky long ago, and how Sky withheld rain for seven years, until crops withered and the dead could not be buried because the hoes broke on the stony Earth. At last Vulture was sent to plead with Sky, and to soften his heart with a song of the suffering of the sons of men. Whenever Nwoye's mother sang this song he felt carried away to the distant scene in the sky where Vulture, Earth's emissary, sang for mercy. At last Sky was moved to pity, and he gave to Vulture rain wrapped in leaves of coco-yam. But as he flew home his long talon pierced the leaves and the rain fell as it had never fallen before. And so heavily did it rain on Vulture that he did not return to deliver his message but flew to a distant land, from where he had espied a fire. And when he got there he found it was a man making a sacrifice. He warmed himself in the fire and ate the entrails.

That was the kind of story that Nwoye loved. But he now knew that they were for foolish women and children, and he knew that his father wanted him to be a man. And so he feigned that he no longer cared for women's stories. And when he did this he saw that his father was pleased, and no longer rebuked him or beat him. So Nwoye and Ikemefuna would listen to Okonkwo's stories about tribal wars or how, years ago, he had stalked his victim, overpowered him and obtained his first human head. And as he told them of the past they sat in darkness or the dim glow of logs, waiting for the women to finish their cooking. When they finished, each brought her bowl of foo-foo and bowl of soup to her husband. An oil lamp was lit and Okonkwo tasted from each bowl, and then passed two shares to Nwoye and Ikemefuna.

In this way the moons and the seasons passed. And then the locusts came. It had not happened for many a long year. The elders said locusts came once in a generation, reappeared every year for seven years and then disappeared for another lifetime. They went back to their caves in a distant land, where they were guarded by a race of stunted men. And then after another lifetime these men opened the caves again and the locusts came to Umuofia.

They came in the cold harmattan season after the harvests had been gathered, and ate up all the wild grass in the fields.

Okonkwo and the two boys were working on the red outer walls of the compound. This was one of the lighter tasks of the after-harvest season. A new cover of thick palm branches and palm leaves was set on the walls to protect them from the next rainy season. Okonkwo worked on the outside of the wall and the boys worked from within. There were little holes from one side to the other in the upper levels of the wall, and through these Okonkwo passed the rope, or *tie-tie,* to the boys and they passed it round the wooden stays and then back to him; and in this way the cover was strengthened on the wall.

The women had gone to the bush to collect firewood, and the little children to visit their playmates in the neighbouring compounds. The harmattan was in the air and seemed to distil a hazy feeling of sleep on the world. Okonkwo and the boys worked in complete silence, which was only broken when a new palm frond was lifted on to the wall or when a busy hen moved dry leaves about in her ceaseless search for food.

And then quite suddenly a shadow fell on the world, and the sun seemed hidden behind a thick cloud. Okonkwo looked up from his work and wondered if it was going to rain at such an unlikely time of the year. But almost immediately a shout of joy broke out in all directions, and Umuofia, which had dozed in the noon-day haze, broke into life and activity.

'Locusts are descending,' was joyfully chanted everywhere, and men, women and children left their work or their play and ran into the open to see the unfamiliar sight. The locusts had not come for many, many years, and only the old people had seen them before.

At first, a fairly small swarm came. They were the harbingers sent to survey the land. And then appeared on the horizon a slowly-moving mass like a boundless sheet of black cloud drifting towards Umuofia.

Soon it covered half the sky, and the solid mass was now broken by tiny eyes of light like shining star-dust. It was a tremendous sight, full of power and beauty.

Everyone was now about, talking excitedly and praying that the locusts should camp in Umuofia for the night. For although locusts had not visited Umuofia for many years, everybody knew by instinct that they were very good to eat. And at last the locusts did descend. They settled on every tree and on every blade of grass; they settled on the roofs and covered the bare ground. Mighty tree branches broke away under them, and the whole country became the brown-earth colour of the vast, hungry swarm.

Many people went out with baskets trying to catch them, but the elders counselled patience till nightfall. And they were right. The locusts settled in the bushes for the night and their wings became wet with dew. Then all Umuofia turned out in spite of the cold harmattan, and everyone filled his bags and pots with locusts. The next morning they were roasted in clay pots and then spread in the sun until they became dry and brittle. And for many days this rare food was eaten with solid palm-oil.

Okonkwo sat in his *obi* crunching happily with Ikemefuna and Nwoye, and drinking palm-wine copiously, when Ogbuefi Ezeudu came in. Ezeudu was the oldest man in this quarter of Umuofia. He had been a great and fearless warrior in his time, and was now accorded great respect in all the clan. He refused to join in the meal, and asked Okonkwo to have a word with him outside. And so they walked out together, the old man supporting himself with his stick. When they were out of earshot, he said to Okonkwo:

'That boy calls you father. Do not bear a hand in his death.' Okonkwo was surprised, and was about to say something when the old man continued:

'Yes, Umuofia has decided to kill him. The Oracle of the Hills and the Caves has pronounced it. They will take him outside Umuofia as is the custom, and kill him there. But I want you to have nothing to do with it. He calls you his father.'

The next day a group of elders from all the nine villages of Umuofia came to Okonkwo's house early in the morning, and before they began to speak in low tones Nwoye and Ikemefuna were sent out. They did not stay very long, but when they went away Okonkwo sat still for a very long time supporting his chin in his palms. Later in the day he called Ikemefuna and told him that he was to be taken home the next day. Nwoye overheard it and burst into tears, whereupon his father beat him heavily. As for Ikemefuna, he was at a loss. His own home had gradually become very faint and distant. He still missed his mother and his sister and would be very glad to see them. But somehow he knew he was not going to see them. He remembered once when men had talked in low tones with his father; and it seemed now as if it was happening all over again.

Later, Nwoye went to his mother's hut and told her that Ikemufuna was going home. She immediately dropped the pestle with which she was grinding pepper, folded her arms across her breast and sighed, 'Poor child'.

The next day, the men returned with a pot of wine. They were all fully dressed as if they were going to a big clan meeting or to pay a visit to a neighbouring village. They passed their cloths under the right armpit, and hung their goatskin bags and sheathed matchets over their left shoulders. Okonkwo got ready quickly and the party set out with Ikemufuna carrying the pot of wine. A deathly silence descended on Okonkwo's compound. Even the very little children seemed to know. Throughout that day Nwoye sat in his mother's hut and tears stood in his eyes.

At the beginning of their journey the men of Umuofia talked and laughed about the locusts, about their women, and about some effeminate men who had refused to come with them. But as they drew near to the outskirts of Umuofia silence fell upon them too.

The sun rose slowly to the centre of the sky, and the dry, sandy footway began to throw up the heat that lay buried in it. Some birds chirruped in the forests around. The men trod dry leaves on the sand. All else was silent. Then from the distance came the faint beating of the *ekwe*. It rose and faded with the wind—a peaceful dance from a distant clan.

'It is an *ozo* dance,' the men said among themselves. But no one was sure where it was coming from. Some said Ezimili, others Abame or Aninta. They argued for a short while and fell into silence again, and the elusive dance rose and fell with the wind. Somewhere a man was taking one of the titles of his clan, with music and dancing and a great feast.

The footway had now become a narrow line in the heart of the forest. The short trees and sparse undergrowth which surrounded the men's village began to give way to giant trees and climbers which perhaps had stood from the beginning of things, untouched by the axe and the bushfire. The sun breaking through their leaves and branches threw a pattern of light and shade on the sandy footway.

Ikemefuna heard a whisper close behind him and turned round sharply. The man who had whispered now called out aloud, urging the others to hurry up.

'We still have a long way to go,' he said. Then he and another man went before Ikemefuna and set a faster pace.

Thus the men of Umuofia pursued their way, armed with sheathed matchets, and Ikemefuna, carrying a pot of palm-wine on his head, walked in their midst. Although he had felt uneasy at first, he was not afraid now. Okonkwo walked behind him. He could hardly imagine that Okonkwo was not his real father. He had never been fond of his real father, and at the end of three years he had become very distant indeed. But his mother and his three-year-old sister . . . of course she would not be three now, but six. Would he recognize her now? She must have grown quite big. How his mother would weep for joy, and thank Okonkwo for having looked after him so well and for bringing him back. She would want to hear everything that had happened to him in all these years. Could he remember them all? He would tell her about Nwoye and his mother, and about the locusts . . . Then quite suddenly a thought came upon him. His mother might be dead. He tried in vain to force the thought out of his mind. Then he tried to settle the matter the way he used to settle such matters when he was a little boy. He still remembered the song:

> Eze elina, elina!
> 　　Sala
> Eze ilikwa ya
> Ikwaba akwa oligholi
> Ebe Danda nechi eze
> Ebe Uzuzu nete egwu
> 　　Sala

He sang it in his mind, and walked to its beat. If the song ended on his right foot, his mother was alive. If it ended on his left, she was dead. No, not dead, but ill. It ended on the right. She was alive and well. He sang the song again, and it ended on the left. But the second time did not count. The first voice gets to Chukwu, or God's house. That was a favourite saying of children. Ikemefuna felt like a child once more. It must be the thought of going home to his mother.

One of the men behind him cleared his throat. Ikemefuna looked back, and the man growled at him to go on and not stand looking back. The way he said it sent cold fear down Ikemefuna's back. His hands trembled vaguely on the black pot he carried. Why had Okonkwo withdrawn to the rear? Ikemefuna felt his legs melting under him. And he was afraid to look back.

As the man who had cleared his throat drew up and raised his matchet, Okonkwo looked away. He heard the blow. The pot fell and broke in the sand. He heard Ikemefuna cry, 'My father, they have killed me!' as he ran towards him. Dazed with fear, Okonkwo drew his matchet and cut him down. He was afraid of being thought weak.

As soon as his father walked in, that night, Nwoye knew that Ikemefuna had been killed, and something seemed to give way inside him, like the snapping of a tightened bow. He did not cry. He just hung limp. He had had the same kind of feeling not long ago, during the last harvest season. Every child loved the harvest season. Those who were big enough to carry even a few yams in a tiny basket went with grown-ups to the farm. And if they could not help in digging up the yams, they could gather firewood together for roasting the ones that would be eaten there on the farm. This roasted yam soaked in red palm-oil and eaten in the open farm was sweeter than any meal at home. It was after such a day at the farm during the last harvest that Nwoye had felt for the first time a snapping inside him like the one he now felt. They were returning home with baskets of yams from a distant farm across the stream when they had heard the voice of an infant crying in the thick forest. A sudden hush had fallen on the women, who had been talking, and they had quickened their steps. Nwoye had heard that twins were put in earthen-ware pots and thrown away in the forest, but he had never yet come across them. A vague chill had descended on him and his head had seemed to swell, like a solitary walker at night who passes an evil spirit on the way. Then something had given way inside him. It descended on him again, this feeling, when his father walked in, that night after killing Ikemefuna.

> [To resist the missionaries and the encroachment of white rule, the men
> of Umuofia destroy the church.]

Chapter Twenty-Three

For the first time in many years Okonkwo had a feeling that was akin to happiness. The times which had altered so unaccountably during his exile seemed to be coming round again. The clan which had turned false on him appeared to be making amends.

He had spoken violently to his clansmen when they had met in the market-place to decide on their action. And they had listened to him with respect. It was like the good old days again, when a warrior was a war-rior. Although they had not agreed to kill the missionary or drive away the Christians, they had agreed to do something substantial. And they had done it. Okonkwo was almost happy again.

For two days after the destruction of the church, nothing happened. Every man in Umuofia went about armed with a gun or a matchet. They would not be caught unawares, like the men of Abame.

Then the District Commissioner returned from his tour. Mr Smith went immediately to him and they had a long discussion. The men of Umuofia did not take any notice of this, and if they did, they thought it was not important. The missionary often went to see his brother white man. There was nothing strange in that.

Three days later the District Commissioner sent his sweet-tongued messenger to the leaders of Umuofia asking them to meet him in his headquarters. That also was not strange. He often asked them to hold such palavers, as he called them. Okonkwo was among the six leaders he invited.

Okonkwo warned the others to be fully armed. 'An Umuofia man does not refuse a call,' he said. 'He may refuse to do what he is asked; he does not refuse to be asked. But the times have changed, and we must be fully prepared.'

And so the six men went to see the District Commissioner, armed with their matchets. They did not carry guns, for that would be unseemly. They were led into the court-house where the District Commissioner sat. He received them politely. They unslung their goatskin bags and their sheathed matchets, put them on the floor, and sat down.

'I have asked you to come,' began the Commissioner, 'because of what happened during my absence. I have been told a few things but I cannot believe them until I have heard your own side. Let us talk about it like friends and find a way of ensuring that it does not happen again.'

Ogbuefi Ekwueme rose to his feet and began to tell the story.

'Wait a minute,' said the Commissioner. 'I want to bring in my men so that they too can hear your grievances and take warning. Many of them come from distant places and although they speak your tongue they are ignorant of your customs. James! Go and bring in the men.' His interpreter left the court-room and soon returned with twelve men. They sat together with the men of Umuofia, and Ogbuefi Ekwueme began again to tell the story of how Enoch murdered an *egwugwu*.

It happened so quickly that the six men did not see it coming. There was only a brief scuffle, too brief even to allow the drawing of a sheathed matchet. The six men were handcuffed and led into the guardroom.

'We shall not do you any harm,' said the District Commissioner to them later, 'if only you agree to co-operate with us. We have brought a peaceful administration to you and your people so that you may be happy. If any man ill-treats you we shall come to your rescue. But we will not allow you to ill-treat others. We have a court of law where we judge cases and administer justice just as it is done in my own country under a great queen. I have brought you here because you joined together to molest others, to burn people's houses and their place of worship. That must not happen in the dominion of our queen, the most powerful ruler in the world. I have decided that you will pay a fine of two hundred bags of cowries. You will be released as soon as you agree to this and undertake to collect that fine from your people. What do you say to that?'

The six men remained sullen and silent and the Commissioner left them for a while. He told the court messengers, when he left the guardroom, to treat the men with respect because they were the leaders of Umuofia. They said, 'Yes, sir,' and saluted.

As soon as the District Commissioner left, the head messenger, who was also the prisoners' barber, took down his razor and shaved off all the hair on the men's heads. They were still handcuffed, and they just sat and moped.

'Who is the chief among you?' the court messengers asked in jest. 'We see that every pauper wears the anklet of title in Umuofia. Does it cost as much as ten cowries?'

The six men ate nothing throughout that day and the next. They were not even given any water to drink, and they could not go out to urinate or go into the bush when they were pressed. At night the messengers came in to taunt them and to knock their shaven heads together.

Even when the men were left alone they found no words to speak to one another. It was only on the third day, when they could no longer bear the hunger and the insults, that they began to talk about giving in.

'We should have killed the white man if you had listened to me,' Okonkwo snarled.

'We could have been in Umuru now waiting to be hanged,' someone said to him.

'Who wants to kill the white man?' asked a messenger who had just rushed in. Nobody spoke.

'You are not satisfied with your crime, but you must kill the white man on top of it.' He carried a strong stick, and he hit each man a few blows on the head and back. Okonkwo was choked with hate.

As soon as the six men were locked up, court messengers went into Umuofia to tell the people that their leaders would not be released unless they paid a fine of two hundred and fifty bags of cowries.

'Unless you pay the fine immediately,' said their headman, 'we will take your leaders to Umuru before the big white man, and hang them.'

This story spread quickly through the villages, and was added to as it went. Some said that the men had already been taken to Umuru and would be hanged on the following day. Some said that their families would also be hanged. Others said that soldiers were already on their way to shoot the people of Umuofia as they had done in Abame.

It was the time of the full moon. But that night the voice of children was not heard. The village *ilo* where they always gathered for a moon-play was empty. The women of Iguedo did not meet in their secret enclosure to learn a new dance to be displayed later to the village. Young men who were always abroad in the moonlight kept their huts that night. Their manly voices were not heard on the village paths as they went to visit their friends and lovers. Umuofia was like a startled animal with ears erect, sniffing the silent, ominous air and not knowing which way to run.

The silence was broken by the village crier beating his sonorous *ogene*. He called every man in Umuofia, from the Akakanma age-group upwards, to a meeting in the market-place after the morning meal. He went from one end of the village to the other and walked all its breadth. He did not leave out any of the main footpaths.

Okonkwo's compound was like a deserted homestead. It was as if cold water had been poured on it. His family was all there, but everyone spoke in whispers. His daughter Ezinma had broken her twenty-eight-day visit to the family of her future husband, and returned home when she heard that her father had been imprisoned, and was going to be hanged. As soon as she got home she went to Obierika to ask what the men of Umuofia were going to do about it. But Obierika had not been home since morning. His wives thought he had gone to a secret meeting. Ezinma was satisfied that something was being done.

On the morning after the village crier's appeal the men of Umuofia met in the market-place and decided to collect without delay two hundred and fifty bags of cowries to appease the white man. They did not know that fifty bags would go to the court messengers, who had increased the fine for that purpose.

Chapter Twenty-Four

Okonkwo and his fellow prisoners were set free as soon as the fine was paid. The District Commissioner spoke to them again about the great queen, and about peace and good government. But the men did not listen. They just sat and looked at him and at his interpreter. In the end they were given back their bags and sheathed matchets and told to go home. They rose and left the court-house. They neither spoke to anyone nor among themselves.

The court-house, like the church, was built a little way outside the village. The footpath that linked them was a very busy one because it also led to the stream, beyond the court. It was open and sandy. Footpaths were open and sandy in the dry season. But when the rains came the bush grew thick on either side and closed in on the path. It was now dry season.

As they made their way to the village the six men met women and children going to the stream with their waterpots. But the men wore such heavy and fearsome looks that the women and children did not say 'nno' or 'welcome' to them, but edged out of the way to let them pass. In the village little groups of men joined them until they became a sizeable company. They walked silently. As each of the six men got to his compound, he turned in, taking some of the crowd with him. The village was astir in a silent, suppressed way.

Ezinma had prepared some food for her father as soon as news spread that the six men would be released. She took it to him in his *obi*. He ate absent-mindedly. He had no appetite; he only ate to please her. His male relations and friends had gathered in his *obi*, and Obierika was urging him to eat. Nobody else spoke, but they noticed the long stripes on Okonkwo's back where the warder's whip had cut into his flesh.

The village crier was abroad again in the night. He beat his iron gong and announced that another meeting would be held in the morning. Everyone knew that Umuofia was at last going to speak its mind about the things that were happening.

Okonkwo slept very little that night. The bitterness in his heart was now mixed with a kind of child-like excitement. Before he had gone to bed he had brought down his war dress, which he had not touched since his return from exile. He had shaken out his smoked raffia skirt and examined his tall feather head-gear and his shield. They were all satisfactory, he had thought.

As he lay on his bamboo bed he thought about the treatment he had received in the white man's court, and he swore vengeance. If Umuofia decided on war, all would be well. But if they chose to be cowards he would go out and avenge himself. He thought about wars in the past. The noblest, he thought, was the war against Isike. In those days Okudo was still alive. Okudo sang a war song in a way that no other man could. He was not a fighter, but his voice turned every man into a lion.

'Worthy men are no more,' Okonkwo sighed as he remembered those days. 'Isike will never forget how we slaughtered them in that war. We killed twelve of their men and they killed only two of ours. Before the end of the fourth market week they were suing for peace. Those were days when men were men.'

As he thought of these things he heard the sound of the iron gong in the distance. He listened carefully, and could just hear the crier's voice. But it was very faint. He turned on his bed and his back hurt him. He ground his teeth. The crier was drawing nearer and nearer until he passed by Okonkwo's compound.

'The greatest obstacle in Umuofia,' Okonkwo thought bitterly, 'is that coward, Egonwanne. His sweet tongue can change fire into cold ash. When he speaks he moves our men to impotence. If they had ignored his womanish wisdom five years ago, we would not have come to this.' He ground his teeth. 'Tomorrow he will tell them that our fathers never fought a "war of blame". If they listen to him I shall leave them and plan my own revenge.'

The crier's voice had once more become faint, and the distance had taken the harsh edge off his iron gong. Okonkwo turned from one side to the other and derived a kind of pleasure from the pain his back gave him. 'Let Egonwanne talk about a "war of blame" tomorrow and I shall show him my back and head.' He ground his teeth.

The market-place began to fill as soon as the sun rose. Obierika was waiting in his *obi* when Okonkwo came along and called him. He hung his goatskin bag and his sheathed matchet on his shoulder and went out to join him. Obierika's hut was close to the road and he saw every man who passed to the market-place. He had exchanged greetings with many who had already passed that morning.

When Okonkwo and Obierika got to the meeting-place there were already so many people that if one threw up a grain of sand it would not find its way to the earth again. And many more people were coming from every quarter of the nine villages. It warmed Okonkwo's heart to see such strength of numbers. But he was looking for one man in particular, the man whose tongue he dreaded and despised so much.

'Can you see him?' he asked Obierika.

'Who?'

'Egonwanne,' he said, his eyes roving from one corner of the huge market-place to the other. Most of the men were seated on goatskins on the ground. A few of them sat on wooden stools they had brought with them.

'No,' said Obierika, casting his eyes over the crowd. 'Yes, there he is, under the silk-cotton tree. Are you afraid he would convince us not to fight?'

'Afraid? I do not care what he does to *you.* I despise him and those who listen to him. I shall fight alone if I choose.'

They spoke at the top of their voices because everybody was talking, and it was like the sound of a great market.

'I shall wait till he has spoken,' Okonkwo thought. 'Then I shall speak.'

'But how do you know he will speak against war?' Obierika asked after a while.

'Because I know he is a coward,' said Okonkwo. Obierika did not hear the rest of what he said because at that moment somebody touched his shoulder from behind and he turned round to shake hands and exchange greetings with five or six friends. Okonkwo did not turn around even though he knew the voices. He was in no mood to exchange greetings. But one of the men touched him and asked about the people of his compound.

'They are well,' he replied without interest.

The first man to speak to Umuofia that morning was Okika, one of the six who had been imprisoned. Okika was a great man and an orator. But he did not have the booming voice which a first speaker must use to establish silence in the assembly of the clan. Onyeka had such a voice; and so he was asked to salute Umuofia before Okika began to speak.

'*Umuofia kwenu!*' he bellowed, raising his left arm and pushing the air with his open hand.

'*Yaa!*' roared Umuofia.

'*Umuofia kwenu!*' he bellowed again, and again and again, facing a new direction each time. And the crowd answered, '*Yaa!*'

There was immediate silence as though cold water had been poured on a roaring flame.

Okika sprang to his feet and also saluted his clansmen four times. Then he began to speak:

'You all know why we are here, when we ought to be building our barns or mending our huts, when we should be putting our compounds in order. My father used to say to me: "Whenever you see a toad jumping in broad daylight, then know that something is after its life." When I saw you all pouring into this meeting from all the quarters of our clan so early in the morning, I knew that something was after our life.' He paused for a brief moment and then began again:

'All our gods are weeping. Idemili is weeping. Ogwugwu is weeping, Agbala is weeping, and all the others. Our dead fathers are weeping because of the shameful sacrilege they are suffering and the abomination we have all seen with our eyes.' He stopped again to steady his trembling voice.

'This is a great gathering. No clan can boast of greater numbers or greater valour. But are we all here? I ask you: Are all the sons of Umuofia with us here?' A deep murmur swept through the crowd.

'They are not,' he said. 'They have broken the clan and gone their several ways. We who are here this morning have remained true to our fathers, but our brothers have deserted us and joined a stranger to soil their fatherland. If we fight the stranger we shall hit our brothers and perhaps shed the blood of a clansman. But we must do it. Our fathers never dreamt of such a thing, they never killed their brothers. But a white man never came to them. So we must do what our fathers would never have done. Eneke the bird was asked why he was always on the wing and he replied: "Men have learnt to shoot without missing their mark and I have learnt to fly without perching on a twig." We must root out this evil. And if our brothers take the side of evil we must root them out too. And we must do it *now*. We must bale this water now that it is only ankle-deep . . .'

At this point there was a sudden stir in the crowd and every eye was turned in one direction. There was a sharp bend in the road that led from the market-place to the white man's court, and to the stream beyond it. And so no one had seen the approach of the five court messengers until they had come round the bend, a few paces from the edge of the crowd. Okonkwo was sitting at the edge.

He sprang to his feet as soon as he saw who it was. He confronted the head messenger, trembling with hate, unable to utter a word. The man was fearless and stood his ground, his four men lined up behind him.

In that brief moment the world seemed to stand still, waiting. There was utter silence. The men of Umuofia were merged into the mute backcloth of trees and giant creepers, waiting.

The spell was broken by the head messenger. 'Let me pass!' he ordered.

'What do you want here?'

'The white man whose power you know too well has ordered this meeting to stop.'

In a flash Okonkwo drew his matchet. The messenger crouched to avoid the blow. It was useless. Okonkwo's matchet decended twice and the man's head lay beside his uniformed body.

The waiting backcloth jumped into tumultuous life and the meeting was stopped. Okonkwo stood looking at the dead man. He knew that Umuofia would not go to war. He knew because they had let the other messenger escape. They had broken into tumult instead of action. He discerned fright in that tumult. He heard voices asking: 'Why did he do it?'

He wiped his matchet on the sand and went away.

Chapter Twenty-Five

When the District Commissioner arrived at Okonkwo's compound at the head of an armed band of soldiers and court messengers he found a small crowd of men sitting wearily in the *obi*. He commanded them to come outside, and they obeyed without a murmur.

'Which among you is called Okonkwo?' he asked through his interpreter.

'He is not here,' replied Obierika.

'Where is he?'

'He is not here!'

The Commissioner became angry and red in the face. He warned the men that unless they produced Okonkwo forthwith he would lock them all up. The men murmured among themselves, and Obierika spoke again.

'We can take you where he is, and perhaps your men will help us.'

The Commissioner did not understand what Obierika meant when he said, 'Perhaps your men will help us.' One of the most infuriating habits of these people was their love of superfluous words, he thought.

Obierika with five or six others led the way. The Commissioner and his men followed, their firearms held at the ready. He had warned Obierika that if he and his men played any monkey tricks they would be shot. And so they went.

There was a small bush behind Okonkwo's compound. The only opening into this bush from the compound was a little round hole in the red-earth wall through which fowls went in and out in their endless search for food. The hole would not let a man through. It was to this bush that Obierika led the Commissioner and his men. They skirted round the compound, keeping close to the wall. The only sound they made was with their feet as they crushed dry leaves.

Then they came to the tree from which Okonkwo's body was dangling, and they stopped dead.

'Perhaps your men can help us bring him down and bury him,' said Obierika. 'We have sent for strangers from another village to do it for us, but they maybe a long time coming.'

The District Commissioner changed instantaneously. The resolute administrator in him gave way to the student of primitive customs.

'Why can't you take him down yourselves?' he asked.

'It is against our custom,' said one of the men. 'It is an abomination for a man to take his own life. It is an offence against the Earth, and a man who commits it will not be buried by his clansmen. His body is evil, and only strangers may touch it. That is why we ask your people to bring him down, because you are strangers?'

'Will you bury him like any other man?' asked the Commissioner.

'We cannot bury him. Only strangers can. We shall pay your men to do it. When he has been buried we will then do our duty by him. We shall make sacrifices to cleanse the desecrated land.'

Obierika, who had been gazing steadily at his friend's dangling body, turned suddenly to the District Commissioner and said ferociously: 'That man was one of the greatest men in Umuofia. You drove him to kill himself; and now he will be buried like a dog . . .' He could not say any more. His voice trembled and choked his words.

'Shut up!' shouted one of the messengers, quite unnecessarily.

'Take down the body,' the Commissioner ordered his chief messenger, 'and bring it and all these people to the court.'

'Yes, sah,' the messenger said, saluting.

The Commissioner went away, taking three or four of the soldiers with him. In the many years in which he had toiled to bring civilization to different parts of Africa he had learnt a number of things. One of them was that a District Commissioner must never attend to such undignified details as cutting down a hanged man from the tree. Such attention would give the natives a poor opinion of him. In the book which he planned to write he would stress that point. As he walked back to the court he thought about that book. Every day brought him some new material. The story of this man who had killed a messenger and hanged himself would make interesting reading. One could almost write a whole chapter on him. Perhaps not a whole chapter but a reasonable paragraph, at any rate. There was so much else to include, and one must be firm in cutting out details. He had already chosen the title of the book, after much thought: *The Pacification of the Primitive Tribes of the Lower Niger.*

Study Questions

1. Why does Okonkwo kill Ikemefuna, and what traditions does this reflect? Does it seem just?
2. Why do the men of Umuofia feel justified in destroying the church?

3. When the District Commissioner imprisons Okonkwo and his men (through trickery), it seems fair according to colonial standards and law. How do the jailed men regard it?

4. What role does indigenous and colonial religion play in the conflict?

5. Why did Okonkwo kill the messenger, then take his own life? What concept of justice is being expressed?

Schindler's List

Director: Steven Spielberg

Screenplay: Steven Zaillan

Based on the book by Thomas Keneally

For information on the director, Steven Spielberg, please see the headnote preceding Saving Private Ryan.
      The film Schindler's List, *a synopsis of which follows, was adapted for the screen from a 1982 biographical novel by Thomas Keneally. The title character, Oskar Schindler, was a real person, and Steven Zaillian's screenplay departs very little from the actual events of his life. Starting as an entrepreneur willing to work with the Nazis as suppliers of Jews for his factory, Schindler develops into a saintly individual who protects hundreds of Jews from extermination. Spielberg tells the story as though we were witnessing history, never intruding in the narrative but allowing the scenes of horror and triumph to speak for themselves.*
      Schindler's List *won seven Academy Awards including Best Picture, Best Cinematography (Janusz Kaminski), Best Adapted Screenplay, Best Original Score (John Williams), Best Editing (Michael Kahn), and Best Art Direction. Liam Neeson was nominated as Best Actor and Ralph Fiennes as Best Supporting Actor, and the film received nominations for Best Costume Design, Best Sound, and Best Makeup. In addition to the Academy Awards,* Schindler's List *was also honored by the Golden Globes and the New York Film Critics Circle.*

Synopsis

The twentieth century has seen enormous advances, principally in science, technology, and medicine, but the horrors committed against the world's peoples are also part of its legacy. It was a time of unprecedented violence and atrocities with large-scale wars, rebellions, and ethnic genocides, the introduction of tanks, planes, and submarines in combat, the employment of nuclear, chemical, and biological weapons, and the displacement, maiming, and starvation of enormous numbers of people.

      We have seen 12 million people killed by the Nazis in Europe, 4 to 5 million killed in the Soviet Union and another 4 to 7 million peasants starved to death, 1.7 million killed by the Khymer Rouge in Cambodia, 1.5 million killed in China's cultural revolution, 1.5 million Hindus and Muslims killed in Pakistan, 1.5 million Armenians and 100,000 Kurds killed in Iraq, 1.3 million killed in the Sudan, 1 million killed in Ethiopia, 1 million Muslims killed by Serbs in Bosnia, and hundreds of thousands killed in Namibia, Tanzania, Uganda, Burundi, East Timor, Guatemala, and Rwanda.

The Holocaust is probably the prime expression and symbol of evil in the twentieth century. The Nazis deliberately murdered six million Jews during World War II, not as collateral damage but systematically and for ideological reasons. According to Nazi theory, Jews were engaged in a financial conspiracy against Germany and Europe at large and had to be eliminated. Moreover, they were accused of having killed Christ and were judged as an inferior people like Negroes, homosexuals, Slavs, and gypsies. The Nazis considered themselves the "Aryan" master race, destined to rule the world, while Jews were thought to be a traditional menace and not fully human. Consequently, they could be used as slave labor and ultimately exterminated in a "final solution."

Schindler's List is one of numerous films such as Jan Kadar's *The Shop on Main Street* and Alan Pakula's *Sophie's Choice,* that have documented and dramatized the horrors of the Holocaust. However, many critics regard it as the finest and most powerful film ever made about the atrocity. The black and white photography enhances the documentary feel of the film, and augments the realism; blood flowing from a head wound is somehow more affecting in black while avoiding tastelessness. In addition, the music selected and composed by John Williams provides a haunting score. Popular Hungarian songs such as "Gloomy Sunday," the German's favorite march "Erica," and Hebrew songs played by Itzhak Perlman provide a fitting background for the events depicted.

The story begins with Oskar Schindler (Liam Neeson) ingratiating himself to Nazi officers in an art deco cabaret in occupied Poland. It is the beginning of World War II, and Schindler wants to make important contacts so he can open a factory, using Jewish workers at slave wages. As a failed businessman in Czechoslovakia (a Sudeten German), he is gambling his remaining funds on war profiteering, and his charisma enables him to win over those with the power to help him. By the end of the evening, he has joined the tables of the cabaret together in a drunken party, and everyone comes away impressed with his strong, physical presence, expensive clothes, and *bon-vivant* manner.

Schindler is subsequently appointed Direktor of a plant that manufactures enameled cooking utensils in Krakow for the German army: Emailwarenfabrik. He hires an accountant named Itzhak Stern (Ben Kingsley) to recruit Jews for the work force and later to manage the factory for him. He himself knows nothing about manufacturing cookware; his genius lies in courting the Nazi authorities. The Jews are grateful for the job, even at starvation pay, because unless they are employed as "essential workers" contributing to national defense, they will be deported or imprisoned. Occupations such as teachers and musicians are classified as non-essential while those contributing to the war effort are protected. Schindler meanwhile, by having low labor costs, begins to amass a fortune.

To maintain his position, Schindler builds strong ties with the Nazi hierarchy through bribery and luxurious gifts: Beluga caviar, Hennessey cognac, Dom Perignon champagne, Cuban cigars, fresh fruit, chocolate, and German cigarettes—all obtained through contacts on the black market. With each box of gifts he encloses a note:

> (Schindler's voice-over) It is my distinct pleasure to announce the fully operational status of Deutsche Emailwaren Fabrik—manufacturers of superior enamelware crockery, expressly designed and crafted for military use, utilizing only the most modern equipment. DEF's staff of highly skilled and experienced artisans and journeymen deliver a product of unparalleled quality, enabling me to proffer with absolute confidence and pride, a full line of field and kitchen ware unsurpassable in all respects by my competitors. See attached list and available colors. Anticipating the enclosed bids will meet with your approval. And looking forward to a long and mutually prosperous association. I extend to you, in advance, my sincerest gratitude and very best regards. Oskar Schindler.

Schindler also hires a staff of eighteen women who function as secretaries and hostesses at parties for the Nazi officers; in addition, they serve as an ever-changing stable of mistresses for him. Schindler has a photograph taken with them outside the factory, dressed impeccably as usual, wearing a Nazi party pin in his lapel and projecting an air of power and success. His aim in everything is to become rich, and with his parties, women, and gifts as well as the cheap labor in his plant, he manages to accomplish it.

When a family is evicted from their luxurious apartment and relocated in a slum dwelling, Schindler takes it over as his own. He stretches out on the bed amidst elegant furnishings, glistening woodwork, and French doors commenting, "It couldn't be better," while the displaced Jewish family comfort themselves by saying, "It could be worse."

When his wife Emilie (Caroline Goodall) comes to visit from Czechoslovakia he tells her that his father at his peak had only fifty employees whereas he has "350 workers on the factory floor with one purpose . . . to make money—for me." He declares that people back home in Czechoslovakia will say of him

> He did something extraordinary. He did something no one else did. He came here with nothing, a suitcase, and built a bankrupt company into a major manufactory. And left with a steamer trunk, two steamer trunks, full of money. All the riches of the world . . . There's no way I could have known this before, but

> there was always something missing. In every business I tried, I
> can see now it wasn't me who was failing. Something was miss-
> ing. Even if I'd known what it was, there's nothing I could have
> done about it, because you can't create this sort of thing. And it
> makes all the difference between success and failure.
> EMILIE: Luck.
> SCHINDLER: War

As the pogroms intensify and people are sent to the death camps for
extermination, Schindler's factory becomes a way for Jews to stay alive.
Nevertheless, saving Jews is not Schindler's intention but a consequence
of their employment; to his mind, they are merely instruments for making money, expendable and replaceable. If a Jew is shot, that's the loss of
a worker. However, very gradually, the means become the end, and he
feels a humane connection to the Jews as they suffer and are murdered,
individually and collectively.

The transformation occurs through a series of incidents, some large-
scale, others personal. After a machinist is brought to his office, to thank
him for the opportunity to work, he tells Stern, "Don't ever do that to me
again. Did you happen to notice that the man had one arm. What use is
he?" Later, however, when the man is shoveling snow and shot by a
guard as useless, he regrets the man's death. In similar circumstances,
Schindler intervenes several times to save people's lives, saying, "He's a
metal press operator, quite skilled," and in the case of children, "They
polish the inside of shell casings."

In another incident, he becomes furious at a woman who asks obse-
quiously that her parents be transferred from a concentration camp to
work in his plant. The woman pleads, "They say that no one dies here.
They say your factory's a haven. They say that you are good." Schindler
threatens to have her arrested for making such a request, and she runs
terrified from his office, but later he has her parents brought to work
for him.

Schindler also saves Stern, his accountant/plant manager, from
deportation, removing him from a cattle car that is headed to a concentration camp. The clerk and soldier he intimidates into stopping the
train say, "It makes no difference to us, you understand. This one, that
one. It's the inconvenience to the list. It's the paperwork." To Schindler,
however, the Jews are becoming individuals and not a bureaucratic
category.

Following the scene on the train platform, the camera follows the
luggage as it's wheeled into a shed. Here the suitcases are emptied and
the contents sorted into piles: paintings, jewelry, photos, watches, precious stones. A pile of teeth is poured out in front of a jeweler, so the gold
fillings can be extracted.

In one of the most horrific scenes in the movie, Schindler sees Jews in the Krakow ghetto being brutally murdered. The incident is shown with graphic realism, and Schindler, overlooking the scene on horseback from a hill, is appalled at the butchery. By contrast, this "liquidation of the ghetto" is regarded as a triumph by the Nazis, for something that had existed for six centuries and fostered business, science, education, and art is now consigned to history.

As Schindler grows in his moral responses and understanding, we see his opposite in the person of a S.S. Commandant of the Plaszow camp, Amon Goeth (Ralph Fiennes). He helps Schindler establish his factory within the prison camp but only because he gets a cut of the profits, and his sadism almost makes him the embodiment of Nazi evil. In summary executions, he shoots an engineer for making a suggestion, treating it as arguing, and he kills every other man from a barrack where a worker tried to escape—some twenty-five men at point-blank range. In one incident, he tries to shoot a worker for some infraction, and when his gun jams, he clubs him with the butt end almost incidentally. In the most chilling scene, Goeth shoots several workers from a parapet of his house overlooking the work yard, apparently as sport or target practice, then sets down the rifle and returns to a woman waiting for him in bed. He kills without remorse or regret, and any pity he might have felt has been buried beneath Nazi doctrine.

Several chinks do appear in his armor, however. In a half-drunken conversation Goeth tells Schindler that, "They fear us because we have the power to kill arbitrarily," to which Schindler replies, "Power is when we have every justification to kill and we don't." He is trying to influence Goeth toward being merciful, and his words do have some effect. Goeth pardons two offenses, that of a girl smoking on the job and a stable boy who puts a saddle on the ground, but he quickly reverts to type and first forgives then shoots a boy for not removing stains on a tub. Doing his duty as camp Commandant seems to coincide with his own temperament and proclivities; he savors the cruelty needed to make the Nazi machine run efficiently. Goeth has believed what he was told about Jews because it was what he wanted to hear.

A common practice among oppressors is to label a despised group as subhuman, and reduce them to an animal state; this then justifies their being treated as animals, slaves, or objects. The opposite process occurs when members of a group are suddenly regarded as persons; then one can identify with their suffering and feel compassion for them as fellow human beings.

Goeth's closest approach to humanity occurs in his relationship with a Jewish servant, Helen Hirsch (Embeth Davidtz). Because of her attractiveness, he picks her out of a lineup to be his maid and, despite himself, he feels sympathy for her situation. In one definitive scene,

Goeth almost yields to his softer feelings, but in the end his hardness prevails.

> I would like so much to reach out and touch you in your loneliness . . .
> What would be wrong with that? . . . I know that you are not a person in
> the strict sense of the word. When they compare you to a vermin and a
> rodent and lice, they make a good point . . . Is this the hair of a rat, are
> these the eyes of a rat? Has not a Jew eyes? . . . No, I don't think so. You
> Jewish bitch, you nearly talked me into it.

Goeth is obviously conflicted. He is drawn to Helen, probably in love with her, but according to Nazi dogma she is the enemy and beneath consideration. Throughout his speech, Helen says nothing, but he claims she "nearly talked me into it." In fact, his own natural feelings had made him respond to her as a woman. Goeth then beats her, transferring his guilt to a scapegoat. By punishing her he is trying to drive out what he regards as impure feelings, suppressing emotions that he perceives as weakness. If Goeth had been able express his love, he might have reclaimed his humanity.

Itzhak Stern occupies the other end of the spectrum, a composite figure who functions as the good soul in the film. He and Schindler have a wary respect for each other that grows more authentic through the years, but their relationship always remains unspoken and understated. Their conversation when Schindler first hires Stern is typical of their interaction.

> SCHINDLER: There's a company you did the books for on Lipowa
> Street, made what—pots and pans?
> STERN: By law, I have to tell you, sir, I'm a Jew.
> SCHINDLER: Well, I'm a German, so there we are. (Schindler pours
> a shot of cognac into the cap of his flask and offers it to Stern—
> who declines.) A good company you think?
> STERN: Modestly successful.
> SCHINDLER: I know nothing about enamelware, do you?
> STERN: I was just the accountant.
> SCHINDLER: Simple engineering, though, wouldn't you think?
> Change the machines around, whatever you do, you could make
> other things, couldn't you? Field kits, mess kits, army contracts.
> Once the war ends, forget it, but for now it's great. You could
> make a fortune, don't you think?
> STERN: I think most people right now have other priorities.
> SCHINDLER: Like what?
> STERN: I'm sure you'll do just fine once you get the contracts. In
> fact, the worse things get, the better you will do.

At one point, Schindler thanks Stern for managing the factory, saying he could not have done it without him, but Stern does not respond, feeling perhaps too ambivalent about his role to accept praise. He is also fearful because his situation is so precarious. When Schindler says "Someday this is all going to end . . . I was going to say, we'll have a drink then," Stern replies, "I think I'd better have it now."

Throughout their association Stern maintains a steady, quiet presence, disciplined, ascetic, patiently doing his job. He first acts out of self-preservation, then because he realizes that the more the factory succeeds, the more lives can be saved.

Aside from the characters of Schindler, Goethe, and Stern and the events surrounding them, there are numerous moments in the film that are both numbing and indelible. Ashes that consist of human remains drift down on people like snow from crematorium chimneys; Jewish women use their own blood to rouge their cheeks and give an appearance of health; bodies are stacked on wheelbarrows while fires burn all around; a boy hides in a latrine, waist-deep in excrement. There are quick images of a little girl's red garment at the beginning of the film and at her death at the end—notably one of the few shots in color. We see people summarily shot if they offer any resistance to being dragged from their apartments; a Polish woman shouting "Goodbye Jews" as trucks full of men, women, and children pass on the street; and a boy running his finger across his throat as cattle cars full of Jews roll along the tracks.

Schindler's apotheosis meanwhile has become complete, and while he must maintain good relations with the Nazis, including Goeth, he actively works to help the Jews. We see this in different ways. For example, at a train station one hot afternoon, when he and some Nazi officers are sipping cold drinks and watching overloaded boxcars with their human freight, he realizes that the people inside are dying of suffocation and thirst. With the help of some soldiers he manages to spray the cars with water from a fire hose, cooling them down and allowing the people to drink the drops. This amuses the Nazis rather than offending them because they know the Jews are being sent to their deaths in Auschwitz. So does Schindler, of course, but he tries to relieve suffering where and when he can. Oddly enough, Schindler seems jovial as he does this, as though his benevolence is an extension of his spirit and flamboyance.

Schindler's most significant act of compassion occurs when the war is beginning to wane. He spends his entire fortune buying his Jewish workers from Goeth, intending to take them to his Czech factory as essential workers. In this way he saves over eleven hundred lives, including that of Helen Hirsch who he wins from Goeth in a bet. Stern, who types Schindler's list, realizes that these Jews are being rescued from extermination. "This list is an absolute good," he says, "The list is life."

When the train carrying the women is mistakenly diverted to Auschwitz, Schindler uses his influence to bring them to Brinnlitz,

Czechoslovakia. At this point his motive is wholly humanitarian, and his previous goal of profiting from slave labor has been completely supplanted.

Later, when he establishes his new factory, his rules include no summary executions and no guards on the shop floor, ostensibly because it might interfere with production. In fact, he wants more humane working conditions and secrecy so that he can miscalibrate the shells; for seven months his factory is "a model of non-production." When the war ends, he saves the workers by telling the guards that they can now leave or else commit wholesale slaughter according to their orders. Predictably, the soldiers choose to go home.

The final sequences of the film have been criticized as somewhat soporific. Schindler breaks down in tears as he bids farewell to his workers, and he berates himself for not saving more. His gold Nazi pin could have saved two lives, his car five lives. Schindler's contrition seems rather excessive since he did risk his life to save hundreds of Jews as well as sabotaging the German war effort.

Schindler's List as a whole brings home the horror of the Holocaust and shows the successful efforts of one man to oppose the atrocities and redeem himself. A message on the screen reads that the Jewish population of Poland today is four thousand, while there are now six thousand descendants of the Jews that Schindler saved. (Ninety-nine percent of Polish Jewish children were annihilated during the war.) At the end of the film we see some of these descendants paying tribute to his memory by laying stones on his grave. Schindler died penniless in 1974 after trying (and failing) to run a farm in Argentina, and the *Schindlerjuden* cared for him until his death.

One intriguing aspect of the film has to do with the transformation of Schindler's character. We wonder how a high living, war-profiteer who begins by exploiting the persecution of Jews in order to enrich himself, ends up spending all his money to rescue Jews from death, at great personal risk. Is it too cynical to speculate that Schindler simply enjoyed the heroic role and grand gesture, whether that meant being a devil or a saint? The more customary interpretation is that, because of the barbarism he witnessed, he underwent a fundamental change from an opportunistic businessman to a caring human being. The metamorphosis does remain an enigma, however, just as we wonder how decent, cultured Germans could have abandoned the moral principles of civilization and become Nazi monsters.

Whatever his motivation Schindler acted while others were uninvolved or paralyzed. Elie Wiesel, who has written extensively on the Holocaust, has called indifference the greatest sin. The Catholic Church in Poland remained silent as did most Poles, and many Germans and citizens in occupied countries claimed they did not know what was happening. The political philosopher Hannah Arendt wonders why the Jews themselves were so passive, and filed to their deaths without greater protest. Schindler at least did not stand aside but behaved righteously against the Nazi terror.

One of the indicators of the worth of a political society is how it treats its minorities, especially if they are disliked. If we operate only in terms of the interests of the majority, then the needs of the minority can be overridden; we can even persecute, imprison, and execute people who lie outside the main group. However, if we function in accordance with moral principles, then we behave considerately toward all human beings; everyone is entitled to rights such as that of life, property, health, work, justice, and happiness. The fascist politics of Nazism affirmed an ethic of power without such moral authority, and in an atmosphere of this kind Jews could be consigned to gas chambers as an unpopular minority. This is one of the lessons in political philosophy that can be drawn from the Holocaust experience: We are obliged to respect for all people as equally deserving of humane treatment.

This realization prompted Schindler's conversion, like Paul on the road to Damascus, and in describing exceptional people like him one survivor wrote,

> We live in a shaky and uncertain world, a world that offers little help in choosing life values. In such a setting, knowledge and awareness about noble and self-sacrificing behavior may help restore some shattered illusions. Indeed, mere awareness that in the midst of ultimate human degradation some people were willing to risk their lives for others denies the inevitable supremacy of evil. (Tec Nechama, *When Light Pierced the Darkness*)

Study Questions

1. Do you think we can generalize about groups of people—races, nations, ethnic or religious groups (such as Jews)? Is it legitimate, for example, to characterize the French as people who love good food, the Japanese as industrious, Americans as friendly? Can we differentiate between generalizations and stereotypes? Should we only make positive generalizations and not negative ones about people such as the Japanese during World War II?

2. What rights were taken away from the Jews in Nazi-occupied countries such as Poland? Is it ever morally justified to deprive people of their rights—convicts, military personnel, the mentally ill, foreign nationals of a hostile country?

3. At the Nurenburg Trials, many Nazis argued that they simply obeyed orders as soldiers should and therefore that they should not be held responsible for the atrocities they committed. Is this a sound argument? Why?

4. If Schindler had been discovered helping Jews, he would have been killed as a traitor for violating the laws of the state. Under what conditions do you think the law should be broken?

5. Should the Polish people have helped the Jews, even at the risk of their own lives? Is that asking too much of people?

B. THE IDEAL STATE: WHAT IS THE BEST FORM OF GOVERNMENT?

Aside from issues of freedom and equality, the larger question in political philosophy is what would be an ideal form for the state to assume. That is, what type of government, legal structure, civil organization and so forth would be best for promoting human well being? As Aristotle wrote "a state exists for the sake of a good life, and not for the sake of life only."

All of the major political philosophers have proposed theories of the ideal state from the first speculations of Plato in the *Republic* to Thomas Hobbes in *The Leviathan*, Jean Jacques Rousseau in *The Social Contract*, and Karl Marx in *The Communist Manifesto*. Aristotle in his *Politics* maintains that any one of several states can be best depending on the circumstances, and his typology of governmental forms is a useful launching point for discussion.

1. *Monarchies* are arguably the oldest form of government. One person is designated as the sovereign, having a hereditary right to rule as head of state throughout his or her lifetime. In Europe during the Middle Ages monarchies were the accepted political structure, supported by the doctrine of "the divine right of kings." According to this view, monarchs are appointed by God as his representatives on earth, and they are responsible only to God not to the will of the people. The monarch is the final authority on all secular matters, and in Protestant countries after the Reformation, on religious matters as well. In some Asian and Eastern nations such as ancient Egypt and Japan, the king himself was regarded as divine.

In most cases, monarchies were dynastic with power transferred from the king to his eldest son, and these inherited monarchies were supported by nobles or by financial interests that wanted a monolithic government. If the king rules by the will of God, and he maintains order, protects the nation, ensures prosperity, and keeps the peace, this can be a popular and effective political system.

In defense of monarchy Thomas Hobbes wrote in *The Leviathan*, "In a state of nature with no intervening authority people quarrel and engage in perpetual warfare of "omnium contra omnes" (all against all). Therefore the life of man is "solitary, poore, nasty, brutish, and short." For this reason people willingly accept the restraint of a sovereign in "the foresight of their own preservation, and of a more contented life thereby."

In the fifteenth and sixteenth centuries, King Henry VIII and King Louis XIV ruled as absolute monarchs, but by the seventeenth and eighteenth centuries the power of kings began to be limited, sometimes as a result of revolutions. The dissatisfaction came about mainly because of the abuse of power. A benevolent, well-informed monarch who rules by the dictates of God is certainly desirable, but if he is self-serving and corrupt, then his authority is undermined.

This is the degeneration that Aristotle describes. Monarchy can be an excellent form of government, preserving wealth, property, and power, but it tends to become a tyranny in which the monarch functions only in his own interest.

2. In *aristocracy*, a small number of individuals are given governmental authority rather than having power vested in a single individual. These few people are considered the most capable of ruling by virtue of their intelligence, nobility, education, character, or other type of qualifications. *Aristos* means best, *kratos* is power, so aristocracy translates as governmental power exercised by the best among the citizens. In its classic form it is not based on birth but power is conferred upon the most meritorious individuals in a society.

Aristocracies existed in Athens from the fifth to the third centuries B.C., in Rome from the sixth to the first centuries B.C., and perhaps in England from the seventeenth to the nineteenth centuries. Plato, of course, presented the most famous justification for aristocracy in *The Republic*, basing his political philosophy on his metaphysics.

As we saw in Chapter I, Plato maintains that the basic reality consists of the world of Ideas which is accessible through rational thought. Philosophers are the people best suited to understand these Ideas because they have logical, reflective, and inquiring minds, and for this reason they should become the rulers. The philosopher is especially qualified for governance because he tries to comprehend the idea of justice, and using that model, to create a just society on earth.

Plato therefore advocates an intellectual aristocracy as the ideal form of government. He recognized that philosophers have no power besides their minds, which most people do not respect, so they would not rule very long—if they got to rule at all. Furthermore, the military would revolt against them using their forces, the masses would attack them using their numerical superiority, and the rich would oppose them using the leverage of their wealth. Despite these practical problems, Plato maintained that if people had enough restraint and foresight to let philosophers rule, the result would be a just state. As an intelligentsia they would be vulnerable, nevertheless they would create the finest type of government.

In criticizing aristocracy in the *Politics*, Aristotle feared that it could degenerate into oligarchy in which a dominant class or clique, especially the wealthy, would seize control for selfish reasons. Plato had safeguards against this in his system, making the rulers' lives extremely austere rather than luxurious, so it would attract only those dedicated to the social good. Nonetheless, the idea of entrusting government to a group of superior people makes many people uncomfortable.

3. Referring again to Aristotle's scheme, *democracy* is another possible form of government, and it can be desirable or undesirable. In the form of constitutional democracy in which the majority of the people

exercise power within the framework of constitutional restraints, it can produce an excellent result. In general, the people as a whole can be trusted more than the few, provided that justice prevails in accordance with law and legislation. Aristotle writes "The many . . . may very likely be better than the few good, if regarded not individually but collectively, just as a feast to which many contribute is better than a dinner provided out of a single purse."

However, democracy can impede human development if the poor, needy, and lower classes are in the majority, and they use the power of numbers to ensure their own good rather than the common interests of society. A popular democracy of this kind means a tyranny of the majority. This is why we need a constitutional democracy in which the best interests of the state and its citizens are legally protected. Ideal democracy is lawful rule by the majority, but in popular democracy we have what Plato called mob rule.

Democracy was instituted in Greek city-states for a brief period but it flowered in the nineteenth and twentieth centuries in Europe and the United States. The Magna Carta (along with the Declaration of Independence and the French Declaration of the Rights of Man) established the foundation for democracy, while the Enlightenment, and the American and French revolutions provided the catalysts for establishing democratic governments. Most of these became representative democracies in which citizens exercise their rights through chosen representatives rather than by direct vote. In this way, the people's voice is heard although the leaders are still able to use independent judgment. Ultimately, the representatives are accountable to the people through regular elections, and to limit power most democracies have a system of checks and balances—in America between the executive, legislative, and judicial branches of government. In this way, there is a "coincidence of interest between the rulers and the ruled."

One inherent tension in any form of democracy is whether the will of the people should be followed or whether certain rights such as civil liberties should be safeguarded. If the two coincide then there is no conflict, but suppose the majority votes to exterminate the minority as in Germany when Hitler was democratically elected? Should people be given what they want or what is best for all? This is when constitutions are important.

In any case, Aristotle judged the worth of a state, whether a monarchy, aristocracy, or democracy according to whether it served the public interest, and this varied from nation to nation depending on the temperament of the people. Sometimes it meant one ruler, sometimes a few, and at other times government by the majority of citizens.

In our age, additional forms of government have arisen, most notably totalitarianism—a strong centralized government that exercises control over people's freedom, will, and thoughts, and is intolerant of dissent. We have seen the rise of the totalitarian governments of fascism and of communism, and each has been rejected after terrible wars of resistance costing millions of lives. Fascism is a right-wing, militaristic movement that asserts the absolute primacy of the nation-state and the submission of the individual; the major examples are Nazi Germany and Mussolini's Italy. In communism, an authoritarian government is needed to establish and maintain a centralized economic system. A self-perpetuating political party and a dominant leader establishes rigid control over the state, as occurred in Russia, China, and Cuba.

Is Aristotle right in thinking that different governments can be right for different societies, or is there an ideal form of government for securing human welfare? Is the cynic right in saying that we have a choice between the corrupt few or the ignorant many? In the United States, we often assume that democracy is best for every nation, but doesn't democracy require an educated electorate? Not all countries have an educated citizenry or even a literate one.

As we can see, determining what constitutes a good state is extremely difficult, in fact the most difficult question in political philosophy. Obviously, neither philosophy nor the nations of the world have settled it.

In the selection from the *Politics* in Section Two, we can see Aristotle's ideas developed more fully and the reasoning behind his conclusions.

In *Brave New World* by Aldous Huxley we are thrust into a totalitarian state of the future, a dystopia in which the government has complete control over the individual. Every person's genetic inheritance is predetermined, and each is psychologically conditioned for a specific role in society.

The final excerpt, from the film *Born on the Fourth of July*, portrays a crisis in democratic government when a large number of citizens, mainly the young, profoundly disagree with the decision of the leaders to go to war. How responsive should a democratic government be? How much dissent can a democratic government tolerate?

The Politics*
Aristotle

Aristotle (384–322 B.C.) along with Plato is considered among the foremost philosophers of ancient Greece. He profoundly influenced St. Thomas Aquinas in building his foundations of Christian theology as well as contributing to philosophic theories of language, rules of validity in logic, astronomy and biology, poetry and literary criticism, ethics and political philosophy. Almost all of Aristotle's early writings for the general public have been lost, but we do have his later work in the form of lecture notes that were preserved and arranged by subsequent scholars. Because this body of work is technical and fragmented, Aristotle's writings are sometimes regarded as dry, dogmatic, and rigid. In fact, he willingly recognized problems in his theories and continually revised his work, taking into account the ideas of his predecessors and common opinions.

Aristotle's theory of science is contained in his Physics, *and his concept of the nature and structure of reality appears in the* Metaphysics, *including his concept of God as "prime mover." The* Nicomachean Ethics, *dedicated to his son Nicomachus, contains his ethical theory; with the doctrine of the "golden mean" and its various applications it is almost a handbook of morality. Every investigation of aesthetics begins with Aristotle's* Poetics, *and his* Politics *is a basic reference point in the study of political philosophy.*

Aristotle argues in the Politics *that, contrary to the Utopia described by Plato in* The Republic, *no perfect form of government can be found. Rather, various forms of government exist, and the circumstances of the society should dictate which one is adopted. Factors such as the customs, education, ideals, laws, and so forth will determine which government is best for a particular society, but there is no one abstract ideal that holds true for all societies.*

. . . We have next to consider how many forms of government there are, and what they are; and in the first place what are the true forms, for when they are determined the perversions of them will at once be apparent. The words constitution and government have the same meaning, and the government, which is the supreme authority in states, must be in the hands of one, or of a few, or of many. The true forms of government,

7. Forms of government, true and perverted.

2

*Translated with marginal analysis by B. Jowett.

therefore, are those in which the one, or the few, or the many, govern with
a view to the common interest; but governments which rule with a view
to the private interest, whether of the one, or of the few, or of the many,
are perversions[b]. For citizens, if they are truly citizens, ought to participate in the advantages of a state. Of forms of government in which one
rules, we call that which regards the common interests, kingship or royalty; that in which more than one, but not many, rule, aristocracy [the rule
of the best]; and it is so called, either because the rulers are the best men,
or because they have at heart the best interests of the state and of the citizens. But when the citizens at large administer the state for the common
interest, the government is called by the generic name,—a constitution
[πολιτεία]. And there is a reason for this use of language. One man or a
few may excel in virtue; but of virtue there are many kinds: and as the
number increases it becomes more difficult for them to attain perfection
in every kind, though they may in military virtue, for this is found in the
masses. Hence, in a constitutional government the fighting-men have the
supreme power, and those who possess arms are the citizens.

Of the above-mentioned forms, the perversions are as follows:—of
royalty, tyranny; of aristocracy, oligarchy; of constitutional government,
democracy. For tyranny is a kind of monarchy which has in view the interest of the monarch only; oligarchy has in view the interest of the
wealthy; democracy, of the needy: none of them the common good of all.

But there are difficulties about these forms of government, and it
will therefore be necessary to state a little more at length the nature of
each of them. For he who would make a philosophical study of the various sciences, and does not regard practice only, ought not to overlook or
omit anything, but to set forth the truth in every particular. Tyranny, as I
was saying, is monarchy exercising the rule of a master over political society; oligarchy is when men of property have the government in their
hands; democracy, the opposite, when the indigent, and not the men of
property, are the rulers. And here arises the first of our difficulties, and it
relates to the definition just given. For democracy is said to be the government of the many. But what if the many are men of property and have
the power in their hands? In like manner oligarchy is said to be the government of the few; but what if the poor are fewer than the rich, and have
the power in their hands because they are stronger? In these cases the
distinction which we have drawn between these different forms of government would no longer hold good.

Suppose, once more, that we add wealth to the few and poverty to
the many, and name the governments accordingly—an oligarchy is said
to be that in which the few and the wealthy, and a democracy that
in which the many and the poor are the rulers—there will still be a

---

(a) The true forms.

3

(I) Royalty, or the rule of one.

III. 7.
(2) Aristoc-racy of a few.

(3) 'Polity' of the citizens at large.

4
1279b.

(But all for the sake of the gov-erned.)

5

(b) The per-versions.
(1) tyranny,
(2) oligarchy,
(3) democ-racy.

8. The divi-sion however must not be made to de-pend merely on a principle of number (quantity).

2

3

III. 8.

4

Wealth and poverty (quantity) must also be considered.

---

[b]Cp. Eth. viii. 10.

difficulty. For, if the only forms of government are the ones already 5 mentioned, how shall we describe those other governments also just mentioned by us, in which the rich are the more numerous and the poor are the fewer, and both govern in their respective states?

The argument seems to show that, whether in oligarchies or in 6 democracies, the number of the governing body, whether the greater number, as in a democracy, or the smaller number, as in an oligarchy, is an accident due to the fact that the rich everywhere are few, and the poor numerous. But if so, there is a misapprehension of the causes of the difference between them. For the real difference between democracy and oligarchy is poverty and wealth. Wherever men rule by reason of their wealth, whether they be few or many, that is an oligarchy, and where the poor rule, that is a democracy. But as a fact the rich are few and the poor many: for few are well-to-do, whereas freedom is enjoyed by all, and wealth and freedom are the grounds on which the oligarchical and demo- 7 cratical parties respectively claim power in the state . . .

The qualitative is the essential and the quantitative the accidental difference, though in fact they generally coincide.

1280a.

But a state exists for the sake of a good life, and not for the sake of 6 life only: if life only were the object, slaves and brute animals might form a state, but they cannot, for they have no share in happiness or in a life of free choice. Nor does a state exist for the sake of alliance and security from injustice[c], nor yet for the sake of exchange and mutual intercourse; for then the Tyrrhenians and the Carthaginians, and all who have commercial treaties with one another, would be the citizens of one state. True, 7 they have agreements about imports, and engagements that they will do no wrong to one another, and written articles of alliance. But there are no magistracies common to the contracting parties who will enforce their engagements; different states have each their own magistracies. Nor does one state take care that the citizens of the other are such as they ought to be, nor see that those who come under the terms of the treaty do no wrong or wickedness at all, but only that they do no injustice to one another. Whereas, those who care for good government take into considera- 8 tion [the larger question of] virtue and vice in states. Whence it may be further inferred that [a]virtue must be the serious care of a state which truly deserves the name[a]: for [without this ethical end] the community becomes a mere alliance which differs only in place from alliances of which the members live apart; and law is only a convention, 'a surety to one another of justice,' as the sophist Lycophron says, and has no real power to make the citizens good and just . . . It is clear then that a state is 12 not a mere society, having a common place, established for the prevention of crime and for the sake of exchange. These are conditions without which a state cannot exist; but all of them together do not constitute a state, which is a community of well-being in families and aggregations of

III. 9.
1280 b.

It is more than a mere alliance designed for the protection of life and property.

but much more than these, viz, a community of well-being.

[c]Cp. c. I. § 4.

families, for the sake of a perfect and self-sufficing life. Such a community can only be established among those who live in the same place and
13 intermarry. Hence arise in cities family connexions, brotherhoods, common sacrifices, amusements which draw men together. They are created by friendship, for friendship is the motive of society. The end is the good
14 life, and these are the means towards it. And the state is the union of fam-
1281 a. ilies and villages having for an end a perfect and self-sufficing life, by which we mean a happy and honourable life[a].

15 Our conclusion, then, is that political society exists for the sake of noble actions, and not of mere companionship. And they who contribute most to such a society have a greater share in it than those who have the same or a greater freedom or nobility of birth but are inferior to them in political virtue; or than those who exceed them in wealth but are surpassed by them in virtue.

Those who contribute most to such a society have the greatest claim to power.

From what has been said it will be clearly seen that all the partisans of different forms of government speak of a part of justice only.

10. Who are to have supreme power?

There is also a doubt as to what is to be the supreme power in the state:—Is it the multitude? Or the wealthy? Or the good? Or the one best man? Or a tyrant? Any of these alternatives seems to involve disagreeable consequences. If the poor, for example, because they are more in

III.10. number, divide among themselves the property of the rich,—is not this
2 unjust? No, by heaven (will be the reply), for the lawful authority [i.e. the

Difficulties: any class having the power may act unjustly; is its authority to be deemed just?

people] willed it. But if this is not injustice, pray what is? Again, when [in the first division] all has been taken, and the majority divide anew the property of the minority, is it not evident, if this goes on, that they will ruin the state? Yet surely, virtue is not the ruin of those who possess her, nor is justice destructive of a state[a]; and therefore this law of confiscation clearly cannot be just. If it were, all the acts of a tyrant must of necessity be just; for he only coerces other men by superior power, just as the mul-
3 titude coerce the rich. But is it just then that the few and the wealthy should be the rulers? And what if they, in like manner, rob and plunder
4 the people,—is this just? If so, the other case [i.e. the case of the majority plundering the minority] will likewise be just. But there can be no doubt

The rule of the good men will exclude the other citizens.

that all these things are wrong and unjust.

Then ought the good to rule and have supreme power? But in that case everybody else, being excluded from power, will be dishonoured. For the offices of a state are posts of honour; and if one set of men always
5 hold them, the rest must be deprived of them. Then will it be well that the one best man should rule? Nay, that is still more oligarchical, for the number of those who are dishonoured is thereby increased. Some one may say that it is bad for a man, subject as he is to all the accidents of

---

[a]Cp. i. 2. § 8; N. Eth. i. 7. § 6.
[a]Cp. Plato Rep. i. 351, 352.

human passion, to have the supreme power, rather than the law. But Even the rule
what if the law itself be democratical or oligarchical, how will that help of the law
us out of our difficulties[b]? Not at all; the same consequences will follow. may only represent a party.

Most of these questions may be reserved for another occasion. The 11.
principle that the multitude ought to be supreme rather than the few best III. 11. Why
is capable of a satisfactory explanation, and, though not free from diffi- the many should have
culty, yet seems to contain an element of truth. For the many, of whom power. They
each individual is but an ordinary person, when they meet together may are wiser
very likely be better than the few good, if regarded not individually but than any one man,
collectively, just as a feast to which many contribute is better than a dinner provided out of a single purse. For each individual among the many
has a share of virtue and prudence, and when they meet together they be- 2
come in a manner one man, who has many feet, and hands, and senses; 1281 b.
that is a figure of their mind and disposition. Hence the many are better
judges than a single man of music and poetry; for some understand one 3
part, and some another, and among them, they understand the whole.
There is a similar combination of qualities in good men, who differ from 4
any individual of the many, as the beautiful are said to differ from those
who are not beautiful, and works of art from realities, because in them
the scattered elements are combined, although, if taken separately, the
eye of one person or some other feature in another person would be
fairer than in the picture. Whether this principle can apply to every 5
democracy, and to all bodies of men, is not clear . . .

. . . Let us begin by determining (1)[a] how many varieties of states 4
there are (since of democracy and oligarchy there are several); (2)[b] what A new begin-
constitution is the most generally acceptable, and what is eligible in ning: Ques-
the next degree[c] after the perfect or any other aristocratical and well- tions to be discussed.
constituted form of government—if any other there be—which is at the
same time adapted to states in general[c]; (3)[d] of the other forms of government to whom is each suited. For democracy may meet the needs of
some better than oligarchy, and conversely. In the next place (4)[e] we have 5
to consider in what manner a man ought to proceed who desires to establish some one among these various forms whether of democracy or of oligarchy; and lastly, (5)[f] having briefly discussed these subjects to the best 6

---

[b]Cp. c. II. § 20.

[a]C. 4–6.

[b]C. 7–9 and 11.

[c]Or: 'after the perfect state; and besides this what other there is which is aristocratical and
well constituted, and at the same time adapted to states in general.'

[d]C. 12.

[e]Book vi.

[f]Book v.

of our power, we will endeavour to ascertain whence arise the ruin and preservation of states, both generally and in individual cases, and to what causes they are to be attributed.

3. Forms of government differ because states are made up of various elements.

The reason why there are many forms of government is that every state contains many elements. In the first place we see that all states are made up of families, and in the multitude of citizens there must be some rich and some poor, and some in a middle condition; [g]the rich are heavy-armed, and the poor not[g]. Of the common people, some are husbandmen, and some traders, and some artisans. There are also among the notables

There are differences of occupation, wealth,

differences of wealth and property—for example, in the number of horses which they keep, for they cannot afford to keep them unless they are rich. And therefore in old times the cities whose strength lay in their cavalry were oligarchies, and they used cavalry in wars[a] against their

2 neighbours; as was the practice of the Eretrians and Chalcidians, and also
3 of the Magnesians on the river Mæander, and of other peoples in Asia.

IV. 3. Besides differences of wealth there are differences of rank and merit, and
4 there are some other elements which were mentioned by us when in

rank, treating of aristocracy we enumerated the essentials of a state[b]. Of these

merit. elements, sometimes all, sometimes the lesser and sometimes the greater

1290 a. number, have a share in the government. It is evident then that there
5 must be many forms of government, differing in kind, since the parts of which they are composed differ from each other in kind. For a constitution is an organization of offices which all the citizens distribute among themselves, according to the power which different classes possess, for example the rich or the poor, or according to some principle of compen-
6 sation which includes both. There must therefore be as many forms of government as there are modes of arranging the offices, according to the superiorities and other inequalities of the different parts of the state.

Two generally reputed types, oligarchy and democracy.

There are generally thought to be two principal forms: as men say of the winds that there are but two—north and south, and that the rest of them are only variations of these, so of governments there are said to be only two forms—democracy and oligarchy. For aristocracy is considered

7 to be a kind of oligarchy, as being the rule of a few, and the so-called constitutional government to be really a democracy, just as among the winds we make the west a variation of the north, and the east of the south wind. Similarly of harmonies there are said to be two kinds, the Dorian and the Phrygian; the other arrangements of the scale are comprehended under

8 one of these two. About forms of government this is a very favourite

---

[g]Or: 'and again both of rich and poor some are armed and some are unarmed.'

[a]Reading either πολέμους with v. tr. (Moerbek) and Bekk. 2nd edit., or πολεμίους with the Greek MSS; cp. c. 13. § 10; vi. c. 7. § 1.

[b]Not in what has preceded, but cp. vii. 8.

notion. But in either case the better and more exact way is to distinguish, as I have done, the one or two which are true forms, and to regard the others as perversions, whether of the most perfectly attempered harmony or of the best form of government: we may compare the oligarchical forms to the severer and more overpowering modes, and the democratic to the more relaxed and gentler ones.

IV. 3. But our classification is more precise.

Study Questions

1. How does Aristotle define a tyranny, and in what way is it a deterioration of royalty?
2. How does Aristotle define an aristocracy, and how is oligarchy a perversion of it?
3. Democracy is described as a form of government in which the many and the poor are rulers. Why does Aristotle consider this to be a bad thing? What would be an advantageous form?
4. What is the purpose of the state or political society?
5. Would you agree that different governments suit different societies, or do you think there is an ideal form of government for human beings in general?

Brave New World (Chapter II)
Aldous Huxley

Aldous Huxley (1894–1963) was a British novelist who is best known for his futuristic novel Brave New World, *but is also celebrated for such works as* Crome Yellow, Antic Hay, *and* Point Counter Point, *which are clever, urbane, and outrageously comical. In his later years he wrote* The Perennial Philosophy, *a serious study strongly influenced by Hindu and mystical thought;* The Doors of Perception, *dealing with the hallucinogenic drug mescalin; and* Island, *a utopian novel which contrasts sharply with his earlier pessimistic vision.*

Huxley styled himself a "Pyrrhonic aesthete" who was merely amused by the direction the world was taking, but it is difficult to see only detachment and not censure in his writings. In Brave New World, *a chapter of which appears below, Huxley portrays the insidious process of psychological conditioning that molds human behavior; in the society depicted it is used as a deliberate political device.*

Mr. Foster was left in the Decanting Room. The D.H.C. and his students stepped into the nearest lift and were carried up to the fifth floor.

INFANT NURSERIES. NEO-PAVLOVIAN CONDITIONING ROOMS, announced the notice board.

The Director opened a door. They were in a large bare room, very bright and sunny; for the whole of the southern wall was a single window. Half a dozen nurses, trousered and jacketed in the regulation white viscose-linen uniform, their hair aseptically hidden under white caps, were engaged in setting out bowls of roses in a long row across the floor. Big bowls, packed tight with blossom. Thousands of petals, ripeblown and silkily smooth, like the cheeks of innumerable little cherubs, but of cherubs, in that bright light, not exclusively pink and Aryan, but also luminously Chinese, also Mexican, also apoplectic with too much blowing of celestial trumpets, also pale as death, pale with the posthumous whiteness of marble.

The nurses stiffened to attention as the D.H.C. came in.

"Set out the books," he said curtly.

In silence the nurses obeyed his command. Between the rose bowls the books were duly set out—a row of nursery quartos opened invitingly each at some gaily coloured image of beast or fish or bird.

"Now bring in the children."

They hurried out of the room and returned in a minute or two, each pushing a kind of tall dumbwaiter laden, on all its four wire-netted shelves, with eight-month-old-babies, all exactly alike (a Bokanovsky Group, it was evident) and all (since their caste was Delta) dressed in khaki.

"Put them down on the floor."

The infants were unloaded.

"Now turn them so that they can see the flowers and books."

Turned, the babies at once fell silent, then began to crawl towards those clusters of sleek colours, those shapes so gay and brilliant on the white pages. As they approached, the sun came out of a momentary eclipse behind a cloud. The roses flamed up as though with a sudden passion from within; a new and profound significance seemed to suffuse the shining pages of the books. From the ranks of the crawling babies came little squeals of excitement, gurgles and twitterings of pleasure.

The Director rubbed his hands. "Excellent!" he said. "It might almost have been done on purpose."

The swiftest crawlers were already at their goal. Small hands reached out uncertainly, touched, grasped, unpetaling the transfigured roses, crumpling the illuminated pages of the books. The Director waited until all were happily busy. Then, "Watch carefully," he said. And, lifting his hand, he gave the signal.

The Head Nurse, who was standing by a switchboard at the other end of the room, pressed down a little lever.

There was a violent explosion. Shriller and ever shriller, a siren shrieked. Alarm bells maddeningly sounded.

The children started, screamed; their faces were distorted with terror.

"And now," the Director shouted (for the noise was deafening), "now we proceed to rub in the lesson with a mild electric shock."

He waved his hand again, and the Head Nurse pressed a second lever. The screaming of the babies suddenly changed its tone. There was something desperate, almost insane, about the sharp spasmodic yelps to which they now gave utterance. Their little bodies twitched and stiffened; their limbs moved jerkily as if to the tug of unseen wires.

"We can electrify that whole strip of floor," bawled the Director in explanation. "But that's enough," he signalled to the nurse.

The explosions ceased, the bells stopped ringing, the shriek of the siren died down from tone to tone into silence. The stiffly twitching bodies relaxed, and what had become the sob and yelp of infant maniacs broadened out once more into a normal howl of ordinary terror.

"Offer them the flowers and the books again."

The nurses obeyed; but at the approach of the roses, at the mere sight of those gaily-coloured images of pussy and cock-a-doodle-doo and baa-baa black sheep, the infants shrank away in horror; the volume of their howling suddenly increased.

"Observe," said the Director triumphantly, "observe."

Books and loud noises, flowers and electric shocks—already in the infant mind these couples were compromisingly linked; and after two hundred repetitions of the same or a similar lesson would be wedded indissolubly. What man has joined, nature is powerless to put asunder.

"They'll grow up with what the psychologists used to call an 'instinctive' hatred of books and flowers. Reflexes unalterably conditioned. They'll be safe from books and botany all their lives." The Director turned to his nurses. "Take them away again."

Still yelling, the khaki babies were loaded on to their dumb-waiters and wheeled out, leaving behind them the smell of sour milk and a most welcome silence.

One of the students held up his hand; and though he could see quite well why you couldn't have the lower-caste people wasting the Community's time over books, and that there was always the risk of their reading something which might undesirably decondition one of their reflexes, yet . . . well, he couldn't understand about the flowers. Why go to the trouble of making it psychologically impossible for Deltas to like flowers?

Patiently the D.H.C. explained. If the children were made to scream at the sight of a rose, that was on grounds of high economic policy. Not so very long ago (a century or thereabouts), Gammas, Deltas, even Epsilons, had been conditioned to like flowers—flowers in particular and wild nature in general. The idea was to make them want to be going out into the country at every available opportunity, and so compel them to consume transport.

"And didn't they consume transport?" asked the student.

"Quite a lot," the D.H.C. replied. "But nothing else."

Primroses and landscapes, he pointed out, have one grave defect: they are gratuitous. A love of nature keeps no factories busy. It was decided to abolish the love of nature, at any rate among the lower classes; to abolish the love of nature, but *not* the tendency to consume transport. For of course it was essential that they should keep on going to the country, even though they hated it. The problem was to find an economically sounder reason for consuming transport than a mere affection for primroses and landscapes. It was duly found.

"We condition the masses to hate the country," concluded the Director. "But simultaneously we condition them to love all country sports. At the same time, we see to it that all country sports shall entail the use of elaborate apparatus. So that they consume manufactured articles as well as transport. Hence those electric shocks."

"I see," said the student, and was silent, lost in admiration.

There was a silence; then, clearing his throat, "Once upon a time," the Director began, "while our Ford was still on earth, there was a little boy called Reuben Rabinovitch. Reuben was the child of Polish-speaking parents." The Director interrupted himself. "You know what Polish is, I suppose?"

"A dead language."

"Like French and German," added another student, officiously showing off his learning.

"And 'parent'?" questioned the D.H.C.

There was an uneasy silence. Several of the boys blushed. They had not yet learned to draw the significant but often very fine distinction between smut and pure science. One, at last, had the courage to raise a hand.

"Human beings used to be . . ." he hesitated; the blood rushed to his cheeks. "Well, they used to be viviparous."

"Quite right." The Director nodded approvingly.

"And when the babies were decanted . . ."

"'Born'," came the correction.

"Well, then they were the parents—I mean, not the babies, of course; the other ones." The poor boy was overwhelmed with confusion.

"In brief," the Director summed up, "the parents were the father and the mother." The smut that was really science fell with a crash into the boys' eye-avoiding silence. "Mother," he repeated loudly rubbing in the science; and, leaning back in his chair, "These," he said gravely, "are unpleasant facts; I know it. But then most historical facts *are* unpleasant."

He returned to Little Reuben—to Little Reuben, in whose room, one evening, by an oversight, his father and mother (crash, crash!) happened to leave the radio turned on.

("For you must remember that in those days of gross viviparous reproduction, children were always brought up by their parents and not in State Conditioning Centres.")

While the child was asleep, a broadcast programme from London suddenly started to come through; and the next morning, to the astonishment of his crash and crash (the more daring of the boys ventured to grin at one another), Little Reuben woke up repeating word for word a long lecture by that curious old writer ("one of the very few whose works have been permitted to come down to us"), George Bernard Shaw, who was speaking, according to a well-authenticated tradition, about his own genius. To Little Reuben's wink and snigger, this lecture was, of course, perfectly incomprehensible and, imagining that their child had suddenly gone mad, they sent for a doctor. He, fortunately, understood English, recognized the discourse as that which Shaw had broadcasted the previous evening, realized the significance of what had happened, and sent a letter to the medical press about it.

"The principle of sleep-teaching, or hypnopædia, had been discovered." The D.H.C. made an impressive pause.

The principle had been discovered; but many, many years were to elapse before that principle was usefully applied.

"The case of Little Reuben occurred only twenty-three years after Our Ford's first T-Model was put on the market." (Here the Director made a sign of the T on his stomach and all the students reverently followed suit.) "And yet . . ."

Furiously the students scribbled. *"Hypnopædia, first used officially in A.F. 214. Why not before? Two reasons. (a) . . ."*

"These early experimenters," the D.H.C. was saying, "were on the wrong track. They thought that hypnopædia could be made an instrument of intellectual education . . ."

(A small boy asleep on his right side, the right arm stuck out, the right hand hanging limp over the edge of the bed. Through a round grating in the side of a box a voice speaks softly.

"The Nile is the longest river in Africa and the second in length of all the rivers of the globe. Although falling short of the length of the Mississippi-Missouri, the Nile is at the head of all rivers as regards the length of its basin, which extends through 35 degrees of latitude . . ."

At breakfast the next morning, "Tommy," some one says, "do you know which is the longest river in Africa?" A shaking of the head. "But don't you remember something that begins: The Nile is the . . ."

"The - Nile - is - the - longest - river - in - Africa - and - the - second - in - length - of - all - the - rivers - of - the - globe . . ." The words come rushing out. "Although - falling - short - of . . ."

"Well now, which is the longest river in Africa?"

The eyes are blank. "I don't know."

"But the Nile, Tommy."

"The - Nile - is - the - longest - river - in - Africa - and - second . . ."

"Then which river is the longest, Tommy?"

Tommy bursts into tears. "I don't know," he howls.)

That howl, the Director made it plain, discouraged the earliest investigators. The experiments were abandoned. No further attempt was made to teach children the length of the Nile in their sleep. Quite rightly. You can't learn a science unless you know what it's all about.

"Whereas, if they'd only started on *moral* education," said the Director, leading the way towards the door. The students followed him, desperately scribbling as they walked and all the way up in the lift. "Moral education, which ought never, in any circumstances, to be rational."

"Silence, silence," whispered a loud speaker as they stepped out at the fourteenth floor, and "Silence, silence," the trumpet mouths indefatigably repeated at intervals down every corridor. The students and even the Director himself rose automatically to the tips of their toes. They were Alphas, of course; but even Alphas have been well conditioned. "Silence, silence." All the air of the fourteenth floor was sibilant with the categorical imperative.

Fifty yards of tiptoeing brought them to a door which the Director cautiously opened. They stepped over the threshold into the twilight of a shuttered dormitory. Eighty cots stood in a row against the wall. There was a sound of light regular breathing and a continuous murmur, as of very faint voices remotely whispering.

A nurse rose as they entered and came to attention before the Director.

"What's the lesson this afternoon?" he asked.

"We had Elementary Sex for the first forty minutes," she answered. "But now it's switched over to Elementary Class Consciousness."

The Director walked slowly down the long line of cots. Rosy and relaxed with sleep, eighty little boys and girls lay softly breathing. There was a whisper under every pillow. The D.H.C. halted and, bending over one of the little beds, listened attentively.

"Elementary Class Consciousness, did you say? Let's have it repeated a little louder by the trumpet."

At the end of the room a loud speaker projected from the wall. The Director walked up to it and pressed a switch.

". . . all wear green," said a soft but very distinct voice, beginning in the middle of a sentence, "and Delta Children wear khaki. Oh no, I don't want to play with Delta children. And Epsilons are still worse. They're too stupid to be able to read or write. Besides, they wear black, which is such a beastly colour. I'm *so* glad I'm a Beta."

There was a pause; then the voice began again.

"Alpha children wear grey. They work much harder than we do, because they're so frightfully clever. I'm really awfully glad I'm a Beta, because I don't work so hard. And then we are much better than the Gammas and Deltas. Gammas are stupid. They all wear green, and Delta children wear khaki. Oh no, I *don't* want to play with Delta children. And Epsilons are still worse. They're too stupid to be able . . ."

The Director pushed back the switch. The voice was silent. Only its thin ghost continued to mutter from beneath the eighty pillows.

"They'll have that repeated forty or fifty times more before they wake; then again on Thursday, and again on Saturday. A hundred and twenty times three times a week for thirty months. After which they go on to a more advanced lesson."

Roses and electric shocks, the khaki of Deltas and a whiff of asafœtida wedded indissolubly before the child can speak. But wordless conditioning is crude and wholesale; cannot bring home the finer distinctions, cannot inculcate the more complex courses of behaviour. For that there must be words, but words without reason. In brief, hypnopædia.

"The greatest moralizing and socializing force of all time."

The students took it down in their little books. Straight from the horse's mouth.

Once more the Director touched the switch.

". . . so frightfully clever," the soft, insinuating, indefatigable voice was saying.

"I'm really awfully glad I'm a Beta, because . . ."

Not so much like drops of water, though water, it is true, can wear holes in the hardest granite; rather, drops of liquid sealing-wax, drops that adhere, incrust, incorporate themselves with what they fall on, till finally the rock is all one scarlet blob.

"Till at last the child's mind *is* these suggestions, and the sum of the suggestions *is* the child's mind. And not the child's mind only. The adult's mind too—all his life long. The mind that judges and desires and decides—made up of these suggestions. But all these suggestions are *our* suggestions!" The Director almost shouted in his triumph. "Suggestions from the State." He banged the nearest table. "It therefore follows . . ."

A noise made him turn round.

"Oh, Ford!" he said in another tone, "I've gone and woken the children."

Study Questions

1. In trying to create a Utopian society, wouldn't it be desirable to create different types of people to perform various types of job using genetic engineering? Wouldn't it also be desirable to condition them to perform those jobs happily and efficiently?
2. Why are the children being conditioned to avoid books and flowers?
3. What do the limitations on sleep learning indicate about the human mind?
4. Are we conditioned to dislike people of a higher or lower class, and to prefer those in our own class? How does our society stream people into different occupations?
5. What essential elements are missing from this ideal society?

Born on the Fourth of July

Director: Oliver Stone

Screenwriters: Ron Kovic and Oliver Stone

Oliver Stone (1946–) is a celebrated director and screenwriter who has presented controversial interpretations of major events in twentieth-century America. He has won three Academy Awards, one for Midnight Express *as best screenplay, and two as best director for* Platoon *and* Born on the Fourth of July. *The latter two films were based on Stone's own experience of combat during the Vietnam War. Stone also wrote the screenplays for* Conan the Barbarian, Scarface, Year of the Dragon, *and* 8 Million Ways to Die.

Among the more provocative films he directed are Salvador, *that criticizes American involvement in Central America, and* JFK, *that portrays the Kennedy assassination as the result of a conspiracy between the government and intelligence communities.* JFK *provoked a national debate on the responsibility for Kennedy's death and whether Stone had the right to present his theory as a quasi-documentary. His more recent films,* Heaven and Earth, *the third in his Vietnam trilogy, and* Natural Born Killers, *about America's fascination with serial killers, received less attention.*

Born on the Fourth of July is based on the best-selling autobiography of Ron Kovic, who collaborated with Stone on the screenplay. Like the protagonist in the film, Kovic came home from Vietnam paralyzed from the chest down, underwent a metamorphosis in his attitude toward the war, was thrown out of the 1972 Republican convention (with his wheelchair), and addressed the Democratic national convention in 1976.

Synopsis

The question of (1) rebellion and revolution, and (2) dissent and disobedience is one that should be addressed in deciding on the structure of an ideal state. When citizens disagree with their government, are they still obligated to carry out its mandates, even when it means endangering their lives? On what grounds can states require citizens to support the government and to obey laws that are unjust? Can states force their people to fight in wars that they oppose?

(1) The first question, that of rebellion (open, organized and armed resistance to a government) and revolution (a forcible overthrow and replacement of a government), has arisen at various points in world history. In the United States, we agonized especially over the Revolutionary War, the Civil War, and the Vietnam War. *Born on the Fourth of July* deals with the last, of course, which was a particularly bitter crisis in our society.

At that time, between the mid-60s and 70s, dissidents began thinking the unthinkable: the violent overthrow of the United States government.

The broad issue in political philosophy is whether and when citizens can use violence against their government. As mentioned in the introduction, Hobbes argues in *The Leviathan* (1651) that the state demands absolute submission to its laws, so that neither rebellion nor revolution is ever justified. When societies were first formed, people surrendered such power to a supreme ruler in exchange for protection from each other's aggression. In a state of nature constant warfare takes place, so people pledge their loyalty to this sovereign who maintains the peace. The sovereign rules in accordance with divine law and as required by man's selfish and violent nature.

His contemporary, John Locke in his *Second Treatise of Government (1689)*, takes an opposite position with regard to the state of nature and the foundation of government. To Locke, human beings are naturally peaceable and possess inherent rights. They enter into a social contract to safeguard those rights, especially property and religion. The government they establish exists by the consent of the governed and fosters the people's mutual interests. If that trust in government is broken, then people can legitimately revolt. Ultimately, it is not the state but the people who retain sovereignty, and they can remove officials or change the government if their rights are violated.

Whenever nations are in civil turmoil the question arises as to who is correct: Hobbes or Locke. Governments will often suppress revolts in the name of authority and law and order, while the opposition will argue that an uprising is appropriate and necessary for the sake of social justice. In recent history China put down a demonstration in Tiananmen Square in Beijing, declaring all dissent illegal; about seven thousand people were shot to death. In our own country, the National Guard fired on students at Kent State University who were protesting the Vietnam War, killing four and wounding nine. The numbers are relatively small, but the nation was shocked that U.S. troops had killed college students to quell a demonstration. (In the war itself over fifty-eight thousand Americans were killed.) Can civil protests be allowed, including outright rebellion, opposing the authority of the state?

(2) The related issue of dissent (expressed political differences in doctrine or opinion) and disobedience (refusal to comply with governmental rules) is less severe but equally vexing. The first philosophic discussion of this issue occurs in the *Crito*, a Platonic dialogue in which Socrates discourses about right and wrong while awaiting execution. Socrates had been accused of corrupting the youth, unfairly convicted, and sentenced to death by drinking poison (hemlock). One of his followers, Crito, urges him to escape from prison, arguing that he would not want to lose a cherished friend and that people would blame him for not bribing the guards, thinking he did not care for Socrates enough. He also

argues that if Socrates allowed himself to be executed he would play into the hands of his enemies and, furthermore, abandon his children, leaving them orphans.

Socrates questions Crito in his customary way to determine whether escaping from prison would be right. By doing so he would be opposing the court's ruling, and he wonders whether citizens have a debt of loyalty to the state, even when they disagree with its decisions. Should we be faithful only when we obtain benefits and not when the state's laws go against us?

> SOC. Then consider the matter in this way: Imagine that I am about to play truant (you may call the proceeding by any name which you like), and the laws and the government come and interrogate me: "Tell us, Socrates," they say; "what are you about? are you going by an act of yours to overturn us—the laws and the whole State, as far as in you lies? Do you imagine that a State can subsist and not be overthrown, in which the decisions of law have no power, but are set aside and overthrown by individuals?" What will be our answer, Crito, to these and the like words? Anyone, and especially a clever rhetorician, will have a good deal to urge about the evil of setting aside the law which requires a sentence to be carried out; and we might reply, "Yes; but the State has injured us and given an unjust sentence." Suppose I say that?
>
> CR. Very good, Socrates.
>
> SOC. "And was that our agreement with you?" the law would say, "or were you to abide by the sentence of the State?" And if I were to express astonishment at their saying this, the law would probably add: "Answer, Socrates, instead of opening your eyes: you are in the habit of asking and answering questions. Tell us what complaint you have to make against us which justifies you in attempting to destroy us and the State? In the first place did we not bring you into existence? Your father married your mother by our aid and begat you. Say whether you have any objection to urge against those of us who regulate marriage?" None, I should reply. "Or against those of us who regulate the system of nurture and education of children in which you were trained? . . . And because we think right to destroy you, do you think that you have any right to destroy us in return, and your country as far as in you lies? And will you, O professor of true virtue, say that you are justified in this? Has a philosopher like you failed to discover that our country is more to be valued and higher and holier far than mother or father or any ancestor, and more to be regarded in the eyes of the gods and of men of understanding? also to be soothed, and gently and reverently entreated

when angry, even more than a father, and if not persuaded, obeyed? And when we are punished by her, whether with imprisonment or stripes, the punishment is to be endured in silence; and if she leads us to wounds or death in battle, thither we follow as is right; neither may anyone yield or retreat or leave his rank, but whether in battle or in a court of law, or in any other place, he must do what his city and his country order him; or he must change their view of what is just: and if he may do no violence to his father or mother, much less may he do violence to his country." What answer shall we make to this, Crito? Do the laws speak truly, or do they not?

CR. I think that they do.

SOC. Then the laws will say: "Consider, Socrates, if this is true, that in your present attempt you are going to do us wrong. For, after having brought you into the world, and nurtured and educated you, and given you and every other citizen a share in every good that we had to give, we further proclaim and give the right to every Athenian, that if he does not like us when he has come of age and has seen the ways of the city, and made our acquaintance, he may go where he pleases and take his goods with him; and none of us laws will forbid him or interfere with him. Any of you who does not like us and the city, and who wants to go to a colony or to any other city, may go where he likes, and take his goods with him. But he who has experience of the manner in which we order justice and administer the State, and still remains, has entered into an implied contract that he will do as we command him. . . .*

Socrates' position may be persuasive but it might also be questionable. He opposes escaping and affirms his loyalty to the state based on three arguments: that by not leaving Athens previously he had tacitly promised to obey the state's laws; that he has a debt of gratitude toward the state for the benefits it conferred upon him; and that the consequences would be disastrous if citizens refused to obey the law.

Each of these points can be challenged. In terms of the first argument, that of a tacit promise, the fact that people remain in a country does not mean that its laws are just or that they thereby consent to obey all of them. There can be a loyal opposition that refuses to follow those laws it considers unjust. This is not necessarily traitorous since one wants for unfair laws to be revoked and to be proud of one's country. "Love it or leave it" is therefore a thoughtless slogan; people may choose to remain in the country they love and work to improve it.

*Translation: Benjamin Jowett.

As for the second argument of gratitude, citizens are not necessarily indebted to the state for benefits they receive, and may not be required to repay them. If someone gives you a gift, that does not always place you under a moral obligation to them, especially if you never asked for the gift, it was a general benefit to others beside yourself, and it advances the interests of the giver. You certainly do not have any debt of gratitude if the gift is something to which you have a right. In fact, if you deserve it anyway, it ceases to be a gift and becomes an entitlement.

The privileges of marriage, nurture, and education that Socrates refers to may be rights of citizens along with health, liberty, life, and property. Perhaps the state safeguards such rights rather than conferring them, and people should not be grateful for that which is due to them.

The third argument, that the state would collapse if its citizens disobeyed the laws, is an argument from utility. To allow people to disobey laws, it is argued, would be "the thin edge of the wedge," a first step on "the long slippery slope" toward anarchy. However, Socrates is not fomenting a general revolution, and if some people at some times oppose some laws, that would not be a serious threat to the state. In fact, if a country's bad laws are changed in response to protests, that could increase people's satisfaction with the government and strengthen its hand. Furthermore, if citizens protest openly, they are not engaging in criminal actions that undermine the state but using public, democratic methods to stimulate discussion about the merits of a law. Freedom of speech and assembly seems a healthy means for bringing about change.

In the *Apology*, Socrates' compares himself to a gadfly that stings the sluggish horse of society into awareness. Perhaps his metaphor can be used against him in this context. If the horse is sound, the sting will just stimulate him or, at worst, be a nuisance. Only the unhealthy horse is threatened by the gadfly—the unsound state that cannot survive criticism.

Based on such considerations, many people throughout history have defied their government's laws, and this issue furnishes the philosophic context for *Born on the Fourth of July*. The setting is the controversial Vietnam War (1965–75) and its attendant protest movements and civil disobedience in the United States. The war provoked anti-war demonstrations all across the country, and there were equally passionate pro-war sentiments by "the silent majority." The nation was divided, bitter, and confused, with sentiments running high both for and against our involvment. The government was determined to win the war, even if that meant deforesting combat zones, using napalm, and giving dubious information to the public about our successes (e.g., body counts).

Meanwhile the American people were growing increasingly uneasy about our warrant for being in Vietnam. Was it really necessary to risk injury or death to our sons in an internal conflict in a foreign country? Was it in our national interest to stop communism in southeast Asia before the "domino effect" brought it to our shores? The cost in human suffering was horrendous, televised for all the nation to see, and people questioned whether the carnage should include civilians, which seemed contrary to American values.

Above all, the country struggled with the question of whether the war was just, and whether opposition to it was disloyal or a higher patriotism. Should young men escape to Canada to avoid the draft? Would that be an act of cowardice and desertion or a courageous act of conscience and good sense? Should we dissociate ourselves from shameful acts by our nation or say "my country right or wrong"? Where does patriotism end and blind obedience begin? People also wondered how much dissent a democracy can tolerate, and when elected leaders should defer to the will of the electorate.

Born on the Fourth of July tells the particular story of Ron Kovic who fought in Vietnam and returned paralyzed from the chest down; his experiences are recounted in his autobiography, and he collaborated with Oliver Stone in writing the screenplay. However, the film functions as a general metaphor for the experience of the country. At first, America was enthusiastic about the war, then wounded and crippled by it, and finally conflicted, disillusioned, and, in varying degrees, repentant. Although the nation never apologized for the youth it sacrificed, its artists did.

At the start of the film, we see Ron Kovic (Tom Cruise) trying to decide whether to enlist in the marines and fight in Vietnam. As a teenager, raised in a small town and nourished by values of family, God, and country, he is strongly attracted to the prospect of combat, especially as a marine, the emblem of toughness and masculinity. Like most boys, Ron regards war as the crucible of courage, and he is eager to prove himself a man, establish a mature identity, and come back a celebrated hero. The marine recruiter (Tom Berenger) plays into such feelings and, by being ambivalent, his parents (Raymond Barry and Caroline Kava) encourage him to enlist by default. In his search for guidance, Ron turns to God in prayer, but even He seems to remain silent.

INT. LIVINGROOM

MOM in the bedroom, DAD watching the news, a newspaper in hand, dozing, exhausted from work. Waking now as RONNIE shuffles in, watching the NEWS CLIP—an Infantry COLONEL is being interviewed at a base camp someplace, TROOPS moving or convoying in the background; shades on his eyes, a green baseball cap over close-cropped hair, a revolver in his shoulder holster, thick forearms:

COLONEL: . . . no question 'bout that. The 82nd Airborne and the First Cavalry Division are the newest concepts in mobile warfare. One division is worth about 2½ Russian and six Chinese divisions . . .

NEWSMAN: But how well do you think the individual soldier will hold up in Vietnam, Colonel?

COLONEL: I've never seen anything like it. I been in World War II—in Korea, these boys—they're gung ho, they wanna eat nails—the finest combat troops we've ever had! It's an honor to lead them.

RONNIE has sat down facing his DAD. A pause between them.

RONNIE: What do you think, Dad—about that?

NEWSCASTER: Do you think, Colonel, the war here will be over soon?

DAD: Oh . . . I don't know—13,000 miles—it's a long way to go to fight a war—

COLONEL: Well, that's a hard question to answer. But without being overconfident, I'd say at the outside, yes—about a year—Course it's a guerilla war so you can't force . . .

RONNIE: But if we give them Vietnam, they'll take the rest. That's the way they are. It's the domino theory, Dad. They'll nibble us up piece by piece. We gotta stop them someplace.

NEWSCASTER: But do you think these people—the Viet Cong—who've fought the Japanese and the French and lived in these caves and tunnels for thirty years—do you really think Colonel . . .

DAD (sighs): Maybe . . . I just hope they send you to Europe or Korea or someplace safe . . .

COLONEL: I think that anything that lives in a tunnel can be weeded out. It takes time and patience, and the support of the people back home—and the support of the press—

RONNIE: They can't Dad! They gotta send me to Vietnam for 13 months, that's the way it is—

NEWSCASTER: Colonel, do you mean . . . the Press is not . . .

DAD: Well, maybe they'll put you on garrison duty someplace . . . an embassy?

RONNIE: Yeah, but they *won't* Dad! Every Marine has a tour over there, it's not like the Army (stronger now) What's *wrong* with everybody around here? Don't you remember what President Kennedy said, Dad, we're not gonna have an America anymore unless there's people willing to sacrifice. I love my country, Dad.

MOM has come out into the livingroom.

DAD: I know Ronnie, I know.

COLONEL: I mean that . . . an important part in this war effort . . . is the attitude of the home front . . .

ANOTHER ANGLE—DAD doesn't want to think about it, looks away. RONNIE deeper in frame is exasperated—this mute climate, this failure to beat a drum on the home front, this early silence and sadness about the war . . .

> MOM: It's your decision Ronnie, it's up to you whatever you de-
> cide, we're behind you. We'll pray for you Ronnie but you be
> careful.
> NEWSCASTER: We . . . we all know . . .

She tries to kiss him on the cheek but RON'S eyes are unsatisfied,
on his DAD.

> RONNIE: Dad, do you understand what it means to me to be a Ma-
> rine? Ever since I've been a kid, Dad, I've wanted this, I've
> wanted to help my country. (pause, the rain) . . . and I wanna go.
> I wanna go to Vietnam. I'll *die* if I have to over there . . .
> COLONEL: . . . remember one thing now. Up in Hanoi they don't
> allow newpapers and televisions to cast any doubts on the . . .
> system—the military system.

The silence. Why is life so anti-climactic at moments like this and
words mean nothing?

> DAD: Not a nice night for the prom . . .
> NEWSCASTER: Well, I . . .
> COLONEL: . . . and it seems to me sometimes we forget that.
> NEWSCASTER: Well, Colonel the basic question is do you think the
> South Vietnamese Government is a viable political entity that can
> stand up to . . .
> COLONEL: If we didn't think so we wouldn't be here now would
> we—(Chopper starts coming in overhead, drowning out sound)

INT. RON'S BEDROOM/BATH/HALL—NIGHT (1964)

RONNIE is kneeling in front of the MIRROR with the CRUCIFIX in
his BEDROOM ("Let the Beauty of Jesus Be Seen In Me")

> RONNIE: . . . sometimes God I'm so confused, sometimes I think
> I'd like just to stay right here in Massapequa and never leave . . .
> but I gotta go. You gotta help me Jesus . . . help me to make the
> right decision . . . I wanna do the right thing . . .

THE RAIN lashing against the bedroom window, suggesting a plea
to a barbaric god. RONNIE inside on his knees.

After a brief scene at the prom when Ron and his girl Donna (Kyra
Sedgwick) slow-dance to a sentimental song, filled with youthful longing
and loss, we are suddenly catapulted to a war zone in Vietnam. The shift
from an innocent and idyllic American moment to intense physical combat in a foreign country is deliberate and startling. Ron's platoon is de-
ployed outside a fishing village on the South China Sea, poised to attack
the Viet Cong from across some rice paddies. As they lie on the dunes, a
heavy, monsoon rain is falling, obstructing the view of the activities in
the village.

The fresh-faced LIEUTENANT listens over the radio and barks orders at RON over the wind.

LIEUTENANT: Red Platoon's receiving fire on the northwest edge of the ville. NVA suspects are coming this way . . .

RON alert, listening now to the imagined sound of distant gunfire . . .

LIEUTENANT: (points) . . . set your squad in a line along the dune . . .

He's very excited, repeating his orders.

LIEUTENANT: I think we got 'em, I think we got 'em this time Sergeant?

Their POV—through the rain—the village. Hard to see anything.

A GRAVEYARD.

In the distance, some movement in the village.

LIEUTENANT (very excited now): You see? Look, they got rifles. Can you see the rifles? . . . Can you see them?

RON looking very hard through the rain.

RON: Yes, I see them. I see them.
LIEUTENANT (puts his arm around him): Tell them when I give the order, I wanna light this ville up like a fucking Christmas tree— okay!!! Get going!

Turning back to his radio, overly keyed.

KOVIC running down the line, sinking in the sand, his baggy poncho flopping over the gear on his back.

Suddenly, SEVERAL FIGURES break from the huts, running.

As RON runs down the straggled LINE OF MEN, someone starts firing from the end with his M-16. Now the whole line suddenly erupts, pulling their triggers without thinking, emptying everything they have into the huts across the graveyard.

RON yelling, trying to get his men to stop the fire.

Voices screaming in the distance.

RON looking at the LIEUTENANT running up the line yelling across the sand.

LIEUTENANT: What happened! Goddamn it, what happened! . . . Who gave the order to fire? I wanna know who gave the order to fire!

Everybody is looking at everybody else with that peculiar awkwardness of a platoon without real leadership.

RON: We better get a killer team out there, sir.

LIEUTENANT: All right, all right Sergeant, get out there with Molina and tell me how many we got . . .

The VOICES continue to scream from the village, an eerie vailing amid the noise of rain.

RON moving to assemble FIVE MEN.

The LIEUTENANT on the radio; there seems to be increased fire from the distance, coming across the radio. Incipient panic building . . .

RON leading his five men across the dunes into the edges of the village . . .

. . . The Voices, the screams continuing . . . RON knows something is wrong, the rain beating on his face as he moves cautiously to the lip of the hut . . .

MOLINA is alongside him . . . They both turn into the hut and see it at the same time . . .

MOLINA: Oh God! Oh Jesus Christ!

RON's eyes convey the horror.

INT. HUT—DAY—RAIN

The floor of the small hut is covered with CHILDREN, screaming and thrashing their arms back and forth, lying in pools of blood, crying wildly, screaming again and again. They're shot in the face, in the chest, in the legs, moaning and crying . . .

RON: Oh Jesus . . .

The LIEUTENANT'S VOICE now blasting in on the radio . . .

LIEUTENANT: Tango Two, how many you got?

An old, OLD MAN in the corner with his head blown off from his eyes up, his brains hanging out of his head like jelly . . .

RON keeps looking at the strange sight, he's never seen anything like it before.

A SMALL BOY, next to the old man is still alive, though shot many times. He's crying softly, lying in a large pool of blood. His small foot has been shot off almost completely and hangs by a thread.

LIEUTENANT (voice): What's going on? What's going on up there?
MOLINA (voice): You better get up here fast Lieutenant. There's a lot of wounded people up here.

A SMALL GIRL moaning now, shot through the stomach.

RON feels crazy, weak, helpless, staring at them . . .

The other THREE MARINES are looking, staring down at the floor like it's a nightmare, like it's some kind of dream and it really isn't happening . . .

Subsequently, in the confusion of a firefight, Ron kills one of his own men and then is badly wounded himself. Little is done for him at the understaffed, overcrowded, vermin-infested hospital where he is sent; in fact, the neglect probably causes him to become a paraplegic, confined to a wheelchair for the rest of his life.

When Ron returns home wearing his uniform with medals on his chest he expects a hero's welcome, but although town officials proudly display him on patriotic occasions, people in the anti-war movement treat him as a criminal, adding to the guilt he already feels for killing innocent civilians. His heroism and sacrifice are not recognized by his family and friends either who treat him with gentle pity; his father constructs a special bathroom for him and carries him to bed each night.

Ron is still a loyal soldier and feels betrayed and confused by the conflicting attitudes he encounters, unsure whether the war was worth fighting. For example, while sitting in a bar one night, watching couples on the dance floor, he expresses his bitterness and is attacked for it:

> RON: . . . It was the wrong fucking war when you gotta come back to a dogshit hospital where they don't give a fuck if . . . when it was just a waste of fuckin' time, and it was all one big fuckin' mistake right and I'm sorry but you can take your Vyet Nam and shove it up your ass . . .
>
> MAN #2: Why don't you shove it up *your* ass pal . . . okay? Just 'cause you're in a fuckin' wheelchair you think everybody's gotta feel sorry for you?
>
> RON: What?
>
> MAN #2: You ain't the only Marine here. I was on Iwo Jima. We lost 6,000 the first day. So don't go crying in your fucking beer to me. You served, you lost, and now you gotta live with it. You're a marine, semper fi, they didn't pick you, you picked them so stop moaning and pissing about it!
>
> RON: . . . I think guys like you are assholes that's what I think.
>
> MAN #2: Yeah, I bet you do buddy, you sorry motherfucker . . . 'cause you know if they win . . . it's guys like you they're gonna put up against the wall first . . . 'cause they know you sure as hell can't trust a traitor.

Ron becomes dissolute as he becomes disillusioned, and for a time he joins a group of drunken veterans in Mexico. He also travels to Syracuse University to visit his ex-girlfriend Donna who is now heavily involved in the anti-war movement. He explains to her why he went to war, and here Oliver Stone suggests that a boy's motives for fighting have more to do with his manhood than with patriotism.

> RON: I wanted you to see me at my best, I don't know why that is with people, but . . . you know it's like . . . it's never enough . . . It's

like you do something at twelve 'cause you wanna show everybody you can be fifteen, and when you're fifteen you wanna be
eighteen, and when you're eighteen you wanna be twenty-one,
you really wanna be a man so you go out and join up and you go
to . . . War . . . and War is like this big secret see—it's something
only a few people in this country really know about—and you
think if you know what that secret is . . . then you think ah! Then
finally at last, I'll be a man . . . and when I'm a Man—then I'm
gonna have you "Donna"— . . . like you're part of a timepiece you
know . . . when I'm twenty-one I'm gonna have Donna and that's
just the way it is . . . and everything . . . *everything* I ever did, hitting
that home run that day you were up in the stands with that stupid
guy and that crazy song playing "awalking in the rain . . . awhooo
whooo whoo whoo . . ." was for you Donna . . . it was for you.
(pause). I wanted to *shine. I really wanted to shine* for you, Donna . . .
'cause I loved you . . . goddamnit I really *loved you* . . . I just never
told you . . . (exhales, a long beat) Jeesus!

Donna comforts him as he cries, but the intervening years and the
past difference in their politics make it impossible for them to be together
as they once were. The way she and the country have changed is made
clearer by a rally at Syracuse that same day. The protest moves Ron further to question the rightness of the war, and we see him gradually becoming radicalized.

The STUDENTS have taken over a BUILDING—waving protest
banners and flags from the windows. Starting to trash the place
now—desks, papers, file cabinets being thrown out the windows
onto the lawns.

CHANTS: FUCK THE PIGS! FUCK THE PIGS! ONE - TWO -
THREE - FOUR WE DON'T WANT YOUR FUCKING WAR!!
FIVE - SIX - SEVEN - EIGHT, WE DON'T WANT TO ESCA-
LATE!

The COPS are forming at two ends of the quadrangle, emptying out
of their vans . . . LOUDSPEAKERS shouting orders . . .

. . . as RON looks on with DONNA and her BOYFRIEND, a tall, lean
intellectual young man of pleasant demeanor . . . "Peace Now" and
"Stop the War" buttons. They are in a LARGE GROUP in the center
of the quadrangle listening to one of the SPEAKERS, a young, black
Veteran in cut off fatigues, his medals pinned to his chest.

On the platform behind him are OTHER YOUNG VETS mixed with
STUDENT LEADERS, the UNIVERSITY REVEREND, and a few
TEACHERS . . .

The SPEAKER is a fiery, moving man, waving a document in the air.

SPEAKER: It says right here People—in the Declaration of Independence, if the Government fucks you over, it's not only your RIGHT but YOUR FUCKIN DUTY, PEOPLE . . . to BRING IT DOWN!!!

A huge roar from the agitated crowd, sensing the POLICE closing in.

CHANTS: RIGHT ON! POWER TO THE PEOPLE MAN! REMEMBER KENT AND JACKSON STATE!

RON has never heard words like this . . . his eyes hungrily roving through the crowd . . .

. . . to a FEW HIPPIES all painted up, long hair, flowers, one of them breast-feeding a BABY . . . A tab of acid being passed in a priestly manner.

. . . guys and girls passing joints . . . a guy beating a drum . . .

. . . a

SPEAKER: . . . If Jefferson and Tom Paine and those dudes were here today, d'you think they'd be with Nixon or with us? (ad lib answers "WITH US!") Shit yes, Nixon's the same as King George!

On the loudspeakers, the COPS are advising the STUDENTS to get out of the Dorms . . .

LOUDSPEAKER: YOU ARE ORDERED TO DISPERSE. YOU HAVE FIVE MINUTES. THIS IS AN UNLAWFUL ASSEMBLY. IF YOU DO NOT DISPERSE, YOU WILL BE ARRESTED.

SPEAKER: First he invades Cambodia and bombs the shit out of it, and then he kills four kids at Kent State 'cause they tried to protest. This guy's gotta go!!! (ROARS—"BURN BABY BURN!") Right on! The people of this country been fucked over cheated and lied to by all of 'em, Truman, Eisenhower, Kennedy, Johnson. The whole war is a big rip off . . . people are dying over there to make some fat cat capitalist businessmen rich, this whole generation's being sold out People . . . (MORE) and we GOTTA DO SOMETHING. WE GOTTA GET RID OF THIS GOVERNMENT NOW. (Roars—"BURN BABY BURN! POWER TO THE PEOPLE!").

A YOUNG VETERAN walking through the CROWD, spots RON, comes over . . . Seeing him, RON tries to shrink back as the VET gives him a high-fiver . . . The VET seeming to know RON is a vet.

VET: Hey brother, Larry Boyle, what's happening man.

RON: Ron Kovic.

VET: Welcome brother . . . to the War at home . . . You gotta get up there, man, say a few words to these dudes. Wake 'em up man . . .

RON: No. No. Not today. Thanks anyway . . .

VET (looking him right in the eye): Peace, Ron . . . and welcome home . . .

He goes . . . RON stirred, something in him reluctantly moved by the man . . . DONNA noticing it, smiles . . .

SPEAKER: We're the ones put our bodies on the line—for people who didn't even care about us when we came home. I loved this country once . . .

The SPEAKER now rips the medals from his chest and brandishes them in his hands . . .

SPEAKER: . . . And all this I won over there . . . the Purple Heart, the Bronze Star, all the Commendation Medals and the rest of this garbage . . . *don't mean a thing*. FUCK THIS SHIT.

Shaking with emotion, he hurls them into the distance . . .

RON is shocked. He's never seen or heard something like this. As he catches DONNA'S eyes for a moment.

She has her fist in the air yelling "RIGHT ON, BURN, BABY, BURN!" beautiful yet cruel in her anger, she embodies the revolution, RON looks away.

Stone might have left Ron Kovic an embittered, crippled veteran, getting drunk, taking drugs, paying for prostitutes, and alienating himself from his parents by his obscenity and violence. That could have been an effective protest against the war. However, Stone chose to present a resolution of the conflict, which is what happened to him and the real Kovic after they fought in Vietnam.

For a long time Ron struggles to understand whether love of country entails protest rallies or loyalty (*semper fidelis,* after all, means always faithful), but eventually he turns against the Vietnam War, for very mixed reasons. Personally, the war took away his manhood instead of validating it, and rather than winning Donna he lost her by leaving to fight. Politically, he never really grasped the reasons for the war while feeling duty-bound to enlist, and he gradually comes to doubt the war's justification. The personal and the political, that is, rage at his paralysis and the awareness of his greater responsibilities, therefore come together to make him a radical activist. In a sense, by deciding to be an effective agent for change, he overcomes his paralysis, he recovers.

As the film progresses we see Ron as part of protest group at the 1972 Republican National Convention. Following a procession of ragged young people with pipe and drum whistling, "When Johnny Comes Marching Home Again," Vietnam veterans walk down a boulevard in Miami wearing fatigues and bush hats, long hair and beards, some with medals on their chests, others carrying Viet Cong flags.

The WOUNDED now appear—blind vets, amputated vets, proudly escorted, parting now onto RON and two other PARAS abreast of him in chairs pushed by FELLOW VETS. RON now has a full mustache and is unshaven, his hair longer than ever . . . a banner above their heads: STOP THE WAR—VIETNAM VETERANS AGAINST THE WAR—"hurray! hurrah!" up from the song . . .

As SPECTATORS watch from the sidewalks or porches . . . ANGRY MEN . . . CHEERING MEN . . . OLD JEWISH LADIES on their verandas . . . mostly neutral, curious looks . . .

SECRET SERVICE cars trailing . . . suits, earplugs, walkie talkies.

COPS in full riot gear filing out of a TRUCK on a quiet street. STATIC of a walkie talkie . . . "proceed to 5th and Cyprus . . . cordon off . . . contain . . . separate . . . the hippies . . . marijuana busts . . . traffic violations . . ." . . . SOUNDS of the WHISTLING MARCHERS in the distance.

INT. MIAMI CONVENTION CENTER—NIGHT

Into an ocean of thundering SOUND . . .

RON and the TWO OTHER PARAS are in the hall, wheeling their way closer to the stage . . .

with them is a FOURTH MAN, a redheaded guy with a beard, floppy bush hat, jungle fatigues who is pushing RON at the parade. He's inside now, and helping push RON and the TWO OTHERS.

. . . past the YOUNG REPUBLICANS yelling "FOUR MORE YEARS. FOUR MORE YEARS!!"

. . . past MEN and WOMEN in summer suits with happy Republican pink faces looking with some concern and possibly apprehension at these three scruffy Vietnam Vets rolling into their midst . . .

A NEWS CAMERA filming them. RON angling into the camera, playing the crowd looking for people to listen.

> RON: Do you hear me? Can I break through your complacency? Can I have an *inch* . . . a moment of your compassion for the human beings who are suffering in this war . . . do you hear me when I say this war is a crime . . . when I say I am not as bitter about my wound as the men who have lied to the people of this country . . . do you hear me?

But they hear nothing. Deaf, blind, dumb, roaring for their leader as he now appears . . . the sound waves rolling up the hall . . .

CLIP—NIXON now coming to the podium. A huge smile. A pause before he stretches out his arms in his famous victory pose. The

ROARS pound over RON and THREE COMRADES continuing to wheel closer.

Like assassins, deep in enemy territory; their POV—the hall looming like a jungle far away. The tension in RON—

CLIP—NIXON

> NIXON: Mr. Chairman, delegates to this convention, my fellow Americans . . .

INTERCUT RON speaking at the same time to a NEWS CAMERA.

> RON: WHY DO THEY WANT TO HIDE US? Why won't they let the veterans of that war speak tonight? Because they don't wanna know, they don't wanna see us, they wanna hide us because they've *lied* and *cheated* to us for so long—but we're not gonna run away and hide anymore, we're going to win because we LOVE this country. We *love* this country more than they could ever know. We fought for it, we gave our bodies because we loved it and believed in *everything* it stood for and tonight we're *ashamed* of it, and we've come from all the little towns, thousands of us to get this country *back* again, to make it *whole* again. Truth, honesty, integrity—this is the lost American dream here tonight, and *we're gonna take it back*!

INTERCUT CLIP—NIXON

Talking about Vietnam. The completely counter argument about ideals, patriotism, ideology—the basis of the Cold War. Cognent, coherent, something we've all heard before—and totally false to its core.

INTERCUT RON—to the cameras. He has become a professional 107 orator now, his voice and eyes and overall intensity the same RON but older now, polished, a political leader.

> RON: We're *never never* gonna let the people of the United States forget that war, because the moment we do, there's gonna be *another war and another, and another,* that's why we're gonna be there for the rest of our lives telling you that the war *happened,* it just wasn't some nightmare, it *happened* and you're not gonna sweep it under the rug because you didn't like the ratings like some television show . . . this wheelchair . . . this steel is your Memorial day on wheels, your yankee doodle . . .

A violent confrontation ensues in which secret service agents surround the veterans, blocking their entry to the convention and attempting to prevent TV cameras from covering the demonstration. As the paraplegics chant "STOP THE BOMBING, STOP THE WAR," and people in the crowd shout "THROW THEM OUT . . . TRAITORS . . .

COMMUNISTS," the agents pull the veterans into the street in their wheelchairs. Ron is tipped out of his chair and brutally handcuffed, but when the agents try to throw him into a car several veterans converge and pull him away.

Ron and the other veterans then regroup and prepare to fight the police who face them with nightsticks. The police slowly advance, striking the sticks against their leather gloves, as the camera freezes and fades on drifting teargas and pulsing red lights. We are left with the impression that clubbing and beating are imminent.

In a final scene four years later, we see Ron Kovic addressing the 1976 Democratic National Convention in New York City. By his authority and presence we can assume he has become a leader in the anti-war movement, for he is a mature and seasoned public speaker, advocating a cause. And from the fact that he is allowed to speak we can assume that the country is now listening to dissenters without regarding them as traitors.

One obvious message of the film is that democracies must be able to tolerate opposition to government policy. Such freedom allows the individual and the nation as a whole a chance for redemption.

> RON: I am the living death. Your Memorial Day on wheels. I am your Yankee Doodle Dandy. Your John Wayne come home. Your Fourth of July firecracker Exploding in the grave . . . Twelve years ago when I was 18 years old, I left Massapequa, Long Island and joined the United States Marines . . . I wanted to serve my country . . . I wanted to be a good American . . . I couldn't wait to fight my first war, and I went with the others like our fathers before us with hope in our hearts and dreams of great victory . . .

Blending into the MUSIC THEME now . . . of tragedy overcome. Of life renewed . . .

Study Questions

1. In what way is Ronnie made to feel that it is his patriotic duty to fight in Vietnam? Do states have the right to compel people to risk their lives for their country?

2. Do you think the attack on the village was necessary? If noncombatants cannot be differentiated from combatants, doesn't that justify treating them as the enemy?

3. Is the anti-war protest legitimate, or do citizens have an obligation to support their government's decision to attack another country? Do the police have the right to disburse the protest as unpatriotic?

4. Does the fact that Ronnie fought in Vietnam and was wounded give him greater authority in condemning the war or does it undermine his protest?

5. What are the limits of free speech in a democracy? Can people be allowed to criticize the government, even if that threatens the stability of the state?

Bibliography of Philosophy, Literature, and Films

V. Establishing the Social Order: Political Philosophy

Philosophy

Anarchy, State, and Utopia	Robert Nozick
Abortion, Law, Choice and Morality	Daniel Callahan
Apology, Crito, Republic	Plato
Basic Rights	Henry Shue
Capital	Karl Marx
Capitalism and Freedom	Milton Friedman
"Civil Disobedience"	H. D. Thoreau
Communism, Fascism, and Democracy	Carl Cohen
The Communist Manifesto	Karl Marx
The Enforcement of Morals	Patrick Devlin
Equality and Preferential Treatment	Marshall Cohen
Feminist Politics and Human Nature	Alison Jagger
The Free Society	John Middleton Murray
Freedom of Expression	Fred R. Berger
Justice and Economic Distribution	John Arthur
Law, Legislation, and Liberty	F. A. Hayek
Leviathan	Thomas Hobbes
Libertarianism: A Political Philosophy	John Hospers
Life and Death with Liberty and Justice	Grisez, Germain
Lifeboat Ethics	George R. Lucas
Mortal Questions	Thomas Nagel
The New Atlantis	Francis Bacon
Of Civil Government	John Locke
On Liberty	John Stuart Mill
The Open Society and Its Enemies	Karl Popper
Persons and Masks of the Law	John T. Noonan
Political Power and Personal Freedom	Sidney Hook
Political Violence and Civil Disobedience	Ernest van den Haag
Politics	Aristotle
Property, Profits, and Economic Justice	Virginia Held
Sex Equality	Jane English
Social Philosophy	Joel Feinberg
The Social Contract	Jean-Jacques Rousseau
Socialism	Michael Harrington
To the Finland Station	Edmund Wilson
A Theory of Justice	John Rawls
Second Treatise of Government	John Locke
The Utopia	Thomas More

Literature

Billiards at Half Past Nine	Heinrich Boll
Brave New World	Aldous Huxley
Bread and Wine	Ignazio Silone
Book of Songs	Heinrich Heine
Cancer Ward	Alexander Solzhenitsyn
Clerambault	Romain Rolland
Darkness at Noon	Arthus Koestler
Dirty Hands	Jean-Paul Sartre
Doctor Zhivago	Boris Pasternak
An Enemy of the People	Henrich Ibsen
Erehwon	Samuel Butler
A Farewell to Arms, The Sun also Rises	Ernest Hemingway
Fathers and Sons	Ivan Turgenev
The Flies	Jean-Paul Sartre
From Here to Eternity	James Jones
A Hero of Our Time	Mikhail Lermontov
Lord of the Flies	William Golding
Man's Estate	Andre Malraux
The Masters and Magrita	Mikhail Bulgakov
Mother	Maxim Gorky
The Naked and the Dead	Norman Mailer
Of Mice and Men	John Steinbeck
"The Overcoat"	Nikolay Gogol
Penguin Island	Anatole France
The Quiet Don	Mikhail Sholokov
Soldier's Pay	William Faulkner
The Sleepwalkers	Hermann Broch
Things Fall Apart	Achua Achebe
The Time Machine	H. G. Wells
The Tin Drum	Gunter Grass
Walden II	B. F. Skinner

Films

Absolute Beginners	Julian Temple
Advise and Consent	Otto Preminger
Alexander Nevsky, *Battleship Potemkin*	Sergei Eisenstein
All Quiet on the Western Front	Lewis Milestone
All the King's Men	Robert Rossen
All the President's Men	Alan Pakula
The Angry Silence	Guy Green
Apocalypse Now	Francis Ford Coppola

Birth of a Nation	D. W. Griffith
Blue Collar	Paul Schrader
Boat People	Ann Hui
Born on the Fourth of July	Oliver Stone
The Boys From Brazil	Franklin Schaffner
The Candidate	Michael Ritchie
Citizen Kane	Orson Wells
City Lights	Charlie Chaplin
Closely Observed Trains	Jiri Menzel
The Conformist	Bernardo Bertolucci
The Cranes Are Flying	Mickail Kalatozov
The Deer Hunter	Michael Cimino
Doctor Stangelove	Stanley Kubrick
Easy Rider	Dennis Hopper
Fahrenheit 451	Francois Truffaut
Fury	Fritz Lang
Gallipoli	Peter Weir
Gandhi	Richard Attenborough
The Garden of the Finzi-Continis	Vittorio de Sica
The Grand Illusion	Jean Renoir
Hiroshima Mon Amour	Alain Resnais
The Informer	John Ford
Judgment at Nuremberg	Stanley Kramer
The Killing Fields	Roland Joffe
Kiss of the Spider Woman	Hector Babenco
The Lion in Winter	Anthony Harvey
La Grande Illusion	Jean Renoir
Love and Anarchy	Lina Wertmuller
The Manchurian Candidate	John Frankenheimer
Man of Marble	Andrzej Wajda
The Marriage of Maria Braun	Rainer Fassbinder
Nixon	Oliver Stone
El Norte	Gregory Nava
The Official Story	Luis Puenzo
On the Waterfront	Elia Kazan
The Pawnbroker	Sidney Lumet
A Passage to India	David Lean
Paths of Glory	Stanley Kubrick
Platoon	Oliver Stone
A Raisin in the Sun	Daniel Petrie
The Rules of the Game	Jean Renoir
Schindler's List	Steven Spielberg
The Servant	Joseph Losey
The Shop on Main Street	Jan Kadar

Sophie's Choice	Alan Pakula
State of Siege,	Constantine Costa-Garvas
Z	
Swept Away	Lina Wertmuller
The Thin Red Line	Andrew Marton

Credits

Rainer Maria Rilke. *The Notebooks of Malte Laurids Brigge.* From THE NOTE-BOOKS OF MALTE LAURIDS BRIGGE by Rainer Maria Rilke, translated by M. D. Herter Norton. Copyright 1949 by W. W. Norton & Company, Inc., renewed © 1977 by M. D. Herter Norton Crena de Iongh. Used by permission of W. W. Norton & Company, Inc.

Akira Kurosawa. *Rashomon.* © 1950 by Akira Kurosawa and Daiei Motion Pictures, © 1952 RKO Pictures. English screenplay ©1969 by Grove Press, Inc.

Hermann Hesse. *Siddhartha* by Herman Hesse, from SIDDHARTHA, copyright ©1951 by New Directions Publishing Corp. Reprinted by permission of New Directions Publishing Corp.

Federico Fellini. *Juliet of the Spirits.* From JULIET OF THE SPIRITS by Federico Fellini, translated by Howard Greenfeld, copyright © 1965 by Grossman Publishers for the English translation. Used by permission of Viking Penguin, a division of Penguin Putnam Inc.

Margaret Atwood. *The Edible Woman.* From THE EDIBLE WOMAN by Margaret Atwood. Copyright © 1969 by Margaret Atwood. By permission of Little, Brown, and Company, Inc.

Wachowski Brothers. *The Matrix.* Silver Pictures/Warner Bros. © 1997. Used by permission of Warner Brothers Studios.

Jean-Paul Sartre. "The Humanism of Existentialism." With gratitude for permission from Philosophical Library, New York.

Ursula K. Le Guin. "The Ones Who Walk Away from Omelas." Copyright © 1973, 2000 by Ursula K. LeGuin, first appeared in THE WIND'S TWELVE QUARTERS; reprinted by permission of the author and the author's agents, the Virginia Kidd Agency, Inc.

Elia Kazan. *On the Waterfront.* With gratitude for permission from Mr. Budd Schulberg.

Index